Passion for Life

Kenneth A. Walsh

North Country Press

Passion for Life

Copyright © 2024 by Kenneth A. Walsh

All rights reserved. No part of this book may be reproduced or transmitted in any form or by any means without written permission of the author.

ISBN 978-1-943424-84-9

LCCN 2024946217

North Country Press
Unity, Maine

Preface

For as long as I can remember, having passion for life has always been within me, part of my soul and spirit. As time goes by, I realize how precious moments can be. Making the moments into something magical is the way that anchors wonderful memories for a lifetime. I believe one must make those moments happen by seizing the opportunities when presented rather than sitting on the sidelines. My life, a small section of my adventures are in this book. Not all rosy and not all I am proud of, although most of the time I left everything on the field and fully embraced all the challenges that came my way.

I am blessed to have been (and still am) surrounded by tremendous mentors who shaped my life into what it is today. I must say that I chose those mentors to be a part of my life. My choices set the stage for success. They taught me how to challenge myself, never to give up, and strive for greatness. They helped me believe that anything is possible if you put your mind to it and are willing to work hard for it. These mentors became like family that I can count on. Family is what keeps everything together. There is nothing like being with the ones you love. Nothing like holding your babies for the first time and watching them enjoy the first moments of life. Nothing like seeing the sunrise and sunset on the beach or on a mountaintop. Nothing like accomplishing a goal that you put your mind to and made happen. Nothing like the natural energy coming from a challenging workout, where you cannot take another step and you are covered with sweat. I love sharing these gifts and passing them on, "paying it forward" to the next generation and giving them the passion for life so they too can pass it on. Life is a blink of an eye and there never seems to be enough time. Instead of watching time go by, embrace all that you can and enjoy the spirit of life. Make your adventures today, tomorrow, and into the future.

Carpe Diem, Ken

Chapter Index

Passion for Life

Journeys
1. Farm League All-Stars..........1
2. Igniting the Competitive Spark..........7
3. DOC 13
4. Halloween School Invasion..........21
5. Lessons of Failure Leads to Success..........27
6. Gus Mascaro - Mr. Boys Club..........33
7. First Adventure on the Mighty Rogue River 1986..........41
8. Forever Brotherhood – Club Naha 1986..........47
9. Katahdin..........61
10. Tomato Soup..........65
11. Harold Alfond, Maine's Legend..........69
12. Rogue River Adventure 1996..........81
13. The Adventure That Never Happened..........89
14. Fitness Fire TV Show..........93
15. Blizzard Run..........97
16. Unity Sprint Triathlon..........101

17. Grand Canyon Trail Run..........105
18. JFK 50 Ultra Run..........109
19. Mt. Washington Road Race – Only One Hill..........115
20. Goodcellmo..........119
21. K100 Spiritual Journey..........123
22. Shaker Tent Ceremony..........131
23. A True Inspiration..........145
24. Life's New Beginning..........149
25. Spirit of Adventure..........155
26. Mt. Hood Hike..........159
27. K100, Going the Distance..........165
28. Dad and Son's Trip to Motherland..........171
29. Thanksgiving Turkey Trot 10K Road Race..........181
30. Rogue River Adventure #3, Snake Bite "Got Home Alive"..........185
31. Sean Chooses Us..........197
32. Trip to China..........201
33. George Yankowski – 1942 MLB Catcher..........213
34. One Pleasant Surprise - Kate Shine (My Little Angel Katie Kate).....217
35. Barbara Jolovitz - Bubbe's World..........221
36. Left-Handed Tennis..........225
37. Christmas Spirit – 2015..........229
38. Annual Thanksgiving Touch Football Game..........235
39. Steve Waite, The Quality of Courage..........239
40. Sweat Lodge Ceremony, 15 Below Zero..........245
41. Southern California Trip..........251
42. It is Never Too Late..........257
43. An Epic Baseball Day – BP at Fenway Park in Boston..........269
44. The Perfect Season..........275
45. Mr. Baseball – Mr. Fran Purnell..........285
46. Spin The Bottle..........291
47. Colby Baseball Championship Season..........295
48. Dodgertown..........299
49. Maine Black Bears – Roy Hobbs World Series..........307
50. The Journey Forward..........315

Journey 1

The Depot Hill Gang 1974

"And David put his hand in the bag and took out a stone and slung it and struck the Philistine on the head, and he fell to the ground."

Farm League All-Stars

In 1973, baseball was at its peak of importance in my life. More than ever, I wanted to be a baseball player. My skills were beginning to develop, and I was becoming a solid player. That year, I played in the most memorable baseball game of my life.

In July 1973, the New York Mets—the San Francisco Giants' hated rivals—were on top of their division and eventually won the National League pennant as they made a gallant run for the World Series. Tug McGraw, relief specialist for the Mets, coined the phrase, "You got to believe," as the Mets fought to keep their hope of winning the Series alive. Unfortunately for the Mets, they couldn't pull it off, even with the famous Willie Mays.

However, the magical season of my 12th year turned out to be the greatest World Series of my life. I played on the Amenia Giants Farm Team. The Farm

Team was made up of ball players ages 8-12 who did not make the Amenia Little League Team. Mike Rooney and I never had the opportunity to try out for the team because he went to Prep School, and I always came to Amenia too late from Brooklyn and missed callout. The Amenia Little League Team were the best players in the area. Later in life, I eventually played with all of them in Babe Ruth, high school, Legion, and the men's team, the Monarchs.

When I was 12, I played probably the most baseball of my whole life. Every day during the summer, our gang members on the Hill played either baseball, fast pitch wiffleball, softball, stickball or a game of 500 in my backyard. We played the game 500 with 3 to 10 players. A batter threw the ball up in the air and hit it on the fly or on the ground. The players in the field would scramble to catch the ball. On the fly, it was worth 100 points; on the ground it was worth 25 points unless the ball was caught on one hop; that was 50 points. The fielder who earned 500 points won the game. 500 fine-tuned our skills on the field that summer.

We also played many games of catch and monkey in the middle that helped our base running. All of these games were fun, and we never realized how well they prepared us for success in organized baseball. The Depot Hill Gang's baseball skills were more refined than many others' because we ate, slept, and dreamed baseball every day.

That summer, like every summer, the Farm League All-Stars were picked to play the Amenia Little League Team that just won the league championship. Each year, the game drew a big crowd at the Amenia Monarchs' semi-pro baseball field even though it was typically a massacre as the Little League destroyed the Farm League.

Four of the Giants were named to the Farm League All-Star Team: Mike Rooney in outfield, Andy Savage as catcher, Mark Christianson at third base, and me. I got the nod to be the starting pitcher that year for the All-Stars. To me, this was a huge deal and honor.

Each night before the big game, Mike Rooney and I played catch in my backyard between the tree swing and the clothesline. We went over their potential lineup and discussed how I should pitch to each hitter. I knew I could not just blow my fastball by them. I had to be craftier and set the batters up with curve balls, off-speed pitches, and work the edges of the strike zone. Mike would get into his catcher's stance and place his glove at the corners of the plate, so I could focus on hitting his glove at each spot.

We were also going to be using a regulation Little League ball, not the rubber coated ball that we had in Farm League. This was even better for me because we were used to playing with real hardballs on the Hill. Using the Little League ball helped me with my grip on the seams of the baseball. I got a much better spin on my curveball.

Passion for Life

At our practices, we started talking up the game to the rest of the All-Stars. In their hearts, they didn't believe we could win. Mike and I did, even if we were going to do it ourselves. We believed that you only play to win, never to just show up. Soon after a couple of practices, we had the other boys believing we had a chance to win. Excitement began to develop. The spirit of practice brought a wave of encouragement. We knew we had a chance. For the first time in Amenia history, we were going to give the Little Leaguers a run for their money.

The Little League team had the brand-new white-with-red-stripe uniforms with matching caps. Their hat was red with a white "A" on the crest. Our All-Star team only had tee shirts with the team name printed across the chest. All of us wore dungarees and sneakers, no spikes like the Little Leaguers.

The night before the game, I was in the bedroom on the second floor that I shared with my brother Rob. Always one of my biggest supporters, Rob came upstairs while I was planning my pitching selection for the next day, and said, "Kenny, I got something for you to wear tomorrow."

He reached into his drawer and pulled out light grey baseball pants with blue stripes along the side that matched my Amenia Giants tee-shirt. These were his pants that he used when he played in the city league. My eyes almost popped out of my head in excitement. I was thrilled that I would at least look like a player on the mound. Rob then pulled out of the closet a pair of baseball spikes he convinced Dennis Rooney to let me use. For me, it was Christmas in July.

The next day, I cut the grass for our neighbor, Mrs. McEniff and felt like I had the weight of the world on my shoulders because I didn't want to let down the team. It gave me the time to think through each pitch and each at bat before the game. I was going to pitch and I was going to win.

The game was scheduled for 6:00 pm. I dressed three hours before game time and waited patiently for Mike Rooney to come across the street to call for me to make our journey down the Hill to the Monarch ball field in town. Mike stopped by at 4:30 pm. knowing that we had to be there at 5:00 for batting practice and fielding.

The rest of the gang on the Hill talked about this game every night during our regular evening ball games. Most of it was to hassle us about how we were going to get creamed by the Little League team. We knew this was the typical harassment that we all gave each other at times. We knew the gang wanted us to win. We all had the pride of the Hill. The gang arrived that night in full force to give us their support. My cousin, Roger Funk, who was my idol and played catcher for the Amenia Monarch Team, came down in his black convertible Triumph. His car was parked right behind the home plate screen.

We went through our warm-up before the game. I had butterflies in every part of my body as we watched the Little Leaguers go through their warm-up. They were a groomed team with nice uniforms. They seemed extremely calm and confident. That is when my butterflies went away. I looked over to Mike and said, "Let's get 'em!" He responded, "You bet your ass!"

We were the away team and had the chance to bat first. On the mound for the Little League team was Jeff Dunlop. He was the upcoming star for next season's team. We knew we could get to him if we just made contact and kept the game close with solid defense.

In the first inning, we erupted with five runs off Jeff, hitting the ball hard and into the gaps. From then on, it was a total blur. I was so focused on the next pitch that the game seemed to skip forward into the seventh inning. I remember the cars in the parking lot were honking at every new run we scored.

We had the Little Leaguers on the run with a 9 to 5 lead. I had 13 strikeouts heading into the bottom of the last inning. And, it was the heart of their order. I called over Andy Savage, my catcher, to discuss the signs. Gary Murphy, the Little League's slugger who had several homeruns during the season, stepped to the plate. The bases were full. The runner on first was Andrew Erskine, who I had hit in the back with a fastball. The following September, Andrew and I became real good friends, but at that moment we had no compassion for each other.

Andy Savage came to me with the plan to pitch around Gary Murphy like we did in the other innings. We did not want to give Gary a chance to beat us. Andy thought if we walked in a run, it would be better than a potential grand slam that would tie the game.

I said to Andy, "Get back behind the plate, I'm pitching to him." I remember going back to the mound and digging into the side of the plate with my borrowed black spikes. I took a deep breath, walked behind the mound and looked at Mike Rooney playing centerfield. He pumped his fist into his red-white-and-blue glove and said "Go get 'em, Kenny boy! You can do it!" The chants of "hum baby, hum baby" were now coming together in the infield. Every player was on edge; two outs, bases full, bottom of the seventh, the last inning!

I took the mound and Tom Downey, the Amenia Monarch coach, who had the honor of umpiring the game, shouted out, "Let's play ball!" Cars began to honk and the crowd began to yell as it became apparent that the Farm League had a chance to beat Little League for the first time ever.

Like a movie, like a dream, all the voices and sounds were blocked out. I looked into the catcher's mitt, zoned in on the strike zone, went into my full Tom Seaver windup, and threw my fastball with all I had right down the middle. Gary Murphy took a powerful swing and connected squarely to send the ball deep to centerfield. In a regular Farm League game, the game would have been tied, but not that night. I had my best friend, a Depot Hiller, in centerfield. Mike ran back, glided under the ball, and lifted his glove as the ball found the web of his mitt! GAME OVER!

Passion for Life

The Farm League All Stars had beat the Amenia Little League, 9 to 5. Andy Savage and the rest of the team ran to the mound and piled on top of me. Our parents and the Depot Hill gang mobbed the field. Hats and gloves were scattered throughout the infield. It was a dream come true – and we lived it!

Following the game at the annual Farm League Awards Dinner, we had a group photo outside the Fish and Game Club where the event was held. I remember Coach Bida posing right next to me as Mike Rooney stood on the right and Andy Savage stood to my left. The photo did not come across like we were champions, no smiles, just stares.

That afternoon, the Little League coach, Bob Schiffer, asked me to come to the front of the room and he presented me with a Little League ball for my efforts in the game. That ball was the symbol of the "Don't Quit Attitude" that would always stay with me. Like Tug McGraw said, "You Got to Believe!"

Journey 2

J.V. Soccer '75

Coach--Mr. James Waldinger

"The spirit, the will to win, and the will to excel are the things that endure. These qualities are so much more important than the events that occur." Vince Lombardi

Igniting the Competitive Spark

Sometimes it is hard to figure out exactly when the positive foundation blocks of life begin. I must say that with three older brothers in the house and all interested in competitive sports, it was not hard to develop a passion for sports and a passion for life. These early days in life help create the will to win and be ready for the chance to win.

My family grew up in Bensonhurst Brooklyn and in the summer months, we went upstate to Amenia, New York. From the city streets to the country cornfields, I played sports with my brothers and friends. My brother, Rob, gave me a small post card with the Vince Lombardi quote "Winning isn't everything, it's the only thing." I kept this with me and still have it today. I certainly do not believe in winning at all cost, although I do believe that the drive to win propels one to success. Fair play, being humble, and showing sportsmanship bring success as well.

In the summer of 1974, our family relocated permanently from Brooklyn to Amenia. During my freshman year, I tried out for the Webutuck High School

Junior Varsity Soccer team. Since our school was Class D, the Fall sports venue was limited. Students either ran cross country or played soccer. I had no experience playing soccer although most of my friends played and encouraged me to try out for the team. I tried out for the team as a goalkeeper. I figured that I was quick, had good hands, and was not afraid to take a hit. It seemed to be the right fit. The downside was that I was only 5'4" at the time, short for a goalie.

The coach of the team was our Science Teacher, Jim Waldinger. He was a slender man standing around 5'8" with dark brown hair and intense eyes. He was a fiery individual that demanded respect and pushed for team discipline. If a player worked hard and hustled, he was rewarded with playing time. If he was lazy and not putting in 100% effort, Coach Waldinger found a new home for the player on the bench. It was as simple as that.

Our team, the Webutuck Warriors, played in a challenging conference. Most of the teams we played were Class A schools coming out of the Poughkeepsie area. Schools from Rhinebeck and Haldane were the only teams of our size. The teams we played against were much more seasoned and skilled than our Warrior team. However, our class was quite talented with players who had played ball together since grammar school. Our team was led by fast, skilled, and athletic kids. Tom Romano, Jim Krieling, Joe Illiano, Frank Collier, Andy Erskine, and Mike Silvernale brought depth to our team.

During the season, we fought hard and shocked some of our opponents from the larger schools with victories, beating John Jay, Ketcham, Kingston and Poughkeepsie. These wins brought us to the top of the division along with the powerhouse team from Arlington. We lost a blowout game against Arlington at their home field earlier on in the season and now we were scheduled to play them for the championship on our home field.

Most of the season, I was backup goalie to Joe Illiano, the Warrior team captain. He was athletic and tall with a 6'2" frame and good agility. He played outstanding during the season. I watched how he commanded the team and played smart in the goal, leaving the net only when necessary. I came in during most games in the second half when the game was not on the line, and I played well. During practice, I played with fierce energy; diving in the air and leaping between players to keep the ball out of the net. I practiced at 100%, giving it my all each and every day. If I was not dirty at the end of the practice session, I didn't play hard enough. I worked hard to understand the angles of working the net and when to stay in the net or when to chase the ball. I did not have a strong punt or drop kick. I relied more on throwing the ball to players during the game.

Three days before our match with Arlington, Joe suffered a broken hand in gym class. Of course, Coach Waldinger chewed Joe up one side and down the other for not being cautious before the big game. After science class Coach Waldinger pulled me to the side and said, "Walsh, the net is yours. I expect you to step up in a big way this Friday for the team. The team is counting on you."

I said, "Yes sir, Coach, I'll do my best."

Waldinger replied, "Walsh, it may take more than that. You need to dig deep inside and bring that fighting spirit of yours to the net that I see every day in practice." I looked Coach in the eye and nodded with determination.

At practice, I worked even harder with more intensity. Joe stayed at the back of the net giving me tips on positioning. After practicing my best friends, Krieling and Erskine came over to encourage me, saying that I would be great in the goal, and they had my back.

I had a sleepless night. It was game day and I had butterflies all day. I was anxious just to get on the field. The game was in late October just before Halloween on a cool overcast autumn day. This game was the talk of the school. It was truly a David and Goliath matchup. No one in the division felt we, the farm boys, had a fighting chance.

Our team dressed in Kelly green uniforms. We were on the field when the Arlington team bus rolled up to the back of our school and parked at the bottom of the hill in the parking lot for visitor buses. We stopped and watched a maroon wave coming out of the bus doors in single file, all running toward our soccer field on the hill. The big maroon machine ran in unison past us to their side.

Coach Waldinger yelled, "Get to work and pay attention to your game. Come on boys."

The game was on. For us, a small town tucked away in farm country, our crowd grew along the sidelines from the teachers, student body, parents, and our varsity team.

Waldinger put his arm around me, looked at me and said, "Walsh, I need a big game out of you. You can do it."

Coach gathered us off the sideline of the field as we circled around him.

"Men, this is what it is all about. No one expected us to be here playing against the big dogs from Poughkeepsie. You deserve to be here. All I expect is the best that you possibly can be today. Give it your all and you will be victorious. These boys are no better than you. The team who wants it more will win today. Bring it in". Our hands were all placed in the middle and with a shout "Warriors", we were on the field for game time.

The game started immediately with Arlington taking control and driving toward our goal, then firing the first shot just wide of the net. Coach blasted our middies and defense to win the one-on-one match-ups. Arlington was fast with good ball handling and always looking to pass to the open space.

The game continued with Arlington pounding the goal, shot after shot. I was diving from one side of the net to the other. One shot came right from the penalty slash and fired directly toward the right upper edge of the net. Somehow, I was able to get my fingertips on the ball to deflect it from going in, bouncing off the cross bar before Frank Collier cleared it out. Another shot came in with what seemed like a sure goal after the Arlington striker beat our defender for a one-on-one with me and the goal. I charged out, diving at the striker's feet, taking the ball away.

The game went on with the Webutuck crowd shouting at the top of their lungs and giving us support. Our offense had only a few chances against Arlington in the first half. With one minute left and the score still tied zero to zero, Jim Krieling received a pass from Tom Romano playing right wing to his striker position. Jim beat his defender and had a clear shot on the goal. He just missed the shot and hit the goal post, which rolled off for a goal kick.

The half was over, and we had held Arlington to a tie. I ran off the field getting pats on my back from my teammates and spectators as we headed into the locker room. Coach Waldinger gave me an encouraging look. I believed I was playing well, but knew I had some luck on my side as well.

Waldinger immediately talked about what we were not doing and how we needed to continue to beat the other team to the ball and keep control. He said, "You are being played. You need to step it up!" He stopped talking for a moment. There was dead silence as we looked at him.

"Men, dammit, we can beat these guys. Give it your all and play smart and we will win." We left the locker room pumped up and ready to play.

The second half was more of the same with Arlington controlling most of the game. I still had save after save, diving every which way. Our offense picked up a bit and had a few more shots on the goal with no real threat. The weather was getting colder as the sun was setting. Two minutes remained with still no score. The Warrior faithful fans all remained, cheering us on in this exciting thriller.

Then it happened. We threw in from the left side of the field. Rich Cummings attempted to throw the ball down the left side to Silvernale. The ball was intercepted and kicked to the Arlington half back who pushed the ball back to the right corner. The right wing kicked a perfect pass to the striker near the penalty box. I came out charging for the ball. I dove at his feet as he was just kicking. The ball went by my outstretched hands. On the ground, I looked behind me as the ball found the right corner of the net. Score. I just laid there for a moment as the Arlington players joyously celebrated their goal.

During the remaining minutes of the game, we fought hard with two more shots at their goal with no luck. Game over. Arlington 1, Webutuck 0.

When the horn blew, our team walked off the field with heads hanging. Not until the tremendous applause from our fans and the other team, did we realize what an incredible day we had on the field. Players from the other team came over to tell me how great I played. Their respect gave me pride even though we lost.

In the locker room, Coach gathered us together. We were sweaty, dirty, and tired as we listened to Coach. "Boys, sometimes in life we learn much more from losing than winning. You played with your hearts out there. You are all winners. I am proud to have coached you this season."

He then looked at me and said, "Walsh, great job today. You gave it your all".

That October afternoon I learned the tough lesson of defeat. I also learned the lesson of pride. Even though we lost, we came together as a team that fall day. Our team in our small school learned the spirit of working together for a common cause, to sacrifice and to support one another. The chemistry from that day lasted another three years in high school. My classmates went on a few years later, winning championships my junior and senior year in soccer, basketball, and baseball. I became one of the co-captains in both soccer and baseball. In defeat, we learned to be victorious. This has carried on in every phase of my life.

"Success is failure turned inside out." This is a line from the "Don't Quit" poem that echoes in my mind during the challenging times in life.

Journey 3

"Never Judge a Book by its Cover"

DOC

In the spring of 1977, when I was still sixteen years old, I was itching for a real job instead of mowing my neighbor's lawn. Since much of the area land in Amenia was owned by farmers, like some of my classmates and fellow Depot Hill buddies, I decided to try to find a job as a farmhand.

After reading the local paper, I found a position in South Amenia on Joe McLaughlin's farm. My parents recognized the farm and knew the owner since my older brothers and sisters knew their children as well. Unfortunately, the oldest son of Mr. McLaughlin died in a tragic accident when he was hit by a car while hitchhiking. His other child was a girl with not much interest in farming. Therefore, Joe was always looking for additional farmhands to support his full-time workers. Farming was also in my family. I remember as a young boy, my idol, Cousin Roger Funk, worked through the summers on the farm.

When I mentioned to my mom and dad that I had interest in the job, they both looked at me with a smirk. I wondered what that was all about, although it did not take long before I discovered what they were thinking.

I immediately called Mr. McLaughlin and after a short talk he invited me to visit him on the farm. I drove out there on a Saturday morning in early May. I had just gotten my driver's license and borrowed my parents' station wagon. I knocked on the door and Mrs. McLaughlin answered the door. I told her why I was there and after a pleasant smile she turned around and said, "Joe, your appointment is here, the Walsh boy."

Joe came to the door with his worn out light blue hat. He was a big man with grey hair and a long face. He had a relaxed presence about him and seemed to just mosey along. His big, callused hand wrapped around my own with a tight grip.

He showed me around the farm, including the big, long red barn that was home to over 200 cows and a few bulls. Joe showed me the stretch of land that he owned that went as far as my eyes could see to the base of the hillside. He also had land across the road for growing crops and haying. On top of the hillside sat a little white trailer with two light blue stripes along the side. It seemed like the trailer had been there for a while as the black tires were worn and flat. Cedar blocks were stacked up on all corners of the trailer for stability. I soon found out that the trailer was his full-time farmhand's house – Doc.

I met Doc for the first time as we toured the barn. In-between the stalls, the darkened tunnel had light bulbs every 20 feet with nine-foot ceilings. Doc came out of one of the stalls after hearing Mr. McLaughlin's voice.

Doc was a short skinny man around 5'2". He wore a green John Deere hat with "DOC" written on it with black magic marker. He wore thick black rimmed glasses, the left lens cracked in the corner. His rubber boots went almost to his knees covering his blue jeans. He wore a checked black and red flannel shirt over a black tee shirt. He reeked like the barn.

Mr. McLaughlin said, "Hey, Doc, this is Ken Walsh. He will be helping us out on the weekends. I want you to show him the ropes tomorrow for his first day." Doc just turned away looking frustrated and said with a monotone voice, "Yep."

Joe looked over to me with a quick glance, "You'll get used to him. He means no harm. His bark is a lot worse than his bite." I thanked McLaughlin for the opportunity and asked him what time he needed me back in the morning.

"Four thirty will do." "Four thirty in the afternoon?" I said, wondering why so late. He said, "No, A.M."

I tried not to look at him too stunned although I now knew my party days with my buddies were going to end quickly.

The next day came way too early. I was up by 4 am, had a quick donut and OJ and was off in my sister Ellen's white Omni. I did not sleep well the night before in anticipation of the next day's work. I had Elton John's Yellow Brick Road cassette playing in the car on high volume to keep awake along with the windows down and the cool morning air blowing in my face. The back country road to South Amenia was quiet as I was the only car I saw during the 7-mile trip to the farm. It was still dark although the skies were clear and showing the last of the stars for that night.

Passion for Life

I drove up the dirt road and saw McLaughlin's barn lights on like many of the other farms I passed. I drove up to the main door of the red barn and parked the Omni near the main entrance. When I got out, I immediately called for Doc. No answer. I walked into the entrance and looked around. Again, I called out his name. Still no answer. Country music was echoing throughout the dark narrow dimly lit area.

"Hey, Doc, I'm here – Ken Walsh".

Finally, Doc appeared from one of the stalls and just gave me a look like "what do you want, get to work."

I dove into the first stall and started milking my first cow until Doc started yelling at me with some language I had never heard. I am sure it was some colorful language in between his ranting. I assumed he just wanted me to do something else. So, I went to the attic and started throwing down bales of hay. That was not it as Doc raised his voice even louder. I then worked my way down the ladder to the first level and ran toward the end of the barn to the grain storage area and filled the wheelbarrow with feed. Doc looked at me more intently and yelled louder. This time he came over to me and grabbed my arm. I really thought for a moment he was going to swing at me.

Doc pointed me over to the stall and said "Milk". I finally understood what he wanted. He wanted me to begin milking on one end of the stalls while he did the other.

Doc and I had a tough beginning; although after I learned the routine and showed that I worked hard he started gaining respect for me. For the next few weekends, Doc and I would start the milking process, feed the cows, clean the barn by pushing the cow manure into the channel belt and then letting the cows out of the barn for the day. During the rest of the day, we did all sorts of chores from fixing fences, repairing the barn, spreading the manure with the tractor, etc. By 3:30 PM I was done for the day. I began to understand what Doc wanted me to do without him saying a word. His body language or his grunts were enough. Doc started to loosen up and began to crack a smile here and there. I knew things were going well when Doc invited me to his trailer for lunch.

We had just finished a morning full of chores and daily routines. The clear sunny sky was as blue as one could imagine. Not a cloud in the sky with a dry 80 degrees. It was a picture-perfect day in Dutchess County.

"Hey Kenny Boy, I have a real treat for ya today. How about lunch at my place?" I said, "Sure Doc that would be great." "Follow me, son, and let's get some grub," Doc said.

We walked up a dirt tractor pathway leading up to a hill overlooking the farm. The green pasture was on both sides with barbed wire fences dividing each field. I was a couple of feet behind Doc as he hustled up the path. His brown knee-high boots still had manure on them from the day's work.

As we got to his white trailer with the two blue horizontal stripes, I could not help noticing all of the junk he had accumulated around the trailer. Old tires, tin cans, broken outdoor chairs and a wheel barrow without a wheel was on the lawn. I followed Doc to the white rusted metal door. A wooden stump was on the step. Doc had to force the door open as it scraped the bottom of the floor. Looking into the trailer was certainly not a pretty sight. Straight ahead was the kitchen sink. He had everything in the sink from dirty dishes, pots and pans, cups and more. The countertop did not look like it had been clean in years.

"Have a seat while I cook up something better than your grandma's cooking," Doc said as he cleaned newspaper off a wooden kitchen chair. I sat down, afraid to touch anything.

Doc said, "You thirsty?" "Sure Doc," I replied. He grabbed an empty Campbell's noodle soup tin can and ran the faucet. He rinsed it out a few times and then filled the can to the rim.

"Here you go, drink up."

I took the can from Doc's hand, looked inside the can and saw some debris floating to the top. I placed the can on the kitchen table surrounded by used plates and sat worried that Doc would say, "Drink up." Lucky for me he just turned his back and opened the white cupboard door searching for a pan. He finally found what he was looking for and placed a small black cast iron pan on top of the stove and turned the heat on high. He then went to the refrigerator, grabbed a tin foil package and set it on the counter. He grabbed a stick of butter and unwrapped it, then threw it into the heated pan. Immediately the butter sizzled. As he opened the tin foil, I saw fresh, white, gray-looking meat.

I thought to myself, "Oh my God I'm going to die."

Four big pieces of meat were placed in the heated pan, side by side. He turned down the heat and let the meat simmer in the buttery juice.

"Kenny boy, you are gonna love this good old country lunch," Doc said with pride.

The smell of the cooking meat filled the trailer. In a matter of minutes, the meat was cooked and ready to go. Doc grabbed two paper plates. He grabbed the meat from the pan with a fork and threw two pieces on each of our plates. He placed the plate in front of me and the smell of buttery meat was music to my senses. With a fork, I cut into a quarter of the meat and tasted it. My first bite of the tender meat was delicious. It melted in my mouth. Each bite was most enjoyable.

"Hey Doc, this is great. What the hell is this?" Doc looked over his John Deere green baseball cap and said, "Rattlesnake."

I coughed up a bite into my mouth, managing to keep it inside my lips.

"Damn good, isn't it?" Doc continued. "I hunt these suckers each weekend during my-off time. It was my mom's specialty."

"Doc, I must say this is pretty good. No, I mean really good," I replied.

Passion for Life

Doc came back with, "I knew you would like it, even a city slicker like you."

We both cracked up laughing. At that moment, I think Doc and I began to bond. As weeks went by, I got to know Doc better; I always asked him, "How's the snake hunting?" Doc would respond, "Some of those nasty creatures always want a piece of me and stick those fangs in me. But, I'm too damn fast for them." He always invited me to join him for his rattlesnake hunts. Unfortunately, I never did go with him. I regret it to this day.

Unfortunately, my farming days were numbered, not due to lack of work, but lack of experience and key mistakes. One early Saturday morning in June, I arrived at the farm a little late. I was with the boys the night before camping out after celebrating a baseball victory. We drank too much Boone's Farm apple wine. I had to get up at 4:00 a.m. while my buddies continued to sleep it off. With my eyes bloodshot and my body feeling woozy, I got to work 15 minutes late. Doc was in the stalls doing his piece milking the cows. I told Doc that I was sorry and jumped in trying to catch up with my responsibilities. I was working fast going from stall to stall like clockwork. Halfway into the morning, I jumped over one stall without paying attention.

I quickly got down to start using the suction machine on the cow, realizing too late that I was in the bull's pen. Rocko, the bull, was not pleased. I attempted to make a hasty move out of the pen only to be kicked through the fence by Rocko. It happened so fast that the force made me crash through and break the fence barrier. Doc heard the sound of the cracking board and ran to my side. I was down face first, my baseball hat four feet away from me.

"Kenny, you OK, kid? That is Rocko, you fool. He could have killed ya." Doc went over to the broken fence, replacing the fence to keep Rocko in his stall. I was still seeing stars as I rolled over trying to catch my breath.

Doc then started busting my chops, "Hey City Slicker, you need a lesson on anatomy. That animal there sure doesn't have a nipple." Doc belted out with an uncontrollable belly laugh. He continued, "Rocko sure kicked the snot out of you son," as he continued laughing hard holding his belly.

Later that morning after the rest of the chores were completed, I sat down on a bale of hay leaning up against the barn's outside wall enjoying the sun beating on my face. My back and butt were extremely sore from the early morning wakeup call with Rocko. Doc was taking a break and threw Redman chew in his mouth while also sitting near me. He started chuckling to himself. I knew what he was thinking.

"Doc, I am glad I was your entertainment today," as I got up walking to the barn. I thought a nice cup of creamy fresh milk would help my spirits. Fresh milk from the cow is like ice cream. After one of our milk sessions Doc introduced me to this heavenly delight. He just reached into the milk container with a cup and scooped out this wonderful thick cream. It was certainly like nothing I ever tasted before. I never imagined milk tasting that good.

Ken Walsh

The milk truck had just arrived and was draining the milk from the container. I knew I had only a few more minutes to get my cup before it was gone. I went into the barn, opened the container, and reached in with my cup. There was only a quarter left deep down in the four-foot tub. As I reached further in, leaning over and just hanging on by one arm, I slipped. I fell all the way making a milky splash. I quickly got up and jumped out covered completely in milk. Doc came in to see me in this state and said, "You've really done it this time."

Doc quickly went outside to tell the truck driver. Unfortunately, the milk was now contaminated and all of it had to be dumped from the truck to the container. I had to drain what was left in the tub and scrub down the walls to purify the area. Worst of all, Mr. McLaughlin had to be notified that his milk product was wasted. Mr. McLaughlin was good with me although I think he was questioning if I could ever be a good farm hand and worth the risk.

The following weekend answered that question. After morning duties were completed - milking and feeding the cows and cleaning up the barn - I was asked to spread manure in the field across the road from the barn. I was very excited as I had just learned how to drive the tractor. It was one of the old-style maroon tractors with the two wheels in front and the big black wheels in the back. I loved sitting up high and riding in the fields during the early summer days.

I sat on the tractor filled with manure waiting for the signal to go from Doc. He gave me the thumbs up and off I went into the front field heading toward the wire fence separating the road from the next field. The road I had to cross over was a main road with a lot of traffic for a back country road. I approached the slight incline heading to the road with the wagon full of manure in the back. I got over the crest heading into the next big dip to the field when a car flew by beeping its horn and the driver yelling out the window. I thought it was one of my buddies.

I turned quickly around to wave and lost control of the steering. The tractor veered off to the right falling off the side of the steep hill. With the balance completely uneven the tractor began to tip over. I dove off the tractor and watched hopelessly as the tractor went crashing to its side and the wagon tipped and spread the entire manure on the road. Doc and Joe Laughlin just stood stunned at the barn door watching the sight. The tractor stalled and luckily shut off. Joe and Doc walked down the path to me. He just looked over to me and said, "Son, you OK?" I looked over to him sheepishly and nodded my head.

Traffic was backed up for an hour as Doc and I shoveled the manure off the road. I remember how embarrassed I was and how hot it was shoveling. It would be the last straw for my farming career. That afternoon Mr. McLaughlin sat me down and said, "Kenny, I would love to keep you. We like you, but I don't think farming is for you." I agreed and thanked Mr. McLaughlin for the opportunity. Later that summer, I found a more suitable job – lifeguarding.

Passion for Life

Reflecting to the experience I had with farming, I recall now how life teaches you lessons that sometimes one does not realize until years later. One was that sometimes one must discover strengths and weaknesses of abilities. My weaknesses in farming led to my success in lifeguarding and water safety training that I carried the rest of my life. I also realized the most important lesson is to never judge a book by its cover. My first impression of Doc was that he was a hick farmer and thought immediately that I was better than him. It was a very poor way to look at a person before learning about them. I realized that Doc was totally happy in his environment. His life as a farm hand satisfied him. It was simple and enjoyable. He knew where he belonged every moment of his life. Not many people can say that.

I only saw Doc one more time after that summer. I had no real reason to go back to the farm. I got busy with finishing high school and all the activities and social events that go with growing up. One winter evening during my senior year, I ran into Doc. I was filling my car with gas on Route 22 heading to Dover Plains to work at the Old Drovers Inn Bed and Breakfast. I got out of my car and began to pump the gas and on the other island pumping gas was a little man with a green hat and wearing a coat that seemed a little too big for him. Not until he turned to place the gas hose back into the pump booth did I realize it was Doc. I immediately stopped pumping gas in my car and walked over to him, "Doc, is that you? How the hell are you?" He looked up wearing the same cracked glasses and the same John Deere hat. We had small talk and went our separate ways.

As I was finishing college, I learned from my mother while she was attending church that Mr. McLaughlin mentioned he lost one of his best farm hands that was with him for many years. Doc died of cancer. When my mother told me the news, I was quiet for a while. Even though Doc was in my life for only a short period of time, I wished that I had gotten to know him a little more to know more about his life. He was not a well-established teacher, coach, businessperson that our society looks up to. Doc was happy being who he was. He was comfortable in his own skin. He had purpose in life and I will never forget him.

Journey 4

Webutuck High School Seniors: Robbie Alkeman, Andrew Erskine, Gary Murphy, Pat Daughty, Bill Wright, Dan Merwin, Ken Walsh, Rich Cummings, Keith Bradley

"Life is either a daring adventure or nothing at all."   Helen Keller

Halloween School Invasion

In the fall of 1978, my senior year adventures continued with creative mischief. We had just finished our soccer season, successfully playing in the sectionals. We ended our high school soccer career on the field winning the first round against Croton Harmon High School, 2-1. Our team from Webutuck High School, a small school with a student body of less than 400, played beyond expectations by beating many of the Class A schools in the Poughkeepsie area. Unfortunately, our second round against Briarcliff from Westchester County, NY, eliminated us from the tournament and the final run to the championship.

This loss led to a much needed "lift me up" adventure. I called my buddy, Patrick Daughty, and said, "Hey buddy. I have an idea on how to celebrate Halloween, are you in?" "I don't know Ken, what are you thinking?" Patrick replied. I hesitated a moment and said, "A Halloween invasion at Webutuck. A way to make our mark on the school forever from the Class of 79."

A week before Halloween, a few of us drove around our towns, Amenia and Millerton, stealing or as I reminded everyone, "borrowing" pumpkins from as many lawns from the main streets to the back roads. I had my four-door light blue and rusted, unreliable 5-speed Toyota Corona. Many times, I had to park the car facing downhill to start the car. For $350, I got total value for the money along with many headaches of jump starts.

On the Sunday evening before Halloween, Patrick met me at my house after 6:30 pm. I finished dinner and told my mom that Patrick was coming over and we were going out. Mom was glad that I was home for a change since most of the time I either had practice or a game during the months of September and October. My Mom would rather have me stay put for the evening. I gobbled down my breaded chicken cutlets, mashed potatoes and green beans, guzzled my milk as Patrick knocked on the door.

"Patrick is here, Mom, I got to go." I went to the door with the plans to just leave when Mom followed me and said, "Wait a minute." "Hi Mrs. Walsh!" Patrick said. He was wearing his Green Webutuck Varsity jacket that he and I picked out for our class.

"I have a feeling you two are up to no good, what's going on?" my Mom quizzed us. "And why is my basement filled with pumpkins? There must be a hundred of them down there," she went on.

During the week I kept the back part of the cellar opened leading into a 10' by 30' storage area. Usually no one went down into that section of the basement. My Mom was searching for something that Sunday afternoon and she could not help but see all of the pumpkins. We were caught.

"Mom don't worry. We are doing a class project that is due tomorrow," I said.

"You boys be careful; I don't want the State Troopers knocking on my door," she said. "Sure thing Mom, see you later." We ran to Patrick's yellow Dodge Charger, got in and off we went in the darkness of the crisp autumn evening.

"Patrick, right around the corner on Murphy's farm I found the mother load of pumpkins. It must be 100 pounds, the size of a picnic table. It is sitting right on Murphy's front lawn, screaming for us to take it."

Patrick's eyes lit up and said, "You sure we want that one, how are we going to fit that monster in the car?"

"Simple, we'll drive up with your back trunk open, turn off your lights and slowly creep up to the front lawn. I'll get out, grab the sucker, throw it in the back and off we go."

Patrick drove up Lango Road beyond my house, turned right onto Prospect Avenue toward the stop sign at the four corners. On the other side of the road heading down Powerhouse Road sat the Murphy farm. There, under the streetlight, was the mother of all pumpkins. Patrick shut his lights and popped open

Passion for Life

the back trunk. He slowly crept toward the farmhouse's front lawn. As the car approached the pumpkin, I jumped out of the car and reached over the pumpkin. It was much heavier than I thought it would be. I got it up to my stomach with my arms holding it along the side. I turned towards the car struggling to walk, losing my grip. Patrick whispered with a stern voice, "Walsh, come on, let's go."

Just then, the front porch lights of Murphy's house went on as I got to the back of the car. Then a dog started barking from one of the neighbor's house. I got the great pumpkin in the trunk just in time as the door of the house opened. I ran over to the front window of the passenger side door and jumped in with legs dangling out of the window as Patrick sped away. Patrick looked in the rearview window seeing old man Murphy coming out onto the lawn as we were safe and clear.

We then headed to the next town, Wassaic. We were told by one of our friends that an old toilet bowl was on the side of Route 22 in front of a gas station. That was the last piece of the puzzle for our plan. We drove up to the parking lot of the gas station, quickly grabbed the toilet bowl and threw in the back sit. When we got back to my house, we went into my cellar through the back door and placed the toilet bowl near the pumpkins.

Between Patrick Daughty, Keith Bradley and me, we collected most of the pumpkins and delivered them to my house to be stored in my basement until Halloween night. That is when the plan was unfolded to the rest of our classmates who played on our intramural team for the last 5 years. Our High School intramural team was called the Mario Nostrum Fugoroller Gang. We shortened the name to MNF. The name came off a tee shirt I wore to school one day in eighth grade. It was a hand-me-down tee shirt that my Aunt Marie gave me. Since her husband was known to have some connections with the Mafia, I used the tee shirt for bragging rights, wearing it in school. I told my buddies that Mario Nostrum Fugoroller was a gang in Italy. Later during my Junior year, my brother Dennis burst my bubble and told me the real meaning. In Italian, it means "Our Sea". The tee shirt was advertisement for a restaurant in Brooklyn.

It was Monday at school. During lunch recess I got together with the rest of the MNF gang in the cafeteria and discussed the plan for the evening.

At 1:00 am on Halloween morning, cars began to arrive in front of my house. MNF gang members, Patrick Daughty, Tom Flood, Jim Krieling, David Shufelt, David Shufelt, Gary Murphy, Bill Parker, Charlie Matolla, Frank Collier, and Tracy Farrar drove to my house preparing for the assault onto Webutuck High School. One by one they came into the kitchen. I assumed that my mother, who was hard of hearing, was not going to wake at 1:00 am. I was wrong. Even though we were trying to be quiet the early morning ruckus woke up my mom. She came into the kitchen to see all my friends dressed in black head to toe, even with black hats and gloves. It looked like Mission Impossible on a secret adventure.

Ken Walsh

"What are you boys doing? I don't like this. It looks like trouble to me!" said my mother half awake.

"Nothing Mom, go back to bed, we are just hanging out," I replied.

"I don't want to get a call from the State Troopers tonight. Whatever you are doing I don't want to know."

With that said, we all went into the basement and took the pumpkins out from the side door, filling the cars for the trip to Webutuck High School. We took the back road to get there so any sheriff or state police would not be suspicious seeing the line of cars going through Main Street in Amenia, especially with the back seats full of pumpkins.

As we got to the bottom of the hill leading to the school, we all pulled our cars to the side. I had Tracy stay put as the lookout. He had one of the walkie talkies while Gary Murphy had the other. Gary was going to be stationed on top of the roof of the high school to pass the message from Tracy to us of unwanted intruders (Police).

We left Tracy behind and drove to the back side of the building. We parked our cars at the base of the baseball field and unloaded all of the pumpkins to the base of the boy's locker room wall. There was a ten-foot wall leading to the roof that was flat on the backside of the building.

Bill Parker, the tallest of all of us (six feet two inches), helped me get to the roof's edge. I got on his shoulders, reached for the edge and shimmied up with a thick rope around my neck. I tied the rope around the stink pipe of the boy's locker room and threw it over the edge for the rest of the gang. Gary Murphy came up after me to be the lookout. He was getting feedback from Tracy as each car drove past him on Route 22, "No cops, that was just another car." Tom, Jim, David and Charlie climbed up to help me. Frank, Bill, Patrick stayed below throwing up pumpkins to us. Since we all were athletes, we were able to catch most of the orange balls, preventing them from smashing onto the roof. The challenge was getting the big momma of a pumpkin up to us. Bill Parker grabbed the pumpkin and pressed it over his head. Tom and Charlie held on to each one of my legs as I hung over the edge. Once I had the pumpkin in my hands, the boys pulled me up. Finally, the toilet bowl followed using the same method. Once all of the pumpkins and toilet were on the roof, it was time to get them to the other side of the building and drop them into the courtyard. The rest of the boys climbed up the rope and joined us. I noticed Frank having something in his hand. "Frank, what's that?" I asked.

"You are going to like this, Kenny. I made a dummy of Principal Grant. We'll stick his head in the toilet bowl." All of us busted out laughing as we proceeded to get to the other side of the building.

There was no anchor to tie the rope to the roof. Bill and Frank held onto the rope and threw it to the other side. One by one we climbed down. Once we were all down, Bill and Frank threw each pumpkin to us into the courtyard. We stacked all the pumpkins around the cherry tree in front of Mr. Grant's office. The toilet was thrown down crashing into the soft grass while the dummy followed. The last item was the "Big Mamma" pumpkin.

Frank said, "Do you really want this one."

I said, "Frank, come on, just throw it down. I'll catch it. We got to get going."

"OK, buddy here it comes." Frank picked the orange bomb up and let it drop. I was directly under it as it flew toward my chest, 10 feet below. The pumpkin hit my chest exploding pumpkin debris all over me and knocking me flat on my back. As I was lying on my back in pumpkin pie, the gang was laughing uncontrollably. Jim came over to help me up and said, "Kenny you look like you just joined the Orangemen of Syracuse."

We placed the toilet bowl under the cherry tree and tied the dummy to the tree upside down with the head in the towel. Mr. Grant's name was printed on the dummy's belly--"Mr. Grant, Happy Halloween." All of a sudden, Gary said "Tracy is on the horn! A car is coming up toward the school." It was now 2:00 am and we knew it was not any of the administration or custodians. We all stayed still waiting to hear if the car turned into the school parking lot.

Gary said, "Coast is clear, the car drove by."

Our job was done, and it was time to get out of "Dodge". We walked over to the area where the rope was hanging and it was gone. We looked up and could not see Frank and Bill. Tom said, "Are you kidding me. They didn't leave it here."

"No way," I said. "Frank, Bill, come on man, where are you guys?"

They finally appeared out of the darkness, "You guys looking for this?" They threw the rope down to us. We all shimmied up, and in the darkness climbed down the wall, went to our cars to head our separate ways, waiting for the short night to be over to see our prized project during the early morning school hours.

Some of us did not sleep and others just had a few hours of sleep before we all entered the hallways of Webutuck High School the next morning just before 7:00 am. Since we were all seniors, all of us drove our own cars into school that morning. We pulled in and parked right in front of the main doorways going into the school. Buses rolled in one after the other as we hung out until everyone arrived.

As we made our move toward the door, we saw a line of custodians carrying pumpkins out of the courtyard into the hallway and out to the maintenance room. A crowd of underclassmen looked out the tall glass windows, watching with interest. We gathered behind them and heard some of the conversation.

"Last night someone dumped all of these pumpkins in the courtyard. See, there is a toilet bowl with a stuffed dummy upside down in the toilet. It has Mr. Grant's name on it."

"I wonder who had the balls to do this?"

Just then, two custodians took the toilet bowl and cut down the tied-up dummy. We had all sworn to secrecy that no one would say a word. That morning as everyone settled into their home rooms, an announcement came over the PA system.

"Ken Walsh and Andrew Erskine, please come to the principal's office."

Andrew and I were the President and Vice President of Student Council. Andrew did not make it that night to help with our project due to a family commitment, although he was aware of what we did. We walked together down the hall to the principal's office.

"Kenny, what do you think Grant wants?" Andrew asked.

"I don't know. Someone might have ratted us out."

We got into the secretary's office, and she led us into Mr. Grant's office. Mr. Grant sat behind his paper-covered desk looking down with his hands clasped. He was a big man with big chunky hands, looking like an offensive lineman. He had dark wavy hair with his black trimmed glasses. His voice was low and deep. He commanded respected.

Andrew and I sat down quickly directly in front of his desk. Mr. Grant slowly looked up at us. I thought he knew what we did and he was going to give us the riot act. I was thinking I would open my mouth and confess to help limit the agony of the silence. Just then Mr. Grant said as he stared at us with his squinting eyes, "Boys, I need your help. I want you to help me find out who did this. This is not good for school morale."

I immediately spoke up and replied, "Absolutely Mr. Grant, I agree with you. We will do our best to figure this out and get back to you." We left his office and walked back to the hallway trying not to laugh. Andrew said, "You said you were going to help. You are kidding me." As he playfully elbowed me in the side.

1984 Amenia Monarchs Tri-State Champions

Back Row: Jim LaPierre, Greg Hosier, Charlie Thorton, Jim Bud, Larry Murphy, Larry Jackson, Tom Downey, Mike Kourht
Front Row: Ken Walsh, TJ Campion, Phil Carol, Bill Caroll, Joe Caroll, Paul Giroux, Howie Mann

"Failure is not the opposite of success, it's part of success." William Ritter

The Lessons of Failure that Lead to Success

I had a successful year playing baseball at Keystone College in LaPlume, Pennsylvania, my freshman year. I was recruited to Keystone by the soccer coach. After a short period of time in the net with three other outstanding recruits, my college soccer days were over, especially since Fall baseball was happening at the same time. The baseball coach, Mike Mould, talked with the soccer coach and they both agreed that baseball was better suited for me at the college level.

I found myself picking up ground balls at second base while Coach Mould hit infield with a big wad of chewing tobacco in his mouth. I took notice that most of the players around the diamond also were chewing. The first baseman came over to me and said, "You chew, don't you?" I responded, "Yea, of course. What you got?" He pulled out two packs from the back pocket of his baseball pants, Red Fox and Redman. He continued, "What's your pleasure?" "Redman will do," I responded.

I rolled up the Redman in a ball and placed it inside my right cheek. Coach Mould kept firing ground balls at us. I was getting hyper with the tobacco beginning to take effect. For a very short time, I thought chewing was cool until it went straight to my head. I started to get woozy and lightheaded. Then it happened. Coach Mould called out, "OK Kenny boy, here we go" as he hit a sharp grounder to me. The ball took a bad bounce and came up at me, quickly hitting me in the throat. My reaction was an immediate swallow. The players around the infield saw the situation and watched me turn shades of green as I fell to the ground upchucking my lunch on the infield. It was one of the worst feelings I could remember.

Adding to the embarrassment, the Pennsylvania boys gathered around me watching the show as Coach Mould came over and kneeled with his hand on the back of my neck trying to relax me. After a while, I started to come around. I got to my feet and Coach walked me over to the bench. He put his arm around me and said, "Kenny, no need to try to impress the rest of the players by being someone you're not. Chewing is not for everyone." I weakly replied, "Thanks Coach, tough lesson for me today."

That was a tough beginning on the Keystone Giants baseball team, but things did get much better. I made the team and played good fall ball. During the off-season, I stayed in shape and trained hard for the spring season. My quick foot speed and ability to get on base helped me start most of the games playing second base. And when not starting at second base, I was the designated hitter (DH). Our team had a decent season ending up 13-8 going into the regional post- season games. We lost our second-round game to Morrisville, NJ. I ended up hitting a .364 as a freshman.

After the season, I transferred to SUNY Cortland to major in Physical Education rather than my original interest in Computer Science. Coach Mould sat down with me and tried to convince me to stay another year and then transfer. He had his eye on me to play third base. I expressed my appreciation and told him my mind was made up. That summer, I played my first summer for the Amenia Monarchs with some of the legends I watched play when I was a kid: Tommy Downey, Mike Kourht, Charlie Thornton, Paul Giroux and Joey Carroll. I developed a good relationship with the great "Doc" Bartlett, the legendary coach and player for the Monarchs who was now scorekeeper. He was in his late seventies and knew almost everything about baseball. His son Billy went to

Passion for Life

Cortland and was a star pitcher for the team holding the record at that time for the most wins in a season. With this connection, I thought for sure after a successful freshman college start and playing with a seasoned semi-pro team that I was ready for the Cortland Dragon baseball team.

Arriving in the fall of 1980 at Cortland as a sophomore, I was fired up to start the fall baseball season. I was placed in a suite with 8 other students, all transfers from around the state. My two roommates were soccer players, Randy and Gerry, one a striker and the other a goalkeeper. Also in the suite were two gymnasts, an ice hockey goalie and a tennis player. I was right where I needed to be - sharing a suite with a bunch of jocks. Cortland was known for producing strong Physical Education, Recreation and Education majors. Their facilities were new, and the sports complexes were state of the art. The student body was much larger than Keystone, going from 800 residential students to over 7,000. I didn't realize the magnitude of the excellent athletes at Cortland until my first day of tryouts. Cortland's baseball records were impressive led by longtime coach "Sparky" Wallace, a chain-smoking baseball guru. It was disappointing to me that the JV team had been cut out of the budget that past summer. This would have been my fall back if I didn't make the Varsity squad.

I walked out of the field house in my sweats with glove in hand ready to play ball only to see more than 100 players on the field with the same idea. Along with the challenge of competing with so many players, most of the team from last year was coming back. Coach Wallace did not make much of an adjustment and kept his core players, cutting 75 including me. I took it in stride knowing the fall season was short. The winter tryout was when it really counts.

Doc called me up and told me not to worry. He spoke with Coach Wallace and told him that he was going to keep a good eye on me for the winter tryout. I thanked Doc and assured him that I was going to give it my all. During the off season I trained extremely hard. Even though my suite mates were partying quite a bit, I was able to mix the fun times with schoolwork and a fitness regimen to be prepared for the baseball call out. I ran 3 to 5 miles every day. I lifted weights every other day. I went into the field house 3 to 5 days a week taking ground balls and hitting in the cage. I was convinced that once I put my mind to something, I was going to complete the task. I surrounded myself with the current Cortland players and pumped myself up with the Rocky movie and soundtrack. I was prepared mentally and physically for the tryout.

After my first semester at Cortland, I went home for school break. My plan was to shorten my time at home and go back early to continue my regimen until tryouts began. While at home, I went to the high school and continued my training, taking grounders in the gym and hitting off the tee. I even made a makeshift tee in my basement at home. Under the gray painted stairway, I hung a rope from underneath the top stair, drilled a hole through a baseball, put the rope through the hole of the baseball and tied a knot. I placed a net around the stairs and was able to hit into the net as the ball swung back for the next swing. I remember my mother coming down the stairs and saying "Kenneth Arthur, what are you doing? Don't knock the stairs down!"

I arrived in Cortland right after New Year with a strong mind and body. I was anxious to get going. Finally, when the rest of the student body arrived, the schedule for the practices came out. All of the practices were in the field house right next to the football field, Monday through Friday. Coach Wallace had four weeks of tryouts and practices before making his team selection.

This round of tryouts did not have as many players. There were about 50, half as many as the fall call out. I assumed those who got cut either did not try out again or played another sport. Half that showed up were players coming back from last year and most were juniors and seniors. There were only 5 slots open for new players. On top of that, the captain of the team was a senior and all-star second baseman. I looked at it in a positive way. I could learn a lot from him and next year the position could be mine. The challenge would be to beat out a junior second baseman that was already on the team.

All the practices started at 6:00 pm and ran until 8:30. We covered the basic warmups in the first 30 minutes, then did running drills. We were taught the fundamentals of the game with different coaching assistants, hit the batting cages and played our position. The routine continued like that for the first two weeks. My quick speed was able to shine during the drills and steady infield play helped as well. After the first two weeks, Coach Wallace cut the team down to 30 players with two more cuts before the spring Florida trip. I was encouraged that playing for the Dragons was becoming a reality.

The following two weeks I stepped up my game even more. I stayed beyond practice to take more swings in the cage. I took additional grounders. Whatever extra work I needed, I spent time doing it. Within a week, Coach let us know that he had two more cuts to make before he had his final roster. On a Saturday morning with a week to go, the list was up in the hallway across from the entrance of the locker room at the Physical Education Recreation Building. Coach mentioned by 9:00 a.m. the list would be up. On the list were the members still on the team. I remember not going out to the bars that Friday night with my buddies so I could get there to see the list first thing in the morning. Snow was on the ground and the wind was blowing in my face as I jogged almost a mile to get to the building from my dorm. I opened the door of the long hallway and jogged to the front of the locker room entrance. I immediately worked my way from the bottom of the list since every name was placed alphabetically. "Walsh" was on the list. I was pumped up, throwing my fist in the air and howling with excitement. I came back to the list to figure out how many more needed to be cut to get to the 30-man roster. I counted 32 on the list. Only 2 more players to be cut. That sobered me up a bit as I walked down the hall. I knew I had to get through the next week.

Passion for Life

That week seemed to be a blur between classes and practice. I must admit I had no focus on schoolwork. At practice, I was really beginning to gel with the team. I was feeling part of the team. Once again, I did all the extras, spending more time in the cage. The timing of my swing felt good, hitting the tennis ball machine from a close distance. Unfortunately, I did not see any live pitching or breaking pitches. I believed that the next two cuts came down to three possibilities, a freshman pitcher, another sophomore infielder, and me.

Two days before the final cut day, Coach Wallace handed out the spring training schedule for the Florida trip. In eight days, we had a 12-game schedule. I was thrilled to have this chance. For me, it would be the first time in Florida along with a college team, playing ball during spring training.

The last day of practice, we went through our regular routine. As practice was wrapping up, Coach asked three of us to stay for extra time in the cage. It was the three that I thought were prospects for the final cut. Coach had the freshman pitcher pitch to us in the cage. The other infielder batted first. The pitcher threw at him slider after slider. The kid had a good one, breaking at knee level and keeping the ball low. The batter struggled making good contact. I had the same trouble when it was my turn. I had the chance to watch and pick up on his pitches, although I had no luck making solid contact. I did not miss the ball often but I hit the ball foul or on the ground. I looked back at Coach. He was puffing his cigarette and had no expression. He spoke up and said, "Ok we are all set, let's pack it up boys." We picked up the gear and headed over to the equipment room. The lights were turned off and the door of the field house was closed. Try outs were over. The next morning, we would find out the final roster and our fate.

That night my suite mates quizzed me on what I thought my chances were. I said, it was up in the air at this point. I did all that I could although the last batting with live pitching was my best performance. My buddies knew I gave it my all. They said if anyone deserves to be on that team, it is you. That night, I went to bed earlier than usual. I got on my knees and prayed to God to give me the chance to make the team. I never was in this position before, never been cut from a team. I did not want it to be the first time.

Morning did not come soon enough. I was up at dawn and went to the cafeteria by myself for breakfast then headed over to the facility. This time I was really rushing to get there like before. I opened the door and looked down the hall and saw two of the senior players looking at the list. They did not notice me until I was halfway down the hallway. They looked over at me and then glanced down to the floor avoiding eye contact. I gave them a head nod and then looked at the list, once again looking from the bottom up. I could not find my name. In disbelief, I looked again hoping my name was not in alphabetical order. It was not there. One of the players put his hand on my shoulder and said, "That can't be right. You should be on this team. Go see Coach on Monday and talk to him.

It can't be right." My chest felt like it just caved in. I was stunned that I got cut even though I knew that it was possible. I did not want to believe it. I looked up at the player and replied, "Yea I will." Then I just turned and walked away. My steps seemed too heavy like walking in cement shoes. I never felt this lost before.

That day was one of the worst days in my life besides losing my parents. I wandered around the campus and the town for hours. When I got back to the dorm, I tried to drink my sorrows away with tequila. It did not take long for me to be so intoxicated that I spent most of evening in the bathroom singing to the toilet bowl. It was not a good sight.

On Monday morning, I went to Coach's office. He was down the hall in the athletic coach's wing among some of the other sports staff. I popped my head in while he was behind his desk. He was doing paperwork and looked up. I said, "Hi Coach, I see that I was cut." I was hoping at this point that Coach would speak up and say, "No you're not. That's got to be a mistake." That did not happen except for him staring at me through his black-framed glasses. I continued, "Coach is there anything that you can advise me on what I need to do to make this team in the future?"

He paused a few seconds and replied, "Ken you're a good ball player. I had to make a tough choice. I need pitching and you seemed to have trouble with the slider. I hope you try out again."

Now I knew the cut was final and I had to move on. For weeks, I did not know what to do with myself since I put all my thoughts and energy into making the team. I had a huge gap in my life. Eventually, I turned to playing Rugby. The sport seemed to have a good fit for me since I had enough speed to compete. That summer I played again for the Amenia Monarchs and continued playing in the men's league for another eight years before moving to Maine. I made one last attempt to make the team my junior year. This attempt was a feeble one as I missed practices and just did not have heart into the tryouts. I eventually stopped attending the practices all together.

This was a painful lesson in my life. Even when one puts their all into something, it still may not be enough. Sometimes it's timing, sometimes it is just not the right fit. Whatever the case, I found out that I needed to move on. I always believed opportunities present themselves in mysterious ways. Perhaps if I made the team, I would have stayed in Cortland and made another career choice leading to a different opportunity other than the Boys & Girls Clubs in New Rochelle. And that could have led to not moving to Maine, not meeting Suzanne, no Sean, no Kate. If that was the sacrifice for not making the team, I'll take it.

Journey 6

"A mentor empowers a person to see a possible future and believes it can be obtained." Shawn Hitchcock

Gus Mascaro – Mr. Boys Club

After graduating from SUNY Cortland in December of 1984, I interviewed for the Unit Director's position at the Boys and Girls Clubs of New Rochelle, New York. I remember driving down to New Rochelle to meet the new Executive Director, Richard Marano, at the South Side Unit. The position was to run the South Side Unit, which shared the facility with the YMCA. I thought I had a good interview, although I found out later that I was actually their second choice. Lucky for me, the Unit Director at the West End August E. Mascaro Unit quit shortly after Rich's tenure and this opened up the job for the Mascaro Unit. I remember receiving the call when I was in Amenia staying at my parents' house. I was elated to start my first full-time job. I did have mixed feelings about leaving behind a part time offer from the Webutuck School Principal Steve O'Connell who offered me the Varsity Baseball coaching job. The thought of going back to my alma mater to coach baseball was a dream come true. But I could not hang my career on a part time job. Interestingly enough, that year the Warrior baseball team went on to win the sectional championships in the spring of 1985. The coach who accepted the job was our high school former first baseman, Don Herring.

A new job in an unfamiliar city was both challenging and thrilling at the same time. I was the youngest Director the organization had ever hired. The Club was established in 1929 by their first Executive Director, Morton Fuerst. He quickly built a good team around him, including a young Director named August "Gus" Mascaro in which the main facility is now named after. As Gus grew into the position, he eventually took over for Morton as the Executive and hired "Hank Deck" DeClemente as his Operations Director.

When I arrived, Gus was retired. He was well in his eighties although he still was on the payroll as a consultant to help the new Executive, Richard Marano, get his feet wet. Mr. Italiano, who I replaced, was a Boys Club Alumni who worked at the Club for seven years after he retired from the Post Office. He was given the job by another retired post office worker who at the time was the Executive Director, Jerry Valenti as part of the agreement with Jerry retiring from the Executive Director's position, Jerry was appointed as my Program Director at the Mascaro Unit. Rich had his hands full being a young Executive at 30 years old and just hired young replacements for the Club's Units. The Boys Club Alumni, being primarily Italian men, were already skeptical about the new leadership and direction of the Club. I also had an Irish last name even though I am half Italian. Kenny Walsh stood out like a sore thumb in the Italian neighborhood.

I remember one of my first meetings with the alumni one Sunday morning. At 10:00 a.m., Rich asked me to come to the Mascaro Unit to meet the Alumni. They were all in the basement of the Club in the community room. I walked in the narrow hallway past the kitchen toward the room and I could see the room was filled with about 40 older men. I clearly could see smoke filling the air and loud conversations as if everyone were talking over each other. Rich opened the door and some of the men yelled over to him, "Hey Richie how ya doing? Who you got there with you?" Rich asked everyone for their attention. Chatter was still going on so he repeated, "Gentlemen, can I get your attention please," in a much louder voice. Most of the men stopped what they were doing and looked up although some were still talking.

Rich went on, "Men I want to introduce you to our new August E. Mascaro Unit Director, Kenny Walsh." At this point everyone stopped what they were doing. The silence was deadly. The Walsh surname instantly got their attention. Even the cigar fell out of the mouth of Gate Datillo, a long-time alumnus. I really do not remember what I said, but I remember the looks on their face - total disbelief. For years, the Boys Club was run by one of their own. This was a bold move on Richard's part to hire a young new director with a surname other than an Italian name. Past directors on the plaques included names such as Mascaro,

Passion for Life

Valenti, Clemente, Italiano etc. For the next few months, the alumni kept their distance although I was always under a watchful eye.

Even with the awkward beginning, I immediately began to transform the activities at the club. I began engaging the youth members with a teen leadership program. I ran into a young teen, Mike Poretta, who had been expelled from the club for misbehavior numerous times by the former director. Mike was an Italian kid with dark hair, brown eyes, dark complexion in a lanky body with a foul mouth and unable to control the "F" word. He tested me a few times early on and each time I brought him to my office for a one-on-one talk, respecting him and telling him I just didn't respect his behavior. Mike slowly began to trust me; leading some of the neighborhood kids to pay attention to my interest in them. Mike eventually became my leader and I named him Youth of the Month even though the current staff was puzzled why I tolerated his attitude. I just told the workers "watch the magic when you begin to believe in them." Mike was someone during my early days at the Club who began to look out for me and gave me heads up on issues before they mushroomed into bigger issues, especially some of the gang activities in the area. Years later when I announced I was leaving to head to Maine, Mike pulled all of the "West End" boys together and surprised me with a going away party at the Centerfield Pub. Mike put together a cassette tape with music from the eighties that reflected the days I was at the Club. I still have that cassette as one of my treasured gifts.

Since I was new to the community and a young director, Rich Marano assigned me to the former retired Executive Director as my mentor. Jerry Valenti's new position was the Youth Coordinator. Jerry and I spent hours talking about the history of the community and the club. Jerry, in his early 70's, didn't have the energy to run with the kids although he was good at organizing the activities and keeping control. I enjoyed Jerry and his easy-going nature immensely. We worked great together on scheduling, discipline issues, and working on the Boys Club alumni. They trusted Jerry even though they did not know how to take me. Rich also suggested another veteran community leader to help in the evening hours with the teens. Terri Swanson lived right around the corner from the Club. She had four children of her own and cared about activities for the area children. We also grew close and as time went by, I called her "Mom". She was my second mother and a mother to all the teen members.

Activities at the Boys & Girls Club began to explode with participation and programs for all ages. During after-school hours between 3 and 5pm, we had youth in the facility from the ages of 6 to 12 years and during 7:00 to 9:00, the 13- to 18-year-olds had the facility. We offered programs that included boxing, karate, flag football, basketball, roller hockey, volleyball, wrestling, weightlifting, dance, arts & crafts, game tournaments and drama. I started a Tri Club competition consisting of the three Units, AE Mascaro, South End, and Remington.

Ken Walsh

In the spring of 1985 during the softball season, I made a bold move that I believed changed the culture and philosophy of coaching and parent participation early in my youth development career. The softball program had the largest involvement of any youth members and volunteer coaches. The Alumni Association paid for all the uniforms for the 200 kids, and longtime umpire, Gate Datillo, was the head umpire at every game. Gate's heart and soul was certainly there for the kids and he tried to enforce sportsmanship. Unfortunately, the coaches and parents took control of the game with too much negative attitude. After watching the first night of games and seeing a fight erupt between two coaches and parents on the sideline, I took drastic measures. The next morning, I met with Rich Marano and told him I wanted to ban all parents from the game and kick out any coach who speaks inappropriately to the umpires, players, or other coaches. Rich backed me. I held a meeting with the coaches and Gate that afternoon and laid down the law. Gate was pleased with my direction although some of the veteran coaches quit in disgust thinking that would change the course of action. For a week I did not allow the parents to watch the games. Rich was flooded with phone calls, but he still backed my actions. In the meantime, I took on coaching one of the teams along with other staff members. At 23 years old, I took on old bad habits and created new behaviors. It was bold and I truly believed what I was doing was right. In a short period of time, sportsmanship was the new focus with kids enjoying the game more with respect shown to the coaches, umpires, and players. I started the line-up handshake at the end of the game in which both teams lined up and congratulated each other. The number of disgruntled parents and coaches were overwhelmed by the set of parents showing gratitude for the new direction. The softball program continued to thrive years after I left and Gate continued to umpire for years later.

The Boys Club Alumni started to take notice. Each evening the Club gym was shut down for the Bingo fundraiser. The Club Alumni Association, led by Sam Lababarra and his core group, Joe Trottier, Charlie Brewer, Sam Brancia, Jerry "Figs" Figlutsie, Dan and Grace Grosso volunteered to raise funds for our programming. Hundreds of people from the area would show up and fill the gym. I hated the atmosphere mostly due to the smoked-filled gym and the aggressive attitudes that some of the participants showed during the evening.

One Wednesday, in late May, Sam came up to the second floor off the game room to see me. Seventy-year-old Sam tapped on my door. What I knew of Sam from some of the short interactions with him was that he was a man of few words. He was short and to the point. I really did not know much about him although he was very organized and directed his volunteer crew with respectful control. I knew he had lived in the neighborhood for years and was known for going into the 4th Street corner building that seemed to be the hangout for many of the alumni. The rumor was that gambling was conducted in this establishment among other questionable activities. I was told it was just a rumor.

"Kenny, me and the boys downstairs want to talk with you," Sam said. "Sure, Sam, now?" I asked. "Come on down and let's talk," he responded.

I asked Jerry Valenti if he would not mind looking over the game room while I talked with Sam. Jerry just winked as if he knew what was about to happen. I was a little nervous knowing that there was much talk going around in the neighborhood of my aggressive changes at the club.

We walked down the circular stairway leading to the first floor off the gym. We entered the narrow hallway and walked to the end. I looked behind me as Joe Trottier and Figs followed. Sam stopped at the last door on the right that was always locked. This was the one door that I did not have a key for. He opened the door. Joe and Figs were right behind me. Inside the door six steps away was another door with another lock. Sam opened that door and turned on the light. The 8 by 8-foot room had bingo supplies and two chairs. In my mind I thought, "Well it's been a good life." Sam reached to one of the shelves and pushed aside a small box. He reached in and pulled out a bottle of Sambuca. He grabbed four shot glasses, opened the bottle without saying a word and poured the shots. Sam handed the shot glasses to us as we stood in the dimly lit room in a semi-circle and he said, "Kenny this is to you. We are impressed with what you are doing for our Club, Salute." Down the shot went. I was relieved and excited to be recognized and supported. From that point on, Sam and I became great friends. He was an avid biker and even asked me to join him for his daily twenty-mile ride.

A few weeks passed when Sam asked me to come over to his home on Lockwood Avenue where I had an apartment on the same street behind the Club, off Feeney Park. It was early afternoon right after lunch. Sam called me early one morning, "Hey Kenny, what are ya doing this afternoon?"

I responded, "I have some paperwork before the kids get in. Otherwise, I'm free." "Come over to my house. I want to show you something."

I arrived at Sam's two-story brick house shortly after noon. I walked up his steps to the front door and rang the doorbell. I waited a few moments and rang the bell again. No answer. I walked down the steps to the alleyway leading to the back yard and yelled Sam's name. "Sam, Sam, are you there?"

"Kenny, get back here. We are in the back yard." I thought to myself, "We?" I walked down the alley, looked to the left and saw Joe Trottier and Sam in a big barrel looking like they were dancing. "Kenny, get in here and help us out. Take your shoes and socks off first." When I got closer, I couldn't believe my eyes. There was Joe and Sam in a big barrel stepping on grapes and making wine the old-fashioned way.

"I bet you've never done this before. This is how you make wine, New Rochelle style," as he and Joe started laughing at the shocked look on my face.

Ken Walsh

For the next forty-five minutes I had my pants rolled up to my knees massaging grapes with my feet, staining them a purple color that lasted for weeks. I knew at this point I was part of the family. Sam, Jerry, Joe and his crew supported me throughout my tenure in New Rochelle.

Early on at the Club, Gus Mascaro, who worked mainly in the early morning until early afternoon focusing on alumni and city relations, stopped by my office to say hello. Gus was still a tall man at eighty-two with a full head of grey hair that was combed back. He always wore a suit and tie. Many of his ties had burn marks from his cigar ashes. He had a stern but gentle voice that got his point across without being too aggressive. What I noticed most was his large hands and firm handshake. He always looked you in the eye as he greeted you. Gus often invited me up to his office on the third floor for an early afternoon chat to discuss philosophies of mentoring youth. He was the real deal. He strongly believed in giving every child a fair shake. He told me a few times, "You show me a poorly behaved child and I'll bet most of the time it comes from the household." He said, "Kenny, you invest in them and your payback will be more than money can buy." I always listened intently and remembered his advice. He was a legend for the Boys Club movement not only for his accomplishments of building the organization of three units serving thousands of youths but what he stood for. He believed that it was better to build boys and girls rather than mend men and women.

My understanding is that Gus at age 19 was hired at the Boys Club of New Rochelle and helped develop many of the programs including a strong Boxing Club. I was told by some of the alumni that he did everything from supervising the programs to housekeeping and maintenance. When the roof needed to be fixed, Gus was on top of the roof banging nails. He was recruited after several years in New Rochelle to run a club in Washington, D.C. He was there for seven years building a nationally recognized youth marching band. He was then asked to come back to New Rochelle and was promoted to Executive Director.

One Sunday afternoon in the springtime, Gus invited me over to his home. It was a second-floor apartment not far from the Club that he shared with his younger brother. They prepared a spaghetti dinner. Even out of work time, he was dressed in a suit. During dinner, we spoke mostly about family. His wife Mary, who passed away a few years back, left him reminiscing about some of the things that he regretted. He said that he wished he spent more time with his two boys and wife. Gus explained how he was so committed to the mission that he sometimes forgot about the things that meant the most. I was only 23 years of age but I will never forget those words. I had Gus in my life for 3 short years. Those years were a of wealth of knowledge and positive spirit. He was a mentor, a friend that I keep with me always. The thought that comes to mind during a difficult decision with the Boys & Girls Club always makes me reflect to the thought, "What would Gus do?"

Passion for Life

Gus passed away in 1988. Even though I knew he was dying, it hit me like I lost my own father. I felt like a hole was missing in my soul for months. His spirit lives on with me and always will until the day I die.

Journey 7

My brother, Dennis, paddling through Wild Cat Rapids

"Life begins at the end of your comfort zone."   Neal Donald Walsch

First Adventure on the Mighty Rogue River 1986

After living in New Rochelle for a year, I was getting extremely antsy to get out of the city rat race and explore this big country of ours. I was only 25 years old and I knew that New Rochelle was not going to be my permanent stop to settle down and raise a family. I needed to have open space, see rugged mountains, and swim in clean rivers. My cousin, Roger, sensed my thoughts at my Mom and Dad's house during Christmas of 1985 and suggested that I get out to the big country and join him for a river run down the mighty Rogue River in southern Oregon. I was more than intrigued and wanted to learn all about it. I had never adventured down a river with sizable rapids and this seemed to be a potential trip of a lifetime. Roger also convinced my older brother, Dennis, that this would be an excellent trip for him as well.

After the New Year, we put the plan in place for Dennis and me to fly out to Oregon in mid-August for two weeks and take up Roger's offer to paddle down the Rogue River. During the spring, Roger sent me the Rogue River Handbook that describes the rapids and history of the canyon. Inside the front cover was a quote from James M. Quinn that has stayed with me forever and prepared me for this trip and for my life:

"A river may be compared to life; always moving, ever changing. The rapids represent the obstacles and hardships we all encounter from time to time, the challenges to be faced squarely and taken with enthusiasm. The slow peaceful stretches are like the quiet uneventful days we never see enough of. Often the river breaks up into several channels and one must decide which course is best. In life, as on the river, we can never be sure what lies ahead around the bend, but we can look forward to the unknown as a challenge and an opportunity rather than a possible disaster. Watch and study the river. It has much to teach about life."

The Rogue River has a long history of individuals attempting to run it with boats, to trap fish, or to search for gold along the river. The first record of a visit from white men was in 1825, by French explorers and they referred to the Native Americans along the river as Rogues, thus calling the river the Rogue River. The wildlife along the river is abundant including black bears, coyotes, cougars, bobcats, black-tailed deer, Roosevelt elk, otter, raccoons, osprey, hawks, eagles, and salmon among other many species. It also has hazardous plants and creatures along the Rogue such as Poison Oak, rattlesnake and scorpion. What I have discovered from my four decades of paddling down the Rogue is that the River is heaven on earth, but not respecting the river or the surroundings can get one in a lot of trouble in a heartbeat.

After my second season running the summer camp program at the New Rochelle Boys & Girls Clubs and a full summer season playing Men's baseball with the Bronx Braves along with studying the martial arts with Master Javier Diaz, I was ready for a change of scenery. At the end of camp, I packed my bags, jumped on a flight out of LaGuardia airport and flew to San Francisco to meet up with Dennis. There we rented a car to make the 5-hour drive up Highway 5 to Oregon. We were both very excited right from the start to get on the river.

Once we arrived in Medford, Roger already had many adventures planned that included hiking the 9,495 feet of Mt. McLaughlin of the Cascade Range in southern Oregon along with a journey to Crater Lake, a huge crater lake created by a volcano eruption centuries ago. We also spent time paddling the middle section of the Rogue down Nugget Rapid to practice being used to paddling in an inflatable.

Our trip lasted for 4 days on the river and once we started there were no take-outs. Roger had photos at the house showing the powerful rapids, 100 of them carving their way through the 100 to 200 feet of canyon walls. After seeing many of these photos and hearing Roger's stories of challenges of some of his trips, Dennis and I were not totally sure if we were going to make it through this vacation.

We met up with Roger's friends, Dennis, and Charlene, gathered our supplies that included all of the camping gear, food, two inflatables, one hard shell kayak and one raft. Charlene and her husband Dennis were on the supply ship that had all of our gear on it while Roger was in his hard shell, and Dennis and I were in the inflatables. The weather and temperature were perfect, in the nineties with clear blue skies.

After the 2-hour road trip to Grants Pass and into the National Forest, we arrived at the place for the put in. It didn't take long for us to pump up the raft and inflatables, secure the raft with our supplies and begin the paddle. The first part of the river was calm with a fast-moving current. The river looked cold, dark and wide. The cold river was nothing to complain about especially with hot 100-degree temperature of the Oregon sun beating upon us.

The first part of the trip started with a series of Class Two rapids. Before entering the first rapids, Roger pulled Dennis and me over to the side to give us the final instructions before we descended the mighty Rogue River. Roger asked if I would switch inflatables with Dennis. He thought my inflatable floated better. We switched and I found that it was a little harder to control. The rapids were ahead of us now as we paddled down the middle of the river. The raft went into the rapids first. I was next, followed by Dennis and then Roger. The lineup stayed that way throughout the trip insuring safety for Dennis and me. I headed into the rapids following the tongue of the water successfully through Grave Creek rapid. Dennis followed and immediately got hit by a side wave, flipping him into the water. I paddled after him down Grave Creek Falls. I headed over to him across stream only to be hit by a side wave and flipping me as well. We swam to shore with our paddles in hand. We gathered our inflatables and continued the journey. We had a long way to go on this four-day adventure and we already flipped on the first rapid.

Not too far from the beginning of the journey, Rainie Falls, the impossible rapid, was looming. Rainie has powerful hydraulics with strong recirculating water that eats boats and people. We cautiously worked around the Falls bringing our inflatables and raft down the smaller technical rapid called Fish Ladder. It was a strong narrow bony current leading around the falls.

The next set of rapids was Tyee rapids. We managed to get through them and then pulled to the side for lunch while Roger played in the hole with his little blue kayak, pulling off a few good pop ups. Pop ups are when you place the head of the kayak in the recirculating water pushing the nose of the kayak down and bringing the back end up causing a "pop up." It was fun watching the master at work. Shortly after the break, we were at it again down Wildcat rapids. Dennis had a good run staying in the middle of the tongue of the rapids and riding the rollercoaster waves. The sun was now beginning to fall behind the canyon and Roger thought it was best to find the next available campground before darkness. Shortly around the bend, we found Russian Creek campground on river left. The campground and rapids were named after a Russian gold prospector who once lived there.

As we approached the campground, we saw a female deer with her fawn. It was wild kingdom at its best. After we set up camp and ate dinner, we sat around looking up at the tremendous evening sky filled with stars and telling stories as our laughs echoed through the canyon. That night I did not sleep well with the fear of black bears invading our campground. Dozing off and on, my ears were alert to night movements around our camp. The Oregon morning came early, although peaceful. The opening of the tent screen door led to a sandy beach with the sun peaking over the mountainside. My bare feet felt good on the cool sand and the music of the Rogue River was upon us. As peaceful as that moment was for Dennis and me, the next day the roar of the rapids was upon us, and for me, a near death.

After a nice circle of conversation around breakfast and a cup of coffee, we packed up and paddled right into the Russian rapids. We took them head on with ease, leading to foolish cockiness after successfully paddling through Montgomery and Howard rapids. Shortly after that, Slim Pickens rapids ate me. I followed Roger to the right of the big boulder located in the middle of the rapid, but instead of going river left, I followed Roger to the right and a big side wave flipped me. I recovered well and quickly got back into the saddle just in time for a challenging set of falls called upper and lower Black Bar rapids. I ran those well and we pulled Dennis out of the Eddie along the shoreline after he flipped in lower Black Bar.

There was another series of rapids that followed right before Horseshoe Bend rapids. I didn't think much of Horseshoe, only that Roger said don't flip it in the beginning otherwise you will have a long swim ahead of you. That note was not taken seriously enough.

Horseshoe Bend had three stretches of the mile-long rapid with the last part of the rapid being the most dangerous. Roger told me to follow his path with Dennis behind me and the raft last. The plan worked well for the first 100 feet of the entrance to Horseshoe until Roger decided he wanted to play in a hole with his hard shell and work on his surfing. That's when I got into trouble.

Horseshoe Bend has many submerged boulders that are surprising as they seem to suddenly appear out of nowhere. One of the boulders came upon me too quickly before I could react and maneuver around it. The boulder caught the front of the inflatable and flipped me hard and propelled me out of the boat. Now I was in for a long swim at the beginning of the rapid with the most dangerous section coming up. I held onto my paddle with one hand and grabbed the boat with the other, attempting to position myself on my back with my feet going downstream and hoping to kick off rocks with my feet when needed. The waves and holes continued to pound me as I held onto the paddle and boat with a death grip. I was sucking in lots of water as wave after wave hit my face sometimes submerging me. Then the most dangerous part of the rapid was on me. This is where a dangerous boulder has taken several lives and many boats. The strong current pushed me toward the left bank into the boulder. I turned my body, so the boat was in front as I went crashing into the boulder. The inflatable took most of the impact, but the current took me under the water, thrashing me in the white form. I swallowed a ton of water and felt like the end was near just as the rapids settled down. I came up gasping for air and began to wonder if I had crossed over to the other world, as there in front of me under the clear blue sky along the base of the canyon wall was a large black bear with a salmon in its mouth. The bear was looking at me with much curiosity. I thought the curious look was the bear contemplating to continue enjoying his salmon catch or to go after the struggling human in the current. Lucky for me, the salmon must have tasted pretty good. The bear cocked his head to the side, glanced at me one more time, and with grace and ease propelled up the side of the mountain disappearing into the trees.

I gathered my strength and swam in the calm water to the shore. When I got there, I was spitting up water just as Roger arrived with Dennis and the raft immediately behind him. "There you are. That's a good place for us to take a break," said Roger. Then he looked at me, blue in the face, and said, "You OK? You must have had a tough long swim." I just nodded my head and laid back on the rocks, catching air and being thankful for my life.

For the remainder of the afternoon, we paddled through more class 2 and 3 rapids - easy enough to handle and helping me gain my composure. Dennis was eaten by another rapid, Kelsey Falls, although he recovered well. The day flew by as daylight started to diminish. We pulled off river right at the Mule Creek checkpoint. It was a rather large campground on a sandy beach sitting on water's edge. Around the bend was Mule Creek Canyon rapids.

After dinner, Dennis and I were cleaning up the dishes from our meal and like a movie scene a beautiful doe walked into our campground. She cautiously came to me as I offered a carrot. She gently ate out of my hand. Another wonderful moment in time. The sun faded behind the mountainside and we stayed up for a short period of time thinking about the next day. The two most challenging rapids were ahead of us, Mule Creek Canyon and Blossom Bar. Being our first time going down the Rogue, we could only imagine what was ahead of us. Roger gave us a pep talk about what to expect and what to plan for. I remember him saying, "Just stay in the boat." It felt like going to war, not sure if we were ever going to make it back.

The morning came too early. We had a long day of challenging paddling and Mule Creek canyon was right on us with no warmup. The lineup order for the morning was Roger, Dennis, me, and the raft sweeping from behind. The roar of the rapids sounded like a freight train. The opening gate was a major rapid called "Jaws", a boat eater. And it did!

Dennis did not stand a chance as Jaws immediately flipped his inflatable and now he was swimming for his life before Telfer's hole. The strong hydraulics push boats toward this hole and Roger knew Dennis was in deep trouble. He quickly paddled to Dennis and had him hang on to the kayak skirting him away from the hole where several men have lost their lives. I followed Roger's lead as did the raft. We got through Mule Creek as well as pushing through the "Coffee Pot" rapid that resembles turbulence of boiling water. The water attempts to push boats into the right canyon walls. This is where one must put their head down and paddle hard. We did and all were safe in the calm pool of water. We swung our paddles in the air, hooting for victory.

The remainder of the day was not as dramatic and we all paddled down Blossom Bar, the most technical rapid, in good form. Roger elected to have Dennis jump into the raft this time for his own safety. We gathered ourselves after Blossom and descended Devils Stairs rapid which was a fun little drop leading to a quiet pool of water. The rest of the day was a nice easy paddle through Higgins Canyon after Paradise Lodge, a year-round commercial place to stay over and have a meal. The jet-powered mail boats would bring customers to the lodge daily.

That late afternoon, we camped at Tate Creek campground area and had the opportunity to hike up to the most tranquil spots on the river. Approximately 200 yards along the creek was a natural slide that was so smooth we were able to slide down the 25 feet into a deep refreshing pool of water. I have great memories of this site and photos to go along with it. It would not be my last time enjoying this moment.

Our last night at the shores of the Rogue was a relaxing bittersweet time. We stayed up a little later that night talking about many things, mostly about making these moments happen and not taking life for granted. While on the beach shoreline, hearing the water rush by us, our time that evening was still, even though our lives rush by us sometimes before we stop and "smell the roses." The Rogue River in my life has and always will be the perfect time out. The next day, I knew I was going to be back on a plane heading East, back to work, back to the grind of life. Although, for me, I never saw it as work. I love what I do, having a small part of helping shape the lives of others. The Rogue River helped me gas up and be a better person for it.

Journey 8

"Brothers in arms are brothers for life." Clone Cadets

Forever Brotherhood – Club Naha 1986

<u>***Black Belt Test – January 29, 1989***</u>

While working one morning in the early summer months of 1986 at the New Rochelle Boys & Girls Club, I met my first martial art teacher, Javier Piscil Diaz from Mexico, and a new world opened up to me. I looked out from my office window onto Fenny Park in the West End of New Rochelle and saw a man running laps around the park. He spotted me and started heading my way toward the Club. I sat back in my office chair as he came in. He had a pleasant smile on his face and in Spanish said something to me that I did not understand. I said, "Hi, I'm Ken. Can I help you?" He did not respond either, frustrated with the lack of communication. He simply turned around and left.

In that moment, I did not think much of it. An hour later, he came back with a friend. His name was Carlos. Carlos explained that Javier was visiting from Mexico and he was a Karate Teacher. Through Carlos, Javier wanted to know if I had interest in having him teach my Club kids at the NRBGC. I explained to Carlos that it would be quite difficult without Javier having command of the English language. In Spanish, Javier talked with Carlos and asked Carlos to convey to me that he would then like to teach me first. I thought about it for a moment and agreed. I always wanted to learn the art and I thought I would give it a try. Javier seemed to be very pleased.

That following day, I woke earlier than usual on a typical Sunday although I was still late for my appointment with my new Karate Instructor. It was 8:30 a.m. and we were supposed to meet at 8:00. I rushed to get out of my apartment around the corner from the Club. I ran out of my second-floor apartment, running through Fenny Park and saw Javier waiting in front of the building. He gave me a look of disappointment indicating that it was disrespectful to be late. I apologized as we walked through the doors of the Club. Our training area was off the gymnasium in the fitness room near the lockers. It was not a big space although it had to do. It had mats and offered privacy for our training.

Javier immediately started teaching the practice of Karate using Japanese terms. He started with simple Japanese terms: work out area – Dojo, teacher – Sensei, numbers, opening mediation and commands for movements. I thought this was so cool learning from a passionate, skilled Sensei and learning a new language at the same time. We mostly communicated in Japanese, not English or Spanish, even though Javier had the thirst for learning the English language and was constantly asking me for new words. I knew at this point that teaching the Martial Arts to my BGC kids would work. They would learn discipline, respect, and self-defense as well as learn Japanese at the same time. It was a perfect combination.

The workouts with Javier were intense. It was training with wrestling-like intensity workouts. Sensei pushed me on my flexibility, taking my limbs to the max each time. I was never so sore in my life. The cardio training through the karate movements of stances, blocks, pushes, kicks and kata drained me during the two-hour, one-on-one sessions. At that moment I did not realize the great privilege it was to have Javier as my instructor. He was one year older than me and was in tremendous shape. He demanded perfection. Our training continued for three times a week throughout the summer of 1986. During that time, Javier and I became great friends. I respected the teacher-student relationship at the same time. His English improved and I convinced the Executive Director of the NRBGC, Rich Marano, to begin a Karate curriculum at the Club in the coming fall with Javier teaching. Javier was thrilled. We began advertising our summer camps and placing posters throughout New Rochelle.

During the same time, I was still playing baseball for the Bronx Braves. I credit the new Karate skills and workouts that gave me my best year, finishing the season with a .429 batting average with two home runs. For me, a smaller infielder, hitting long balls was not my strength. I usually am a slap hitter and could spray the ball to the different fields as a leadoff. With the Karate training, my focus and hip quickness came into play, and I was driving the ball much better. The ball seemed like a large grapefruit coming into the plate.

Passion for Life

Javier and I continued our extensive training throughout the summer leading into the fall. I realized that the Martial Art training for our Club kids could be a real advantage. In the 80's karate was not well known in the Boys & Girls Club curriculum. Boxing still held court as the major activity besides basketball. I had a little convincing to do with our Executive Director. He gave me the go ahead only if I was directly involved. His worry was about teaching tough kids the means to be more dangerous. I knew if the Martial Arts was taught properly, focusing on discipline, respect, and using methods of meditation, it would have the counter effect of any kind of violence.

We did not have a real dojo (karate studio) to practice. I was able to find space for evening classes in the senior citizen area on the third floor of the Club. The floor was hard although the lighting was great. Classes started the first week in September right after Labor Day weekend. Javier recruited a dozen new students including an FBI agent, Bob Gruber and his two sons, Bob Jr. and Dan. Also in the original group were two of our youth Club members, Dennis Racanello and Erica Swanson. The classes were scheduled for an hour and a half, but we were never out in time. The classes went into 2 hours of extreme workout. It was challenging to practice on the tile floor especially the running, jumping, sit-ups, knuckle push-ups, and judo throws on the floor. Yet, we all adapted well and expected the soreness in the morning. Our uniforms were drenched with sweat after each workout. The practices went on for three days a week until Thanksgiving. The confidence in my skill level developed rapidly. I believe the rest of the students had the strong confidence as well. Sensei had a special gift for teaching and taking one to the limit of their physical and mental abilities. He also demonstrated his skill level at appropriate times at the right teaching moment. He was lighting fast with great power, agility, focus, and flexibility. He also set the bar high and always wanted perfection with each move. Javier focused a lot on flexibility. His workout focused the first 40 minutes just on stretching.

In November, Javier informed me that his VISA was running out and soon he would have to return to Mexico, even though his dream was to open a Karate school in the US. The challenge to get a working VISA was too difficult for the time frame even though we had Bob Grubert working on all fronts to make it happen. By Thanksgiving, Javier was heading back to Mexico. We were all sad to see our teacher go. I vowed to keep the training going even though I was promoted only to the next Kyu (white belt 2 stripes). Javier promised to be back with hope to stay much longer.

Our classes continued into the following year, but it was not the same. I did my best to continue to motivate although the command and knowledge from Javier was not there. Then, in mid-January, a man from New Zealand came into our Boys and Girls Club and offered to volunteer. During our conversation, I was describing our programs and Karate came up. I told him that we lost our instructor and that got his attention. Ian Reid said, "Hey I teach Karate, mate,

I'm a black belt. Perhaps I can help here." I could not believe the timing. It was perfect. Sensei Ian and I worked out the schedules and again we had a full martial art program. The difficulty was the change in the style from Shudokan (Japanese) to Wonwha-do (Korean). Since we were all beginners, it did not take long to pick up the new katas and self-defense as many of the basic moves were the same.

We converted the third-floor weight room into the new Karate Dojang (dojo). Most of the original group stayed with the program. We added more classes in the afternoon so many of the younger kids could also participate. With new donations of mats and equipment, we had a strong program that grew from session to session. By spring, over one hundred kids were involved. Dennis and Bob continued to excel in their development and took on more leadership roles in the classes. Ian brought other guest instructors including Gordon Kelly, a tall 6'4" Black Belt.

In the spring of 1987, Ian and Gordon invited me to train at their Dojang in Tarrytown, about 30 minutes from New Rochelle. I gladly accepted their invitation and was anxious to work out with the Wonhwa-do Black Belts. The address they gave me was on Route 9 on the Hudson River. Practice was at 8:00 p.m. I drove to the area in the dark and pulled into a long driveway with a security check point to the left. The 10-foot iron gates were closed as I approached a security officer. He asked my name and then called his supervisor in order to let me travel in. I drove around the campus following a narrow, paved road past a large mansion overlooking the Hudson River. I pulled in front of the practice area. The building was an old church. I got out of the car and was greeted by Ian. "Hey, mate, you made it."

We walked into a two-story building and up to the second floor. Ian showed me the changing area located on a balcony overlooking the Dojang. While changing, I looked over to the wall in front of me. There was an American flag to the left, a Korean flag to the right and a big, framed photo of Dr. Reverend Moon in the middle. I said to myself, "What have I gotten myself into?"

Dressed in my Karate uniform, I followed the stairs down to the dojang. The entire floor was around 600 sq. ft. and covered with an off-white canvas springy mat. It was a great floor for throws. Much of the Wonhwa Do's curriculum was built around Judo since the Grandmaster Dr. Joon Hoo Suke was a Judo champion in South Korea. The practice with my new friends, mainly all Black Belts, went well. Most of them were Martial Artists from around the world. They welcomed me and never pushed their religious teachings on me during any of the practices. I was very cautious about the Martial Art style being affiliated with Dr. Moon. Ian and Gordon made sure the religion was never discussed at the club and was sensitive to the concern.

The months that followed became more intense. I accepted a new full-time job in the fall of 1987 to teach physical education at St. Benedict's school in the Bronx. Having two full-time jobs, Club and St. Benedict's, was taxing on me while also studying the martial arts. For over a year, I worked from 7:00 a.m. to 9:00 p.m. and took Martial Art classes twice a week until 11:00 pm. I was promoted to my Green Belt in late fall, skipping my yellow belt testing and earning a Blue Belt in the spring.

Meanwhile, the karate classes at the BGC continued to grow. Our kids entered their first tournament that summer and I was asked to compete as well. In the Wonhwa Do International Tournament held at Brooklyn College, twenty students from the Boys & Girls Club participated. The gym was packed with participants from around the world. This was the first time we met Wonhwa Do's Grandmaster Dr. Joon Hoo Suek and Head Instructor Kensaku Takahichi. The kids were all pumped to be there to meet these legends in the art. Our club kids did extremely well and brought home lots of medals and trophies.

As a Blue belt, I competed in the advanced belt level against other Blue and Brown belts. I fought in kumite (sparring) against all Brown belt competitors. My first bout was against a tall German fighter. He quickly scored a point with an ax kick to my eye, giving me a shiner. I was able to regain my senses and score the next three points to win the match with reverse punches and a front snap kick to the solar plexus. My next bout was against a Korean who challenged me to the end although I scored the final point to win 3 to 2. I was in the semifinals against a martial artist from Japan. We hooked up in a fierce battle. We were tied with the time running out. The next point would win. I came at him hard with a roundhouse kick to the body only for him to block it with a leg. As I hit him, I felt a sharp pain in front of my left shin. I learned later that evening that I fractured my leg from that kick. I continued to fight and lost from a punch to my mid-section. I was pleased in my first competition that I fought good bouts against skilled martial artists from around the world.

The 1987-88 season was rewarding and challenging all at the same time. I felt burnt out at times due to the intense work schedule and my pursuit to earn my Black Belt. In the late fall of 1988, I decided that I would give up my job teaching at St. Benedict's after the holidays. At the same time, I was promoted to Assistant Executive Director of the NRBGC. The new salary was around the same for both positions. In the spring of 1988, I was promoted to my Brown Belt level, one step away from my black belt.

In January of 1989, I decided it was time to move out of New Rochelle and find a home further north in Westchester County. I found a small three-bedroom house on 31 Fox Hill Road in Cortlandt Manor and moved in on January 26. While unpacking after a long day of moving, the phone rang and Ian Reid was on the phone. He said, "Ken, Kensaku Takahichi told me it's your time. You have been invited to test for your Black Belt in Red Hook, NY, tomorrow morning. I was caught off guard and my heart began to pump an extra beat in anticipation.

Ken Walsh

At 6:00 in the morning, a station wagon pulled up to my house loaded with seven other Wonwha do black belts. I jumped into the back seat and we headed to Red Hook. With the combination of the winding narrow roads and the crazy reckless driving of our driver, I thought I would never make it to the Black Belt test. We arrived at the Red Hook campus around 7:30 a.m., 30 minutes before the testing. I walked into the auditorium with the other black belts to see the entire auditorium filled with spectators and Black Belts on the main floor stretching, getting ready for battle. I saw Kensaku Takahachi at the main judges table with other senior black belts milling around him. I walked over to him to show my respect and bowed. He shook my hand and said good luck. I found a spot on the mat to stretch and warm up for the testing. At 8:00 sharp, we were instructed to line up in front of the judges table, shoulder to shoulder, facing Kensaku. We bowed and knelt to meditate. With our eyes closed, we spoke the tenets of Wonwha Do:
1. To be filial and loyal to God.
2. To be filial and respectful to your parents.
3. To love your brothers and sisters.
4. To make sincere efforts to achieve unity between mind and body.
5. To overcome every difficulty with perseverance.
6. To be courageous for the cause of rightness.
7. To fight against any injustice with indomitable spirit.

The eight hours of testing began with stretching, cardio and then basic stances, strikes and blocks. We continued throughout the day with kata, one step sparring and the required skills for the Black Belt, repeatedly. By 3:00 p.m., my uniform was drenched in sweat, my legs were shaking, and my energy depleted. Then came the formal black belt initiation. I had to fight 21 Black Belts, one after the other, scoring 3 points for each one. I was at a disadvantage immediately, already fatigued from the testing. The first seven fights, I held my own, then I ran out of gas. The Black Belts from all different nationalities tested my skill along with my will and gave me unanswered strikes to my stomach and head. I was bleeding from my lip and my eyes were swollen. I thought that the Black Belts that I trained with all along would have mercy. Unfortunately, they came at me full on and did not let up. I looked down at my uniform and saw blood on the right thigh of the white uniform. My white sparring hand pads were covered with blood, mainly mine. I kept pushing on, one fight at a time. I struggled getting to the last fight. My legs were wobbling, and my arms could not be lifted. I was out of breath from the one hour of straight continuous fighting. Ian Reid had the pleasure of being the last fighter. Once again, he did not lay off. He picked me apart with strikes and blows to the body.

The crowd was chanting, giving me encouragement to continue and to fight with whatever I had left. After a few minutes I scored my second point with only one point to go to earn the Black Belt. Ian worked hard the entire bout to make it the hardest point of my life, dancing around me with his skill and speed, striking at will. I finally mustered up all the energy I had left and chased him down, tackling him to the floor. While on top of him, I landed the final point to his solar plexus. The judge shouted out "point"! I rolled off Ian totally drained. Ian got up and offered his hand to help me up. We embraced each other while other Black Belts came over to congratulate me as well. The crowd stood and clapped. After handshakes and pats on the back, we all lined up for the closing ceremony. I stepped to the front of the line as Kensaku reached over to my belt, took off the Brown Belt and presented the Black Belt to me This was one of the proudest moments of my life. I vowed from that moment on that I would inspire others and help motivate them to achieve their goals. I wanted my students, especially kids, to experience the moment that I had that day. And for over thirty years, I have done that through our Naha three-day Black Belt challenges.

Naha Black Belt Weekend – Discovering the inner spirit

In 1991, before leaving New Rochelle to accept my new position as the Executive Director of the Boys & Girls Club of Waterville, Maine, I needed a plan to sustain the Karate program at the New Rochelle Club. Our top student at the time was Dennis Racanello, a talented young man who showed leadership skills and the other martial artists respected him. He was my choice to hand over the baton. He was named our Club's Youth of the Year in 1989 and the current administration trusted him for his loyalty, passion, and work ethic to help continue the program.

At a goodbye ceremony at the Mascaro Boys and Girls Club in February before leaving for Maine, in front of all my students, I awarded Dennis the assignment. The timing was fitting especially with the good energy of the hundred students and parents present. Eighteen-year-old Dennis Racanello was up for the challenge. He also had great support from adults Bob Grubert and Nick Demeo to push the program forward. And he did just that. Dennis went on to not only become an excellent teacher and one of the best martial artists I have ever seen, he was also lightning fast with extraordinary flexibility. In January of 1992 I promoted Dennis to first-degree black belt and I vowed to make it back to New Rochelle to conduct a Black Belt test for Bob. In 1993, I did return and conducted Bob's test in HenSan Ryu. HenSan Ryu was a style created with the help of Master Tommy May that combined Wonwha-Do and Shudokan along with other styles including Judo and JuJitsu.

HenSan Ryu continued for eight years in Maine as our style at the Waterville Club. HenSan Ryu was then transformed in 2001 back to the focus on Shudokan (Club Naha) when my original instructor Javier Diaz Piscil came to Maine to help develop our Martial program to a new level. Our most dedicated Naha student, Craig Sargent, (one of my first students, like Dennis Racanello) took our program to a new level. On the weekend of December 1, 1995, I conducted the first Black Belt test in Maine for candidates Craig Sargent and Dave Panarelli.

I met Craig Sargent shortly after I arrived in Waterville to manage the Club. My meetings with him were not all positive in the beginning. He was a disruptive young 12-year-old attempting to find his way. His home life at times was challenging, living in public housing. He was kicked out of the Club many times due to his behavior.

When I arrived at the Club, the first action item was to develop new programs. The Boys & Girls Club was located on Main Street in Waterville, an old Club held together by duct tape. It was a tired building and some rooms off the gym were used only for storage. Within my first few weeks, I cleared out four rooms and created programming space. I called up Kennebec County Sheriff Frank Hackett and asked to use his inmates to assist. He gladly agreed as part of their civic engagement program. Within a few weeks the rooms were cleared, and new programs were established: Dance, Teen Club and Martial Arts.

Shortly after the rooms were cleared in April 1992, I started the first martial art classes. Since it was the beginning, all the classes were for novice and divided into two age groups, one for the youth and the other for adults. Youth classes were held twice a week, one during a weekday and the other on Saturday morning for an hour. The adult classes were held twice a week in the evenings and were more intensive, lasting at least two hours with hard-core training. I believed that if the students were not drenched in sweat at the end of class, I did not do my job. Therefore, the first hour of class was meditation, warm up, stretching, tons of push-ups, sit-ups, and running. It was two hours of boot camp. The second hour was the introduction of self-defensive techniques, kata, judo and point sparring. With adults, point sparring became quite aggressive at times, although under control of my watchful eye. I made my point that egos had to be checked at the door and poor attitudes were not tolerated.

One of my first students in Maine was our Boys & Girls Club Program Director Rich Levine. Rich, like my training with instructor Sensei Diaz, was conducted one-on-one as I was grooming him to assist with teaching classes. Rich was eager to learn and picked up the teaching lesson plan and philosophy quickly. This was helpful for me since I was a new Executive Director of the Club and many times in the upcoming year, I had to attend meetings. Rich ended up teaching many classes the following year. He was responsible for engaging Craig Sargent and bringing Dave Panarelli into the Dojo. Craig was the youngest in the adult class and for the most part held his own during sparring. Craig embraced the martial art. Club officials, teachers and volunteers started to see Craig's attitude change and become more positive. He wanted to absorb more about Eastern philosophy and studied the art outside of the Dojo. He stopped skipping classes and soon transferred from alternative education to mainstream classes at

Passion for Life

the junior high. Teachers at the school talked about how more respectful and engaged he was in classes.

Rich Levine eventually left the Boys & Girls Club for another career and Craig, at 14 years old, took on Rich's role in the Dojo. Even though he was young, the parents and students respected him for his dedication and knowledge of the art. He spent endless hours training as did Dave Panarelli. They progressed on their promotions and obtained their Brown Belts in December 1994. They were like brothers. In the fall of 1995, I announced to them that they would be the first Maine students to be tested for a Black Belt.

As I thought about the purpose of the Black Belt test, I began to develop the criteria that I thought would be more than just challenging skill-wise, but more about engaging total commitment of the mind, body and spirit. I thought once a student reached a level to be tested, his/her skill level should be at the black belt level. The true test centered about the spirit of the candidate. Do they have what it takes to overcome any extreme challenges that life bestows upon us? Will they have the skill set to help fight through these obstacles and move on? I wanted the black belt test to be something they can reflect back to during the most difficult times in life and always remember that if they were able to get through this test, they could get through anything in life. They also will know that the brotherhood of Naha would always be there with them during their challenges. From this philosophy, I created a three-day test, to test the limits of each candidate. My plan was to find their weakness and focus on helping them overcome that weakness to help build the foundation of strength for the future.

On Friday, December 1, 1995, Dave Panarelli and 16-year-old Craig Sargent started their three-day Black Belt test. I told them that they needed to know all their levels of practice as close to wansung (perfection) as possible. Developing students come in three phases: sunsang, jungsung and wansung, (formation, growth and perfection). These are the stages that were taught to me and that I handed down in my training. Besides informing them of this responsibility, I also made sure they knew that they were going to be up against a challenge they never had before. I knew that anticipation of the unknown can bring individuals to feelings of nervousness and fear. I also know that if someone wants something bad enough, they will overcome that fear and do whatever it takes to cross the finish line.

The week before the testing was to begin; I told Dave and Craig to meet me at my house on Snow Pond at 4:30 am. They looked at each other bewildered because of the time request, but said nothing. I also told them to bring their sleeping bags, snacks and beverages needed for three days, warm clothes, hiking shoes, and all their Karate gear.

On that cold December morning, both Dave and Craig arrived at my house before sunrise. After they unloaded their supplies in my finished basement, their home for the next three days, we went outside along the cold waterfront. In darkness, with the wind blowing off the shoreline, we meditated. In silence, breathing slowly and being still in the moment, the warriors were gearing up for battle. After ten minutes of meditation, I called out "Yame", they opened their eyes and we bowed.

I explained the tasks at hand. I told them they would be given assignments to test their strength and spirit. I told them that their mind would be tested and at times they would want to quit. Besides being tested on their physical Naha skills, they would have to complete 3,000 sit ups and push-ups, run up mountains, paddle in the cold water, take a three-hour written exam, and battle all day in the dojo on day three. I added, if you fail on any one of these tasks, your test will be over. I concluded by saying that they can be the first Maine Club Naha Black Belts, an honor to hold forever.

"Gentlemen, your first task this morning is to work as a team. I want you to grab that canoe and paddle together around the first island as quickly as possible. I will be timing you. If you happen to fall into the water, blow the whistle. The PFD will keep you afloat and I will be there to assist." I looked at them, said, "Good Luck. Begin."

After putting on their PFDs, headlamps, whistle, hats and gloves, they pushed off into the frigid water. The north wind pushed them to the island quickly, although around the island was thin ice that they had to chop and it slowed them up considerably. Once they paddled around the island, they were up against the thin ice with a strong wind in their face. It took them less than 20 minutes to get to the island, although on the way back it took 30 minutes. Since it was their first task, they pushed hard, demonstrating their eagerness to succeed.

They pulled their canoe to the shore. They were sweating from the hard work. They were feeling good about their accomplishment and ready for the next challenge. They came up to the house. I was in the hot tub with a cup of coffee. They got excited thinking that they were going to join me. I said, "Nice job, you completed your paddle in 50 minutes and 23 seconds. That was a nice warm-up. Now, for the real test, get back into the canoe and complete the same task in less than 48 minutes. If not, the test is over."

Craig and Dave looked at each other in shock knowing that they thought they had given it their all the first time. Now they had to shave off more than two minutes of time. They got back in their canoe. On my signal, the stopwatch started. They put their heads down and paddled with all their might toward the island. They made great time getting to the island, but again the wind was not their friend as they circled the island on the way back. They finally broke through the thin ice, paddling hard and headed back to the shoreline with ten minutes to spare. I yelled across the water, "You are at 38 minutes, 10 minutes to go!"

Paddling against the wind, with the cold water splashing with every stroke, they had their head down, paddling rapidly to me. It was going to be close. With

100 feet left, they were at 46 minutes. They pushed hard fighting the wind. They approached the shore at 47 minutes 33 seconds. They got out, high fiving each other, drenched in sweat and celebrating their victory as the sun was rising over the horizon.

I said, "Great job boys. To celebrate your accomplishment, it's time to jump in the lake. Get into your bathing suits and jump off the dock." Dave responded, "Really?" I said, "Really!"

As instructed, they stripped down to their suits and walked over to the dock. Both hesitated as their mind was not allowing them to take the next step. Dave glanced over to Craig and said, "Let's just get this over with." They both made a victory shout as they plunged into the frigid water. Their heads came to the surface with both in shock from the extreme temperature.

After they dried off, we went back into my house as I had the hot tub on. This was a welcome sight, although they cautiously went in not knowing if it was a trick. It wasn't a trick. It was time to reflect and after breakfast prepare for the next challenge.

At 9:30 a.m. we drove to the next town, Belgrade, where we took a short hike to French's Mountain overlooking Long Pond. There I had Craig and Dave continue to do their push-ups and sit-ups, complete all their kata and self-defense on top of the rocky, slippery cliff. After a short break at noon, we drove over to Blueberry Mountain overlooking the valley of Belgrade and both Long Pond and Great Pond. This is one of my favorite places in the world. Besides the stunning views, there is a sense of solitude. The snow was falling as we meditated in the silence of nature at the beginning of winter. After we completed our meditation, I had them suit for sparring. My objective was to get them prepared for the Dojo work of extensive fighting on Sunday morning against another martial artist. Their task at this moment was to spar against each other for ten rounds of 3 minutes each with 30 second breaks in between rounds. The snow fell on top of these two driven Black Belt candidates as they battled against each other, trading blows with skillful technique and respect. They were covered in sweat even though the temperatures were around freezing. Their arms and legs were heavy during the last round as they put every bit of their energy in sparring. They completed the last round, bowed to each other and respectfully shook each other's right hand.

The physical activity for the day was completed except for working on their push-ups and sit-ups. On their own, they continued to practice their kata and self-defensive techniques. We landed at my house on Snow Pond later in the afternoon. After dinner, they started their 30-page exam that tested them on Korean and Japanese martial art terms, writing out all their katas, self-defense, reciting the history of our style, and mapping out their vision for their life. As the test has progressed over the years, I made the test include that all students write down their "100 bucket list" items. The purpose is to engage the Black Belt candidates in personal goal setting and to have the zest of life to accomplish things that are important to them. Every goal had to have to timeframe to it. Dave and Craig finished their test before midnight. The next day was going to be another challenging adventure.

At 8:00 a.m. on Saturday morning, I had each of them place gloves, hats, a jug of water, a change of clothes and one apple in their back packs. After they each knocked off 500 sit-ups and 200 push-ups, we jumped into my car and headed northwest to the Mt. Blue Mountain range located in Weld, Maine. Tumbledown Mountain was waiting for us. In the Waterville area during this time, we did not have much snowfall, although in the western mountains there was plenty. I don't believe any of us were prepared for the next challenge, even me who was conducting the test. We parked at the base of the mountain off the dirt road looking straight up the rugged climb. When we got out of the car, I told them we needed to get to the top of the mountain by 11:00 a.m. or the test was over. That gave us a little more than an hour to accomplish the goal.

We grabbed our backpacks and followed the slightly covered snow path upward. The first 15 minutes was easy going until the path elevation increased and more dense snow amounts grew as we traveled further inward and upward. As time went on, we went from stepping in 6 inches of snow to mid-thigh. At times, we would step and stay on the surface of the snow while other times we fell deep up to our waist. Even though the temperatures were below freezing, we were sweating hard. Layers of our clothes came off while we continued the journey to the top. No one stopped for water as time was ticking. I heard each of their heavy breaths as the last part of the climb was upon us. This was treacherous going, especially the last 100 yards. We were climbing hand over fist, covered in snow and sweat and the wind began to blow harder as the tree line disappeared.

We finally made it to the top within the timeframe allocated to see the glorious views. With mostly cloudy skies, both Craig and Dave enjoyed the view especially the surprising view of the pond located on the top of Tumbledown Mountain. The wind was blowing harder bringing the temperature in the teens to feel even colder. I wanted to make sure they continued moving. We moved over to the flat portion near the pond where I told them to go through all their self-defense and one step sparring techniques. Within ten minutes, they completed the request. They were red in the face and the winter chill was getting to them. At that point, I told them to change into their dry clothes and meet me near the cliff rock shelter overlooking the valley. The rock shelter prevented us from being in full wind impact. We huddled in. They were hungry, cold, and tired. I told them, "In life we take simple things for granted, like warmth, food, and water. Always appreciate what you have, not what you don't have." With that, I pulled out water for each of them and one apple. The water was a welcome gift as well as the apple. The apple could have been a bucket of gold the way they treasured each bit down to the core. Watching their faces was all I needed to see as their expressions showed total satisfaction.

We headed down the mountain. It did not take us as long as we glided and slid down all the way to the car. They had a sense of victory from this task. Mission accomplished.

Journey 9

"We don't grow when things are easy; we grow when we face challenges."
Anonymous

Katahdin

In early March, 1992, I made my move to Maine. I quickly engaged with my work, spending endless hours at the Waterville Boys & Girls Club. During this time, I did not really get the chance to explore Maine. The Board President, Phil Roy, a Maine native, said to me, "Have you been to Mt. Katahdin yet?"

With my thirst for outdoor activity, this was all it took to jump on that hook for my newest adventure in Maine. We decided that Memorial Day weekend would be a perfect time for the hike. My Westchester County, New York, softball and football buddy, John "Gus" Guscoria, decided to drive up from NY to visit, play tennis and join Phil and me for the hike.

Gus took the seven-hour drive on that Friday and stayed with me in my apartment that night. We hit the town for dinner and beverages before ending the day around midnight. We decided to play a tennis match at Champions

Fitness Center on Saturday morning before we joined Phil for the 2 ½ hour ride to Baxter State Park in Millinocket that afternoon. Perhaps this was a bad choice.

Gus and I have had long, drawn-out tennis matches in the past. We are both baseline players coming to the net infrequently. Our good foot speed kept the rallies going. For old-time sake we decided to play best out of five; first to three sets wins. We thought this would take around two hours to finish. All evening and into the morning, we had our usual smack talk that continued on the court.

The match was grueling. We played toe to toe throughout the entire match, both winning our service games and ending in a tie breaker for each set. After 2 ½ hours in a stuffy indoor court with a gallon of water chugged and a change of shirts, we were tied two sets to two. 6-7, 7-6, 7-6, 6-7. I had Gus on the ropes the fourth set to win, up 40 – 15 serving and leading 6 games to 5, Gus battled back to win the game and forced the fourth game into the tie breaker.

After the fourth set, both of us were drained, sweaty and worn out. We looked at each other knowing it might be best to call it a tie. That thought was considered for two seconds before we knew that it was unacceptable to leave any match at a tie.

We had to meet Phil at 2:00 p.m. at his house to drive to Baxter State Park. So, we had to get moving and play the final set to determine the winner. We were like two heavyweight boxers in the final round of a drawn-out hard fight. Our legs were wobbly and our energy low. We kept the ball in play early on as the final set went on, each of us tried to play a winning point to finish the game, which caused more forced errors. I was up five games to four with Gus serving. Gus made a few quick errors, hitting the ball long over the baseline to give me a 40-15 advantage on his next serve. I hit the ball deep to his backhand side and came to the net, one of the few times, waiting for the ball to execute a perfect half volley to win. We were both exhausted. We walked over to the sideline, sat in the metal chairs and drank our water. We both knew that was one of the best matches we had ever played. In fact, that was the last match Gus and I played against each other. He ended up moving to Virginia as I stayed in Maine. We did not run into each other until ten years later in 2012 at a hotel in Chicago. As I was coming out of the elevator, I recognized my old buddy as he was going down the hallway. We went to the bar for a quick beer and to catch up on life. Of course, we discussed the marathon tennis match. After ten years, we had different memories of who won. Gus insisted that he took the final set.

We met Phil and drove together, both of us falling asleep along the way. We stayed overnight at the Atrium Hotel in Millinocket. The plan was to get up at 4:30 a.m., drive to the gate at Baxter State Park, and begin our hike up Abol Trail to Katahdin at 5:30, still in the dark. The alarm woke Gus and me up way too early. Phil was used to that time since he owned a dry-cleaning business and that was his normal wakeup hour. We rolled out of bed, drank coffee, ate an energy bar, filled our backpacks with extra socks, wind breaker, an apple, and plenty of water. I had climbed mountaintops of 10,000 feet in Oregon, so I did not think much of this hike. I assumed it was going to be a piece of cake.

I shared my excitement of whitewater paddling with Phil and his payback was to take me to Katahdin. Phil and I had several adventures during his tenure on the Board of the Boys & Girls Club. Since I was getting into whitewater kayaking, I was working on learning how to perform the Eskimo roll. During the afternoons, we would practice the rolls in the Boys & Girls Club pool. He was in his "overflow kayak" and I was in my "Red Dancer". We practically drowned each other attempting to roll over and over without success. At times we were close to being out of breath before the other would flip the boat over from an unsuccessful roll attempt. During one stormy mini-hurricane summer day in Maine, we decided to practice our kayaking skills down the Kennebec River, putting in above The Forks, a common place for rafting and kayaking trips. The river was a good class 3 plus. We had our eyes set on the weekend in early July that we were both available. On Friday we got the news that the weather conditions were going to be hurricane-like, with high winds and lots of rain. Neither of us were afraid of the challenge and decided to still go. When we got to the put-in Saturday morning we both looked at each other like "you sure you want to do this?" The male ego got the best of us. Phil paid the price. Right from the start Phil flipped his overflow kayak and started to swim in the downpour windy rain. The roar of the river seemed to be accented much more by the weather. Unfortunately, this continued for the next 2 miles down the river. Phil would get in the boat and flip again. I would rescue him, pull off to the side of the river, dump his boat and then within minutes a side wave would flip him again. Toward the end of the rapids, Phil was beat up. I believe his kayaking career ended on that trip. I had to give him lots of credit for his perseverance.

We continued to drive in darkness for twenty-five miles to the head of the trail. The weather was a cool 49 degrees at the base of the mountain for May 30th. We all had shorts on and long sleeves expecting to heat up quickly with the steep climb ahead of us. We saw the ranger at the beginning of the trail warning us that the weather can change rapidly. He said beware of snow. "Snow, in May?!" I thought.

The first hour was a nice walk with increased incline for half a mile. Phil said Abol Trail was the quickest way to the top but the most difficult. Gus's legs and mine were burning from playing three-and-a-half hours of tennis. We started to feel it as we continued. The trail became rockier with large boulders to maneuver around. The weather started to turn from a foggy morning to an overcast sky and a very cold breeze came from the west. As we were climbing hand over hand, the first sign of snow started in a form of flurries. We kept moving along and the snow began to come steadier and in our face. Phil stopped leading us and said, "We might want to consider turning back. Katahdin can be quite unpredictable at the top. Gus said, "That's OK with me. I'm heading back." I said, "Phil, if you are game, I'm game, let's do this."

Off we went as Gus headed back down the mountain. The snow was now even steadier. We attempted to climb fast to make it to the top quicker although we were cautious of the snow-covered rocks making the footing very slippery. My hands started turning red and numb along with my legs. I reached into my backpack and pulled out my extra socks and used them as gloves to finish the journey.

We made it to the top as the wind really picked up to a blizzard, pelting us sideways. We quickly took a photograph of us and headed immediately back down the path. The photo shows how the background was a complete white-out. We kept our eye on the trail markers making sure we did not leave the trail heading down. The footing was slick and dangerous. It took us more time than we liked to work our way downward. As we reached the tree line, the snow turned into a cold drizzle. We were both glad after four hours of battling the elements to finally get back to the parking lot. Gus was hanging out, patiently waiting for us. "I was worried about you guys. I was about to stop into the Ranger station to get some help," said Gus.

"I am sorry you couldn't make it to the top, you wimp," I said, as I looked over at Phil and said, "He must be a flatlander from New York." I was the pot calling the kettle black.

Journey 10

"Enjoy the little things in life, because one day you will look back and realize they were the big things."   Anonymous

Tomato Soup

In March of 1993, I was invited by a Boys & Girls Club Board member, Dave Lovejoy, to join him on a two-night snowshoeing trip into the White Mountains along the Presidential mountains. Since it was March, (in New York that meant spring), I thought that would not be too bad for a journey into the woods.

Dave loved the outdoors having lived most of his life in Maine. While in college, he lived out West climbing sheer cliffs and paddling down Class 5 waters. To top it off, while in the Armed Services, he was in the Special Forces of the Marines. He and his best buddy, Barney, were going to be guiding me during this trip. Barney and Dave were two peas in a pod. They loved the outdoors and loved any adventures the wilderness playground had to offer.

In the winter of 1993, Dave called me up out of the blue when I lived on Snow Pond. The ice was just frozen over with seven miles of clear smooth ice. It looked beautiful. The wind was quite strong on this blue-sky day. "Hey Ken, do you have ice skates?" I said, "Yea." Dave said, "Good I'll be right over."

Dave arrived at the house ten minutes later with skates and two personal floatation devices over his shoulder and an umbrella. He led me down to the shoreline and we got on our skates. I said, "Dave, you are sure the ice is thick enough?"

"Well, we will see, won't we? If one of us goes in the PFD's will keep us up long enough to be pulled out. Just follow me. Let the wind take us for the ride."

Aimlessly, I followed his instructions. Off we went on the ice. It was amazing! We were tied to each other with ten feet of distance in between. Dave held out the umbrella. We flew down the thin ice in the middle of the lake with the wind blowing us down the west side of the lake. We were hooting and hollering and having a ball. Someone yelled out from one of the windows of a local house. "Hey, what the hell is wrong with you guys? The ice is too thin." We just waved and continued. From that day on, I knew any adventures with Dave would be interesting.

That night I packed my blue hiking framed pack with my sleeping bag and tent, along with other warm clothes. Dave and Barry were going to take care of the dinner meals. Dave offered to drive and meet me at my house Friday morning. I threw my backpack in the back of his Chevy. Dave looked at the backpack and instantly grabbed the tent off the frame and said, "You won't need this."

We met up with Barry at his house in Western Maine. Off we went toward Mt. Washington National Park. The temperature outside was warmer than usual for Maine in early March. Outside it was a raw 39 degrees. Not cold enough for snow but cold enough for freezing rain. I had no idea where we were going. I was just going for the ride. We pulled up to the trail marker and the signed indicated "Eagle Crest" loop. I was not as prepared as I should have been with no waterproof gear. I knew that I was going to get soaked.

We arrived late in the morning, put our snowshoes on and started as the freezing rain came down at a steady pace. Dave and Barney were hoping as we climbed higher into the peaks that it would turn into snow. Otherwise, the trip would be miserable. Every step with the snowshoes was awkward. I was sliding all over the trail now with the icy glaze on top. I remember trying to stay up with them as their stride was much longer than mine as both men were well over six feet tall. My "Rocky" attitude kept me within 10 yards from them as they pushed on. I was warm and sweating from the workout. Three hours of the hard, strenuous work was under our belts. It was starting to get darker on the hillside. Barry and Dave decided we should hike to the lean-to at the base of Eagle Crest and camp for the night. The lean-to was a welcome sight.

I arrived drenched in sweat and my clothes soaked. Dave and Barry were worried about me going into hyperthermia. They knew the temperatures were going to fall quickly and my sweat would cause my core temperature to drop. They suggested that I get out of my clothes immediately and change under cover from the downpour of freezing rain. I put on dry clothes although I was still chilled. That night I do not remember much about dinner. I remember getting

Passion for Life

into my sleeping bag and trying to stay warm until the morning. By early morning, the sky did clear but the temperature had dropped by 15 degrees.

Our plan for day two was to hike to Eagle Crest ridge and follow the mountaintop for the remaining part of the journey. My clothes that I took off were frozen when I awakened. The smell of coffee that Barry was brewing was a warm welcome to the start of the day. He also cooked up a bowl of oatmeal for all of us for our supply of energy for the morning.

We had an early start. I stuffed my frozen clothes in a plastic bag into my backpack, put my snowshoes on, and followed Dave and Barry up the path. The path was even more difficult now that ice had formed on top of the snow from the freezing temperature. It was a beautiful, sunny but cold day. I could see my frozen breath as I exhaled.

We had a tremendous day working our way to the top. The terrain became steep and we had to remove our snowshoes. When we did get to the crest of the hillside, the sights were outstanding. We saw for miles along the Presidential Range with the vision of Mt. Washington upon us. That made it all worthwhile.

At the end of the day, Dave and Barry agreed on a spot to settle for the evening. We found a set of smooth flat rocks just below a ridge protecting us from the west wind. As the sun started to set, the cold winds picked up, and the temperature began to drop. We had no fire for the evening. Dave and I leaned up against the rock wall while Barry heated up dinner with his little propane stove.

Dave asked, "Hey Barry, what's on the menu tonight? I'll have lobster tails if that's available tonight." "Sure thing buddy, coming right up although I know you would rather have instant tomato soup instead, right?"

I heard the words "tomato soup" and thought, "Oh boy! I'm going hungry tonight." I had hated tomato soup ever since my childhood. I was tired, cold and hungry. If it was only tomato soup, I was ready to force it down.

The sun was setting. We all were against the rock ledge sitting up in our sleeping bags. The clear sky showed the brilliant stars. Barry handed over a cup of tomato soup to each of us. I grabbed the coffee mug with the hot soup in my hands. It felt great having the warmth of the cup in my hands. I put my nose near the edge of the cup and smelled the tomato soup. For the first time in my life I realized how good tomato soup smelled. My senses were alive. I took my first sip of the soup and truly was in paradise. At that moment, the soup was more important than the finest treasures of the world. It was the treasure. The warm taste of the tomato soup exploded in my mouth and warmed my belly. Sipping the soup, looking into the sky and seeing the wonders of the universe was a perfect moment in life. At this moment, nothing mattered except for this time, nothing else. It was perfect. Tomato soup and being on top of a beautiful mountain range with a star-filled night. We spent the remaining part of the evening talking about our lives, adventures, and future journeys to explore.

The next morning we headed out and downward towards the final loop of the trail to Dave's truck. We got back around noon at the trail's head to travel back home. As we were driving back listening to a Crosby, Stills, Nash and Young cassette tape, I was reflecting on the trip. Obviously, I was not prepared for the snowshoeing trip. If I was alone, I might have been in big trouble dealing with the elements. I did learn something about myself. I must continue to open my mind to what is offered in life. Not trying things in life will always make me question what could have been. I knew that life's treasures are ones to explore. Dreaming is one thing but implementing a plan to take on the dreams is more important.

Finally, my thoughts were around the simple pleasures of life. I will never forget the tomato soup. On a normal day, tomato soup would disgust me. In the setting on top of Eagle Crest it was the best meal I could have ever wanted. These days, the smell of tomato soup brings me right back to the rocky ledge looking up into the beautiful star-filled sky.

Journey 11

Harold with Cal Ripken Jr., his son Bill Alfond, me,
Dr. John Winkin, and Governor John Baldacci

"Heroes come and go, but legends are forever."   Kobe Bryant

Harold Alfond, Maine's Legend

    In life we are sometimes lucky to come upon an individual that is unique to mankind. A man whose life positively makes an impact on an entire generation. That man to me was Harold Alfond, a successful businessman and philanthropist--- a game changer.

    When I moved to Maine, the first words out of many peoples' mouths as I was trying to bring breath back to the Boys and Girls Club of Waterville was that I needed to meet Harold Alfond. Mr. Alfond could make a significant difference in any organization. The Waterville citizens were certainly right.

    In the Fall of 1993, the great John "Swisher" Mitchell, who was a legend in his own right playing for the New England 1944 Basketball Waterville Championship Team as well as playing for the University of Rhode Island against Hall of Fame Celtics star Bob Cousy, offered to make the introduction to Mr. Alfond.

Swisher and Harold went back decades as Harold followed the 44 team during that championship season. Harold offered Swisher many job opportunities as he invested in people he trusted to get the job done. Swisher not only worked in the Waterville School system and at the Waterville Boys Club as the Director, but also was one of the first organizers of the Waterville Little League with HOF Collegiate Coach Dr. John Winkin. Mr. Alfond loved sports and baseball seemed to be his favorite.

One fall Sunday afternoon, Swisher said that Harold was ready to meet me at his home and invited me to watch the New England Patriots play. Harold at the time was 79 years old and still owner of Dexter Shoe company as well as the majority minority owner of the Boston Red Sox. The story goes that when the Red Sox were looking for an investor from the State of Maine, Mr. Alfond's name was number one on the list.

Mr. Alfond stood around 5'6" and was round but not overweight. He had white hair cut short and balding on top. He usually wore a baseball cap of all different sorts and different teams. What I noticed most about Mr. Alfond was the twinkle in his eye. This twinkle was a sign that he had ideas floating through his head. I described him as the 21st century Santa Claus, most fitting for the many dreams he made come true. What I liked most about Harold was that he did not showboat his wealth. On the contrary, he lived in a very modest humble way for a wealthy man. He loved challenging the community and institutions if he had trust in the leadership within the organization. I was blessed that I developed that trust over the years with Mr. Alfond.

When I arrived at Mr. Alfond's house with Swisher, we were invited in by his longtime caretaker Alice. She introduced me to Dorothy "Bibby", Harold's wife, and we walked into the living room. Harold was in his recliner already watching the game with a fire in the forefront. Swisher advised me not to start a conversation but to take his lead. We sat and watched the entire first half with little conversation. The Quarterback for the Patriots, Drew Bledsoe, scored a TD. Harold turned to me and asked, "What do you want?" Before I could reply, he said, "I'll tell you what I could do for you. I'll give you $50,000 for the next five years for the Boys Club, no questions asked, or I'll challenge you to raise $500,000 in one year to be matched by me dollar for dollar. Which one do you want?" I replied, "I'll take the challenge." He said, "Alright then, you'll have one year to raise the $500,000. Cash in the barrel, no pledges."

Swisher and I left during half time. While we were driving in the car Swisher said, "Kenny that was a good choice. I think Harold liked that."

So, I was off on the first official Capital Campaign of my career. Long story short, we raised the $500,000 three days before the deadline. During that time, Harold and I started our relationship that lasted 14 years until his death in 2007. After the challenge was met, Mr. Alfond came to my office on a surprise visit and told me that he wanted to challenge me to build the best Boys Club in the country in a new building. From that conversation, we discussed the vision to merge the YMCA, the Club and the city's Park and Recreation together under one roof. That vision brought national attention and was a major success. I was the CEO of the finest youth and family organization in the country called the Harold and Bibby Alfond Youth Center. I could go on about this amazing feat although I want to share the connection and amazing opportunities that Harold brought to my life. Most of it was around the sporting games we loved.

During the time of the Capital Campaign, Harold and I had the opportunity to get to know each other. Our love of sports helped us bond along with the drive to succeed on projects. In 1995, Harold was nominated to receive the National Football Foundation Gold Medal Award from NCAA as one of the most outstanding people in the country. The event was held at the Waldorf Astoria Hotel in NYC. Athletes and coaches from around the country attended this special event. I was honored that Mr. Alfond asked me to attend the ceremony with him. We flew to NYC along with his sons, Teddy, Billy and Peter, and his close friend's baseball coach of the University of Maine John Winkin and Johnny "Swisher" Mitchell. Harold's newly hired attorney, Greg Powell, also joined us. Harold's nephew Peter Lunder was to meet us there.

For me, this was one of the most superior hotels that I ever stayed in during my life. I stayed in a two-bedroom suite with Winkin, Mitchell and Peter Alfond. I bunked with John Winkin. John, one of Harold's best friends, was the most fit individual I have ever met. Even in his 70's, John worked out every day before fitness fads hit our culture. He always stood upright, shoulders back, clean cut and chose his words with purpose. He brought his University of Maine baseball teams to the NCAA World Series several times even though the season in Maine was short. Ninety-two of his players were drafted into the Major Leagues including star pitcher Billy Swift and shortstop and teammate of Cal Ripken Jr., Mike Brodick. I enjoyed discussing baseball with Coach Winkin. He had an amazing baseball mind. Coach was certainly ahead of his time. He started the pitch count at Colby College way before it became a practice in the Major Leagues.

Before the major event that evening, Greg Powell and I walked to Rockefeller Center to see the Christmas tree and to get to know each other. At that time, I had no idea how important Greg was going to be regarding administrating Harold Alfond's Foundation. After Harold passed away in 2007, Greg became the President and CEO of the Harold Alfond Foundation and responsible to evaluate and fund many of the applications that came by the office. He and the trustees have supported a tremendous number of projects well into the hundreds of millions of dollars.

Later in the afternoon, we all gathered in Harold's suite. This suite has hosted many dignitaries, including Presidents of the United States. I have a photo standing behind Harold Alfond in my tux with Harold sitting in John F. Kennedy's rocking chair. At the crowded pre-party, I met the famous BYU Football

Coach LaVell Edwards who had an overall record of 257 wins coaching at BYU from 1962 to 2000, 38 years along with winning a National Championship in 1984.

At dinner, we had our table center stage to the podium. Many top stars were there. Sitting across from us was the All Star and former Pro Football player from Oklahoma, Billy Sims. This was a formal event in which everyone was in black ties and elegant gowns. When it was Harold's time to talk, he did a fantastic job with his light joking and being grateful for his success.

Harold was very successful building his shoe company empire although his most famous deal came from the negotiation with the Billionaire Warren Buffet selling his company for Berkshire Hathway stock and making Harold a fortune overnight. The deal was legendary, made on a plane heading north from Florida.

Harold knew I loved the game of baseball. I shared with him the days I played farm team, Babe Ruth, legion, high school, college and semi-pro baseball. And he opened at times to talk about how he was a third baseman for his high school team in Swampscot, Massachusetts. I came to Maine following the Yankees and proudly waved my Yankee advertisement with flags outside my home, my office decorated in Yankee colors and my license plate sharing my love for the Yankees. My Board members of the Boys & Girls Club warned me to be cautious being too outward especially around Mr. Alfond. I was not worried as Harold and I used to jab back and forth about his Red Sox and my Yanks. I always ended many of our conversations on "How many World Series has the Red Sox won. It's been a long time since 1912."

On August 28th, 1998, Harold called me and said, "Ken, since you and your "Boys Club" team have done such a good job, I want to treat you to a game at Fenway Park. Bring along seven others with you." This was going to be my first time going to see the Red Sox play. They had an evening game against the Minnesota Twins with the great future HOF player Paul Molitor in town playing his last season.

As I drove up to the Waterville Airport, there sat on the runway, a Red Sox jet. The Red Sox emblem was very pronounced on the back wing. Boston here we come. I went with other Board members as the copilots led us onto the jet. Inside the small jet lining both sides were leather couches and leather seats in the back. It seemed to seat 10-12 people comfortably. Harold had the jet stocked with beverages and snacks. He arrived with his driver Alice in an older Blue Buick that usually took him around. He was wearing his blue, Red Sox baseball cap, off-white slacks and light pink polo shirt. The game was a 7:05 pm start. We planned to get to Fenway by 5:00 to watch batting practice.

"Hey boys, are you ready for the game tonight? We are going to show this New York boy what Red Sox baseball is all about." Harold said, with a slight belly laugh.

Passion for Life

The trip down to Boston was less than 45 minutes. Looking at the Maine landscape along the coastal flight was fascinating. I was amazed by all the islands off the coast. A van was waiting for us when we arrived at the airport just outside of Boston. We all got in for the 10-minute ride to Fenway. As we approached the stadium, already there was a buzz going on around Yawkey Way. We pulled into the players' parking lot. We got out and Harold led us to the field. My first view was stunning, looking down to the field right behind home plate at the Green Monster wall. The stadium was not as enormous as Yankee or Shea Stadium. Any seat in the house seemed to be a good one. Until now, my only view of Fenway had been on TV during the 1975 Reds and Red Sox World Series. Being there looking out to the Red Sox taking batting practice blew me away with excitement. The sounds of the bats cracking and echoing during batting practice had my hair standing up on the back of my neck.

Harold said, "Come on boys, let's get on the field and meet some of the players." In my mind, I said "Are you kidding me?" I was a kid in a candy store. We approached the entrance near the Red Sox dugout and out came the Red Sox Manager Jimmy Williams and General Manager Dan Duquette. "Hi, Harold," they both said. Harold shouted out, "Hey boys," referring to Jimmy and Dan. "I want you to meet the guys from Maine who are building the biggest Boys Club in the Nation."

After greetings and small talk, we went onto the field. The Red Sox management gave us each a ball for signatures and off we went to meet the players. We talked with first basemen Mo Vaughn, John Valentin, Normar Garciaparra, Troy O'Leary, Jason Varitek, and the great Pedro Martinez, I walked over to the batting cage and watched batting practice right next to the HOF Jim Rice, as their batting coach, was giving instructions to Valentin. I was out of my mind.

One of the biggest highlights was talking with HOF player Paul Molitor as he was stretching before the Twins turn for batting practice. I walked over to him and said hello. I said, "Paul, it's an honor to meet you." I told him it was my first time at Fenway and he immediately engaged into the conversation with no arrogance at all. I asked him how much longer he thought he was going to play. He told me he thought this would be his last.

We then went into the dugout and struck up a conversation with the great Pedro Martinez. He was so easy to talk with. He had great enthusiasm and joked with us about being from Maine. He said how it's got to be damn cold up there. He played for Montreal for several years.

Harold said it was time to get to our seats. We took the elevator up to the Dexter Shoe Company's owner's box right next to the Red Sox owner, John Harrington's box. It was hard to imagine that we were watching a game from the owner's box. Inside was a buffet spread of all kinds of food including lobster as well as all types of beverages and snacks. Inside the main area was a big screen TV with couches along with coffee tables stacked with Red Sox baseball hats as gifts. A sliding glass door led out to the outdoor seats. Harold's box was just to the left of home plate. Each of the owners' boxes along third base side was divided by glass. We sat most of the time outside and could look into the Red Sox owner's box. Dan Duquette and John Harrington and other Red Sox brass were there. Then, HOF catcher Carlton Fisk came in. We all elbowed each other and could not help but to stare at Carlton. As the game went on, Fisk came over to our box to say hello to Harold who introduced us all.

The Red Sox and the Twins pounded out many hits that night with several home runs winning 13-12. Tim Wakefield started the game although he got knocked out early giving up seven runs in four innings. That night's attendance was almost at full capacity with close to 33,000 people seeing this exciting finish. We left around the seventh inning, as Harold was famous for not staying to the end and wanted to get home without traffic delay.

On the flight back to Maine, I could not get over the unbelievable evening. Later in life, I appreciate more and more how fantastic it was meeting five Hall of Fame Players and watching my first game at Fenway in an owner's box. That evening, my interest was growing for this Red Sox team. Not too long after numerous repeats of this type of experience, the Yankee flag came down in front of my house.

Harold continued to push his views to me on what real baseball was all about and where the real house of baseball is played. The following year, in 1999, the Red Sox were on the hunt for the first time fighting towards the World Series since 1912. They had to go through their arch enemy, the New York Yankees. Already the Yanks were ahead in the series 2-0 before heading back to Fenway. Harold called me on a Friday and said, "Ken, pack your bags. We are heading to Boston to watch our beloved Sox." I replied, "Harold, your beloved Sox." He also invited the Alfond Youth Center Board Chair, Joe Jabar Sr., to attend as well. Harold did these nice gestures to volunteers of the Alfond Youth Center as a thank you. Harold and Joe go way back. Joe played for Colby College and was drafted by the Seattle Mariners as a hard throwing fastball pitcher. He played in the Cape Cod league during his summer months while in college and the great Yankee captain Thurman Munson was his catcher. After one year in the minors, having had a good season and not being called up to double A, he thought it was best to hang up the cleats and go to law school. Harold knew that Joe would enjoy this great matchup between Pedro and Roger Clemens.

This matchup was discussed on talk radio and in the media all week. Pedro was the new Red Sox pitching star and the "Rocket" Clemens was the Red Sox star from the past. Since the Red Sox management let Clemens go, thinking his better days were in the past, the Rocket dominated the league as a Blue Jay and a Yankee, winning CY Young awards.

Passion for Life

The Red Sox faithfuls were geared up for this matchup of the century and Joe and I were thrilled to be a part of this at Fenway in Harold's owner's box. This was certainly a fantasy trip that I would never forget, thanks to Harold.

Game time was 1:05 p.m. This series had it all including all the great announcers and past players Tim McCarver, Bobby Murcer, Ken Singleton, Jerry Remy, and Jim Kaat. Yankee owner George Steinbrenner was still alive with the HOF coach Joe Torre leading the Yanks while Jimmy Williams was back for another year with the Red Sox.

We got to Fenway early enough, flying in the Red Sox jet again and arriving around 11:30 a.m. to watch batting practice from the Red Sox dug out. In the Red Sox dugout stood Varitek, Stanley, Garciaparra, Nixon, Saberhagen, and Martinez in the bullpen. The Sox went back to the dugout and out came the Yanks leading with Jeter, Bernie Williams, Scott Brosius, Chuck Knoblauch, Tino Martinez, Paul O'Neill, Daryl Strawberry and Mario Riveria, Roger Clemens could be seen in the bullpen warming up as the Red Sox faithfuls were giving him hell.

Joe and I went to the owner's box after watching batting practice and taking in the energy from the field level. The box had all you could eat and Red Sox wildcard baseball caps for Harold's guests. We were like little kids ready to watch the fight of the century between two of the best pitchers of that time during one of the greatest rivalries of any sport teams in the biggest sporting events of the year.

The packed house at Fenway was electrifying. This arena was going to erupt at the first hit by the Sox. And the Sox did. Jose Offerman led with a triple off Clemens bringing the noise level to waves all the way to Maine. Then Valentin homered off the Rocket causing an earthquake of sound to San Francisco. By the third inning, Clemens was driven off the mound to the dugout with the Fenway fans shaking the stadium with the chant "Where is Roger? In the Shower!" On the other hand, Pedro pitched outstanding going into the 7th and allowing only two hits and no runs. The Sox won 13 to 1. There is no doubt in my mind that this was the most memorable game that I ever witnessed. I did realize quickly that the fan base of the Red Sox nation were well educated baseball fans with a powerful loyalty and the hunger for a World Series win. These fans could taste it that night.

Instead of taking a cab back to the Four Seasons hotel after the game, Harold wanted to walk to enjoy the celebration among the fans. Harold was not a young man. He was 85 and a spirited individual after this great win. I remember Joe telling me that he would get in front of Harold and I was going to be behind him to protect him from the rowdiness. And it was certainly rowdy - Boston was in party mode. The chanting and singing went on all night long on the streets and in the bars. We made it back to the hotel safely. We found out the next day while sitting around the pool that we were staying in the hotel where most of the Yankees were staying.

Sunday's game was at 7:00 p.m., so Joe and I went to one of the local pubs near the stadium to watch the Patriots play against the Miami Dolphins before heading over to Fenway to meet Harold. We watched the Patriots lose a tough game 31-30. The crowd in Boston was disappointed although they had hope for another fantastic Red Sox victory that evening to tie up the series with the Yankees. But that was not to be as the Yankees scored six in the top of the ninth to win a blowout 9 to 2. The Yankees put the dagger in game five winning 6 to 1 to win the series and off to the World Series against the Atlanta Braves. The Yanks went on to beat the Braves in four straight games winning yet another World Series title.

Even though being a Yankee fan in my heart, my love for the Red Sox was growing. Harold Alfond was spinning his magical web and I was caught in it. Mr. Alfond continued to give these priceless gifts to me. I believe he got just as much gratification watching my enjoyment during these incredible moments. My payback would come later in 2007.

A few years later another tremendous sporting gift came from Mr. Alfond. While visiting with me at my new house during the summer of 2000, an 1860 colonial home in China Village, Harold noticed a Fighting Irish of Notre Dame flag waving in the wind on my flagpole outside. "You like Notre Dame?" asked Harold. I said, "Of course, I'm Irish. The interest came from my dad watching many of the Irish football games as a kid. I have never stopped following them."

"Well, the former Athletic Director of University of Maine is now the Notre Dame AD. Maybe we'll have to go visit Kevin White one of these days," Harold said. A few weeks later I got a call from Harold on Wednesday September 6th. "Ken, what are you doing this coming weekend," Harold asked. Before I could answer he said, "Pack your bags. We are heading on a journey for a few days." I asked, "Where?" Harold replied, "Don't worry, just bring yourself and meet me at the airport at 8:00 Friday morning."

I arrived on a beautiful Maine day at the Waterville airport where there was always just a few small planes sitting near the runway except for today the Red Sox small jet was getting ready for a journey. At the airport also waiting was his Attorney and Director of his Foundation Greg Powell. I walked up to Greg and said, "Where are we going?" Greg smiled with a chuckle and replied, "You mean Harold didn't tell you? South Bend, Indiana, for the Notre Dame - Nebraska football game. We will be staying with Kevin White, the Athletic Director." "You're kidding me!" was all that I could say.

Harold arrived with his grandson, John, son of his oldest Teddy. John was in his twenties and a big football fan. The flight to South Bend only took 2:15 hours. At the airport, Kevin White was waiting for us and then took us to his home off campus. His large home was in a new development and John, Greg and I slept in a finished basement bedroom off the recreation room with big TV's and a pool table. Harold had a room on the second floor.

At noon, we were invited to the Notre Dame Pre pep rally luncheon with many of the alumni attending to show support before the game. We had a table off the main elevated Dias where Coach Bob Davie and his key players, Julius Jones, Grant Irons sat. The coach got up after lunch and talked about the upcoming season and how this game against Nebraska was going to be tough against the number one ranked team in the nation while ND was ranked 23.

Later that afternoon the Irish held a pep rally at the stadium that started at 6:00. This would be my first step into the stadium at South Bend. Before the rally, Harold wanted to go to the NCAA Football Hall of Fame in downtown South Bend. We all went and enjoyed ourselves reviewing the tremendous history of the game. The many hallways and open rooms brought me back to many of the great bowl games I watched as a kid on the small black and white TV in Brooklyn and in Amenia.

We arrived at the stadium around 5:30 p.m. and found our seats on the fifty-yard line. Harold was escorted onto the field by Kevin White as Greg, John and I took our seats. Over 30,000 people showed up just for the rally. The Fighting Irish band came marching onto the field at 6:00 sharp and the announcers introduced the players and coaching staff. The crowd was jacked up for the big game.

After the rally, we headed over to Kevin's house for the post rally party. When we got there, the house had a few guests but not for long. People started to arrive from all different directions including the marching band and the Irish leprechaun. The band stayed outside and played the Irish traditional Notre Dame Fight songs. I could not believe the neighbors would tolerate the level of noise being created. Either they were all invited to the party, or they expected this during home games. We did not get to bed until after midnight. The game time the next day was at 2:30 p.m.

After a big breakfast at Kevin's house, John and I headed over to the stadium early to go to the gift shop and enjoy the tailgate parties while Greg Powell and Harold went with Kevin to sit in the President's box at the stadium. Also in the President's box was Shawn Walsh, the University of Maine Hockey Coach who won the NCAA championship and was admired by Harold. Shawn was battling cancer and unfortunately died within a year after the game. At the student union, Notre Dame memorabilia and dress wear was all over the place. I couldn't help myself and bought an overpriced jacket, a hat and sweatshirt.

John and I then went to the stadium and started walking around the parking lot that was packed with tailgaters. Everywhere we went beers were offered to us which we gladly accepted and joined some of the parties. I was anxious to get to the stadium and be a part of this unbelievable moment. We finally drank our last beer and went into the stadium packed with 80,000 fans. I was surprised to see that there was a huge wave of Nebraska fans on the other side of the stadium. They had to buy up a ton of tickets to show support to their number one team.

We had great tickets, eight rows up from the Notre Dame fifty-yard line. The game was one of the best; a see-saw battle trading scores back and forth. Nebraska had a good quarterback, Eric Couch, leading the way, completing 7 of 15 passes along with rushing for 116. Nebraska entered halftime with a 14 to 7 lead. Notre Dame battled back and tied the game in the fourth quarter 21 to 21 with a fantastic punt return for 83 yards resulting in overtime. Unfortunately, for the Irish, Notre Dame lost in overtime 27 to 24. The stadium was rocking during the whole game. The energy level matched the Red Sox playoff game against the Yankees.

Once again Harold provided another classic moment in my life, one that will be forever cemented in my soul. I could never have dreamed of being part of this opportunity, especially reflecting to the days when I was a little kid in front of a black and white TV in Brooklyn watching the Irish. In those days, thinking of being at Notre Dame stadium was a fairy tale.

After building the Alfond Youth Center, we started developing our Camp Tracy location with a new capital campaign thanks to the New Balance Foundation 1-million-dollar match. Steve King a former Boys Club alumnus who worked for the New Balance company opened the door by making a pitch to owners Jim and Ann Davis. After reaching the fundraising challenge and building a new campus including climbing walls, rope courses, outdoor theater, waterfront lodge, a main four-season lodge and cabins on McGrath Pond in Oakland, Maine, I knew something was missing. It was simple. A new ball field was needed to round out the camp.

I brought Mr. Alfond over to Camp Tracy to see what we had accomplished. He was pleased and I shared my idea about building a ball field. He said, "Ken, I'll give you $50,000 to pay for the study." I replied, "Harold, thanks for the support, although I'm turning down your money this time because I want this to be a gift for you in your honor." He gave me that Harold Alfond twinkle and a smirk, enjoying the bold statement.

My attempt to give a billionaire an appropriate gift was challenging. There was only one thing to do: build a baseball stadium that was a replica of Fenway Park. I approached the current Board Chair of the AYC, Mike Runser, and the Building and Grounds Committee Chair, Fred Stubbert, about this concept. Both were great Red Sox baseball fans, although Mike was more cautious than Fred. Fred was an engineer and he jumped all over the project and worked with another board member, Al Hodsdon, who had his own engineering firm. We began to plan the design of Fenway.

As the men began the design phase, I reached out to the Director of Marketing for Major League Baseball, John Brody, a former Boys and Girls Club alumnus (his father was a Board President in the past) to help with the process.

Passion for Life

John helped push through the licensed agreement with MLB after months of going through MLB administration and attorneys. Once we got the licensed agreement, the fundraising efforts were open for presentations. Thanks to Paul McClay, the secretary of the Maine Sports Legends and on the Board of Gardiner Savings Bank, we were able to obtain our first 100K. The Cal Ripken Sr. Foundation, through the leadership of their CEO Steve Salem and Board member Robbie Callaway donated another 100K.

Then donations from the Red Sox and Yawkey Foundations along with other local businesses helped us raise the necessary funds to build our Mini Fenway. Steve Aucoin, a city councilor, who later worked for us as our Unit Director of our North End Public Housing Unit, was our main carpenter. I quickly realized that the community wanted to be a part of this unique project and it became a real grass roots effort to build this only replica of Fenway in Maine. Within five months, the project was completed. I called up Harold and said, "Are you ready to see the field that we've been building in your honor?"

In late August, Harold met me at Camp Tracy for his first viewing of Fenway. He was taken to the field by his oldest son Teddy along with Ted's son-in-law. I was waiting at the entrance to show off the field. He came down the road in Ted's black SUV. At 93 years old, Mr. Alfond was battling cancer and was weak from his treatments. The SUV stopped where I was standing. Harold got out with help from Teddy. He looked over to the field seeing the Green Monster Wall, the Fisk Pole, the Pesky Pole, the score board built just like Fenway's and the big sign in Center Field with his name on it, "The Harold Alfond Fenway Park." The field was the exact 66% replica of Fenway from color codes to every angle of the field.

Harold just stood staring at the field just repeating, "Beautiful." I could see his eyes watering with joy. I knew at that point I had accomplished my goal. I gave a gift that Mr. Alfond really appreciated and left a lasting impression and legacy in his honor.

On September 7, 2007, we held the official dedication of the Harold Alfond Fenway Park. We were able to engage Cal Ripken Jr., the Iron Man of Baseball and Hall of Fame star to be our honored guest. Unfortunately, that Saturday was a miserable day with steady rain but over a thousand people showed up for the dedication, lining up to see Cal Ripken Jr. and extend gratitude to Harold Alfond. The Governor, a Congressman, local dignitaries, little league teams, and even the Boston Park Rangers Mounted Unit along with many guests surrounded the field on this wet day.

Before the 1:00 p.m. start time, Cal Ripken Jr., Steve Salem, Bill Alfond, Coach Winkin and I met in Harold Alfond's living room at his home on Great Pond. This memory will always be a powerful one for me reflecting on seeing the Iron Man of Baseball standing up in the middle of the living room with Coach Winkin discussing the strategies of the game. I looked over to Harold sitting in his recliner. He had a big smile on his face. Seeing the two greats of the game passionately talking about the game was a sight to see.

The dedication went well even with the rain. Off the second base area, we had a big tent set up for the speakers. Cal and Harold arrived and marched over to the tent. Cal stopped for a moment and went over to see my wife and my 3-month-old son, Sean. I have a great photograph of Cal and Sean. Weeks later Cal sent me a signed baseball for Sean, it said, "To Sean, Discover Baseball, Cal Ripken Jr." That was not the first signed ball Sean has received. The day after Sean was born Harold called me and said he had something for me. I met him in the parking lot of the Alfond Youth Center. He rolled down the window and threw out a baseball. He said, "Ken, I wanted to make sure that Sean got his first signed baseball from me."

At the podium the day of the dedication, Mr. Alfond was very thankful and pleased. Cal was wonderful speaking about Mr. Alfond and about sportsmanship. We all thought that Cal would leave after the speeches due to weather and head back to the Alfond Youth Center for the event's dinner. Since the round robin baseball game for the kids had to be canceled, Cal asked all the players from the four teams to line up to hit three balls off him attempting to hit over the Green Monster Wall. The kids lined up at the edge of the short stop area of the infield and took their swings. With the rain pouring down and no one left to see this unbelievable moment, Cal could have gone but he wanted to make an impact. He certainly did. In the paper the next day was a photo of Cal kneeling down pitching to batters in the downpour rain.

Harold Alfond passed away two months later. Before he died, we spent some quality time. He told me that he was not planning to go to Florida and wanted me to help him with a fitness plan. I met with him at his camp with his nurses and physical therapist to discuss a plan. During one of our meetings, he introduced me to one of his helpers. He said, "This is Ken Walsh, he is like a son to me." I looked at Harold and thanked him and said, "That is an honor for you to say that." He said, "I meant that."

That day late in October would be the last afternoon I would see Harold Alfond alive. I never imagined Harold Alfond ever dying. He was much larger than life. The memory that I reflect upon quite often is the time he and I came back to my house in China Village in the fall of 1999. He and I sat on my front porch just talking about life. Our discussion had nothing to do with work, projects, or sports. It was just about the important things in life--people who mean something to you. I did not realize at the moment how much Harold Alfond meant to me.

Journey 12

"When you know what's important it's easy to ignore what's not." Anonymous

Rogue River Adventure – 1996

    During the winter months, a friendship developed with another tennis player at Champions Fitness Center. Bill Lord had a great sense of spiritual energy that I enjoyed and many times after a match, we discussed our common bond about life over a beer. He had two sons, Zack and Tyson. That fall, Tyson at 13 years old, came home one afternoon after school to find his mother dead on the couch from an aneurism at the age of forty. I remember Joyce playing doubles with Bill and others at Champions. She was fit and seemed to have many years of life ahead of her. Her death was a shock to our community. Bill had his own business selling medical supplies. After his wife's death, he sold it and began work on getting his degree in therapy, a healthy way of dealing with the tragedy. He focused much of his time watching over his boys and being a single father. The healing process from the Vietnam War where he served as a medic was now added to the challenge of losing his wife. Bill explained, "I lost my soul mate. The only person who could keep me centered."

    During our conversations, I would speak with him about my martial art meditation practice in which Bill believed in, as well as catching good energy from the river. I shared my Rogue River experience in 1986 and my plans to go back the summer of 1996 and asked him to join me. Bill liked the idea and the challenge. He thought it might be a good experience for him and the boys to reconnect and refocus on their lives. Once Bill decided that he was serious about the Rogue River trip, I called Roger about our intentions. Roger was always up for another excuse to get on the river. He was excited about adventure and looked forward to meeting Bill and his family. My brother, Dennis, also decided to join us.

The Summer of 1996 did not come soon enough. Bill and I continued to play tennis throughout the winter into spring. In the spring, Bill bought an overflow whitewater kayak to prepare for the rapids. Instead of jumping on the raft, he was up to paddling the mighty Rogue with me. I was feeling much more confident in the boat these days spending many hours paddling with friends on the Dead, Penobscot, and Kennebec Rivers. Bill and I spent some time in the Boys & Girls Club pool practicing rolls and defining our paddling skills. We went down the mid-section of the Kennebec at the Carry Brook outlet a few times to prepare for the big water, 100 rapids in three days. Bill held his own, despite not really having a combat roll. However, at times he was able to roll the kayak back up in still water.

Bill's boys were excited to join the adventure. Tyson at 13 was 100 lbs with lots of pent-up energy. His brother Zack was much taller, approaching 6 feet, and his hair was long and past his shoulders. During the trip, my brother Dennis nicknamed him Jesus.

In July, the Lord family and I flew together out of Portland, Maine, to San Francisco and rented a car for the 5-hour journey to Medford, Oregon. Dennis flew in from NY to Medford where we all met at Roger's A-frame home nestled in the hillside of Talent, Oregon. The first few days we hung around Roger's house getting our whitewater gear and supplies together. We took a practice run down the Northern California Rattlesnake River to warm up. There was one section that was tricky, otherwise, it was a smooth river run for that very hot dry July day. We were ready and pumped for the Rogue.

We packed our gear in the afternoon until early evening. We planned to take one large raft that Roger would paddle that included our sleeping gear, food, and supplies for three nights. Roger's Toyota pickup hauled the raft and gear while we crammed in the front and back seats. It was a tight squeeze with seven of us in the truck. Thank God Roger had air conditioning as the temperatures were expected to be in the 90's the day we were leaving for the 2-hour ride.

On the journey to the Rogue River Grave Creek, Dennis could not help talking up the Rogue River rapids and how he swam more than he wanted the first time. I shook my head and Roger laughed out loud. Bill's boys started getting nervous hearing Dennis talk about Mule Creek Canyon and Blossom Bar and how some return from the trip in a body bag. I do not think Bill appreciated the conversation, but he just laughed it off. Roger added that thousands of paddlers go down the river each year and all come home safe.

After we arrived at Grave Creek, we unloaded the raft. Tyson, Zack and Dennis paddled the inflatables while Bill and I were in hard shell kayaks. Roger took command of the raft. After all was settled with unpacking, we moved into the river and practiced our paddling, working on catching our eddies and bracing. Bill and I worked on our Eskimo rolls. I had my roll down this year and was ready for my revenge from the 1986 Horseshoe rapid thrashing. Bill on the other hand had about fifty-fifty success with his roll. His skill level was where I was back in 1986.

Roger pulled us together along the shoreline while he was in his raft and we were in our boats ready for battle with Mother Nature's river. Roger reminded us, "When a wave comes at you, lean into it, not away. Don't stop paddling in the rapids. Paddle hard into the eddy. Point the nose of the boat up stream coming out of the eddy for a good peel out. If you dump it, hang on to the paddle and boat and we will get to you. Use the boat for cushion if going toward a wall or rock. But most important, have fun." With that we were off!

We started at Grave Creek. Bill, Tyson, and Zack didn't have time to prepare for the class three. All of us found the middle of the river following the tongue of the rapid, and a side wave flipped us for a rude awaking. I flipped chasing Dennis as he was swimming in the rapids. I was able to roll back up with the others. It was my first combat roll.

At the end of the rapid, Roger encouraged us with hooting and howling as an initiation. Rainie Falls followed shortly afterward, an extremely challenging class 5 plus in 2200 CFS. We chose to portage around Rainie and it was a wise move. Many kayaks and rafts have been totally trashed attempting to go through Rainie Falls and feeling the pain afterward. We watched a kayaker make the attempt, while we stopped on the rocky shore for lunch. We watched his gallant effort, and he ended up getting destroyed. He finally had to pull out of his kayak and swim in the strong unforgiving waves. Getting caught in the rapids is like being caught by an ocean wave and tossed in all directions under the water not knowing when the rapid will release. It is not a good feeling. It is a helpless feeling being pounded by water pressure at the same time.

The first day was a successful day for our team led by Captain, Roger Funk, as he guided us and gave us tips running through the first day of rapids that were Class 3 or 3 plus. Dennis, Tyson, Zack and Bill all dumped, coming out of their boats during different rapids with no real danger. The class 4 Tyee rapid got all of us. I had to roll up for the second time. I followed Roger's raft too close heading down river and too close to the rock wall. The strong turbulence flipped me easily. I pulled out of the kayak after attempting to roll a few times. I banged up my left knee bad. When I got to the shoreline, my knee swelled up. Roger provided some pain relievers and by the end of the day, my knee was back to normal. Shortly after Tyee, we paddled into Wildcat rapids, one of the most exciting flows with nice size waves and holes that made us stay on edge as we paddled hard through it. The day went on as we continued to hit one rapid after the next. Fatigue started to hit us all. For some of the other rapids, they all swam a little more before being rescued by our fearless leader and the safety raft.

The day ended at Big Windy Creek camp area. We found a terrific place left of the river on top of a rocky hill. The sun was going down after a full day of dry, hot weather. The water was in the fifties. Water temperature was nice during the middle of the day although in the evening it felt cold. We set up camp next to a cool stream with fresh water. Across the way on the other side of the river were beautiful rock ledges, perfect for cliff jumping. Heights were from twenty to forty feet. We had a hoot jumping at different levels until the water became too cool to continue. Our voices and joyous yells echoed through the valley. We were a team enjoying the wonders of mother earth. Time stayed still at that moment as we enjoyed a piece of heaven.

We dried off and set up camp. I spent time soaking my left knee in the cool stream. We then had a great evening dinner around the fire. Roger prepared the meal and the rest of us cleaned the dishes. That night after everyone went to bed, Bill and I stayed around the fire drinking a few beers with the clear, starry sky and listening to the strong rapids roaring in the valley. Bill opened up to me and discussed how he got in the hard-shell kayak not caring if he lived or died. He missed his wife Joyce and wanted to be with her. He was being reckless because he was hurting.

Bill said, "Ken, this trip helped me realize I have so much more to live for. I need to be there for Tyson and Zack." I just remember putting my arm on Bill's shoulder and not needing to reply. He was where he needed to be. It was a perfect evening to reflect. We had another perfect moment in life where everything made sense.

Even though the evening was a perfect one, the roar of the river and the next day Class 3 rapids upper and lower Black Bar Falls were upon us. Bill told me in the morning that the rapids kept him up all night in anticipation. We had another perfect sunny hot dry day on the river. After breakfast, we packed the raft, and we were on the river by 10:30 am. We headed down the rapids and Bill was knocked out of his hard shell for good. The next thing I knew, I was looking over to see his blue dancer on top of Rogers raft and Bill riding along. He told me later that the fear of getting hurt and not being there for his kids was his decision to call it. He did not want to take the chance. I was left as the only one in a hard shell, but I understood Bill's decision.

After a few Class Two rapids I faced my fear from ten years ago on the rapid that beat me up pretty good – Horseshoe Bend. I flipped my inflatable in the beginning of the rapid in 1986 and had the long painful swim. I was prepared this time. I was mentally willing to take on the challenge. This was one of my personal goals to complete this rapid without flipping my kayak. This time going down the rapids I evaluated each hole, catching eddy after eddy working down the river. Finally, after the mile rapid was completed, I pulled over to river left in a pool of calm water with a big "Ya- Ho!" The other inflatables and raft followed as we celebrated together. Roger took a photo of me completing the rapid pulling into the eddy. This is one of my most treasured photos.

The next series of rapids were mainly Class 2's and 3's that led to Mule Creek Canyon, a solid Class 5 rapid. I was getting a little cocky paddling easily through the number of rapids until Mother Nature brought me back to reality. In front of me was Chinamen's Fall. On the river description, it is a simple Class Two with a small drop. I paddled over the ledge not focusing on keeping the paddle in the water. And then out of nowhere, I was hit by a wave flipping me unexpectedly. While under the water and still in the hard shell, I set up for my roll and suddenly, my face hit a rock under the water opening up the side of my face. I recall seeing trickles of my blood coming from my face, rising upward to the surface. I was stunned enough that I immediately pulled out of my kayak and swam toward the shoreline. Roger retrieved my boat and paddle as I sat along the rocky edge of the river. I was clearly shaken up and everyone noticed it. Besides that, the side of my face was swollen with a nice gash over my lip.

Mule Creek Canyon, one of the most difficult rapids, was still in front of us and my confidence was now in question. It would have been easy to join Bill on Roger's raft and call it good. I got back in my dancer and put my helmet back on. In the eddy, I redirected my thoughts to a meditative silence. Everyone left me alone for a few moments. Roger came up to me and said, "Are you ready to go?" not giving me much time to think too much. I said, "Let's go." Bill told me later that evening that he saw the focus in my eyes that I was not going to quit and I was going to make it through the rapid.

Roger led the way down to Mule Creek Canyon. As we got closer, it sounded like a jet taking off. The sound of the rapids was deafening. Mule Creek lived up to its reputation. The first part of the rapid "Jaws" ate Dennis immediately and he was now swimming at the beginning of this dangerous river just as he did in 1986. Roger backed his raft toward Dennis's floating body yelling to him to grab on as Bill yanked him into the boat. I successfully glided through the heavy hydraulics into the strong flow of the canyon. I followed the channel watching the raft fifty feet in front of me as the rapid sent me toward Telfer's Hole. This killer hole sucked me in. I just put my head down and paddled with all my might to break its grip. Then, shortly afterward without warning, I enter the Coffee Pot which is a very unpredictable rapid that boils up and down and all around. It is not a section that I wanted to hang around in too long. Finally, I was out in a flow of small rollercoaster waves leading into calmer waters.

Another celebration was had with my paddle above my head circling with yells of honor. We all paddled over to the canyon to the left in which we indulged in the waterfalls placing our bodies underneath and getting pounded by the cool fresh water.

After lunch, we all paddled forward feeling good about our accomplishments in the second day of our journey down the Rogue, although in front of us was another Class 5 rapid that takes at least one life each year. The previous year a woman on vacation fell out of her inflatable before the Picket Fence rapid of Blossom Bar and dropped into the hole. The rapid continued to hold her in the depths of the water before it decided to release her. Her body was found days later. I was aware of the dangers and suggested to all that we need to follow Roger's instructions to the tee. We scouted the rapid, river right from the high rocky mound. Roger told us to follow the tongue until we see the first large rock and catch the eddy there before going down the chute.

Roger and Bill's raft guided the group as we all stayed close behind. The directions worked perfectly as we found the eddy right before the Picket Fence and followed the tongue of the rapid through the rest of Blossom Bar. The rolling waves wove between the rocky gardens to the open calm water. Once again, we celebrated going through the Class 5 waters with yells of victory. It was all short lived as Devils Staircase rapid came up right way. It was a quick steep drop with a big hole to river right. After the raft went down, I followed behind the wave successfully. Dennis and Tyson got swallowed up as Zack plowed through the wave. We recovered Tyson and Dennis in the calm pool of water, helping them back into their boats.

The rest of the trip was calm with many choppy Class Two rapids. Some of the rapids were surprising to us as they caught us off guard with small holes that flipped some of the inflatables. On the last night, we camped right before Paradise Lodge on a nice sandy beach area at river left. As we set up camp, the air was getting cooler, supper was being cooked, and a black bear family appeared across the river. We all stopped what we were doing to watch nature play its role in life. The bears were hunting for food as the two little cubbies followed shortly behind mom. Wild kingdom was at our doorstep. The evening fell upon us as the sun went down. The cool Oregon sky was as clear as any night I could remember. The stars were brilliant, filling the sky with no light pollution. It was a perfect moment being around the campfire with beer, baseball caps on, and sharing adventure stories. We all laughed, smiled and were on solid ground. I think we were all relaxed also knowing the most challenging rapids were behind us and proud of our accomplishments working as a team going down the mighty Rogue River.

The next day was another clear, warm and sunny day as we set forth for the last part of the journey. We mostly played in the rapids, pulled off to the shore, and hiked along the riverbed past Tate Creek to a beautiful spot for a swim. Two

Passion for Life

hundred yards up the creek was a natural slide where water flowed down its smooth surface. Each of us climbed to the top of the 25-foot drop, sat into the slide, and flew down the chute into a deep fresh pool of water. It was another gift from nature without waiting in line and without paying money for an amusement ride.

We took out at Foster Bar Landing early in the afternoon. I think we were all reluctant to get out of our kayaks, inflatables, and raft knowing the trip was over. We hung around the shoreline and played a little bit as Tyson and Zack dumped Dennis from his boat. Bill got in my dancer and practiced his roll and finally nailed it. After we packed up, we had a scenic drive over the mountain back through Grants Pass to Roger's home in Talent. We had another day before we all took off to San Francisco and Eastern bound.

The day was spent walking around Ashland and visiting this lovely town. Our main goal was to get our film developed. The one-hour photo was not quick enough as we were anxious to see the photos and reminisce of our adventure. We picked up the film and walked through Lithia Park sharing the photos like little kids sharing their baseball cards.

After heading home, we all went our separate ways and back to our life's routines. Roger, Dennis, and I kept in contact because we are family. Many times, the friends you have at any moment may drift away due to life situations. Bill and his boys grew closer, I believe due to the Rogue River trip. They had the opportunity to bond together and become the new family pressing on with life. Zack went on to college and became a Chef. Tyson eventually did the same and moved south. Bill remarried a wonderful lady. I bought a house in China Village a couple of years after our trip. It was two doors down from Bill. At times, I would pop in to say hello and share a bear hug. Each night as he drove by the house, I would always hear the honk of his Saab.

I eventually moved away from China Village and our contact slipped away. Although each time we run into each other it rekindles our brotherhood in a spirit that will never go away. In life we all run into people we are spiritually connected to, no matter how often you see them, or how less often you see them, the connection is made from within and carries on for a lifetime. Bill Lord is a soul brother to me. After I moved away, I would travel down the China Village Neck Road and look to the left at Bill's yellow ranch. Looking straight up the driveway when his garage door was open, I could see his yellow overflow hard-shell kayak hanging from the rafters. That always made me smile.

Journey 13

Dorado Beach, Puerto Rico with Peter Alfond

"In the end we only regret the chances we didn't take." Anonymous

The Adventure That Never Happened

A trip to the Himalayas is always an adventure of a lifetime. Back in 2000, during one of my annual trips visiting my friend and philanthropist Peter Alfond at Dorado in Puerto Rico, we started planning the ultimate spiritual trip to the base camp of Mount Everest. The trip was not going to be about the climb, but more about finding our inner spirituality with spiritual leaders guiding us along the way. The trip would be one month long. Peter was going to use his personal jet to fly the team he assembled to Hong Kong, then to Katmandu, before renting out a helicopter to the mountaintops and the base of the Himalayas. Peter also offered to cover all the costs.

Peter's purpose was to have the time and insight to write a non-fiction book about the adventure. For it to be worthwhile, we needed a cast of journeymen to be part of the story. We assembled the following team of spiritual leaders.

Jose Irizarry

Jose was a longtime friend of Peter's. When Peter moved to Puerto Rico to run Dexter Shoe Company, Jose befriended Peter and the relationship grew stronger every year. Jose was an Ironman triathlon athlete who competed in world competitions including the famous Kona Ironman. He was in great shape but more importantly, he had a wonderful soul and great insight. During many of my trips to Puerto Rico, Peter, Jose and I would be drinking coffee early in the morning before sunrise discussing the philosophy of life.

Javier Diaz Piscil

Javier was my first Martial Art Karate instructor going back to 1986. He was an intense individual in his field and only believed in the best. His martial skills and teaching abilities were outstanding. He and I also trained in Reiki to round out the Ying part of the art. Javier is a very spiritual person and very sensitive to mankind. He would be a great fit to the group. He was another person in tremendous shape.

Elaine

One of Peter's spiritual advisors was a woman named Elaine. She was a Reiki master and gave Peter lots of insight on life. He respected her and thought having a female present would round out the group. She was also going to be the writer and journalist for the trip, providing leadership during the campfire discussions.

Buddhist Priest

Rounding out the group was the hiring of a Buddhist priest. Peter researched and discovered individuals who would go on the trip that had spiritual training. This individual would be helpful especially from the outside of this group. The Buddhist priest would give a different perspective for the trip.

The plan was for the team to meet in Boston and fly out together. When we arrive in Katmandu, we would hook up with the Buddhist priest for the helicopter flight to the base of the Himalayas. The trek to the base of Everest would take around four weeks. We hoped to all gain insight about ourselves, life, and our souls.

This trip was an adventure of a lifetime. I always wanted to go to Everest and even dreamed of climbing to the top. This trip seemed to be even better. The opportunity to be around inspirational people would give positive energy that would last a lifetime. Then, of course, the views of the mountain, the highest peaks in the world would be right in front of us. That energy by itself would be thrilling.

For months after my winter visit with Peter, we continued our planning, months of e-mails, phone calls, interviews with Buddhist priests and discussions

Passion for Life

on the format of the proposed book. We were set to leave at the end of the month in September 2001. We would be gone until Thanksgiving.

Then it happened. I had a trip heading to Las Vegas for a Boys & Girls Clubs of America national meeting on September 11, 2001. My original scheduled trip was the typical flight that I took for many of these trips, Boston to LA then LA to Las Vegas. However, this time and for no apparent reason, my secretary booked me out of Portland, Maine, to Detroit then to Las Vegas.

I left first thing in the morning with the arrival time in Las Vegas set for early afternoon. As the plane flew by NYC, the sky was as blue as I had ever seen it. It seemed to be a perfect day to fly. We landed in Detroit and were about to taxi to the gate when a horrifying announcement came over the PA from the Captain.

"Can I have your attention for a moment? The Twin Towers in NYC have been hit by planes along with the Pentagon. We must have you exit the plane immediately. All flights across the country have been grounded. Once you get to the terminal more instructions will be given."

I stepped out of the plane and saw everyone heading toward the gate area. It was a mess. I waited in line for the phone to make hotel reservations. All flights were cancelled until further notice. All local reservations to hotels were booked. I could not find any hotels except for sixty miles away at a Best Western.

In the meantime, in Waterville, the AYC staff gathered around the TV in the Teen Center watching the moment-by-moment broadcast. Many of my staff initially thought I was on the flight that crashed to the Twin Towers since it was the flight that I typically took going from Boston to LA. When they received my call two hours after the crash, they were relieved. They had me dead for two hours.

I hailed a cab and off I went outside of Detroit to a Best Western hotel. I wasn't sure what I would do once I got there or how long I was going to be stuck in the Detroit area, but at least I had a place to stay. I checked in and thought it was a good time to get a run in. As I was walking down the hall looking into the bar, I couldn't believe it, there was my neighbor Mark Ford. I saw him staring at the TV. I yelled out, "Hey Mark, can I buy you a beer?" He looked at me with eyes widened, "You're kidding me. Walsh, what are doing here?"

We traded stories about how we ended up at the hotel. Mark was coming from Chicago to Maine when he got detoured. He said he had rented out a car and tomorrow he and two other guys were heading east via Canada then down into NY and across to New England. I was invited to join them and left with them the next day.

After being home for a few days and thinking of our spiritual journey, I got a call from Peter Alfond. "Ken, I hate to do this, but I was strongly advised by my attorney and family to postpone our trip due to the world unrest."

I understood, of course, but was very disappointed. 9/11 changed all our lives. What we remember of world freedom was now disrupted by terrorists. The most powerful nation in the world was attacked in the financial district of NYC. Our country now was vulnerable for terrorist attacks. And, our way of life was no longer. The adventure that might have been was now gone.

Considering the heartache for the thousands of people who lost loved ones during that horrific day, our cancellation was meaningless. For years after, Peter and I discussed the possibility of rescheduling this adventure. The last time I saw Peter was the spring of 2017. He had moved from Puerto Rico to West Palm Beach, Florida. I visited with him that April. His passion was all about wellness and developing teaching kitchens.

In July 2017, he and his oldest brother took a trip to Africa. Peter arrived back to the States and became very ill. Within a week Peter died, as he had contracted Malaria. He was only 65 years old. This was a very unfortunate tragedy demonstrating how life is so precious and time on earth is so fragile. I reflect often how we all must live for today and appreciate every minute that we have and the people that we share life with. As time goes by, the people that we care and love for will pass on. What stays with us will be their impactful memory.

Journey 14

Preparing for Fitness Fire Show segment:. John Guimond, me, Suzanne, and Eva Grover

Fitness Fire TV Show

After the Alfond Youth Center was built in 1999, the AYC staff and programs were settling into the new facility. The new building was equipped with a triple gymnasium, gymnastics center, two indoor pools, a karate dojo, dance studios, a full-service childcare center along with a large dining and kitchen area.

I wanted to spread the word about the AYC activities and had an idea to develop a TV show. I was training hard in the gym for triathlons and marathons and I thought the show should focus on wellness. Little did I know that this show was ahead of the wave of fitness programs that would come upon us a decade later.

In Maine, one of the local stations was Channel 9 out of the Maine State capital city of Augusta. One afternoon I called the station to discuss my idea with the station manager and pitch the concept. He thought it was good enough to pursue.

My concept was to break the 30-minute show into three parts. The first part was a fitness element where each episode would have a specialist working out with me in the gym with weights, karate class, yoga, tai chi, swimming, running etc. This would be followed with a talking head – a person that was inspirational, had a good message, and was a mentor in wellness. Finally, our 4'10" little General from our kitchen program, Eva Grover, and I would cook up a healthy meal to share with the viewers.

The filming of the show started immediately after I met with the producer and the camera crew. I started off with an introduction of what Fitness Fire was all about. I used the letters of

F.I.R.E. as the theme of the show.

F – Always **FOCUS** on your goals and work on your success one step at a time.

I – Whatever you do, do it with full **INTENSITY**.

R – Have proper **REST** in order to heal and recover.

E – **EAT** right to give you the proper energy to improve your fitness.

The opening of the show had Bob Seger's song "The Fire Inside" as the opener and ended the show with the same music and credits. Commercials were in between each segment. From that point, I had to line up my guest for the fitness part and the interviews. This was not hard to do with my circle of friends and the individuals that I knew in the fitness world. I included others that have improved their fitness and were an inspiration to those who were thinking about starting a wellness routine. I interviewed many different State of Maine wellness inspirational people including:

John Jenkins – a Martial Art Hall of Fame fitness guru.

Chief Barry Dana – The Penobscot Nation Chief and ultra-marathon runner and world class paddler.

Marty Brown – At the age of eighty, she was a world senior competitor in swimming and triathlons.

Doc Brown – Marty's husband who was the state racket ball champion, well into his 80's.

Others interviewed were Bruce Chase, Bob Benner, Julie Omsberg, Dave Turnage, Nicole Guimond, Gerry St. Amand and Lisa Patterson.

The fitness portion was mainly done by me, John Jenkins, and Bob Benner. The show went on for 24 episodes (two years) and aired a few times a week running a month long for each episode.

I had the most fun with the show on the last segment with Eva Grover in the kitchen. Eva was responsible for developing our Kid's Kitchen at the Alfond Youth Center. She begged and borrowed from businesses and individuals to provide a full hot meal to the kids in the after school program. She also recruited volunteer senior citizens to help serve the 100 plus meals a day. Eva was in her mid-seventies and as a grandma, she wanted the kids' bellies to be full and she got great satisfaction seeing smiles on their faces. Even though nutrition was a big piece of my show, she did not agree that cakes, pies, and ice cream should be eliminated from their dinner. Having a sweet tooth, I selfishly agreed. During many Kids Kitchen mealtimes, I would get caught in the cookie jar having my hands swatted playfully by Eva.

A few shows were filmed in the dead of winter cooking on a grill outside in Hawaiian outfits with Beach Boy music playing while cooking salmon and snow blowing behind us. Another episode, we were on China Lake building our own ice cream sundaes concluding with Eva on the dock wearing water skis as if she was going to water ski. I had one of my teen Black Belts, Shawn Norton, wear a white wig to resemble Eva with the camera shooting Shawn on the skis being pulled by the boat. It looked as if Eva was water skiing. That day the AYC received calls wondering if it was really Eva. Viewers were amazed that Eva was water skiing.

Once again, I never thought in a million years that I was going to produce a TV show. It just came to me and I implemented a plan. In life, one can sit on their hands and dream of making things happen or get in the ring and make it happen. I prefer to make things happen.

In 2005 our little General left the organization. After a few years I called Eva, and we went out for coffee. We had the chance to discuss the good old days. In 2012, Eva passed away. Her family asked me to host the celebration of life in the AYC second floor library. I talked about her drive, dedication to our kids and her passion for life. I will never forget Eva and the spirit she brought to all of us. I nominated Eva into the AYC Inspirational Hall of Fame, and she will forever be remembered.

I still have copies of the 24 episodes on VHS of all the Fitness Fire Shows. Occasionally, I pull one out and watch some of the shows and recall the great memories.

"Be spontaneous. Be crazy. Leave your comfort zone and live with no regrets." Unknown

Blizzard Run

Like many of us during a winter storm, no less a winter blizzard, we hunker down in the comfort of our homes to stay warm, dry, and out of the cold. Not me.

The forecast called for a blizzard to hit Maine early on a Sunday morning and would last throughout the day. A foot of snow was predicted along with high winds and all of the news stations advised everyone to stay off the roads and remain at home until the storm subsided.

I woke up that morning in my old 1860 farmhouse nestled in the historic China Village to heavy snow in the air and on the ground. I went to the kitchen, made a cup of coffee, and sat at the kitchen table looking out the window to the street. I noticed that a few inches were already building up and more was coming down fast. I also noticed the strong wind blowing from the west and blowing the snow sideways.

After half of my cup of coffee, I had a hankering to go out and get a run in. That is all that it took. The idea excited me, knowing that not too many people in Maine right then were thinking of this kind of activity. I was anxious to get outside for my morning run especially since I was training heavy for ultra runs. I decided that a 5-mile run would do the trick in this weather and was a short enough time in the subzero temperatures and snowy conditions.

I quickly went upstairs to the bedroom, pulled out warm under-layer clothes, my black winter New Balance running top and pants, gloves and running hat. I was getting pumped knowing that I would have the entire road to myself. I did not want to run along the streets around town. I wanted to run Moe's Mountain. Moe's Mountain is one of my favorite runs with Suzanne. It is a 4.5-mile loop with the last mile being a straight 12-degree grade hill to finish the workout. The loop was approximately a six-mile drive from the house. The plan was to drive my Bravado four-wheel drive to the starting point and begin the run.

I pulled the Bravado out of the garage into the heavy snowfall and took my time driving to the destination. I quickly learned within a few minutes of driving that this was a real storm to be concerned about with visibility almost zero. I drove in the middle of the road since there was no other traffic in sight. It took a good 30 minutes or so to get to Moe's Mountain. Thankfully, the 4-wheel drive was able to plow through the deep snow. I parked the car along the side of an abandoned farm on top of the hill, put on my gloves, hat, and a face mask and off I went.

The wind on top of the hill that looks over China Lake was howling and cold. I would guess the temperatures were in the single digits and much less with the wind gusts. I did not waste must time to get on the road and begin the run. I noticed immediately that the road and area was very still and quiet except for the sound of the wind. A beautiful winter wonderland was in front of my eyes. Even though there were houses that I passed along the way, I could not see them. They were hidden by the blinding snow as if they did not even exist. I worked on keeping a steady pace, keeping my footing in the middle of the road. I was running a lot slower than my usual sub-8-minute mile pace.

I was looking ahead trying to find the red stop sign for my left turn to circle back to finish the loop and was getting nervous that I might have run by it, heading to the next town another eight miles away. I had no interest running that long in this weather. Finally, out of the blue with only a few feet to see in front of me was the red stop sign caked with snow and swaying with the wind. I turned left and knew I had a mile more along this part of the run and then a left turn up the steep part of Moe's Mountain.

I was feeling fantastic that I was doing something so out of the ordinary and unique, which most people would say was foolish. I knew within 20 minutes or less I would be back at the car and back home to the warmth of my home and the fire.

I stayed in the middle of the road with my head down keeping the snow and wind from blinding me and then out of nowhere appeared a black sedan right on top of me. Lucky for me he was going slow, and I was able to sidestep the

Passion for Life

car to the passenger side. The driver stopped the car and rolled down the window. An elderly gentleman said, "Hey, you OK? I almost hit you. What are you doing out here – do you need help?"

I replied, "Yea that was close. No, I'm OK. Just going for a run. Thanks for asking."

He just looked at me in bewilderment like I was speaking a foreign language. I said thanks again and just continued to run. I noticed he stayed in the same place for a moment and then drove off. I am sure he was trying to comprehend what just happened. I could only imagine that he arrived back home to his wife and told her he met some crazy fool running in the blizzard and how he almost hit me.

The last part of the run was the most challenging. I was running straight into the wind with the snow hitting me sideways. I approached Moe's Mountain and started my final ascent. Since there was so much snow on the road with every step I took, I slid back a half foot. On any normal run up Moe's Mountain, my heart seemed to bust out of my body from the steep incline. With the weather conditions and the incline being the same, it was even more challenging. My heavy breathing and my arms pumping at a rapid rate helped keep me warm, in fact, it made me sweat. By the time I got to the car finishing my run, the sweat was frozen and covering my entire face with ice. I looked like a winter Mountain Man.

I got back in the Bravado, took off some of my layers of my running gear, started the car with heat blasting and I went home. When I arrived home, I felt the awesome feeling of the body fully cleansed from a good workout. Mentally, I felt even better knowing that I did something that I could not imagine. Yes, I could have stayed home like most people, but the passion to have the spirit to take on another challenge made me feel exhilarated.

Journey 16

"Never, never, never give up." Winston Churchill

Unity Sprint Triathlon

Besides training for ultra-marathons, I had interest in competing in triathlons. My ultimate vision was to compete in the Ironman in Kona, Hawaii – 2.4-mile swim, 110 bike race, and a 26.2 marathon run. I thought it was best to start with the basics and enter my first Sprint Triathlon in ten years. My last triathlon was the Bud Light event held in Belgrade when I was 31. Now I was 41. At that event, I witnessed a real act of courage and perseverance by an 80-year-old woman, Mardie Brown, she lost her bike chain halfway through the 26-mile bike race. Instead of quitting, she continued on, walking the bike to the transition point and finishing the run portion of the race. Seeing Mardie's will to fight stayed etched in my mind. How could I complain about unfortunate circumstances that may come up at any time?

To start my training, I looked online to find all the triathlons in Maine for that season. One of the first ones was in Unity, not too far from my house. It was a simple course and an easy distance, ¼-mile swim, 15-mile bike and a 5K run.

I gladly accepted Suzanne's offer to attend the race with me to help during the transitions. It is always nice to have someone near your bike to organize your gear before the next stage of the race. We got there that day around 8:15 am, 45 minutes before race time. I set up my bike along the racks with all the others. I found a place for my helmet, energy drink, bike cleats and running shoes for the last stage. Even though it was June, I was going to wear a full wet suit, which made me look like Batman. Underneath were my riding shorts to help with the quick transition.

It was a beautiful summer day in Maine. The temperature was around 70 degrees early in the morning with a few clouds in the sky. I stretched out a little bit before putting on my wet suit. It was a snug fit. Coming out of the water, I knew it would be challenging to get it off quickly. According to the rules of the race, no one can help during the transition of the race. They could be there during the switch of activities, but could not provide any hands-on help with the gear during the competition. Luckily, the wet suit that I wore came with the long pull tag to help with the zipper in the back.

Ten minutes before the beginning of the swim, we were all called down to the water's edge for instructions and rules. The small 2-mile pond was calm as the sunshine reflected off the water into our eyes. The 100 competitors lined up for better positioning to get a good start before the starting horn went off. I positioned myself in the front end of the group and put on my swim cap along with my goggles. The first buoy was to the left followed by the next one to the right and the final one to the far right, making the course a triangular swim. I was nursing a slight calf strain from one of my previous workouts, so I made sure I massaged the area well before the horn went off.

When the horn went off, everyone made a mad dash to the water. The elite swimmers immediately took the lead and were the front pack, completing the ¼-mile swim easily. The amateur swimmers like me were fine letting them go, hoping to catch up with them during the bike or run phase of the race. The real novice swimmers stayed back and waited for the commotion to pass. I did well right from the start and led the middle pack, with my eye on chasing down the leaders. I kept my head down, sprinted with my arms and legs at a steady pace following the six leaders.

As I came around the last buoy heading for shore, I gained on a few of the leaders coming into the last stretch. They all got out of the water in front of me although I was not too far behind. I ran quickly to the bike transition area where Suzanne was waiting. She was quite surprised to see me out of the water so quickly. "Wow, you're doing great! How do you feel?" she asked. I told her I was feeling terrific and needed to get on my bike quickly to try to catch the lead competitors.

Passion for Life

The batman suit came off easily without much of a struggle. I jumped on the bike, quickly riding down the road. The lead racers were well ahead of me with a two- to three-minute advantage. As I raced toward them, I could see the last of the two, about a quarter of a mile ahead of me. Once again, I was giving it my all to gain some ground during the 15-mile bike portion of the race with the hope to catch a few of them on the run portion.

The last four miles of the bike loop brought us back onto Main Street heading to the park where the race started. I made my turn and in front of me were two of the lead competitors only 30 yards away. I had them in my sights and knew I could pass them especially now with the road going slightly downhill. I was pumping rapidly with a plan to upshift for more speed. This is where I made a crucial mistake. Instead of upshifting, I downshifted. My right sore calf pushed down extremely hard expecting resistance, however, instead there was hardly any resistance at all, which caused a horrible pull of the calf muscle. I immediately felt the pain and knew I was toast. I yelled out and reached down to grab my calf. I stopped pedaling and let the bike coast. I attempted to push down but could not. I glided as I drifted further behind the racers in front. Soon the other bikes from behind caught up and raced past me. I gently and slowly just tried to finish the race biking the last 3.5 miles on a damaged leg. By the time I got to the final transition point, I was in the middle of the pack rather than the top seven. Suzanne knew something was wrong after seeing many of the bikers come in before me. When I arrived, I told her that I pulled my right calf.

I pulled up next to her to stop the bike and that is when my cleat got stuck on my right pedal and I crashed to the ground with the bike. According to the rules, no one can help you or you will be disqualified. Suzanne came over to help and I yelled out, "No, you can't. I'll be disqualified!" as I was rolling on the ground clutching my leg. My rolling around and yelling drew quite a bit of attention from the spectators. Afterward, Suzanne and I joked about how comical it looked. I looked like a fish out of water just flapping around on the ground.

I finally gained my composure and moved the bike out of the pathway. I did the best I could to take off my bike cleats and replace them with my running shoes. At this point, Gerry Cormier, the Finance Director of the Alfond Youth Center came in as he was in the back part of the group. He saw me and said, "You OK, Bud?" We had trained together in the pool for the last few weeks before this race. He sometimes competed in these races although not looking to be competitive but to finish.

By the time I got on my running shoes, Gerry was ready to run as well. He was tired and I was injured. It ended up being a good partnership as we walked the first ¼ mile, which helped loosen up my calf. The 5K, which I hoped to finish around 23 minutes, took Gerry and me 29 minutes. I had no push-off on the right leg and just strolled with an easy pace.

Ken Walsh

I was proud to be able to finish this race even though I was extremely frustrated knowing that I could have finished in the top seven. I could have easily stopped after the injury but the thought of Mardie Brown at age 80 finishing her race stayed with me. Perseverance and the Don't Quit Attitude was the lesson for that day. After reviewing the outcome, I was just as proud of this race as I was with ones that I excelled at and finished in the top of the heat.

Journey 17

Grand Canyon, Bottom of Angel Trail, early morning

"Running allows me to set my mind free. Nothing seems impossible. Nothing unattainable." Kara Goucher

The Grand Canyon Trail Run

My anticipation of seeing one of the Seven Wonders of the World did not prepare me for the awesome sight when I got out of my car and followed the path that commanded the tremendous view of the canyon. Photographs in magazines and photos by friends do not do justice to the first sight of the Grand Canyon. Endless ripples of sandcastles unfold as they continue to run endlessly in the horizon with deep gorges that make way for the robust Colorado River. Individuals from around the world travel to get just one glimpse of this wonder. Along these enormous cliffs, people hold tight to the rails feeling insecure from the uncontrollable strength of nature. Rock formations are abundant.

For the rock climber, this is heaven. Each ledge presents a new challenge. Brilliant colors from earth leave you speechless. The colors of the horizon change by the minute as the sun plays on each canyon wall and in the valley. For those of us who love adventure, the Canyon has it all. It would take years to explore and hike each mountaintop and valley. And for the hang glider, each cliff is a fantastic new jump. A jump takes you to 190 miles of canyon walls, pathways, the Colorado River and the beautiful blue sky. It is a time to soar with the eagles above.

Unfortunately, I was not able to soar like eagles. My plan was to connect with Mother Earth at the floor of the canyon. Morning broke just before 5:00 am on a Saturday. I had a night of no sleep with apprehension of the planned assault to the bottom of the Canyon. At this time of day, the canyon floor lures only a few individuals as many of the tour guides do not begin until mid-morning. I felt the wind call my spirit, the descent and the ultimate run back to the top.

I prepared my backpack with six power bars, beef jerky, two full bottles of water and a towel. I got into my car, drove the short distance to the canyon pathway, got out in the darkness of the morning, tucked my car keys in my backpack, and followed the dirt path. I traveled with a quick pace down the Bright Angel Trail in the valley of darkness as just a hint of morning sun appeared on one of the faraway peaks. The travel down seemed to go for endless miles, snaking from one ridge to the other. The thought of the run back up was intimidating and shook my confidence. In an hour and fifteen minutes, I reached the bottom and was joined by native elk enjoying the morning before the 100-degree heat forecasted. The two worlds of dark and light are vivid in my mind as I came to the end of the valley and approached a path leading to the river.

I entered Indian Garden, a camper's heaven at the Grand Canyon. This is a place of spiritual peace. Here in the rocky earth are vibrant green trees and shrubs that bloom in the shade of the Canyon. A clear, cool stream dances past the campground and eventually finds its home in the Colorado River. I had only 1.5 miles to go to the end of the walking journey to see my first glimpse of the river. The pathway looked endless and seemed to fall off the edge of the earth. No one was around and it was peaceful, but eerie. One could get absorbed in this massive area and never be found. The sun peeked from the Canyon wall. At 8:00 am, I knew the sun would be with me as a friend and as an enemy. My full backpack gave some comfort. Constant intake of fluid would be key for the run later on in the hot sun.

Looking back six miles later, I turned to see the distance I had traveled. It was hard to fathom I came from the bright blue mountaintop. Now, the run to the top does not seem possible. I had reached the end of the trail that leads to the river. No one is around and I want to show proof that I was at this wonderful place on earth. Proof for only myself, knowing perhaps this is a once in a lifetime journey. A selfie (before selfies were a thing) was taken with my triumph in the background. I wore a Grand Canyon hat and Native American feathers attached to my backpack. I had made the first half of the journey. The final shot in my camera is the one of the river, the brown cold river that has carved its way through this countryside for millions and millions of years. A river that I hope to travel down some day.

After the last photo of my journey down, my run, my true journey began. What I learned from my involvement with my Native American friends is that challenge runs are not about a race or about time. It is about your commitment to the spirit behind the race. Many times, the journey is about healing or the challenge to start something new. I did not know how long I would last; not knowing if my injured right knee from the K-100 would prevent my 6-mile run on the rocky dirt terrain that would bring me back to the blue sky at the top of the ridge.

The energy and spirit of the Canyon brought me contentment. The run was not about a race or another challenge. It was about me and the new reborn life that was ahead of me. It was a life that I had yet to experience. With all these thoughts and feelings deeply embedded into my heart, I moved toward the Bright Angel Canyon walls to the journey upward.

On this hot dry 100-degree day, I ran with my backpack as one unit. Each step on the heavily traveled path from the visitors throughout the world brought new energy that moved me forward. My breath and sweat was at an extreme level as I quickened the pace and began my incline to the steeper walls. I passed hikers who traveled upward from the night before, as they left Indian Garden campground. They attempted to escape the mid-day sun while I ran past the numerous other tourists on their way down for a day hike. Each of the individuals looked at me a bit confused and questioned my purpose as I smiled through my heavy breath and said hello. As I approached the 1.5-mile mark I ran into a Native American man and his family. He gave me a thumbs up and said, "You are looking good, almost there." It was an endorsement of understanding and the inspiration I needed to keep pushing forward.

As I approached the last series of the rim weaving up and around, I saw the hilltop Bright Angel Lodge and the American flag waving in the wind. My pace picked up and my tired legs became more energized. I reached the top and the journey that I thought was a physical challenge was no match for the spiritual journey that helped me complete the run. This journey from the heart became a journey of a renewed life and soul. Running for others is what makes one take that extra step, the step beyond. To have self-worth is to give the ultimate self to others, which is love and the sense of peaceful contentment. The Grand Canyon reassured me that this is possible.

Journey 18

JOHN F. KENNEDY 50 MILER
40th Annual November 23, 2002
"World of Color"

"If it doesn't challenge you, it won't change you." Fred Devito

JFK-50 Ultra Run

I slept in on November 10, 2002, and did not go to my weekly 7:15 am Rotary meeting. I needed the extra sleep and instead woke up at 9:00 am, feeling rested. My mental game plan was starting to kick in. All my training and the anticipation of the run was now coming into the "Red Zone." No excuses, just perform. The only thing holding me back from completion would be injury. Would my battered left knee hold up? I thought my will and determination can carry me through any past injuries without the worry of permanent damage. I thought to myself, if I can get to mile 40 it will be a done deal. I can crawl to the finish line if need be. By noon, if we reach mile 30, it gives us another 7 hours to complete the race before elimination and time rules kick in.

My backpacks are filled with running gear, my New Balance 991's with three pairs of socks, NB running undergarments and pullovers. I also threw in sandals knowing that my toes will be a mess at the end, perhaps even missing toenails. Aspirin and Aleve for pain, vitamins for pre-race and one backpack full of Clif bars, 25 energy shots and mineral juice.

Within an hour, Chief Barry Dana of the Penobscot Nation and Steve Hesseltine would arrive in Waterville to pick me up and the journey of 15 hours to Maryland would begin in the tribal truck. I looked forward to the spirit within as we discuss everything about life and challenges. We are the "Spirit Runners". I had black baseball caps made up that say, "Spirit Runners" on the back with an embroidered eagle feather on the front.

When Barry and Steve arrived, I threw everything in the back of the truck and slid into the back seat. It was non-stop conversation about life as we drove south. We had many inspiring and uplifting discussions on life pathways, challenges and future visions.

Barry discussed his dilemma of how to lead his people as Chief and deal with the management of tribal government. Feelings that grew deep inside began to come out. Chief said during the discussion that I had to write this down, "To the world you may be one person, but to one person you may be the world." So, I did.

Our travels would take us close to the hometown I grew up in, so we drove down I90 towards Route 22 into Amenia, New York. As we drove, I shared some of the cornerstone places on Route 22. We soon arrived at my parents' driveway on Depot Hill and pulled in. My parents at that time were in their late seventies and both were retired from work. I introduced Barry as Chief and my mother said, "Chief of what?" Then she followed up by saying to Steve, "and you must be the Assistant Chief." We all chuckled at her dry humor.

Of course, my dad had to show Steve and Barry his flowers and trees in the back yard. We sat down at my parents' kitchen table where many years of conversation had taken place. My dad asked Barry, "What do you do for work?" Barry responded, "I am the Chief of the Penobscot Nation". My dad repeated his question, "So what do you do for work?" Barry once again responded, "I am the Chief." My dad could not understand that the reservation had a paid Chief who acted like a town manager of a municipality. It was an amusing and interesting visit for sure!

After a bit, we said our goodbyes and stopped by the local pizza place in Amenia. I talked with former high school alumni Karin McEnroe who owned the place. He asked many questions about the JFK 50 race that we were journeying to, and we were happy to talk about it. The next part of the road trip led us into Pennsylvania and down to Maryland. Finally, we arrived at the hotel around midnight and we all shared a hotel room.

We quickly settled in for the night, exhausted after the long day of driving. Sleep was not an issue, but Barry woke with his internal clock at 4:30 am. For Steve and me, sleep was now officially over. Immediately, Steve followed Barry as I laid there hoping they would fall back to sleep. Steve has the amazing ability to talk about anything at any moment. Chief Dana added into the conversation with his morning saying, "In the end, the world will be saved or destroyed by the written word." This is a Penobscot saying.

It was time for me to get up as apparently sleeping in was not part of the plan. So, we got in the truck that early morning and scouted out the trail of the run. We spent most of the day traveling along the 50-mile stretch. We saw some beautiful country with rolling hills and valleys. Barry kept saying, "I am fired up!!"

I called Suzanne and we talked for a while to catch up on things. I gave her a description of the beautiful country and our high energy with anticipation of the run. She and I also discussed sharing a Thanksgiving together that year, including a duck dinner instead of the traditional turkey.

We got back to the hotel late afternoon and Steve headed down to the pool with plans to jump into the hot tub. He returned rather quickly. He said he saw an obese truck driver in the tub with an open can of beer and two unopened ones next to him. Steve laughed and said that the Karma was just not right at that moment.

Electric energy was in the air now as we packed for the adventure. Barry was concerned about calorie intake. He says, "Never enough". You said that we need at least 400 calories per hour and a total of 4,000 for the full run. We were to consume Clif shots and Snicker bars, three every hour along with water and simple carbs. We were all pumped up and knew no one would sleep well this night.

We headed down for the spaghetti dinner at a local Bob Evans restaurant next to the hotel. We got stuffed with carbohydrates and were ready to burn fuel for the next day. That evening after dinner, many thoughts came across my mind while getting ready for bed. The eve of the 50-miler was upon us. All the dedicated training was hopefully going to pay off. I was running through my mind all the different ways to be motivated and to get beyond the pain when it hit, pain that I knew was going to be there especially for a novice runner. I knew once the fatigue hit, it would be time for the mental and spiritual energy to kick in to get beyond the wall. The words, Shugyo "take the step beyond," Kokoro "with all of your Heart," and Kime "focus on the outcome," were my mantra. I did not want to let Barry and Steve down. I knew their spirit and drive would be there for me and I hoped to do my best to hang in there with them. I was a little cautious knowing how I ran into the wall on our 34-mile practice run in Solon, Maine. I had nothing left at the end of that run.

Barry set the strategy for the race. We would run 13 minutes and walk 2 minutes for the entire run. Our goal was to finish within the 8- to 9-hour mark. I went into the local gas station and bought Swisher Sweets cigars and Hawkins chew for the celebration at the end of the run. I assumed that this certainly might not be what my body would be craving at the end, although I could not get out of the thought of a baseball celebration. All I needed was champagne to go along with it. As I laid these items out on the bed, Steve and Barry shook their heads like, "You're nuts, we're not putting that crap in our system."

Steve picked up a can of Barry's Ensure and said, "There are not many things I look at with fear, but I do this." It was funny looking over the pull-out couch of the hotel room and seeing the bundle of food that cluttered the dresser: vitamins, painkillers, gallons of water, popcorn, Clif shots, Clif bars, oranges, bananas, bagels, blueberry pie, coffee, blueberry muffins, Ensure Plus and bags of Snicker Bars.

I spent time taping my toes individually as we chatted. Vaseline was caked between each toe. The last 50 miles during the 100-mile ultra-run in Old Town that past summer resulted in four of my toenails gone and days of hobbling around. I hoped that I learned from that experience. That run was not just a memory of a painful finish. It had lots of inspiring energy, especially the sight of an eagle flying over our heads. We were like the two eagles at the beginning of the K-100 run in September. It was a sign for me to run tomorrow and another reason why the race was not about me.

After this race, I was looking forward to getting back to a normal fitness routine, perhaps stepping up with more weightlifting for the month of December. I had a goal of developing new muscle mass that I lost while training for the ultra. This challenge, the process of training, truly helped with the transition in my life with a new house, new job responsibilities, and preparing for my life ahead.

Finally, it was lights out and we had more small talk before closing our eyes for the night. Steve's obnoxious alarm woke us all up at 3:30 am. We rolled out of bed, drank some water, and ate bagels and peanut butter while we swallowed a few Advil. We hustled downstairs into the lobby. The hotel was quiet and the darkness outside contributed to the stillness. We opened the doors to the very cool early morning and got into the tribal truck. Steve turned the key, blasted the heater and off we went to Boonsboro High School for sign-in and line-up for the race.

As we got to the HS, the buzz was in the air. Cars were pulling into the full parking lot as 1,000 runners from around the world gathered. I noticed a group of military men approaching the doorway of the gym and all decked out in camouflage gear with one solider holding the American flag. We opened the facility doors that opened to a hallway leading into the gym. The gym was packed with people standing or sitting and stretching. The energy was high. I just took in the thought of all the combined hours of running to train for this event that was in this room. It was a powerful thought. We found a little opening on the gym floor to sit down and stretch. The race start time was 5:00 am. We had another 45 minutes before the start gun. That 45 minutes seemed like hours.

Fifteen minutes before the start of the race, we were all asked to leave the gym and head to the road leading to Main Street. It was like herding cattle. We stood together shoulder to shoulder moving in unison. The military runners wearing red, white, and blue headbands were in front of us. One of the runners held the American flag on a wooden pole. It was still dark as we gathered on Main Street, one thousand deep and wide. We were in the middle of the pack crammed in like sardines. Along the side of the street was a platform where the race director said the words we all were waiting for. "Take your mark." Then the horn went off and all the runners slowly began their steps into strides to start the race.

The first mile was on pavement through the town toward the National Park entrance. The next 18 miles were on a narrow trail weaving up and down a mountain and heading toward the Potomac River. As soon as we reached the trail, our running headlights were needed. I saw in front of me a string of lights moving up the mountain. The trail was very narrow so that only one person could pass at a time. Our team stayed with our system of running for 13 minutes and walking for two. All during the race, we leap frogged many runners as we started and stopped running. By mile ten, we were seeing the same runners as we were all now at the same pace. The trail, especially during the darkness, became dangerous at points. A simple trip over the sharp rocks and roots had the ability to take a runner out of the competition. I assumed during these races that runners at times have twisted their ankles, hurt their knee, or tripped and broken a wrist.

As we crested the hill, the sun was coming up and the glow of its light was a beautiful moment. I was running sacred ground and it was overwhelming. The civil war battles were along these mountaintops and valleys and I felt as if the spirit of our ancestors were upon us. These thoughts gave me a boost of energy. I had spring in my legs and added power over the final hill peak before running down the trail to the final valley before the river. At this point, I lost contact with my fellow "Spirit Runners", Barry and Steve, although on the last mile on the trail I saw Steve. He said Barry was just a few hundred feet behind him. In front of me was a big table of oranges at the beginning of the Potomac River trail. Thankfully, these refreshment tables were available throughout the rest of the run. The oranges were refreshing, especially after three-plus hours of Snicker bars and Gatorade. Shortly into the run along the river trail, Barry, Steve and I were all together again. The next twenty-three miles were on a wide packed dirt trail. At this point, runners were spread out and we ran with a pack of marathoners that stayed with our pace.

Every five miles along the way, there was a road crew with tables full of water, sandwiches, salted potatoes or soup. By mile 35, fatigue was setting in and our legs were getting weary. At mile 42, the end of the Potomac trail, our legs were all but rubber. Unfortunately, the nice soft trail now turned into hard pavement and the final eight miles on tired legs were to be on pavement heading to the finish line. Barry pumped us up knowing we were running out of daylight and it was time to dig deep into our soul and run for glory to finish this race strong. We stopped our 13 – 2 strategy and ran the last 8 miles without stopping. Our energy and our pace picked up. Where we got this new energy, I have no idea. It felt great to be able to cruise after 42 miles and over 8 hours of running. The darkness started to move in during the last two miles. We smelled the finish line and ran a sub-8-minute mile to the end. The last hundred yards in darkness was up a slight hill towards the lighted finish. We ended like we started, together as a team, the "Spirit Runners." We did it and it felt awesome!

We celebrated with hugs and high fives as the JFK 50-mile medals were placed over us. My official time was 10 hours, 13 minutes and 15 seconds and I placed 365 out of 993 runners - not bad for my first official ultra-marathon run. After the run, we entered the high school for the post-race meal. They served fried chicken that we absorbed quickly. We hung out for a bit and then decided it was time to head home. We were back in the tribal truck and on the road for the long trip back. Needless to say, it didn't take time for our legs to stiffen up. We drove through the night arriving back in Maine as the sun rose from the eastern sky.

Getting out of the tribal truck after not having the chance to stretch during this length of time was the hardest part of the race. I climbed the stairs, hobbling at each step although understanding the tremendous accomplishment was worth the pain. The bond and brotherhood that was developed during this trip will never be forgotten. Our connection will be forever cemented through this adventure and spirit journey.

Journey 19

"It does not matter how slowly you go, as long as you do not stop."
Confucious

Mt. Washington Road Race – Only One Hill

There is "Only One Hill." That is how they market the Mt. Washington Road Race, the road up the highest mountain in the East of America. It certainly is one big hill: 7.6 miles to the top, 6,288 feet, and 4,650 vertical feet with an average incline grade of 11.5%. There is not one section of the run that is a flat plateau to catch your breath, just straight up. The race was first held in 1936. Since then, thousands of individuals across the world take on the challenge.

After months of running and training, Suzanne and I thought that taking on the Mt. Washington Road Race would be a good challenge. The race date was

Ken Walsh

June 15, 2002. We were lucky enough to get in the lottery to enter the race as thousands of runners apply each year, and only one thousand runners are selected.

Suzanne and I trained locally, mainly running up and down Moe's Mountain off one of the side roads near China Village. The grade for this hill was like what we were going to fight against in New Hampshire. Unfortunately, Moe's hill was only 1 mile long. We ran up and down this hill for months thinking we were prepared for the big race. Were we wrong!

On a cloudy morning, Saturday June 15th, we took our drive along the winding roads of Maine into New Hampshire. The temperature was around 55 degrees with light rain. While driving, we discussed our strategy to run the hill. Suzanne always believed in a slow, steady pace and building momentum as the race continued to unfold. I always believed in starting out fast with the front pack to get an early advantage. We finally agreed to stay together and pace ourselves slow and easy.

After turning left in the village of Gorham, New Hampshire, we drove along the Presidential Highway into the White Mountain National Forest leading to the base of Mt. Washington. We pulled in to see hundreds of cars, tents, porta-potties and runners registering for the race and hanging around. After we registered, we ran into a few Waterville running club members – "The Central Maine Striders." I saw David Benn who has been a long-time runner in the community and has run the Mt. Washington Road Race numerous times. I tried to get his insight on his approach to the race. His advice was simple, slow and steady. Suzanne just smiled hearing the advice that my pig-headed Irish stubbornness would not accept.

As race time approached, the race director came over the loud speaker to inform us that the race had to be modified due to the weather at the top of the mountain. The air temperature at the base of the mountain was 50 degrees, but on top of Mt. Washington, it was 28 degrees with a wind chill in the teens along with sleet and snow. The race length was altered to 3.8 miles, halfway up the mountain. Although disappointed that it would not be the full race, I immediately saw it as an advantage. My strategy to run steady and slow was no longer part of my new plan.

Anxious runners, including us, were preparing for the race to begin. The loud horn went off indicating that it was time to line up at that start line. The thousand runners all walked over to the paved road and lined up under the entrance of the Mt. Washington Auto Road. We were packed in like sardines. Some runners ran to the latrine one last time. At this point, I felt the energy of all the runners anticipating the beginning of the race. Some runners were running in place while others stretched, some were setting their watches for the start. Suzanne and I were side by side when the gun went off.

Passion for Life

And in typical fashion, I could not help myself and shot out fast working through the crowd. I left Suzanne behind me. She just let me go. The first quarter mile was deceiving with a somewhat flat terrain until the road veered upward and upward and steeper and steeper. The 11.5% grade started. And that was just the average grade. The first set of hills is much greater than 11.5%. Some even reach 22%. I passed many runners early on, feeling good. Then my heart rate increased intensely after only one mile and the runners I passed started to pass me including some that were much older than me. I had it in my head that I was not going to walk at all, not once. After another half mile and my heart feeling like it was going to explode, I gave up on that plan as well. As I approached mile two, I walked for the first time. My new plan now was to walk for 2 minutes and run for 10 minutes. That lasted only another half mile and I changed that to a 2-minute walk, 5-minute run. I thought I was in good shape until this run. The upward grade of the hill was relentless. At mile three, I heard a sweet, familiar voice from behind me.

"There you are! How are you doing?" Suzanne spoke in a composed voice as if we were jogging together at an easy pace. I was red in my face, breathing heavy and trying to get air into my lungs. I replied, "This hill is a killer. I'd rather run the NYC Marathon twice."

Suzanne wanted to stay with me, but I waved her on and told her that I would see her at the finish line. I wanted to focus on pulling it together. So, she reluctantly took off. I saw her pass a few runners and disappear ahead of me.

Suzanne finished 74 of 212 women with a time of 48 minutes and 10 seconds, pace 12:41 per mile. While I ended up 502 of 666 male runners, time 52:37, pace 13.51 per mile. I was certainly humbled by this mountain. And it was only half the usual distance!

Suzanne did not have to say anything as I came through the finish line sucking wind and had the token medal placed around my neck. I thought she might be thinking "I told you so," but she was all smiles and happy to see me finish. It was a grueling race and we congratulated each other on finishing it.

Not long after the run, while we were driving back to Maine, I started talking with Suzanne about next year's race and how better prepared I would be. It was now even more of a challenge for me to conquer. Unfortunately, I found out it never seemed like training was ever good enough. In 2003 and 2005, we ran the race again. Both races these years were the full 7.6 miles. For each race, I started off slow and used the run walk method. Each time I never felt like I had control of my breathing. During many of my discussions I had with Suzanne or other runners, I always said this was one of the hardest runs and challenges. I never ever seemed to catch my breath due to the constant grade of the hill.

I never beat Suzanne up "The Only One Hill." She beat me again in 2003 completing the race in 2:06:55 to my 2:07:16 and then again, our last race together in 2005 beating me 1:53:05 while I had my best personnel time of 2:03:30.

Ken Walsh

Those familiar sounds of Suzanne's footsteps in road races will always be in my mind during our road races together. I always start out in front and then hear her footsteps coming, knowing the conclusion will be seeing her pass me to the finish line. Only during shorter 5K races can I beat her. Her momentum builds as the miles rack up and I am a sprinter, quick out of the gate. We complement each other well and enjoy ribbing each other about our races together. The key is to never give up, not in races, not in life and not with each other. Life is a challenge to be enjoyed and embraced, even when it is tough. It is only one hill!

Journey 20

"A soul mate is not found. A soul mate is recognized." Vironika Tugaleva

Goodcellmo

In Passamaquoddy, Goodcellmo means "I love you." On June 26, 2003, I was heading Downeast to the Passamaquoddy tribe to once again be a part of a sweat lodge ceremony. This day was very special as I was spiritually committing myself to my soul mate and showing my dedication through the ceremony.

I left Suzanne early that morning at 4:50 am, picked up my good friend, John Guimond, who was also my workout partner and the father of one of my Club Naha Black Belt students, Nicole. Today we were meeting with two Natives, Brian "Buck" Altvater and Noel Lewey and a few others for the ceremony. The 200-mile trip took us approximately 3 ½ hours. This small town of Perry is home to the Sipayik reservation of the Passamaquoddy. It is one of the closest US points to Canada and where the sun shines first in the US.

We arrived at Pleasant Point at 10:00 am and met Buck and Noel at Buck's house. We chatted for about 45 minutes before heading to the sweat lodge site. Before going to the sweat lodge, we visited the construction site of the new Boys

& Girls Club that we were developing at the Community Center. The facility was one of the best locations for any club in the nation, sitting right beside the ocean. I also had a $45,000 check from the William and Joan Alfond Foundation to give to the tribe to finish off the project. We stopped by the tribe offices and met with Chief Francis along with other tribal council members. They were thrilled to receive the gift and announced that the official dedication of the new building would be August 8th.

Then, we drove to the field for the sweat. The sweat lodge was located in an open field on native land off a back road. Purple lupine flowers were in full bloom and covered the entire area. Buck and I left John and Noel to gather wood for the fire while we searched out the proper poles for the lodge.

Buck and I drove back to the reservation and went behind the tribal office in search of birch bark poles. There, we found a perfect area with tons of white birch. After cutting down the birch trees with a hand axe, we loaded up Buck's truck and went back to the field. Approaching the field, a billow of smoke had formed in the distance. Noel and John had the rocks baking already with a good strong fire that would give them that hot orange glow. While waiting for the fire to settle, Noel and I struck up a good conversation. He discussed his passion for running and I found out that he is an amazing short and long-distance runner at the young age of 45. Recently, he completed a 7.1 mile run in 39 minutes. He also ran the Boston Marathon in 2 hours and 41 minutes and finished the Vermont 100 ultra in 22 hours. This is impressive.

The sweat lodge was put together with the poles first and then with tarps and army blankets covering the lodge. We were now prepared for the ceremony. Buck entered the lodge first after smudging each of us with sweet grass. He also brought in his bear pipe and drum. We left any of our personal items (rings, necklaces etc.) on top of the lodge before we got in. The intense heat inside the lodge would burn the skin if wearing any jewelry.

We entered the lodge clockwise. Noel – East, John – North, Buck – West, and me – South. The temperatures on this warm June day helped quickly bring up the warmth inside the lodge. With the flap down in the pitch black, the hot rocks increased the temperature dramatically during this first round of four. The sweat immediately poured down our faces, dripping on our laps. Inside the lodge during the four rounds, we prayed, sang and shared our blessings. I thought of my soul mate, Suzanne, and hoped to open my soul to her forever. I focused on bringing this energy from the sweat lodge back home to my future wife.

The end of the sweat left us exhausted, drained physically and spiritually. We crawled out of the lodge and laid on our backs in the field, feeling cleansed and fulfilled. When we got up, we hugged each other like warriors after a hard-fought battle. We took down the sweat lodge and traveled back to Buck's house where his wife, Dee, prepared the most delicious seafood meal. With our full bellies and being totally cleansed, the night led to a very sound sleep at Buck's house. The next day, we planned a day on the bay with Buck in his 18-foot boat.

I woke early the next morning at 6:45 am. I am usually a light sleeper although that night I would have slept through an earthquake. I looked over to the other bed and John was gone and his bed was neatly put together. He eventually came back an hour later after enjoying the sunrise on the shoreline. It was a great way to start the day. He later told me that he was digging deep into his heart to work on some unanswered questions. The sweat helped him to get a better understanding of where he needed to go.

Now that things had settled from a good night of sleep, I recalled more of the conversation I had with Noel when we were having dinner and before he left to go back to Indian Island where he worked as a Computer Tech. We had discussed a lot about relationships.

I shared with him my four thoughts for a strong relationship that I called the Forever Honeymoon:

    1. Don't take each other for granted.
    2. Break the routine.
    3. Be spontaneous.
    4. Have unconditional love.

When John got back, we had breakfast with Buck's family before heading out onto the bay on Buck's boat. Our plan was to head to the other side where the waters opened to the full strength of the ocean near Lubec. Before leaving, Brian was looking for an eagle nest to search for eagle feathers. He said he always looked near this spot and I could see why. Eagle nests were all over the shoreline. Within ten minutes, Buck found what he was looking for. After giving a blessing, he took the feather and we left.

This morning the water was calm on the bay although the temperature was very cool from the ocean breeze. We cruised to the channel heading to open water. We cruised by the islands and saw some unique landmarks. It was hard to believe that for thousands of years Native Americans lived on this part of the earth. They fished in these waters and lived in harmony before the invasion of the white man. The pain of their land being taken away and changing to the white man's ways still haunt many of the natives today.

Unfortunately, when we got to the other side of the island into the open waters, the wind and waves were so strong that we had to turn back. The boat would have easily been tossed around. We thought the wind would die down, but we were wrong. Mother Nature had other plans. The waves grew from smooth bumps to five-foot swells. Buck had us get in the back of the boat as he focused on steering the boat straight back to shore. The waves crashed over the front of the boat. We got wet and cold very quickly. We also knew that the four miles back was going to get rougher. At any moment, I thought the boat would capsize. Buck (with his Philadelphia Eagle's hat on) focused all his energy in keeping the boat straight into the break of the waves to keep us safe. I could not imagine the swim back to shore if we tipped over. Most likely it would have been impossible with the 50-degree water temperatures. Not until we approached one hundred yards away from the shoreline did I start to feel relieved. I looked over to John and his face was also less tense. He just shook his head and said, "That was something else, Kenny Boy." Buck just gazed back at us, and said calmly, "I guess it wasn't our time."

It certainly was not. We all had much more life to live and I was anxious to return to my soulmate and tell her "Goodcellmo," now and forever.

Journey 21

Taking a break, mile 40, changing socks and tape

"A journey of a thousand miles begins with a single step." Lao Tzu

K100 Spiritual Journey

The Penobscot Nation has conducted their spiritual run since the early 1990s. It was inspired by former Chief, Barry Dana. I was first invited in 2001 to be a part of this sacred and challenging journey. During that first year, I decided to bike the entire adventure. With my Black Belt students supporting me, after the opening circle, it took me 9 hours to finish the ride to the mountain by bike. The week before the ride was more mentally challenging than the ride itself as I was invited to my first Native American sweat hosted by Chief Barry Dana at his house in Solon. I gladly accepted although did not know what to expect. I arrived at the scheduled time and did not realize that everyone else was on Indian time and I was not. Indian time as explained to me by other Natives is to never set the clock. One arrives when they are ready, usually late.

The sweat ceremony did not start until two hours after my arrival. All the guests, mainly Native Americans, gathered around the fire and helped set up the lodge behind Chief Dana's log house, just 100 yards away from his pen of a dozen mushing dogs. I did not have any information on how the sweat lodge ceremony was going to be conducted, so I just followed along.

As we gathered around the fire pit, Chief told everyone it was time. He crawled into the 4-foot high and 6-foot-wide circular igloo-like lodge with layers of tarp and blankets insulating the top and sides. There were 15 of us, male and female. I was the only non-native. We all crawled in clockwise. Before going in I saw John Neptune, a Penobscot whom I worked with to develop the first Native American Boys & Girls Club on Indian Island. He grabbed me and said that I should bring in a towel to help during the sweat. I thanked him for the heads up.

I followed John by crawling in on the dirt floor going clockwise. Once inside the lodge, the heat swelled as our 15 bodies crammed into the compact space. In the middle were orange hot rocks giving off dry heat. I immediately began to sweat. The only light coming in from outside was a small ray from the lodge door opening.

Once everyone was settled, Chief Dana asked the keeper of the door to bring down the flap. With the door flap shut, the heat increased in the pitch darkness. I was shoulder to shoulder with two of my native friends, not knowing what to think. I kept repeating in my mind, "You are a Black Belt, and you can handle this." And repeating, "Hang Sang Sim." This means calm cool mind in Korean. Chief then spoke to all of us saying that if anyone needed to leave the lodge at any time just say, "all my relations" and wait for permission. He added that he hoped all could at least wait until the round was over. I listened intently with sweat dripping in puddles onto my lap. I was finally focused when he began splashing water onto the rocks creating a burning intense steam that I had never experienced before. This is when I was about to bail out, although my pride kept me in the game.

The first round gave everyone in the lodge an opportunity to pray out loud and share with others. This was optional, although everyone there had something to say either praying for others or speaking about their own issues. The heat did not subside, but got more intense especially as Chief Dana threw more water on the rocks after each prayer. After about six took their turn to pray out loud, I thought to myself that we were all going to die in here. I was near the end as the turns went clockwise. When I prayed out loud, I was very brief and thanked everyone for allowing me to be part of the ceremony. After everyone was done, I sensed that the participants in the lodge were all ready to leave the lodge for fresh air. Chief Dana ordered the flap open.

Passion for Life

I was so relieved especially seeing the sun's light come through the opening. I was anxious to crawl out, but I had to wait my turn. It was hard to see outside since the lodge was now in a dense fog from the steam. I finally got to the entrance with my body drenched as if I had just gotten out of the shower. I was crawling on my hands and knees to the side of the sweat lodge. I then collapsed to the ground, rolled over to my back and gasped for breath. Steam from my body rose to the atmosphere. I was lying down with others as I tried to gain my strength. This is when I noticed that Chief Dana stayed in. I said to myself, "This guy is a warrior."

I survived my first sweat without bailing out, especially the challenge of the unknown. Then I heard from inside the lodge that it was time for Round 2. My mind screamed, "What, are you kidding me?!" I did not have the strength to go back in for the following three rounds, at least not this sweat. Later, Barry informed me that the sweat lodge is a traditional ceremony practiced for thousands of years by his culture. It was done many times before the warriors were about to go into battle to cleanse themselves for what was ahead. The sweat is so intense for some that it is conducted a week before the challenge so that those who participate in the K100 still have strength to carry on. He said the sweat is physically draining and the ceremony is more spiritual and tests the mind. I was honored to be invited to be part of the ceremony.

The following week, I joined the rest of the tribe and left Indian Island taking part in my 100-mile bike ride to Katahdin while others ran, canoed, or walked. My journey that day was not eventful until the last 30 or more miles as I got cramps in my legs and my back got a little sore. The best part was arriving at the campground to see many of the natives preparing their campsites for the evening feast. The Naha Black Belts and I stayed that night enjoying the ceremonial drumming and bonfire. We were welcomed guests and developed good relations with many of our new tribal friends. Although I knew I was missing something, it seemed that I did not sacrifice enough of my body, mind, and soul for the mission. There was more to give. This became even more apparent when the other Penobscots came in after their 100-mile journey, paddling 64 miles upstream and then running 34 miles into Baxter State Park. When they came all together into the campground with a unified special energy completing their sacred journey, I recognized that was the true purpose. The twenty or so warriors embraced each other, exhausted and proud. They accomplished their journey by giving every bit of themselves. I knew the following year I had to do this again. I had to be a part of digging deep and challenging myself to go beyond my capabilities.

The following year, Suzanne and I decided to do the K100 together and we started our journey to the great mountain on a Friday afternoon after dropping off Gunner, our chocolate lab, at doggy camp and heading north to Bangor. We stayed at the Comfort Inn and had a high carb Italian dinner at the Olive Garden.

After dinner, we headed back to the hotel, taped our toes to prevent blisters and laid out our running gear while watching the Red Sox and Yankee game. Four o'clock in the morning came too quickly.

The next day we traveled north from Old Town to Indian Island where the famous first Native American professional baseball player and a Penobscot Louis Sockalexis is laid to rest. He played for the Cleveland Spiders. They changed their name to the Cleveland Indians after Louis. He had tremendous skills although alcohol got the best of him and shortened his career. We met all the K100 participants at the sacred burial ground located at the north tip of the Island. Suzanne unpacked at the Penobscot Town Hall and we walked in the dark early morning on the dirt road leading to the opening ceremony circle.

The Natives gathered around the fire in the middle. Elder Butch Mitchell proceeded with prayers and began to smudge everyone with the smoke from the burning sweet grass and holding his eagle feather. We then placed our tobacco into the fire for our offering to give thanks for the opportunity to begin the journey to the sacred mountain Katahdin. Chief Barry Dana spoke to the group and discussed the meaning of the spiritual journey. He said, "No one should have negative thoughts."

In mid-June, I thought my pursuit of the K100 run was not possible due to the injury to my left knee sustained while running down Bigelow Mountain. The pain did not go away even though I tried many different holistic, western and eastern medicines available. The alternative was surgery and at that time, I thought the K100 was an undoable feat. I reached deep to continue to push on and let my mental toughness propel forward. I had the best possible positive team surrounding me with this effort; of course, my biggest fan, Suzanne, as well as my JFK 50 buddy Steve Hesseltine with his can-do attitude, and great support from our road crew John, Barbara and Nicole Guimond.

We started in darkness for the 4-mile warmup, running from Indian Island over the bridge to the mainland before turning onto Route 14. We stopped at the gas station before the turn and waited for the road crew support team. Our method to complete this task was planned out. We were going to run 7 minutes and then walk 3 minutes; following this method for the next 96 miles to Katahdin. Early on, my knee felt strong. I felt at this point that with the strong fellowship of our team, nothing was going to stop us from completing our mission.

We were like clockwork, 7's and 3's – the first 15 miles seemed like a cake walk. After 25 miles, things seemed to slow down a bit as we headed in to Howland. Our road crew, Barbara and Nicole, seemed to fatigue. John Guimond cycled into the run and ran with us. We reached the dead zone where a second wind was needed. It was at the turnoff on the way to Chester.

It is well known among the Penobscots that the town of Chester has intense negative energy. It is to be avoided at all costs and if it can't be avoided, one must clear one's mind of any thought of the town. At Chester, the Penobscots do not mention the name of the town. Chief Barry Dana says, "Don't even think of Chester, put your head down and fly by it. That's where you'll have the best chance to survive." It is not possible to bypass Chester on this route to Katahdin, so we put our heads down and pushed onward.

Then, the curse of Chester hit us. John Guimond fielded a phone call from home during one of our 7-minute splits. Their youngest daughter fell off the swing back at home and broke her arm in two places. They had to leave and our road crew was now off and gone. Despite this, we continued. Suzanne and Steve decide that they would take turns driving. Suzanne ran many miles that day, 47 in all, her personal best. She was an absolute machine, although she knew now that her main job was to support me and she happily took on the critical role of road crew.

At the 50-mile mark, my legs became rubber although surprisingly enough, my knee felt fine. The steps forward just seemed to be harder and harder. Mind over matter was the mantra. We turned the corner to see the sign for Medway at mile 60. The sun was setting and we needed to crash for a while. I could not run any more. The dark seemed to drain the energy from all of us. During the last mile that night, I walked with Suzanne and I told Steve that I needed to rest for a while. He agreed, so we found an open area near a field. We pulled the truck in the grassy area for the night. We set up our tent in the cool night air where Suzanne and I slept for the night while Steve stayed in the truck. Our legs were achy and cramped up. My left knee was swollen. At this point, I thought I was through.

In the morning, climbing out of the tent in the wet dew, I saw Steve in his running gear preparing for the day. Steve is a real warrior, a Marine who has seen battle and has run the K100 many times. He knows how to dig deep within and to gain strength with positive thoughts. He was ready to go. I knew I could not leave my buddy out there alone. Steve evaluated the situation and knew that the next 40 miles could be very difficult unless we altered our attack plan. His reasonable solution was to drive the 10 miles to Millinocket, grab some breakfast for fuel and run the final 25 miles. It did not take too much time for all of us to nod our heads in agreement and jump in the truck.

Watching the road fall away from us as we drove by Medway and then East Millinocket into Millinocket, my thoughts wondered if we were ever going to complete the final stretch to Katahdin. After a brief breakfast on this cold Sunday morning, Steve and I set out toward the mountain. Suzanne gave us an approving smile and drove off for the first break a mile away.

My legs felt like lead and walking was difficult, running nearly impossible. After ten miles of torture, I gave in and had Suzanne step in for me for the next three cycles, while I drove the truck. In between the cycles waiting for Steve and Suzanne, I took the chance to lie down and shut my eyes.

After the 3rd cycle, I got out of the truck and Steve took over. Suzanne and I walked the next two miles. As we came over the hill, we saw Steve loading up his backpack, getting ready to run on his own. I told Steve that instead of going it alone, Suzanne and I would be his road crew for him. We did this until the Baxter State Park entrance. I planned to join Steve at the base of Abol Hill (the mile killer hill) for the final challenging assault before the last four miles into the campground. My left knee and quads were still out of commission. We drove about one mile and parked along the side of the road at the first pond in the park. Suzanne offered to massage my leg and I gladly accepted. I took a couple of Advils with a swig of Coke. I laid in the back of the truck and Suzanne's magic helped relieve enough of the pain. Within ten minutes I was ready to go again. The pain subsided and with pure enthusiasm, Steve and I attacked Abol Hill.

We were getting near the Park and looking tired and worn down. Steve and I took a moment to gather all positive energy that we could muster up. We walked a quarter of a mile and then started the run up the hill. We gave it our all. I seemed to be re-energized. Every step up the final assault was with purpose. We used every bit of our positive spirit to propel us upward. Getting to the top was an incredible feeling of accomplishment. The rest of the run was a blink of the eye. We developed a new form of energy as we picked up the pace heading into the Katahdin Stream Campground. You could hear the drumming in the distance which made us pick up the pace even more. As we turned into the dirt road leading to the camping area, we saw the lean-tos, tents, and the gathering point for the other K100 runners, bikers, and canoe teams. And there was Suzanne, anxiously waiting for us. The journey was complete!

Suzanne and I hugged each other and everyone embraced. It took time for it to sink in that we were done, after thoughts of the almost impossible task. I did not complete the entire 100 mile run this time, but ran over 80 miles and the element of pushing on despite adversity and obstacles was the key learning experience that I will never forget. No matter how tough it was at any point, the passion and purpose within got me through and not to quit.

Suzanne and I gathered our sleeping gear and found our site area. Campground Site Number 3 was located on the other side of the stream. It was a quiet location away from the rest of the group. The sound of the stream was the greatest white noise for the day. We happily set up camp and got into the tent for a nap. We awoke later in the afternoon with enough time to watch the final journey of the team coming into camp. Chief Barry Dana's crew who canoed upstream 64 miles and ran the rest of the 36 miles had arrived. They came in to Native drumming and with a surreal energy. It was an inspiring sight.

Following the celebration of the last runners and arrivals, a potluck dinner was held in the center of the campground near the bonfire. Before everyone ate, a naming ceremony was performed for a new baby that was recently born. The meal was delicious with moose meat simmered in gravy and many other wonderful dishes. It melted in our mouths. Suzanne and I went to bed early that evening under the watchful eye of the brilliant star-studded clear sky. Our hearts were full.

The next day was the closing circle where all runners, road crew, and tribal native people get together to offer their thanks for the journey. Everyone told their story of what they learned from the 100-mile trip to the sacred mountain. They shared tears, smiles, and laughable stories. That day everyone was on the same page, the page of giving oneself for others.

Journey 22

"Faith sees the invisible. Believes the unbelievable. And receives the impossible." Corrie Ten Boom

Shaker Tent Ceremony

I awoke on October 24, 2003, to a beautiful crisp and sunny fall day with thoughts of a MicMac sweat and shaker tent ceremony ahead of us. Seven of us shared a cabin along the quiet shoreline along the famous tidal bora in Nova Scotia. Club Naha Black Belts Bob Hartley, Tim Merrithew and Dave Panarelli along with Passamaquoddy Natives, Brian "Buck" Altaver, Newell Lewey and our Karate Parents Association parent and my workout partner, John Guimond were among the individuals on the trip.

The drive to Shubenacadie was eleven hours along the shoreline of Down East Maine and across the US/Canadian Border. We left at 7:00 am on Friday from the Alfond Youth Center parking lot in Waterville and headed north to meet our Native friends. After a few stops, we cruised up the highway and arrived around 6:00 pm. On the way, we saw an eagle flying at us along the highway and a coyote on a hilltop watching us fly up the road. They knew we were coming.

The purpose of this trip was to test two of our Black Belts – Senseis Bob Hartley and Dave Panarelli - to the 3rd degree level and Tim Merrithew to the 2nd degree level. This test was to focus on the higher dimension and enlightenment. This is where Blind Medicine Man Dave Gehue comes in. I had never met Dave before, had only heard of him and his special talents from my Passamaquoddy friends Brian Altvater and Newell Lewey. We were told the Northeast Medicine Man had amazing insight and direct connection with the spirit world. Since two of my Black Belts are traditionalists (Bob and Tim), I thought that this would be a great opportunity to test them to see if they can empty their minds and absorb new enlightenment.

We checked in at the campground, Cabin Number 4 overlooking the Tidal Bore. After settling in, we planned to head to Dave Gehue's house on the Micmac reservation and prepare for the sweat. We gathered water, a change of clothes, towels and snacks, and stepped outside to the clear Canadian sky. The stars were as brilliant as I could ever remember. Brian "Buck" urged us to see the natural wonder of the Tidal Bore that was just a hundred yards away from our cabin. The water during high tide rushes up the channel in the deep gorge of the valley. We walked toward the shoreline. In the distance, the rumble of the incoming water made its way through the shadow of the darkness. Even though we could not see the water, the sound was intense as the thunderous waves came closer to where we were standing. Within minutes, the volume of water increased dramatically creeping up the embankment toward us.

Newell Lewey, the amazing 46-year-old Native runner who had just completed a marathon in Bar Harbor easily under 3 hours, told us while he was kayaking the rush of the water was so fast that he thought immediately of two things: first, I better tighten up my belt and second, it's a good day to die. Certainly, this is one of the most powerful wonders of the world.

We drove to the Micmac reservation to meet up with Dave Gehue. We pulled into his driveway not knowing what to expect. Before coming to Canada to meet Dave, I visualized a medicine man living in a village like the movie "Dances with Wolves". What I was about to see was far different than what I had imagined.

Dave's house was in the heart of the reservation. His street was surrounded by public housing dwellings. We pulled up in front of his house with a yard covered with clutter. Three dogs were chained up in the front yard. Dave's house was two stories with only half of the siding completed and the roof shingles all curled. We walked up to the door. Buck knocked once and then just opened the door and walked in. We entered the living room where four natives sat on a couch while watching TV. The individuals were Dave's wife Melissa, his daughter, son and a granddaughter. The house was a wreck. Papers, crumbs and household items were all over the floor. Books, cups, CDs, old radios and cassette tapes were all over the place.

We walked into the kitchen. The sink was piled high with dishes and the kitchen table was covered with dirty plates. We waited for Dave as Melissa went into the dark hallway to fetch him. Dave's son came into the kitchen proudly showing us the new tattoo on his forearm. The tattoo was red and black of two men looking intently at one another. Behind the kitchen table wall was Dave's Hypnosis certifications. They were all dated between 2000 and 2002.

My thought of what I imagined a Blind Medicine Man compared to what I saw was totally different. I expected to see an old man with long white hair tied in a ponytail with an eagle feather tied to the back, someone with a slight build. When he spoke, it was with elegance and with immediate wisdom.

Dave approached the kitchen coming from the dark narrow hallway. Here was an overweight man with a cigarette hanging out of his mouth. His hair was black, greasy, and messy. He looked like he just got up from a hangover (even though Dave had not touched alcohol for many years). He walked into the kitchen, sat down at the table, and introduced himself. We all walked over to him, told him our names, and shook his hand. Dave talked a little bit about himself and his personal journey to his medicine work. His language was foul, cursing often while smoking one cigarette after another.

Dave shared other thoughts focusing on our Black Belt training. He discussed the power of Chi. He told us that Chi is a universal power shared around the world. He demonstrated his power of Chi on me. He asked me to hold on to his hand as tight as possible. With a flick of his finger, my strength went to weakness and I lost my grip. This was the first sign that my initial judgment was not all correct.

He explained to us his early days in the medicine world. Before Dave lost his eyesight at 12 years old, his father gave him instructions to go into a field and bring back a plant that had special medicine his mother needed as she was very ill. He went to the back of the house as commanded by his dad and found the special plant. He brought the medicine back to the house and his dad boiled the plant to give to his wife in the form of tea. Within a few days, his mother was healed from her illness. From that day on, Dave was interested in the power of healing.

Dave also had interesting beliefs. He believed that death is a choice, when you are ready to die, you die. He also talked about how babies choose their parents not that the parents choose them. We discussed the naming ceremony. Dave told us that once you have been given an Indian name the spirit stays with you until you drink or use alcohol. The spirit will then leave you for four days before returning. Also, after a sweat, a person should not shower and use soap or shampoo for a day, otherwise, the spirits will leave you as they will be washed away.

After our lengthy discussion in Dave's kitchen, we headed toward the area where the sweat was going to be conducted. We drove in two cars following Dave and his wife as we traveled into the heart of the Micmac reservation. We pulled up to a house that was in a densely populated area with many houses. I immediately thought to myself, "you've got to be kidding, we are going to do a sweat here?" Across the street, the sound of three aggressive dogs was our welcome party. The lawn was full of pillow feathers from a dog that had ripped them apart.

We walked toward the side of the house. In the small yard was the sweat lodge at the edge of the property. Last night's hard rain soaked the structure and everything around it. The top of the sweat lodge was open, and the rugs used to sit on were draped over the top of the lodge to dry. Water filled the center pit where the hot rocks would lay. The sweat lodge was not going to be used this evening. After attempting to drain the center pit and fix the wet covers of the lodge, we concluded this was not going to be the night for a sweat ceremony. We would have to wait until tomorrow. We packed it up and headed off to our cabin with the plan to meet up with Dave in the morning around 10:30 at his house.

That night we settled in with thoughts of tomorrow and not knowing what to expect. The first night did not go well. We were all judging Dave for what we had seen so far. We were all tired and looking forward to the end of the day after the long drive. Tim Merrithew and Bob Hartley, two very big men averaging over 250 pounds each, shared a double bed in one room, while Buck and Newell shared the other bedroom. Dave, John and I slept in the living room. Dave and I broke out in uncontrollable laughter thinking of Tim and Bob sleeping together - we called it cuddling kata. We could hear their voices from the closed door as if they were bickering about something. The image of these two hairy Black Belts talking like an old couple in bed together was the breaking point for the laughter.

I slept well and awoke to John Guimond making breakfast of eggs, turkey, bacon and toast. The smell of the bacon and strong coffee got our attention quickly. After breakfast we went back to the shoreline to watch the tidal bore and to start the testing for the Black Belts. We started with Kata, self-defense and fighting (kumite). We finished the training with one minute of round robin continuous fighting with no pads.

The Black Belts went back to the cabin, and I went to the main lodge to make reservations for a January long weekend stay in Cabin #7 with Suzanne. I imagined it to be a perfect getaway weekend full of snow and peace, a time to relax and reflect on our lives. (And, it certainly did snow that weekend creating a long slow journey back to Maine driving in a snowstorm.)

The Black Belts and I decided to stay a little longer around the river before heading out to pick up Dave. We were intrigued by the tidal bore and its enormous power. This day the bore was scheduled to come up the river around 12:30 pm. We all huddled around the shoreline at the dock waiting to hear the rumble of the water making its way inland. In the distance, we saw the thin line of the wave making its way up covering the sandbar in the middle of the river. It was amazing how quickly the water rose. The landmarks disappeared under the volume of the water. It was an awesome sight.

We finally left to pick up Dave, two hours late. Not too long into our trip to the Reservation, Buck's brand-new truck stalled in front of us. Buck's truck had only 11,000 miles on it and the pressure plate malfunctioned. We spent the next two and a half hours waiting around for the truck to be towed. Finally, we got to Dave's after 3:00 pm.

We met at the site where the sweat was supposed to be conducted. When we got there, Buck split us into two groups. One group was to build the Shaker tent while the other group prepared the sweat lodge. Since it was Tim's and Bob's Black Belt test and Dave Panarelli was the other high ranking Black Belt, I thought it best for them to stay together with Dave and another Micmac named Joe. They went to an unknown location to start the construction of the Shaker tent. John, Buck, Newell and I went to pick up wood for the fire. Joe led us to a retreat house at the edge of the reservation. When we got there, I was amazed to see all the big white birch and white pine trees knocked down from the 100-mile hurricane winds that hit a week ago. But there in the middle of the trees looking like toothpicks thrown around, was a sweat lodge, untouched. It was quite shocking, although not for the natives Dave, Joe, Buck and Newell.

As I walked over to the area to check out the sweat lodge, a nice size and well built, I asked Buck why we were not using this one. No work to repair and it was in a perfect location. The lodge looked like it could easily hold 12 people. Buck asked me to ask Joe if it was OK to consider performing the sweat here. Joe did not think it was a problem. I believe fate had us make the change. For the next three-and-a-half hours we set up the area for the fire. Rocks that were in the sweat from the past were used again. We made a line and passed the rocks, 24 of them into the fire pit. In past sweats, I have seen only 12 rocks being used. Since the lodge was so big, Dave wanted to add more heat power.

Buck gave the blessing with tobacco before we started the fire. The rocks were piled in the center and the wood that was split by Newell, John, and I was placed around the rocks. Within ten minutes, a roaring fire covered the rocks. I was told by Buck that rocks cannot be seen when the fire is lit so the rocks can get good and hot. As the fire was burning, I climbed up one of the 50-foot birch trees that had fallen beside the sweat. I was twenty feet high looking down into the fire. The sun began to fade over the horizon and for a few minutes, I experienced another perfect moment in time.

Dave Gehue arrived with the others from their Shaker Tent assignment with two other helpers, a man and a native woman; they followed Dave during many ceremonies and were in training to be assistants. We all gathered around the fire and Newell smudged us with sweet grass before we entered the lodge. Dave and his helpers spent the next 20 minutes explaining the sweat ceremony. He said there were going to be four rounds each lasting 15 to 20 minutes each. He said if anyone at any time wanted to leave the sweat lodge they could. All one must say is "All my relations" before one leaves. He also said that sometimes people see things during the sweat ceremony that may be hard to explain. He said not to worry. No one is intended to get hurt. His job is to keep everyone safe. The spirits will be with us.

We removed our clothes except for our shorts. Dave asked me to come into the sweat without the others. I followed him as he crawled in. We circled clockwise. I got next to him on his left side. He asked me to guide all the hot rocks into the center hole from the extremely hot fire. The rocks came in one at a time and they had the hot orange glow showing in the darkness of the lodge. The first rock was placed in the East, the next, the South, the third, the West and the final one, the North. An offering of sweet grass was placed on each rock according to their direction. The smell of the sweet grass burning gave off a pleasant aroma. The Lodge became hot as the rocks were piled on. In many of the sweat lodge ceremonies, only four rocks are placed for each round, although Dave instructed all 24 rocks to be put into the pit. My body felt as if it was going to melt. I was glad the flap was still open, letting some of the cool air in. The ceremony had not even started and I was soaked in my own sweat.

Dave asked all the participants to come into the lodge now that the rocks were placed in order. To my left in counterclockwise order were Joe, John Guimond, Dave Panarelli, Tim Merrithew, Newell Lewey, Bob Hartley, Buck Altvater and Dave Gehue. The intense energy was beginning especially from the new sweat lodge participants.

Under the direction of Dave, I blessed the water and the pipe with the sweet grass. Once again, I blessed the directions – East, South, West and North in the middle of the rocks. After the blessing, Dave filled his pipe with tobacco and told us if anyone had alcohol in the last four days, they could not smoke the pipe. The spirits come through the pipe and if alcohol is present, it can break the pipe as well as the pipe blowing up in your face. Since I had a glass of wine with Suzanne the day before, I was certainly not going to take any chances. The pipe was smoked and passed clockwise around the dark tent. The smell of tobacco filled the air. The pipe circled the group four times. After the final circle, Dave gave the order to close the flap. Whatever light was in the lodge was now gone except for the slight glow of the rocks in the pit.

Passion for Life

We were in total darkness. The heat continued to build in the air-locked chamber. Dave began with blessings and poured water over the hot orange rocks, which immediately caused intense steam. The sweat came pouring out of our skin. The initial burn of the steamed water was stinging. When Dave stopped pouring water on the rocks, the steam subsided. I remember placing my head closer to the pit letting the steam flow to the top of the lodge and toward the back of me. The coolest area seemed to be on the ground and near the rocks.

Round One – Representing the East, the Eagle

The first round began with heated intensity. As we all were trying to settle into the challenging atmosphere, Dave asked Newell to sing a traditional Passamaquoddy song. His song echoed in the lodge with his drumming keeping the beat. It was intense. The song was easy to catch on so that we all were able to join in. It was a great feeling of fellowship. We sang and sweated together. We were all the same, no difference in color, nationality, or creed. We had harmony. We were a team inside the lodge with the same purpose. The song helped keep the focus away from intense heat. When the song was completed, Dave gave the order to open the flap. The helpers outside wrestled with the covering and finally got the passageway open. The flap peeled away. I looked through the opening to see the outside fire pit and the steam sucked out into the open air. The cool air began to move into the lodge creating a dense fog. The orange glow of the fire outside was present. Round one was over.

Round Two – Representing the South, the Turtle

The water on the hot rocks created a steam bath in the lodge. The mist was dense as the cool air drifted inside the lodge. Sweat poured down our bodies. A constant drip started from my forehead to a straight line down my body onto my shorts. Dave again ordered the flap shut and darkness was upon us as intense heat built up. Dave splashed water on the rocks to create the burning steam. Dave announced the focus of the round would be healing ourselves from aliments.

Over the past six weeks, I had been suffering with pains in my stomach that could not be explained. It seemed to stem from the kidney area. I saw a few doctors and had a number of tests with no conclusive results. I let Dave know of this issue. He asked me to lie down on the dirt floor. His helper, Joe, was asked to lightly hit my stomach with the turtle beads shaker. Dave was chanting and at the same time splashing water on the rocks. The healing process seemed to go on for a few minutes. It stopped abruptly. Dave asked for the flap to go up. I slowly sat up. I was shocked to feel no pain. And, the pain never came back.

Round Three – Representing the West, the Bear.

This was the round to share thoughts of prayer for others. Each of us had the opportunity to speak out loud or keep our prayers to ourselves. I remember most of us in the circle expressed our prayers verbally. I remember giving thanks to my Black Belts and the extended Naha Family. I gave thanks for my friendship to Buck and Newell. I expressed my appreciation to Dave for his work with us and many others. I finally mentioned my love for my family and my soul mate, Suzanne.

Round Four – Representing the North, the White Buffalo

The flap was closed, and Dave asked who wanted a spirit Indian name? I immediately said "Yes" while John and Dave followed and then Tim. Finally, Bob agreed, hesitantly. This round was Buck's training round. Dave asked Buck to assist in the naming ceremony and it was his first opportunity to help provide Native names.

I was the first to be named. Dave asked me where my parents were from. I responded that the Walsh and Tumminelli clan were from Ireland and Italy, respectively. Then he asked what my favorite round was. I said, "The third round." Dave then asked Buck what vision did he have coming from the West. Buck said he saw something flying with clouds above. Dave asked if the clouds were moving. Buck said yes. Dave asked again, how fast? Buck replied, "Rapidly". Dave proclaimed that my Indian spirit name is WESTWIND. Dave went around the circle naming the rest of the Black Belts including John Guimond, our guest. John was given the name "Rolling Thunder." Dave Panarelli was given "Sitting Bear." Tim Merrithew's name was the "Man from the Sea." And Bob was given a name with the most impact, "The Man Who Cures Cancer".

The name given to Bob was quite intriguing especially since Bob had the most doubt with Native beliefs. Bob seemed to be given the most responsibility for mankind. The power of Bob's name would sit still then and into the future.

We closed the sweat ceremony and opened the flap for the last time. The cool Nova Scotia air moved quickly inside. The steam from the sweat flowed outward into the cool sky. We all moved clockwise crawling on our hands and knees to exit the lodge. When we got out, we all grabbed our bags with clothes and put on our dry clothing. We huddled around the hot coals of the fire as we waited until Dave emerged from the lodge. He told us that he was heading home to change before leading us with the next ceremony, the Shaker Tent.

We decided to head back to the cabin for a short respite. We piled into cars and took the ride back that seemed to take longer than yesterday. Perhaps we all had many thoughts circling in our mind from the sweat ceremony. We got back to the cabin with the sky darkening above. We all took part in preparing dinner that included Swedish meatballs and deer stew. Our team huddled around the kitchen counter and enjoyed this delicious meal. Food seemed to dance with our taste buds as our senses were alive from the sweat.

While we were eating, I couldn't help but turn on the TV to catch up with the World Series Baseball game between the Yankees and the Florida Marlins. Florida was winning the game going into late innings as we packed up and headed back out for the shaker ceremony. Later I learned on my journey back to Maine that the Yanks lost the game and the Marlins won their second World Series within ten years.

We drove to the Micmac Reservation and followed the directions from Bob, Tim and Dave as they took us deeper into the backwoods of the tribal property. We followed a dirt road until we came to an opening blocked by a metal fence leading to a field surrounded by pine trees. We followed Bob, Tim and Dave. They were here earlier building the Shaker Tent. Now I realized why it took so long for them to arrive at the sweat lodge. The Shaker Tent was made from birch branches with rope tied around them creating a circle with the limbs secured into the ground. The shape of the circle looked like a woman's dress, wide at the bottom and narrow at the top. Buffalo skin covered the entire area. It looked like sleigh bells hung from the top.

We waited another 45 minutes as Buck left to pick up Dave Gehue. That night, the air was very cool. Luckily, the cloudy sky kept in the heat from the day. While we waited for Dave's arrival, John and I walked on a pathway along the edge of the pine trees. We talked about many things including some of John's family challenges. Tonight he had hope that he was going to get answers to help mend his worries. While we were in our in-depth discussion, out of nowhere we heard a loud crashing sound coming from the dense pines. In the darkness, it was hard to tell what it might be. The sound got louder and much more intense. It headed right toward us. My initial thought was a BEAR and a big one. I yelled at the top of my lungs – Hey, Hey! John turned and ran in the other direction. Then with a hearty laugh, Tim made himself present. The sudden attack ticked off John and me especially since we were having a peaceful walk in the depths of the Nova Scotia field. Tim got a big kick out of scaring the hell out of us. After our heart rate settled down, we continued our walk until Dave arrived with Buck.

Dave asked us to gather around the Shaker Tent. He began to give instructions and what to expect. He was dressed in jeans, a sweatshirt and sports coat. He walked with his Indian stick that had messages carved throughout the wood. Dave began the ceremony by discussing the Micmac traditional legend about Indians that lived over 200 years old. He said it was mainly of choice. People choose to die and when they will die. We only get old because we choose to get old.

The night was getting colder although the sky was still cloudy and Dave began to talk again. He said that when it is time for him to get into the Shaker Tent, the skies will open and allow the spirits into the tent to talk with us. We will have our questions answered. As he talked, I wanted to believe his words, but I had my doubts. My doubt began to chip away as he crawled into the Shaker Tent and John elbowed me to look up at the sky. I looked up in awe as the cloudy area over the Shaker Tent opened up to a clear, starry sky. Was this real? I did not know what to think, although with our own eyes, we witnessed this amazing sight. Timing perhaps, circumstance maybe. John and I looked at each other like we had seen a supernatural occurrence.

Dave was in the Shaker Tent and Buck told us to leave until we were asked to come back one by one. When we did come back, we were to kneel next to the tent and place one hand on a crystal ball and state our spirit name to be recognized by the spirits. At that point, one could ask questions.

Buck went first. We all gathered near the cars around 100 feet away. After 15 minutes or so, Buck came down to us and told me that it was my turn. Buck and I walked in the darkness back to the tent. I looked up to the sky and noticed that the area over the tent was still clear. I thought to myself how bizarre that was. I approached the tent and Buck stayed alongside. In my mind I really thought how wacky this whole process was. Out of respect to Buck and the Native tradition, I thought I would just go with the flow. I knelt and placed my hand on the crystal ball and said this is Westwind. The tent began to move rapidly side to side with the bells ringing. Dave said, "The spirits recognize you, Westwind, what question may you have?"

I said, "I would like to speak with my Grandma Josephine Tumminelli." Dave said from the tent, "She is here, you can ask her any of your questions." I said, "Grandma, I am sorry I was not with you at your death. I should have been there, are you OK?" Dave's voice responded, "She is fine. She wants you to go to Rattlesnake Mountain and retrieve the silver necklace that you put in the tree at the top of the mountain."

At this point, my heart seemed to stop as the hair on the back of my neck stood up. I did not know what to say. I was stunned. The words that came from the tent brought me back twenty-three years ago to the time of my grandmother's death. Her death was very painful for me. She was always there for me and my brothers and sisters while we grew up. She lived in the same house in Brooklyn and took care of us while my parents worked. When she died, a part of me died with her. I did not know how to handle the situation because this was the first time that I had dealt with someone passing away who was truly close to my life.

I got the news of my grandmother's death from my mom. She was at the hospital after suffering from a stroke. She had the stroke while I was away at Water Safety Instruction Training Camp in Lake George. My grandmother was staying in my bedroom on a visit from Brooklyn. She woke up in the middle of the night to go to the bathroom and fell. She was rushed to the hospital. My mom called me the last day of camp to tell me the news. I came home in a panic and went to the hospital to see her. There she lay, a woman with much pride who could not talk or help herself. I could see in her eyes how painful it was for her to not communicate or take care of herself. It made her extremely frustrated. I did not know how to deal with her condition and felt awkward. I was only 19 years old and did not want to face the death of my grandmother.

Passion for Life

In a short week, my grandmother gave up and passed away. She had her final breath without me there and her good spirit left this earth. When I was told, I did the only thing I knew, which was to run away and deal with it in my own way. I climbed up Rattlesnake Mountain. I hiked to the top of the mountain just above where my house was located. When I got to the top, I took off my silver necklace and climbed a pine tree overlooking a cliff. I wrapped the necklace around a tree limb as I broke down in sadness in the silence of the woods. This was my way to show grief, and I never mentioned this to anyone.

How Dave said these words instructing me twenty-three years later to go to the mountain was shocking. I do not recall thinking about that moment for many, many years. If I had mentioned this to some of the Black Belts or even Buck, I could possibly understand the message being relayed, but I had not. This was truly remarkable. My doubts believing that there is something bigger than all of us disappeared rapidly. The spirits within the Shaker Tent clearly explained in detail my inner most secret painful memory and brought it back to life. Was it the spirit of my grandmother speaking to me? I now had no doubt as I had before the ceremony. I felt the spirits that Buck and my Native friends talked about often and they were now alive with me. A new understanding was being developed within.

I finished my questions and thanked the spirits for their time. I left slowly walking down the dirt path heading to others. I really did not know what to say. I was still stunned from what had just happened. As the night progressed, the other Black Belts came back from the Shaker Tent in a similar disbelief of what just happened to them. Our six foot four, two hundred and fifty pound gentle giant Tim Merrithew, a true honest Mainer, came back to the circle after his turn, speechless and almost in tears. He said he spoke with his aunt who he missed dearly and had been gone for years.

Bob was the only one that refused to participate for his own reasons that we all respected and did not pass judgment. The ceremony ended and we helped take down the Shaker Tent. We all thanked Dave and wished him well as we led him to the car.

We headed back to the cabin. I was wired along with John. On the way back to the cabin, we decided to head home even though it was now approaching 3:00 am. It was going to be our road trip. Dave Panarelli decided to join us as well. Once we got back to the cabin, we gathered our stuff, said goodbye to the others, and left for the eight-hour adventure home.

We immediately began an eight-hour non-stop conversation talking about issues, dreams, and goals. As the sun rose and we entered Maine, I could remember thinking this will be a memory that will last a lifetime. We created this opportunity; we created this moment to happen. It was a good feeling. I remember getting back home and seeing Suzanne as I got out of my car. I immediately gave her a big hug and we had some small talk about the trip. I was pleasantly exhausted knowing that I was about to have a very sound sleep even though it was early afternoon. This adventure was ending but it was not finished.

I knew I had to head back to Amenia to climb Rattlesnake Mountain to search for the necklace. I decided the best time for the journey would be Thanksgiving break. On Thanksgiving Day, I left Suzanne and headed south to New York. My sister, Janice, held the family Thanksgiving dinners for many years at her home in Westchester County.

I left at 8:00 am with the plan to arrive around 2:00 pm for dinner. While driving, I had lots of time to think of the conversation with Dave Gehue, the sweat, the Shaker Tent and the drive back to Maine with my Black Belt brothers. I was anxious about the climb to Rattlesnake Mountain. I had not been there in years. I was trying to picture in my mind the pathway that led to the top of the mountain. I imagined the ridge where the pine tree was in which the necklace might have settled. The memory I had now twenty-three years later was that I climbed the pine tree on a cliff overlooking the valley into Sharon, CT. Would I find the tree, the necklace?

When I arrived at Janice and Eddie's home, I had a warm feeling of yester year. Our holidays around the Walsh family gatherings were always festive. It was especially sweet since I have not taken part in the Thanksgiving gathering for two years. I went through the formalities of saying hello to all the family members and friends. It was good to see Mom and Dad looking well. My mom always enjoyed having all her children together. In the piano room den sat my sister Ellen and my brother Rob with his new baby son, Liam. During family activities, all the attention is directed towards the newest addition to the family. This was my first time meeting the little guy.

I spoke with Ellen in length about my sweat lodge experience. I told her of my mission to retrieve the necklace from years ago that was placed on the pine tree. She listened intently and asked lots of questions. She had no doubt that these unusual circumstances were real. This Thanksgiving was typical, lots of chatter and too much to eat. At the end of the evening, my mother took an early ride home with my sister Ellen and her partner Debbie while I followed a half an hour later taking my dad home. We had our usual short talk with not much substance. Dad did talk about his newfound money gained by selling Aunt Lilly's house in Brooklyn.

I shared with Dad that Suzanne and I were planning a trip to Northern Italy. He thought it was a fantastic idea and thought he might come along. I guess he did not realize that this was our honeymoon plan. I went to bed early that night thinking of my adventure the next morning. I was having second thoughts. My Brother Jim worried that I may be prohibited from climbing to the top of the mountain since the Murphys just sold the property. They have restricted some use of their new land. After more discussion over the kitchen table, the place

Passion for Life

where many conversations were held in my family, I went upstairs to bed and quickly fell asleep.

That morning I awoke before anyone. It was a rainy foggy morning in Amenia. I gathered my bright orange rain jacket and cell phone. I headed out the door walking past the houses on Depot Hill to the entrance of the field that leads to Rattlesnake Mountain in the drizzling rain. As I walked along the open farmer's field, I noticed the new development of houses from the distance. At one point, this was all farmland and now houses were beginning to appear along the hillside. I could remember my buddies, Mike Rooney, Mike and Billy O'Connell taking this same path to fish, hike, or camp out. The pathway took me to the old Boy Scout campsite called The Pines. In the mist of the fog, the pines brought back memories of our youth. In my mind, I could hear echoes of laughter and visualize the rowdiness of our times together. All the building structures were now gone except for some of the old wooden foundations.

I looked over the open field thinking of the best approach to the base of Rattlesnake Mountain without being discovered by the owner. The dense fog helped. I walked along the barbed wire fence that had lots of brush and small trees separating the fields and got to the base of Rattlesnake Mountain where the old rusted out pickup truck was left fifty years ago.

I looked back and admired the site of the valley and then continued to climb through the dense woods. It was extremely eerie walking knowing that hunters could be in the area. I wanted to be quiet although not too quiet worrying that I could be mistaken as game. I tried to find the old trail that led to the top, however, everything had changed after twenty plus years. I charged forward and climbed up making my own path. I finally reached the ridge. On top of the mountain, the fog became more dense. I could hardly see twenty feet in front of me. I tried to remember where the pine tree was located. I discovered a worn-down narrow path that I continued to follow that took me to the cliff overlooking Sharon.

I was almost certain that the rocky ledge was the spot of the old pine tree that I climbed years ago. I found several pine trees all grown and tall. I climbed each one of them with no luck finding the chain. I concluded that either the chain was absorbed into the tree or it broke off and fell to the ground buried forever.

I began to ask questions to myself. Why was I summoned to take this journey and not find what I was looking for? Then it occurred to me. I needed to be there on top of Rattlesnake Mountain. I needed to let go of my guilt of not being there with my grandmother as she passed on. I needed to forgive myself. I believed that my grandmother's spirit brought me there to reflect back and look within my soul. It all came together; this was a journey of healing and letting go of the past and continuing to move on in life. We all need to empty the closet, to stop harboring guilty feelings from the past and come to terms in order to live life to the fullest.

Journey 23

My Girl, Suzanne, last mile to go, Alfond Youth Center 5K Road Race

"You know you're in love when you can't fall asleep because reality is finally better than your dreams." Dr. Seuss

A True Inspiration

That is right, I might be biased, but I believe with my entire heart that my wife, my soulmate, Suzanne, is an inspiration for all women as well as men.

Suzanne is a quiet doer never looking for fanfare or a pat on the back. She just does what she needs to do even though the task might be daunting.

Suzanne is the CEO of a large non-profit, community action organization and their mission to end poverty extends throughout Kennebec and Somerset counties in Maine – a geographical territory the size of Connecticut. The work is challenging at times due to the vast differences in economic instability of their clients and the dire impacts of poverty on children and families – not unlike many of the youth I serve at the Alfond Youth Center. Although Suzanne takes it all in stride with her solid and steady leadership to make the best out of any situation, she is a true leader that puts others before self.

Suzanne has been involved in a fitness routine for many years of her life. She has spent most of the time pounding the pavement, running 5 to 7 miles per day for years. When we first met, we consistently ran together during our lunch times and weekends putting in between 30 to 40 miles per week. Many of the workouts led to 5K and 10K races along with longer runs such as the Mt. Washington Road Race and the 100-mile journey to Katahdin. During our runs together, Suzanne was always steady and seemed to get stronger as the run continued. While on the other hand, I typically came out of the box quick and burned out at the end of the race having no kick at the end.

After the birth of Sean and then Kate, our running routine changed due to the needs of our little ones. Workouts became more on an individual basis in which I continued some of the longer races including the NYC, Boston and Sugarloaf marathons. It seemed like every time we had planned to run a marathon together, Suzanne was pregnant with another child and she had to bow out.

When Katie was born, Suzanne was 45 and she was concerned that her fitness level would never be the same. However, Suzanne would not accept that age would make a difference in her health and wellbeing. In 2013, Suzanne started a fitness regimen that she religiously followed, starting her workouts every weekday morning at 4:15 am and a little later on weekend mornings. She knew that if she wanted to be physically and mentally healthy, she needed to get her workout in before the business of the day started. She continues to follow it to this day, however, with the kids getting older, the early, early morning routine has thankfully gotten a little later.

Wherever we have lived, Suzanne and I made sure to have our own fitness center in our home. It includes a treadmill, stationary bike, universal system, free weights, and mats that we both use to train. Since 2013, Suzanne has only missed two days of working out and those were because of my mother's and my father's funerals.

There are so many things to love about Suzanne. She is a loving wife and a devoted mom who cares about family first. Everything else is secondary. It makes her uneasy when she has to be out of town on business away from her family. I know that she unconditionally loves me and her family, no matter what the situation may be.

On top of her family dedication, is being the CEO of one of the largest nonprofit organizations in Central Maine, the Kennebec Valley Community Action Program. Her dedicated 34 years of service to this organization landed her this position even though she was not too sure if she had the leadership skills or the time to become a CEO. The question that was heavy on her mind was how much family time was going to be taken away.

Suzanne's great leadership quickly surfaced and she has demonstrated leading her organization during some of the most difficult times for a nonprofit. She has led her team with confidence and a focused energy to continue to grow the organization that helps thousands of people in need through Head Start, transportation, heating assistance, and housing needs.

Suzanne continues to juggle life's tasks between the immense housework that needs be done in our large homestead, making sure the kids are well dressed, doing their homework, taking care of our two cats and our black lab as well as finding quality time for us as a couple.

We make a point to make magical moments during our vacation time by taking trips with the kids to Disney, Bahamas, Hawaii, and summer camping that gives us the opportunity to spend quality time together. In 2018 during our family trip to Disney, our vacation did not turn out to be a relaxing getaway. We rented out an eight-bedroom home in Davenport, Florida with the Lockwood family. After only two days there, I developed the flu that kept me in bed the remaining time of our trip. Even though I was down and out, Suzanne kept the kids active enjoying the Florida sunshine at the pool and taking them to Magic Kingdom.

Our work schedules create challenging circumstances, especially our work conferences and meetings out of town. I tend to have a lot of meetings and often Suzanne is home alone with the kids juggling work, their school and many of their activities, sacrificing her own time for others. In March 2018 while I was away in Washington DC at a YMCA Advocacy event, a Northeastern blizzard came up the coast locking me in DC while Suzanne was buried in snow with the kids at home. Once again, she made the best of it until three days later, I was finally able to get back to Maine.

Suzanne is an amazing person who truly cares first and foremost about those she loves over her own needs. She is a hero. Her children and grandchildren will realize this someday and will understand, if they don't already, the special person that she is. I will always be grateful to have her as my loving partner and teammate for life. We are truly happy and blessed to have found each other.

Journey 24

Avis Hart, Mitch and Megan McQuarrie, Suzanne and me with Chief Barry Dana
August 8, 2004

Now you will feel no rain, for each of you will be shelter for the other. Now you will feel no cold, for each of you will be warmth for the other. Now there is no more loneliness. Now you are two persons, but there is only one life before you. May your days together be good and long upon the earth. Apache Wedding Blessing

Life's New Beginning

For too many, the wedding union between two partners turns out to be all about everyone else and not for the couple. These external factors weigh heavy during the wedding plans causing much stress among the couple and everyone around them. For Suzanne and me, it was quite different. The main objective was to keep the ceremony about us and not worry about anyone else.

Since I had a strong relationship with the Native American tribe, especially the Penobscot Nation, I wanted something to symbolize the outdoor and native spirit in our ceremony. After discussing with Suzanne, we asked my good friend, Former Chief Barry Dana, if he would do the honors and conduct the wedding ceremony. He accepted and was willing to add the Native American touch to the ceremony. His advice was that I needed to cleanse my mind, body, and spirit to be able to open myself up to Suzanne, now and for years into the future.

Suzanne and I thought that we would like to have the ceremony on top of Moxie Falls located in the Forks near the base of the Kennebec River, which I paddled many times since being in Maine. Moxie Falls was also a sacred place for us. We enjoyed hiking on top of Moxie Falls and it was a special place for us. Therefore, this outdoor church was an appropriate venue to officially unite.

Moxie Falls was off the beaten path on a back road for many of the rafting companies. Getting there was only by foot, a short ¾ mile hike on a narrow pathway. Many people who go there usually hike down to the base of the 60-foot waterfall and hang out among the many rocks, sun bath or swim in the crystal-clear cool water. It was not too far from the top where Suzanne and I enjoyed picnics and time together. The setting is a pleasant quiet surrounding of nature with the sounds of the wildlife and the stream leading to the Falls.

Chief Dana said, "Ken, you must cleanse your soul with a sweat lodge ceremony followed by a two-day fasting in the mountains to discover who you are and how you will continue the journey of life with your new mate."

Two weeks prior to the wedding, Barry invited us and some of our close friends to a sweat lodge ceremony near his home in Solon. The sweat lodge group would include Barry, his wife Lori, Steve Hesseltine (Barry's half-brother), Charlie Giguere and his friend Marvy, Suzanne and me. On a Sunday morning, two weeks before the ceremony, we all gathered in Solon at Barry's sister-in-law's cabin in the middle of the woods. We followed a narrow dirt road with two feet of grass in the middle that led to a small opening with a one bedroom, two story cabin in front of a very small pond. When we arrived, Steve, Barry, and Lori were already preparing the fire to bake the rocks for the sweat. A billow of smoke appeared above the cabin as we pulled in. We all spent the next couple of hours preparing the ground area, building the bear sweat lodge, collecting cedar limbs for the ground area, tying the ends of each pole together, and tending the fire on this hot humid July day in Maine.

The hot orange rocks were ready for the sweat. Everyone crawled into the four-foot-high lodge and sat around the hole in the ground in the middle of the lodge where the rocks would be placed. Chief Dana sat at the far end next to his wife. Suzanne and I were next to them as Charlie and Marvy sat closer to the lodge door. Steve was the lodge keeper, bringing the hot rocks in as well as opening and closing the canvas door before and after each round. For Charlie, Marvy, and Suzanne, this was their first sweat lodge. For many first timers, the anticipation of the unknown is worse than the ceremony itself. Their eyes told the story of nervousness.

The outside air temperature was hot and sticky and made the small confines of the sweat lodge even more uncomfortable. Once the flap was closed, it was pitch dark and our bodies were immediately covered with dripping sweat. I kept telling Suzanne to focus on her breathing, taking shallow breaths and if it got too hot for her to place her face to the ground, the coolest part of the lodge. Chief Dana provided the ground rules. He said if anyone needed to leave the lodge, they may do so but must say "All my relations" before leaving. He explained how the sweat lodge was part of his culture for thousands of years and remains a part of his being today. He also said this is a time for healing and praying for oneself or others, to give the strength to take on challenges and to discover who you may be.

Chief Dana opened with a native Penobscot song that struck our souls with his tremendous passionate voice. He then splashed more water on the hot rocks creating intense steam. We went through four of the rounds together, each one of us continuing with the ceremony. Suzanne and I pledged our love and hearts to each other in our words. When the final round was over, we each crawled out of the lodge and laid down on our backs inhaling every bit of cooler temperature the earth offered to us. Every pore of our bodies was open, the sweat cleansed us. The body felt reborn physically and spiritually. The first part of the cleansing was completed.

The second part of my spiritual cleanse was a two-day fasting in the mountains. I chose Tumbledown as this was also a sacred place for Suzanne and me. This was where we pledged our love for each other after hiking to the top.

The weekend before the wedding, I headed to Tumbledown Mountain in western Maine to camp out, to be by myself without food or water. According to Chief Dana, this will truly discipline my soul for the acceptance of my new mate for my lifetime. I did not mind the thought of being alone in the wilderness, although the idea of no food or water for two days was daunting. I got up at 5:00 am on Friday morning, rolled over in bed and kissed Suzanne goodbye. In a groggy state she said, "Please be safe and you don't need to do this." I smiled, kissed her again and off I went. She knew no matter what she said this was something I needed to do.

The drive to Tumbledown took close to 2 hours. The morning was quiet and the sun was just rising. I love this time of the morning, when things are so still and the earth is just waking up for the new day. I arrived at Weld turning toward the direction of Mt. Blue State Park onto a dirt road heading to Tumbledown. Tumbledown was always one my favorite hills to climb. The trail was well maintained although still rugged with the rocks painted along the hillside. Near the peak sat a beautiful little clear pond with rocky ledges surrounding the pool of water.

    I finally got to the base of the mountain. I drove into the narrow road leading to an open remote camping area, parked my car near an area that I thought would be secluded, and set up my two-person tent. This was my home for the next two days. Already my stomach was growling from no breakfast and lack of any food or water since 9:00 the evening before. It was less than 12 hours and I was already craving food. I thought the best method of not thinking about the craving was a good old hike up Tumbledown. I had all day, so I took my time working slowly up the trail. Typically, the hike took me around 2 hours. I planned to stretch this out and make it a day and climb both peaks Little Jackson and Big Jackson. It was 8:00 a.m. In shorts, a Red Sox blue baseball cap, a good pair of hiking boots and a tee shirt, I ascended upward. I stopped several times to conserve energy and to take in the sights and sounds of nature. A few times, I was tempted to lean over the running brook to wet my mouth. I struggled to discipline myself.

    The most challenging part of the journey was walking along the rocky knoll hiking toward the mountain top pond. There in front of me were blueberry patches as far as I could see in full bloom. I love blueberries, really love blueberries. Here at my feet was my favorite snack calling my name. At this point, I knew the gods were testing me. I just thought to myself, how unfair. I worked myself around the blueberry fields and sat overlooking the pond. It was a beautiful Maine summer day. The sun was shining and there was not a cloud in the sky with the temperature climbing into the mid 80's. I thought this was the perfect time to meditate on the rock ledge opening all my senses to nature.

    I must have been in my meditative state for 20 minutes, when I began to hear the echo of women's voices coming from below at the pond. I opened my eyes to see six young women with camping gear, setting up their campground at the edge of the water, about 400 yards in front of me. I thought they might be local college students from the University of Maine at Farmington. I kept in my meditation state trying to focus although the echo in the valley with their laughter and cheerful voices made it hard and to top it off, they all stripped down to their bathing suits for a swim. At that point, I thought this was a bad joke the gods were playing on me.

    I had to get out of there and redirect my focus. Now I was hungry and feeling fatigued. I found the path to Little Jackson trail. The hike up the mountain was laboring without water and nutrition. I finally got to the top around 2:30 pm. At the top, I looked down and could see the girls at a far distance looking like little ants huddled together. I laid down on a flat rock and fell asleep. I awoke with a windy chill coming across my body. I had slept for 2 hours. It was 4:30 pm. I was glad that some amount of time passed without feeling the pain of hunger or thirst. I got up slowly and felt dizzy. My mind was foggy, and thoughts were unclear. It was now 20 plus hours without food or water.

I slowly and carefully worked myself down the trail. I came across the blueberry crop again. This time the blueberries seemed to be waving in the wind with voices taunting me, "eat me, have just one." In the state of weariness, your mind does strange things. I wanted to get away from the field as soon as possible as I hustled down the path and the trail. By 7:00 pm, I arrived at my campground. With daylight for only another hour, I was just going to enter the tent and call it a day. Instead, I suddenly decided to build a fire and relax. I stayed up until around 9:30 pm, now at twenty-four hours of fasting. I remember looking into the fire, watching the flames dance, and thinking of my next phase of life with Suzanne. My energy was completely depleted.

My heart just took over thinking of how important it is to give my total self to Suzanne and her to me. I had a vision of what it takes for a perfect and lasting relationship, knowing that every relationship needs lots of communication, honesty, and hard work. I knew in past relationships, I did not do these things very well and my immaturity at times did not help foster a good foundation. I pledged to change and work hard to keep the fire going with Suzanne.

The vision I came up with staring at the fire was a term Suzanne and I still use now, "The Forever Honeymoon." The ingredients of the forever honeymoon are as follows.

1. Break the routine of the relationship
2. Be Spontaneous
3. Never take each other for granted
4. Unconditional love

To this day, this saying is in our bedroom as a reminder to pledge to work on these ingredients every day.

That night, I slept well into the morning and spent most of the day into early evening walking around the base of Tumbledown. I meditated and napped off and on. The second day without food and water did not seem as difficult. I was in a fog although the hot sun gave me good energy. I left at 7:00 pm to head back home. I do not remember much about the ride. It seemed to go quickly.

When I saw Suzanne, I gave her a big bear hug embrace and thanked her for giving me this opportunity. I showered, ate a great meal that Suzanne prepared of salmon, asparagus and rice along with BLUEBERRY Pie.

Our wedding was the following week. Before the ceremony, we needed to make it legally official by having a Justice of the Peace marry us. On Thursday, August 4th, our attorney and good friend, George Jabar, met us at the Alfond Youth Center. My staff at the Alfond Youth Center got wind of it and Development Director, Jennifer Buker, and Human Resource Director, Karen Estes, set up an impromptu wedding ceremony behind the AYC. They gave Suzanne flowers and brought in a white wooden archway for George to conduct the wedding vows.

Even though we were now officially married, the real ceremony for us was going to be at Moxie Falls. On Sunday, August 8th, the plan was to start at 10:00 am and everyone who could hike in to meet us at the top of the Falls. Chief Dana would conduct the Native Ceremony.

My brothers, Dennis and Jim, came up from New York on Saturday. On Sunday, Jim, Dennis, and Steve Hesseltine drove with me to Chief Dana's house in Solon early in the morning. Suzanne and the kids followed a bit later and we would meet up at the wedding alter. The weather started out in the morning with a rainy mist, although the forecast called for the skies to break late morning for the rest of the day. Our friends and most of Suzanne's family planned to be there along with her mom.

The groom's party arrived at Moxie Falls a little later than everyone else. We walked in and came to the crowd at the top of the Falls. I was surprised at the amount of people who showed up especially with the weather not being perfect. The mist started to drift away and the sun was breaking through the cloud cover. We followed the path winding down to the rock ledge where Suzanne watched me come down and said joking, "I was wondering if you got cold feet."

Steve Hesseltine brought his guitar and started the ceremony with some of our favorite tunes from the movie Phenomenon and John Denver's song list, "Dance with Life", and John Denver "Rhymes & Reasons". At that point, Suzanne and I went over to where Chief Dana stood at the top of the waterfalls as the stream flowed to the crest and fell quickly down to the pool below. Mitch and Megan along with Suzanne's mom came with us. Barry lit a little fire and burned sage to smudge us. This would purify us before the ceremony. With an eagle feather, he described how our hearts will be joined forever now and into the spirit world.

He said, "Now you feel no rain for each of you will be shelter to the other. Now you will feel no cold for each of you will be warmth to each other. Now there will be no more loneliness for each of you will be a companion to the other. Now you are two bodies but there is one life before you. Go now to your dwelling place to enter the days of your togetherness. And may your days be good and long upon the earth." With that he blessed us with the eagle feather and gave it to us. Today the wedding blessing and the eagle feather is framed on a wall in our home.

We ended the day with a wonderful celebration with family and friends back at our house. Many other guests who were not able to hike into Moxie Falls arrived and gave us warm wishes. Many of my elder mentors showed up— Fred Boucher, Ken and Shirley Eskelund, Lester and Barbara Jolovitz, and Harold Alfond along with his son, Peter. We had a terrific afternoon of fellowship and love. It was a perfect wedding that joined our spirits together, perfectly.

Journey 25

Naha Black Belts Chris and Dave Panarelli

"A strong friendship doesn't need daily conversation, doesn't always need togetherness, as long as the relationship lives in the heart, true friends will never part". Anonymous

Spirit of Adventure

Another trip to Vegas in 2005 once again led me on another adventure into the great West. I had the opportunity to go on a business trip to Las Vegas and then take some personal time to visit one of my first Black Belts who I promoted in the early nineties and now lives in Park City, Utah. Utah was a State I always wanted to visit and now the time was right. Thank you, Dave Panarelli.

I arrived in Las Vegas on a Tuesday night and headed into the casino. I was never interested in gambling. Perhaps because I am compulsive and do not like to lose. This is a dangerous combination for someone in a casino. This venture into a casino was the first time for me. Although I had many business trips to

Las Vegas, I never journeyed into the hall of slot machines. Many of my friends, family and staff have busted on me for not gambling in sin city.

That night I decided to give it a go since I had a free night with no meetings. I went to cash in my bills for coins and then realized that the slot machines had dollar changers. This was another brilliant gimmick to make more money for the casinos. My plan was to play with only $100 and then stop. I picked my spot surrounded by many gray-haired smoking individuals, placed my one dollar into the machine, pulled the lever and all 7's came across the board. I immediately won $300. I grabbed my winnings and walked away. One pull and victorious - game over! I was proud of myself in not getting caught up with the win and losing it all.

For the next two days, I went running after my long meetings with the Boys & Girls Clubs Workers Association. In glitter town, running outside was a challenge since the city streets were extremely hot and the dry air hid the real temperature of the blazing sun. My body's skin took its toll as the dry salt from my skin appeared on both sides of my face. After my eight-mile run, I looked in the mirror and saw two rivers of salt on each side of my face. I was able to continue my long runs with the help of my MP3 player playing my favorite inspirational tunes with soundtracks from the movies Rudy, Rocky, and Field of Dreams.

On Friday morning, I rented a car at the airport and headed north to a place I had never visited – Utah. I was excited to get away from the paved city and head into the mountains, into nature. There I would hook up with two of my Naha Black Belts who were now living in ski town – Park City.

Dave Panarelli and his son Chris Panarelli who had just turned 18 had lived out West for several years. Chris was one of our Black Belts that earned the rank at a young age of 10. It was hard to see them go as they were such an important part of our Naha Karate family. Ten years ago, Dave obtained his Black Belt along with Craig Sargent, two of my first students in Maine. His son Chris followed two years later.

I drove north and saw the snowy mountain range explode before me in the far distance. The Arizona desert was at my back as I approached the Utah boarder. It was a good call upgrading my rental car to an SUV knowing that I was heading into the mountains with snowy conditions. I was cruising at 90 miles per hour just staying up with the rest of the crowd on the highway. The roads on this stretch were straight and I could see many miles ahead.

Signs for Salt Lake City, which leads to Park City, appeared in front of me and the mountain ranges became more pronounced. I got off the main highway following the exit to Park City. This was a beautiful winding road twisting along the mountainside. I was excited to finally arrive in Park City. Everything Dave shared on the phone about his new place of living was true. Park City was located in an area with ski slopes and trails on both sides of the valley. It was an absolute incredible place to relocate.

Passion for Life

I stayed in the Best Western Hotel right off the Interstate. Looking out from the hotel sat a mountain ridge leading to an exclusive community. The road to the top was about a mile long reaching to an 8,000-foot peak. The next day, I convinced Dave to take a run with me for a workout.

That following morning Dave and his daughter Megan picked me up and showed me the sights of Park City. That weekend it happened to be the Snow Board World Championship. Chris, an avid snowboarder, was on the high school team and he was very enthusiastic about the event. The hill was packed with spectators from around the US and the World. Top athletes showed off their stuff. The competition was amazing. The gymnastic flips in the air along with the twists, kept the crowd energized.

It was fun catching up with the Panarelli family. My friendship with Dave had not missed a beat and his son, Chris, cracked me up with his new face. He had a very dark tan all on his face except for his eyes where he wore his goggles. He was a grown adult now compared to the young child I knew. After a long day touring the city and watching the competition, I headed back to the hotel to change up for the mile run to the 8,000-foot elevation. Dave was up for the challenge. I decided to add to my run by running the few miles to his house at the base of the mountain.

We started at the base and our run began immediately upward with a steep incline. During the first 100 yards, we had a good conversation. It abruptly stopped as the elevation got steeper and our heavy breathing took over. The road continued to switch back and forth until we came around a bend and there in front of us was this tremendous view of the Utah Mountains. The sun was fading quickly and the temperature was dropping as well. Our heavy breathing continued with our steady pace. I was impressed by Dave who stayed with me even though he had not run in a while. We finally made it to the top with the reward of the brilliant scenery of the village below. We gathered our thoughts and breath as we admired our accomplishment. At that moment in time, everything was perfect in the silence and peace on top of the mountain.

Then, it was time to find another good moment. That is when the trouble began. We decided to take a different trail down the mountain. This trail led to another side of the mountain into a housing development. We headed in this direction thinking it was going to lead us to the same starting point. We were wrong.

After running a couple of miles through snow, mud, streams and fields, we eventually found our way back. It was nightfall and we were late for dinner. Despite our late arrival, we enjoyed a much-needed steak dinner at the Panarelli's at their mountainside condo.

I headed back to the hotel for one more night before my long journey back to Maine. Dave and I did get a chance to discuss our goals, dreams, and where our lives were heading. We were both in a good place.

Journey 26

Trail Head to Mt. Hood

"The mountains are calling, and I must go." John Muir

Mt. Hood Hike

As we were heading home and our flight passed Mt. Hood at 20,000 feet, I looked straight down and saw the white caps of the North Side. I reflected to my journey hiking up there only two days earlier.

Our family journey with Mitch and Megan began on August 3, 2005, with a stay over in Boston before our flight out. We had a connecting flight in Chicago and then to Portland, Oregon. As we approached the Portland Airport, we flew in between Mt. Hood on the left and Mt. Adams, Mt. Rainier and Mt. St. Helens on the right. The Columbia River Gorge was right below us. The sight was amazing.

Everyone was exhausted by the time we arrived at 1:00 pm. Suzanne, Mitch and Megan were sacked out in the car during the 45-minute drive to the town of Welch where we were staying for the week. While they were sleeping, I was occupied with the beautiful picture-perfect mountain ranges. I drove with Mt. Hood in front of me. My excitement of experiencing the North West Country grew with each mile.

This family trip for Mitch, Megan and Suzanne was the first time they had traveled to the great State of Oregon. I have been coming out to Oregon since 1986 and wanted to share this great land with them. We exchanged our Hawaii timeshare points to rent out a townhouse for a week. The townhouse house with three bedrooms was nestled at the base of the mountains and had a family pool area and sauna. This would keep the kids happy for some of the trip.

We planned a few sightseeing tours, which drove Mitch and Meg crazy riding in the car, but the waterfalls along the river were tremendous. The problem for Mitch and Megan was that there were many of them and we hit them all. In their mind, if you've seen one waterfall, you've seen them all.

One of the highlights of the trip was the ride that Mitch and I took to see Mt. St. Helens, while Suzanne and Megan enjoyed a day by the pool. It is hard to imagine how Mother Nature's unimaginable destruction can cause so much mud. The trees and anything in the pathway from that eruption was pushed around like tall grass in the wind.

Suzanne and I had planned this trip for months by trading our Shell vacation time share points from Hawaii to include Mitch and Megan on a family trip. For Mitch and Megan, the trip to the Northwest was more appealing if it had a pool. Lucky for us, the condo at Whispering Pines had just that along with a sauna, workout room, club house, and all the amenities of a condo.

The first day at Whispering Pines was relaxing. This was our downtime to catch our energy. My cousin Roger and his girlfriend Sue Yeoman were arriving the next day to show us around the area. It was great to see my mentor, who I also call my oldest brother. Roger and Sue were stopping in to see us on their way to Idaho for a six-day rafting trip, typical for Roger. We toured Mt. Hood visiting Lake Trillion and swam while the sight of Mt. Hood jumped out in front of us. It was so perfect that it seemed like a painting. After a cool swim in the crystal-clear lake, we went to the base of Mt. Hood at Timberline Lodge. Many of the top snow boarders in the world train here during the summer months since the snow is plentiful. The lodge was big and beautiful. It is a tremendous four-story log cabin with large windows facing the mountain. According to guidebooks, it takes about 15 hours to hike to the top. Hikers are advised to start at night and reach the top by daybreak to be able to return by the end of the next day. It is also helpful that the frozen snow at night is better for footing. The other major hazard is the crevasses that are endless. One wrong step and you are visiting the depths of Mother Earth. After our adventures, Sue and Roger joined us for dinner. They stayed overnight and headed out the next day for their whitewater river trip.

On Sunday, we stayed around the condo in the morning and then went back to the ski lodge to take a ride down the Alpine slide. We then found a place for miniature golf and ended the day with a movie back at the Condo. The next day, we took a road trip to visit the Gorge and all its landmark waterfalls. After the first three, the kids had enough and were ready to get back. Everything we did with them was under protest - typical for teenagers. We traveled into Mt. Hood Township for lunch before heading back to the condo.

On Tuesday we drove to Portland and went to the Oregon Museum of Science. We met up with my cousin Karly and her husband Doug. The teens seemed to enjoy what the museum had to offer. We discussed taking a trip along the coast to the beach the next day although we sensed that the kids had enough of being in the car. This is when I suggested to Suzanne that she consider hanging out with them at the resort while I find a mountain to climb. Mt. Hood was on my mind and I was tempted to climb as far as possible with the limited time available.

It was getting close to the end of our trip and I felt antsy for not climbing a mountain while in Oregon. I expressed my feeling with Suzanne and she encouraged me to find a trail to climb but cautioned me to be careful. I told her there was only One Mountain to consider – Mt. Hood. After the green light, I picked up a backpack from the store in town, filled it with two peanut candy bars, trail mix, water, an American flag bandana, my cell phone and a sweatshirt. After a kiss goodbye, Suzanne dropped me off at the Timberline Lodge at 12:30 pm and again cautioned me to be careful. I planned to hike two hours up then turn back to meet her in the parking lot at 4:30 pm.

I took the right side of the trail with the intent to hike the far-right ridge. The trail was dry and sandy, an easy trail for athletic shoes. I did not have boots or hiking shoes. The trail was quiet with no one else hiking. At the far left, I saw skiers at the base of the mountain and the maintenance crew grooming the slopes. The mountain ski lodge was at 7,500 feet while the main lodge sat at 6,000 feet. The elevation of Mt. Hood is at 11,250 feet.

Off to my right was the glacier area. I saw a slow-running stream leading to the heavy snow area with a deep crevasse that had wide channels and running water in its depths. I heard the loud sound of water echoing along the sides of the white snow walls. I continued to take a slow jog (I wanted to go as far as I could in 2 hours) following the trail leading over the top of the ski slope. While running, I was thinking on how I could have saved an hour if I took the ski lift, but that would have ruined the purpose of the hike and the sweat behind the challenge.

    I took a water break on top of a little mound and ate my candy bars and then started off to the top of the slope. The chair lift stopped as the final bunch of skiers headed downward. The only people left on the slope were the lodge workers. The big cats cleared the snow-covered walls and pushed the enormous snow down towards the bottom slopes for grooming. I walked along the pathway of snow until I made it to the last stop of the ski lift. I found the next trail heading to a higher peak. This part of the hike was very rocky and uneven with loose, sandy unstable ground in between the rocks. With only sneakers, I was careful not to turn an ankle.

    I came across a few young adults camping out at 500 feet above the ski lift. They were in a two-person tent and they were outside lying on the uncovered rocks taking in the sun's rays during this beautiful blue-sky day. It was now the two-hour mark and I wanted to continue to push on. I called Suzanne on the cell phone and asked what she was doing. She was shopping with the kids in the town of Gresham. I told her that I needed another hour to be able to get in another thousand feet. She was fine with the plan and I went on.

    This part of the climb was more challenging. The grades were steeper with sliding rocks on the unstable ground. Many times, as I stepped on a layer of rocks, they would give way and slide down causing a little avalanche. If other hikers were with me, we would have had to spread out to prevent these sliding rocks from causing a dangerous situation.

    I finally made it to the last hillside at 3:30 pm. The area had manmade rock shelters scattered around to huddle in during the strong penetrating windy days. I am sure many hikers use these shelters for cover during challenging weather. I took a break, drank a little water, and ate some trail mix. While eating I sat on a rock overlooking God's Country. Mt. Jefferson was in perfect view as was the valleys in the West, East and South. Mirror Lake in which we swam a day ago was in view straight below.

    I remember being in total peace at that moment. I was thinking that no matter what circumstances in life I experienced, having these moments gave me respite to the anxiety, the worry, and the stress of life. These times give us the strength to move on and attack the challenges of everyday life. On top of a mountain, it does not take long for me to gain strength, knowledge and wisdom to move forward in life. I concluded during this hike that in order to understand nature's wisdom it is important to tap into what Mother Nature offers such as our mountains, rivers, and the songs of the wind.

    I was happy that I took the moment for this hike and know that these adventures for me will continue. This feeds my soul. The bucket list of adventures must be planned now and into the future. Knowing that something new will be around the corner to look forward to brings a smile to my face. This is something that Suzanne and I instill in our children – to always plan those much sought after adventures in life – the bucket list adventures that feed your spirit and your strength.

September 4, 2005, at the Start of the K100
Steve Hesseltine, Suzanne, me, Barbara Guimond, John Guimond

"Respect the distance or the distance won't respect you! It will eat you up, spit you out and make you beg for mercy."   Unknown

K-100, Going the Distance

At 44 years old, I did not know how much more I had in me to attempt another 100-mile run. After talking with Chief Barry Dana and Steve Hesseltine it did not take too much convincing. Suzanne, Steve, and some of the Naha Black Belts planned to join me to support the effort and to be our road crew.

On the Friday night before the opening ceremony at Indian Island, Suzanne and I decided to stay in Bangor at the Black Bear Inn and have dinner at Bugaboo

Creek Restaurant. The opening circle the next day was at 5:00 am. It was Saturday, September 4th, and a beautiful day. The darkness could not hide the beautiful day ahead. A glimmer of sunshine was coming up from the Eastern horizon as members of the Penobscot Tribe and their guests circled around the open grassy space with the ancient native burial ground to the north and the Penobscot River to the east. Native elders and Chief Barry Dana smudged everyone, fifty strong, as we all stayed in a circle with the fire in the middle. The Native drummers played their warrior song to close out the ceremony for the 100-mile journey to the sacred mountain, Katahdin. The word Katahdin means "great mountain". Many of the Penobscots were going to paddle 66 miles upstream and run the final 34 to the base of the mountain at Baxter State Park.

After the opening ceremony, we walked back to the Community Center where I helped start the first Native American Boys & Girls Club in Maine in 2001 with help from Chief Dana, Tribal Judge George Tomer and John Neptune. Here at the Community Center, we worked out our running strategy, planned who was going to run, and how many miles ahead the road crew would stay in front of us with our supplies.

One of our Naha Black Belts, Derek Carter, who was in his late teen years had lots of piss and vinegar early on with a Gung Ho spirit and did not stay to the eight-minute run, two-minute walk strategy. Derek was ready to run the whole thing. By mile 11, he was toast.

During the first part of the run, everyone stayed together, except for Derek and the conversations were plentiful and upbeat. The early sun was out and we saw two Eagles high in the sky coming off Indian Island. It was time for us to soar and have the strength of the Eagle with us. By mile 15, my ailing right heel became tender, an injury that had not completely recovered from the last 100-mile run. By mile 25 it was downright sore.

During the run, we had to make a detour around the town of Howland onto Route 2. This detour brought us into heavier, more traffic. We had to keep our heads in the game, so we did not drift into the roadway. On our original route, we had the entire road to ourselves.

The town of Chester was coming up marking close to the 50-mile mark. Chester had scored many victims during the K100 spiritual runs. When one arrives in the township, the runner is spent and it is usually getting dark. Stopping here to rest is not an option. The objective was to not look up, keep our heads down and blow right by the town, which we did. Another five miles outside of Chester we decided to take a few hours break to recharge. Black Belt 6'4" Tim Merrithew had his camper with us as part of the road crew. It was filled with all the needs of a mobile home. He, his son Logan, and Derek stayed inside while Patricia and her son Jess, Suzanne, Steve, and I camped under the stars. Patricia and her son Jess were good friends with Chief Barry Dana and offered to be a part of our road crew. They were a valuable part of our overall success, always being there for us. We pulled off to the side of the road in an empty field and set up camp. My heel and left knee were inflamed and my back was stiff. I knew the early morning wake-up process was going to be a difficult one.

The couple of hours of sleep brought hell to my body. I was stiff as a board and the Advil did not relieve the pain. I got up and reached for my running shoes. On my hands and knees, I crawled out of the tent into the cool misty air. I pushed off with my right leg and the pain shot into my heel as if a thousand needles were penetrating the area. I got up and placed my left leg down and immediately went back to the ground as my left knee was swollen and tender. I grabbed the edge of the camper to pull myself back up and tried to stand straight with the pain in both legs. I figured if I could attempt to walk a little, I could get the blood flowing and the pain would ease up. I took ten steps and each step was increasingly painful. At this point in my mind, I thought I was done. I would never be able to continue.

Suzanne followed me outside the tent. I looked at her, disappointed, and said, "It's over for me." She replied, "You don't want to do permanent damage to your body and not be able to do these things again." Good words of wisdom.

As everyone was getting out of their tents and cars, I told them I am now a new member of the road crew. My running days are over for the moment. Tim offered to let me rest in the back of the camper with ice packs on my ailing joints. I took him up on the offer and jumped back into the camper. Steve got his gear ready along with a few other runners and began running once again.

The camper was moving one mile at a time in order to stop to assist the runners, while I was in the back having a cup of coffee and a bologna sandwich. My energy was coming back, and I could not get my head around giving up and not running any more. I thought of others who have experienced similar circumstances and in worse situations might have pulled it together to continue. Now I was getting annoyed that I stopped. By the sixth mile of riding, Tim Merrithew stopped the camper. He pulled off to the side and came back to see me. He was surprised to see that I had my running shoes back on and gear ready to go. He said, "Sensei, what are you doing"? I just replied, "Shugyo, the extra step."

I went hobbling down the road to catch up with Steve. When he finally saw me, he stopped and waited for me. He did not need to say a word. He understood why I was doing this as he was in this situation many times. We started running down a gradual hill into East Millinocket and there, straight in the horizon over us in a ceremony, were two Eagles dancing in the sky.

My energy and spirit level continued to build as we ran towards Millinocket. Big Tim joined us, his bare hairy chest going along with his beard and wearing his Elmer Fudd hat. It looked like the lumberjack road race. We proudly cruised through town, Tim, Steve, Suzanne, Derek, Jess, Logan and me. We were now at mile 75, one more marathon to run to complete the spiritual journey.

The team wanted to stop in town to get supplies, so Steve and I just continued to run. The next 17 miles were the worst. The road to Baxter State Park was crowded and narrow. The traffic was horrible and moving fast as people were anxious to get to the mountain or get home. The running path along the road was an uneven, rocky surface. It was late morning, and the sun was hot. We thought the road crew would catch up with us soon, so we didn't think much of our run alone. We made the mistake of not having any supplies besides our water. Forty-five minutes into the run without the road crew, we were suffering and hungry for energy supplements. By the time they got to us, we could see the big mountain on the horizon.

We stopped for an extended time; Patricia, Jess's mom, was a masseuse and gave Steve and me a quick leg rubdown. The best part of the break was the fresh blueberry and strawberry salad that we brought, and it gave us the bundle of energy we needed to get back on the road.

The last 10 miles into the park was tedious, painful for our legs and the mountain in front of us never seemed to get any closer. When we finally arrived at Baxter State Park Gate, it was late afternoon. My energy was depleted with eight more miles to go. Now we were on a softer gravel surface leading to our destination, Katahdin Stream Campground. Suzanne gave me a leg massage one more time along with another bowl of blueberries and strawberries. Off I went. In front of us was the famous 1-mile ABOL hill. The Natives gave it all and ran up the hill recognizing and honoring their elders. With all our energy and spirit from within, we ran the ABOL one-mile hill. That accomplishment alone was a victory.

We refueled at Abol Campground before making our final approach into the campground, two-and-a-half miles away. We decided to go for it and run the entire time with a strong pace. It seemed we ran like the eagles flying. The lead legs were like feathers.

We heard the native drumming in the distance as we approached the campground. We turned into the roadway and a quarter mile in front of us was a greeting crowd mostly of the Penobscot people celebrating our arrival. The celebration around the fire was already happening. We did it! Hugs, handshakes and bounding spirit were abundant at that moment. This time would be etched into my mind forever.

That night around the bonfire, the drumming and singing brought time to a standstill. I could not be more in the moment. It was one of the many times that I have been in an absolutely satisfied moment. Everything was perfect.

The next morning was another brilliant day full of sunshine with the big sacred mountain over us. We gathered again for the closing circle. The journeymen who ran, canoed, biked, and walked, along with the road crews, friends and families, gathered in the large circle. Chief Barry Dana and his wife Lori sat at the far east of the circle as each of us had our time to talk and share our personal journey to the mountain. We shared our journey; many laughed, cried and celebrated their moments. We all gave thanks for the opportunity to share our sacrifice for others who needed us. That powerful energy was the greatest healing therapy for many who attended.

Journey 28

Dad in his glory with a Jack Russell Terrier in Ireland

"My father didn't tell me how to live; he lived and let me watch him do it." Clarence B. Kelland

Dad and Son's Trip to the Motherland

I was at South Station in Boston waiting for my dad's arrival from Penn Station, NYC. His train was delayed, and his new arrival time was two hours later. Early in the afternoon on October 23, 2005, I left our home in Vassalboro, Maine, to make the three-hour drive to the train station. This trip for me was during a busy work time. However, I was looking forward to an adventure with my dad, perhaps his last trip to Ireland now that he was 81 years of age.

His train finally rolled into the station. I watched as individuals left the train and walked along the pathway. In the middle of the pack was my dad, wearing his Irish wool hat and pulling along his luggage. As soon as he saw me, he gave me a great big smile with his arms outstretched in the air like we just scored a touchdown. He was very excited for the trip. I gave him a handshake and a shoulder bump as my dad wasn't the most openly affectionate individual.

We took the short ride in my car to the airport and waited for our flight to Ireland via Aer Lingus. As we discussed the trip beforehand, I planned to be his personal taxi driver. Wherever he wanted to go, I would take him. I assumed that I had lots of driving ahead of me in Ireland (homeland of my ancestors) driving on the other side of the narrow roads. I was hoping that my immune system could withstand a potentially hectic trip knowing that my dad can be demanding and is very opinionated.

Our flight out of Boston was at 9:00 p.m. with an arrival time of 7:40 a.m. at Shannon Airport. I brought extra sleeping pills for the flight, anticipating that getting comfortable on a red-eye could hinder any decent sleep. I was hoping that I would be able to convince my dad to drive to Galway when we arrived, find a hotel and catch up on sleep before we pushed on. That was not to be.

Dad and I did fall asleep for a few hours on the plane. At the Shannon airport, my dad was amazed with the positive changes since his last visit. The strong economic climate was evident at the airport. As soon as we got there, we rented a car and picked up a Toyota Camry. My father was delighted. He had owned Toyotas for over thirty years and swore by them. Off to a good start!

Driving out of the airport, the sight of new construction of homes and businesses was apparent throughout the land. My dad was interested in finding a woman named Margaret Walsh. He met her years ago during his last trip with my mother back in 1995 when they stayed in her Bed and Breakfast. She lived in the small town of Salt Hill, north of Galway. My dad talked about how he took her Jack Russell terrier named Lucky for a walk. We drove through the town of Salt Hill with no luck finding the Bed and Breakfast. My dad was disappointed. He had high hopes of meeting up again with Margaret and, more importantly, Lucky.

We continued to head west with the goal to reach Clifton. Before we left for Ireland, Suzanne researched this small coastal town nestled within the mountains and the Bay of Galway at the end of the peninsula. We spent most of the time driving in and out of these small villages working our way toward Clifton, and we were lost. We pulled into a driveway to turn around and an old Irishman came out to offer us directions. With a heavy Irish brogue, he asked us where we were from. We told him and he said, "Welcome Yanks, have a good trip." With the new economic development, the Irish heritage and language was embraced and making a strong comeback. The language was now on many of the radios and road signs throughout Ireland.

We finally entered Clifton in the midafternoon and checked into the Best Western hotel right in the middle of town. Downtown was small but quaint. We went to two different pubs on Main Street and had a few pints of Guinness. My dad immediately began to share his family history with me, revealing interesting and funny information I had never heard before. Dad talked about his parents and his grandparents. He brought with him letters that he pulled out of his jacket that were written back in the 1950s. The letters were from his grandfather's family. The "Shine" letters explained about hardships, who was ill and how the weather was dreary.

My father told me a funny story about his grandfather who came over to the US and had never eaten ice cream before. Dad said he took one big bite not knowing what to expect only to feel the immediate cold sensation. He quickly spit out the ice cream saying his mouth was burning. Dad talked about his older and only brother Billy. He never graduated from high school and seemed to always get into trouble with the law. He was part of the anti WWII movement. He finally was forced to join the Army, otherwise he would have spent time in jail feeling the heat from the Federal Government with his pro German support. While in the service, he was stationed on a small island off Bermuda. During his time there, he once again ran into trouble stealing an Army jeep and crashing it off the side of the road during a night of drinking. Dad shook his head recalling the story.

The next morning, we had breakfast at Walsh's bakery on Main Street before leaving town. On the road, we stopped to take photographs of fantastic scenery that included many of the hillsides and rich green fields with sheep and donkeys roaming the land. We stopped at the bridge where famous scenes from the movie "The Quiet Man" was filmed with John Wayne.

We traveled back to Galway and then to Athlone in search of the Shine Family. The last time Dad was in Ireland with my mother, he came upon a graveyard and found many Shine family members buried there. We were in search of this town's cemetery.

Athlone was a beautiful town showing off a castle along the river and a magnificent church that was the center stage of Athlone. The Shannon River divided the town in two. A wonderful bike and walking trail went right along the river. Over the bridge and heading into town was an IRA statue saluting those who fell during the war with England. As hard as we searched, we could not find the Shine family cemetery.

We then headed to Limerick thinking that might be the best place to set up base camp as the center point for our excursions. Limerick was a congested city that made it hard for us to get in and out of, so we decided to head on N24 towards Tipperary. It was starting to get late. The roads in Ireland at nighttime become more challenging in the dark. It was becoming harder to find a vacancy and get something to eat. We settled on a hotel on Main Street in Tipperary above an Irish pub. We asked the concierge for recommendations for a pub and a place to eat. She gave us a winner – "Kickem Bar" with live entertainment with Irish homegrown music every Tuesday night. After a dinner of salmon, salad, and shrimp we were ready for more Guinness.

The bar was a perfect authentic hometown Irish pub. There was nothing commercial about it. As we started drinking our first pint of Guinness, we watched an Irish soccer game on the big screen with a few of the locals. Toward the end of the game more of the elders began to stroll in. Before we knew it, the pub was packed with what seemed like the entire town. I went to the bar for another Guinness and as I looked back, I saw my dad surrounded by the musicians. My dad attempted to get up, but one of the Elders said, "No Lad, stay here with us, it's no trouble. We will be honored if you sit with us while we play."

My dad was in his glory sitting at a long table with nine Irish musicians. They pulled out their flutes, violins, harmonicas, drums etc. The Irish ballads were awesome. I brought the pint of Guinness to my dad and watched from the corner of the bar. My dad had the biggest smile on his face enjoying every minute. That sight is etched into my mind forever. Foolishly, I left the camera back at the hotel, although this vivid memory will always be part of me. As I thought it could not get any better, the loud sounds of the music and the chatter in the pub stopped. I turned around from the bar to see an older Irish woman in her eighties with dyed flaming red hair standing in front of the band. She grabbed the microphone. A young lad stood up and joined her. Then, all of a sudden, she and the lad began to sing "Danny Boy." It was chilling.

The night ended and we had discovered new Irish friends. Everyone began to leave the pub all at once with a few stragglers staying behind for their last pint. Dad and I walked back to our hotel with an extra spirit in our steps leading to a peaceful night of sleep.

The next morning, after a quick breakfast in the hotel, we left Tipperary on N74 toward Cashel. During our drive, I kept telling Dad, it would be one heck of a painting of last night's time. I urged him to think about it. He did agree, but he never did follow up on painting that scene. We both recalled that vivid memory many times before his death.

My dad was a commercial artist during his career, working mostly with spray guns. In 1969 when I was 8 years old during a family picnic at Round Pond in Amenia, Dad painted a scene at Round Pond. I remember him doing this and the painting stayed in our cellar in Amenia for years. A few years before his death, I asked my dad for it and he gladly gave it to me. My wife, Suzanne, had it framed for my fiftieth birthday and now it proudly hangs in our house.

My dad was retracing his footsteps from his trip in 1995. The town of Cashel stood out in his memory where a historic castle had a strong presence in the center of town. Dad was right about selecting this place to visit. The Castle was at the top of the hill overlooking the entire area of Cashel. It was built by the Irish in 1,100 A.D. and taken over by the Normans soon afterward. Old gravestones surrounded the Castle ruins. Years later the Catholic Church controlled the residence of the Castle for many, many years. As we were on top of the hill, an eerie fog came rolling in covering the entire hilltop, adding to the historic presence of the castle.

After spending more time walking around the village and enjoying the stone homes, we got back into the Camry and drove to Fethard. Fethard is a village where the entire town is surrounded by an ancient wall. In Fethard and in many other towns, the Irish government has invested a lot of money to restore their ancient buildings, houses and castles.

We stopped in a local pub in the middle of the town across from the Catholic Church. We pulled up a chair right at the bar and ordered a wonderful bowl of potato soup. This soup was to die for and to top it off we had the best Guinness in Ireland. It was smooth and creamy like no other. My dad continued the feast with apple pie and coffee.

After lunch we walked into town in search of the famous wall. We had a hard time locating it. The funny thing was we were inside it all along and didn't realize this until leaving the town. We immediately got out of the car and walked along the base of the wall looking for a way to get back into the village. We finally found a way through the entrance of the Church of Ireland. They were in the process of renovating the stone wall making it difficult to get around. When we got into the center court of the church, old tombstones filled the ground one after another. I was amazed at the young ages of the deaths of O'Reilly, Murphy, Sullivan, O'Daly, McManus etc. After walking the grounds, we left the town, moving on.

Our next stop was the City of Cork and we stayed the night there. The roads were hard to travel on, only one lane and very narrow. I was always on edge as the Irish speed around corners, narrowly missing the next car. It took a long time to get from one point to the next along the one lane traffic. On the way there, we stopped past a bridge and got out to look at a castle ruin. At the entrance of the bridge was a statue honoring one of their local heroes who was killed during the war with the British. While we were looking over the ruined castle, a friendly yellow lab came over to play. He had a plastic coke bottle in his mouth wanting us to take it from him. He was playful and smart. I got the bottle out of his mouth a few times and tossed it for a game of fetch. The lab certainly knew how to work the visitors in town. We were worried that he was going to take a misstep and walk into the moving traffic. He seemed to know what to do, always staying on the sidewalk and avoiding the dense movement of cars.

We pulled into the city around 5:00 p.m. Cork was an overcrowded city with congested traffic. Not my idea for an Irish vacation. On top of it all, the weather was wet all week. I was getting tired of it and now the exhaust of the cars started to make me a little edgy. I never cared too much for the city life. On the other hand, Dad grew up in the city and worked his entire life in the city. He was enjoying the congestion.

We found a parking garage along the city streets. It was right across from the Clayton Hotel. We walked over to check in only to find out that they were booked. It seemed that many of the hotels were booked as there was a Fall Festival in full swing. The receptionist suggested we try the Imperial Hotel just down the block. It worked! A room was available. We walked back to the garage and drove closer to the hotel for better parking.

After we checked in, we ate at another local pub around the corner of the hotel. Of course, I had my Guinness and fish and chips while Dad had a burger that he did not enjoy. We went back to the hotel for dessert, which ended the evening on a more positive note. The coffee and chocolate cake were delicious.

I was thrilled to be in a real hotel with the hope of a good night's sleep. I was exhausted from the driving and sightseeing. We settled in and had the lights out around 10:00 pm. We were ready for shuteye; however, the city of Cork was just waking up. The noise from down below from partying and traffic provided the worst night of sleep during this trip. On top of the noise, my dad snored throughout the night and got up four times for bathroom breaks. I am a light sleeper and at this point, I gave up the thought of any rest for the trip.

Morning came too fast; we woke early and skipped breakfast. I was happy to leave Cork behind us heading to Killarney. It was another rainy day. We traveled along N71 through Bandon towards Kinsale. Kinsale was a brilliant harbor town famous for the Irish ship that was torpedoed by a German warship killing all on board and starting the WW1 events. Monuments of the fallen sailors were throughout the town. We stopped at a local Bed and Breakfast and had a hearty early meal.

We then traveled up a steep hill for a couple of miles from the town to find an old British fort and spent quite a bit of time walking through it. Dad studied the ruins with intensity. On top of the fort wall we had someone take our only team photo of the trip. Our journey took us up the coast to the west side heading north on N42. The inclement weather prevented us from seeing spectacular views of the countryside. We climbed mountains and traveled along narrow winding roads. The backcountry mountain roads were busy with construction. Lots of money was being put into the infrastructure.

Dad was never at a loss for words during the whole trip. He always had strong opinions on many subjects, speaking his mind with or without facts. His opinion was always the right one. Being a liberal Democrat his entire life, he always denounced any Republican in office and those who supported him. He was affected deeply when John F. Kennedy was shot and more devastated when his brother Robert F. Kennedy was shot in California in 1968 during his bid for

Presidency. He watched helplessly in our living room that early morning when we lived in Brooklyn as he witnessed the assassination on television. Like many, he was in a state of shock for days. I was only 7 years old, although I knew from my dad's face something was not right. He always thought that Robert would have made a better President than John because of his compassion for people. Dad felt he spoke from his heart. He kept saying the Irish loved the Kennedys, loved them!

He could not stand George W. Bush He denounced him, called him evil. My dad's strong opinions were not worth arguing over even if I had a different viewpoint. No win or compromise was going to come out of it, only hard feelings. I learned at an early age in my household that most of the time it was best to not get into it with my dad. It was better to ride out the storm. A week before my dad's death I sat at the end of his bed as he was battling with his last stages of cancer. On the record player, I put on an old 33 album of JFK's speeches. As he was struggling with his breathing, he reflected with me that these were good times. "JFK," he said, "was the greatest." I recorded that conversation on my iPhone.

We began to travel southward, sailing smoothly towards Kenmare. Kenmare was a place where I once rented a house when I visited back in 1998, the last time I was in Ireland. Kenmore seemed to be a progressive town growing by leaps and bounds. It was a town full of life – great food, stores, schools, pubs and churches all at the base of the Ring of Kerry. The house that I stayed in sat on top of a hill looking down onto the Kenmare River and looking outward to MacGillycuddy's Reeks. I climbed Ireland's highest peak in 1998 with the owner of the house I had rented, Joop Dunn. He called the outing a walk. It was much more than a hike. The ridge we climbed was only 1,058 feet although surprisingly difficult and took more than 9 hours to complete the journey. The trail was through fields and rocky grounds challenging to maneuver.

As we drove to Kenmare, I was not sure if Joop and his family were still in the area. We approached Kenmare and I quickly recognized the bridge and the immediate left turn leading to a small narrow road climbing up a small hill about a mile away from Joop's home. As we got to the top of the ridge, I saw Joop's furniture van parked in front of his house. It was now raining hard. We pulled up in front of his house and I showed Dad the rental home I stayed at in 1998. I asked Dad if it was OK to take time to visit Joop. He welcomed the idea.

We got out of the car and walked over to the workshop. The light was on. I opened the door and called out to Joop. I then went to the house and knocked on the door, no answer. I said, Dad, no one is home and turned toward the car. Then the door opened and Joop appeared. He opened the door and immediately recognized me. "Ken?" He looked like he just got up from a nap. I said, "Did we wake you?" He replied, "It's been a long few days, I just got back from

Amsterdam visiting my mom." I introduced him to my dad and he invited us in for a cup of tea. My dad picked up immediately on the wood-burning stove in the kitchen and said, "Boy that throws off lots of heat. What do you burn?" Joop replied, "Nuclear energy." My Dad seemed confused and did not get the joke. Dad said, "What?"

Joop's children were older; one at 14 while the others, 18 and 20, were in college. We talked about the famous local Kenmare Boat Race we had entered where we took 2nd place. We had first place in sight until the wind off the Kenmare River took us off path preventing us from victory, although we did enjoy the second-place victory bottle of wine after the race.

My dad took over most of the conversation, as usual, talking like an expert about Ireland and politics. He never listened to a word from Joop, but I think Joop got a real kick out of my dad and his personality. Joop took us around his workshop. Dad especially liked all the fine projects Joop had going on. I asked Joop if he is still going for walks (hikes) and he said that he is more into cycling now and has competed in a few triathlons. He invited me back for a sprint triathlon that was going to be held in Kenmare. A triathlon group out of Cork puts the event together each year. The event was a 1.2-mile swim, 58-mile bike and 13-mile run, usually held the second week in September. I was excited about the possibility of participating in the event in the future. Joop showed us his guest cottage. It looked great with a reasonable rental price of 660 Euros for the week during high season of May – October and 380 during the down season.

We said our goodbyes and off we went to Killarney. This was a short ride, a little under one hour. We tried to find a hotel as the rain continued to fall heavily. My dad fell asleep in the car and it was a peaceful quiet ride to our next stop.

We found reservations at a hotel in the central part of town on Main Street, a short walking distance to many of the shops and a big mall. My dad had the shopping bug. After we checked in, we went to the Irish Mall. My dad was so impressed with the growing economy of the Irish. He said, "Business is booming here." We stopped by the Barney Mills Outlet in the mall and bought gifts for the family. I bought a CD of the Wolf Tones to listen to for the remaining part of the trip. It had all the Irish rebel songs. One song that we enjoyed most was, "You can never beat the Irish."

We had our dinner at the hotel with our daily Guinness. Dad ordered fish and chips and I had a delicious plate of lamb. We had a decent night of sleep and woke up around 8:30 a.m., had our breakfast and we were off to the Shannon area. The roads to Shannon were excellent, smooth and newly paved. We passed through many quaint towns. The city of Limerick was on the way as we drove on N18 and N19 towards the airport. Approximately 15 minutes from the airport, we pulled into the 2-Mile Hotel. This was a main hotel for tourists. Many buses were arriving around the same time as we walked into the lobby area.

Passion for Life

We checked in and made plans to see the Bunratty Castle. Last time I was in Ireland I was at this same commercial tourist trap. It seems this time there were a lot more people. We stopped into the restaurant and pub right outside of the castle. Dad engaged into a conversation with the waitress and educated her on Irish history. She corrected him a few times, although Dad believed that he was right no matter what she said.

We finished our meal and pint and got our passes to tour the castle. The castle was quite nice since they restored it. The circular stairs climbing from floor to floor were very narrow, steep and dark. I kept an eye on my dad as he climbed up the stairs. The view from the top of the castle was awesome. One could see for miles around. The Irish flag was flying high and mighty, waving on top of the Castle.

We again stopped by Barney Mill Outlet store for one more shopping spree before heading back to the hotel. At the hotel, my dad fell asleep watching CNN. We went to the local pub when he woke up and had a Guinness with chocolate cake. When I got back to the room, I called Suzanne. She was alone with no kids, no dogs, no Ken – a good down time for her to relax. I looked forward to my return and reuniting with her after a long trip. My dad and I fell asleep around 10:00 p.m. and awoke at 7:00 a.m. for our breakfast and the short drive to the airport.

I could see that my dad was depressed about leaving Ireland. He really loved it. I asked him if he had to do it over again and if he were younger, would he consider moving to Ireland. He said without hesitation – "Yes!" For this reason, I feel that is where his spirit lies today.

We arrived at the airport with plenty of time to spare for customs. Since we had more than enough time before our flight, we stopped by the airport pub for one last Irish Guinness stout. Now reflecting back, I never imagined that this would be the last Guinness I had with my dad. We sat at the bar. My dad had on his Irish wool hat, looking at the Guinness with his thick wide glasses and sipping the pint of gold. We asked the waitress to take a photo of us with our Guinness in our hands.

The trip to Ireland with my dad turned out better than I could have imagined. It was the most time I had ever spent with my dad. He opened about his life and thoughts. My dad was never afraid to talk with people. He is the true meaning of an extravert. I believe he really cared about people, although, he did not spend much time listening but always talking. He loved life, loved his Jack Russell Terrier and regretted not having the time to get to Paris and Europe more often. He wished he had the opportunity to live there and experience life there.

His mother May (Shine) was overbearing while he loved his dad immensely. He truly believed in his values and would test your values by playing the other side at times. He was a real hater of war. He cared about the underprivileged and believed that Social Security should be saved for years to come. He believed in universal health coverage. He liked simple foods with no spices. He could eat ice cream every day and drink coffee even into the wee hours of the morning. He liked country living although he got excited about the city life.

We had one discussion about WWII that I believe haunted him. He was a paratrooper in the 11th Airborne. He joined the paratroopers because he had a fear of heights. This was the way for him to embrace his fear and overcome it. His assignment led him to New Guinea fighting the Japanese. While there, after a work detail, he along with another GI asked his commanding officer if it was OK to go for a walk. The commander said fine, but do not get into trouble.

While they were walking through the jungle, a Philippine native saw them and headed their way. He started yelling "Japs are here, Japs are here!" My dad told him to be quiet. He loaded up his automatic rifle and moved to the hillside looking down at the Japanese soldiers. They were leaning over a fire having a meal. My dad took aim with no intention to shoot unless shot upon, although the other soldier immediately began shooting rounds of fire into them. They returned fire and threw hand grenades back at them, but the distance was too far for them to reach. He thought he shot at least two, maybe three of them at the end of the crossfire.

He told me that this moment still bothers him. Taking another man's life is never easy even in war. He told me that only four from his platoon returned home from the war. Soon after he returned, he met my mother, got married, had seven children, struggled with his profession to earn money to support the family, and lived with his Italian mother-in-law in her home. I could see why dad behaved the way he did at times and why our Amenia home was his paradise. It was his solitude.

Not until the tail end of his life did dad share his war experiences. During the summer of 2016, I visited dad a couple of months before his passing. We were sitting in the room off the kitchen. My friend Steve Waite was with me. For some reason, the War was discussed. He told us that when he went to France and visited Normandy, the emotions were overwhelming. As he talked, he broke down in tears explaining how he felt. He said he fell to his knees and cried when he saw all the men that lost their lives and are now at rest at the cemetery. Not many times did I see my dad cry. This time he did not hold back.

With all the daily stresses, he said he loved his work and always looked forward to the next day to complete his new projects and assignments. His job was a love of life. He lived to work, not worked to live.

"Slower runners make faster runners look good. You're welcome."

Thanksgiving Turkey Trot 10K Road Race

In 2005, Suzanne and I discussed our plan for Thanksgiving and finally decided that we were going to stay in Maine this year instead of traveling to New York for the annual Walsh family gathering at my sister, Janice's, house. This Thanksgiving would be just the four of us, Mitch, Megan and Suzanne and me. In an effort to break up the routine of the traditional Thanksgiving dinner, we planned to go to Steve's Restaurant in Waterville after we ran the Champions Fitness Center Turkey Trot 10K road race. Cooking a big turkey for just the four of us seemed like a lot of work and we thought going out would be different and fun. We were also anxious to start developing some of our own unique family traditions.

Weeks prior to Thanksgiving my good friend Charlie Giguere and owner of Champions Fitness Club convinced us to run their 3rd Annual Turkey Trot 10K road race. Suzanne and I had never run this race. Suzanne had been running quite a bit, and she was looking and feeling strong. I was nursing a heel injury from the K100 that had not completely gone away. I had been doing cross training, but not enough to improve my cardio conditioning needed for this race.

During the week prior to the race, Suzanne and I did a test run along the Bog Road, a 10k length. Suzanne blew me away on the hills and ended up around 51 minutes, while I came in around 54 minutes. At least I knew that I could finish the course. During that week, I stayed off my feet except for a one-hour bike ride and a tennis match, nothing to cause too much harm on my ailing heel.

On Wednesday night, the eve of the race, we settled into bed early only to be awakened by a weird howling sound coming from our basement. It was 3:40 am. We got up, went down the stairs to explore where the sound might have come from. We checked Mitch and Megan's rooms; they were both a sleep. Our two dogs, Gunner, a chocolate lab and Shugyo, an Alaskan Husky, were both cuddled up and sleeping on the floor. We looked throughout the house and found nothing. This was haunting. The only thing we could think of was that the Shugyo was howling in his sleep. The disruption of our sleep brought morning way too soon. We looked out the window on this early Thanksgiving morning to see a steady snow falling. This race would prove to be challenging.

We arrived at Champions about 30 minutes before race time. We warmed up on the treadmills inside before we met everyone outside for the start. The snow continued to fall as over 50 runners lined up at the starting line.

When the race started, I went out fast running with the lead pack even though I told Suzanne my plan was to stay back and run with her. My typical strategy, I could not help myself. Suzanne watched me sprint off out of sight while she ran somewhat cautiously as the roads were slippery from the snowfall.

Five of the top runners shot out into the forefront while I stayed with David Benn an experienced Central Maine Strider runner. I stayed on his heels, slightly behind him. I thought his pace was a good one to stay with until I seized the moment to make a move. Julie Bradford, a very good runner who ended up taking first place in the women's and 4th overall ran up to us, stayed with our pace for a short while and then took off. I looked behind me and could not see Suzanne as she was still in the middle of the pack, well behind. The roads were slippery, but the racecourse was flat. The weather conditions could add at least a minute to our times.

The first three miles seemed to work well for me. I was keeping a good pace and was not too far from the lead male runners. When we hit the next town (Fairfield), we took a right turn on West Street heading back toward Champions. I picked up my pace with two and a half miles to go. I passed a runner and then another. I was now in 7th place overall and gaining speed. I focused on my breathing and stride thinking that I could keep this pace to the finish line. However, with a mile and half to go, my legs became heavier and my breathing more rapid. I felt I was now testing my limits. I looked down at my watch. It read 37 minutes with a mile and half away from the touchdown.

At this point, I heard familiar footsteps rapidly approaching. The pounding of the pavement was getting louder and stronger each second as my visitor was coming closer. I had nothing left in me to pick up the pace knowing that I could not hold off this person. I had an idea who it could be and I was right. In typical fashion, Suzanne was getting her second wind and was about to overtake me with a mile to go. She is always a strong finisher.

She came up to me with the intent to run in together. In between heavy breaths, I told her to continue since I would just hold her back. She did not stick around to argue and flew past me heading for the final stretch. I turned onto Armory Road and I glanced over my shoulder to see if anyone else would be challenging me for the last quarter mile. The road was clear and I was in great shape to follow my wife in to take 7th place. Suzanne took 6th place at 50:15 while I followed at 50:35. We were both happy with our times despite the lack of training and road conditions. This was a great way to start our Thanksgiving Day. It opened the door for a big feast and a festive day.

Journey 30

The Rogue Crew ready to start the morning paddle, June 29, 2006

"Life is not what you expect: it is made up of the most unexpected twists and turns." Llaiyaraaja

Rogue River Adventure #3, Snake Bite, "Got Home Alive"

It had been 30 years since I started the wilderness adventures down the mighty Oregon Rogue River back in 1986. Back then it was all new. The entire trip was an unknown. Now thinking back years later and now married with stepchildren, I was embarking on a new type of adventure – a family trip. Suzanne and her children, Mitch 17, Megan 13, joined the journey along with a school friend of Megan's.

Day one was all travel, driving 3 hours to Boston for a flight to San Francisco. Suzanne and the kids were anticipating what lies ahead, but they were distracted by thoughts of exploring San Francisco for two days. By Sunday, they felt tension and excitement about the unknown. We arrived in San Francisco that evening, picked up a rental car, a Chrysler 300 (not what we expected), and drove to a hotel outside the city over the Golden Gate Bridge. The hotel was perfect as it was renovated apartments with a kitchen, two bedrooms, a pool, and fitness room.

We got up in the morning and took the ferry over to Fisherman's Wharf. At the wharf, we split up. Mitch and I went one way while Suzanne, Megan, and her friend went another way with a hook-up time to regroup. San Francisco was crowded this time of day, and the weather was beautiful in the 70's with clear skies. We walked to Chinatown, picked up gifts and then headed back to the ferry. That evening, back at the hotel, I ran a hard 4 miles on the treadmill. The next morning before our 6-hour ride to Oregon, I did the same.

We left early to make the long drive to Oregon that morning. We got turned around a bit as we headed East towards Oklahoma and then found the right route. The journey to Oregon was uneventful on I-5 until we reached the Mt. Shasta area. The towering summit covered in snow presented itself from miles away. Mt. Shasta was the monument towards Oregon. As we drove around the enormous mountains, we saw the largest manmade lake in California. The lake stretched over 40 miles in the vast wilderness environment. If we ever relocated to the West, the Mt. Shasta area would be a possibility.

We arrived at my cousin Roger's around 6:00 pm. He introduced his kids, Linnaea and Spencer, to the others. At first it was a little awkward; however, it did not take long for connections to develop due to Spencer's excitable and charismatic personality. Spencer always stole the show in any situation with his extraverted behavior. After a wonderful cookout of steak and chicken, Spencer had everyone outside and he lined up the evening's fireworks event. The display was enjoyable watching Spencer at work being center stage.

The next day, we all slept in. After we awoke, most of the day was spent gearing up to get ready for the trip down the Rogue River. Suzanne took the kids grocery shopping while Roger and I packed the rafts. Roger had his check sheets outlining all the supplies. Everyone had their own dry and wet bag for the journey. The food and beverages were abundant as well.

That night, Spencer put together a fireworks display that was better than the night before. He wore a red tie over his t-shirt. Once again, he was the master of ceremonies. We all went to bed shortly afterward in anticipation of the next day's adventure. We woke up early that morning with the expectation to leave Roger's home at 8:30 am. The plan was to meet the other Rogue River crew members by 10:00 am at the landing site. As we traveled on I-5 toward Grants Pass and following Roger's trailer with two rafts on top, debris started to fly from the raft. We signaled Roger by cell phone to stop. Luckily, no other items flew off the coolers from the raft. They were strapped down once again as we continued down the highway. We stopped at the Hell Canyon overlook (Vista) and could see the Rogue from 100 yards down below. A series of rapids were exposed as rafts and inflatables danced their way downward. We took a family and group photo from the top showing the beginning of our trip.

We checked in at the Rand Forest Ranger Station in Galice to show our permit and talk with the rangers, then headed back down the road. Roger suddenly stopped as he heard a clicking sound from the trailer. Lucky that he did. When Roger checked, the lug nuts from the left wheel were missing and only one remained. This could have been disastrous on I-5 going sixty plus miles per hour. We pulled off to the side of the road. Roger happened to have three extra lug nuts – go figure! Roger jacked up the tire, fixed the wheel and off we went again.

We pulled into the raft launch area, unloaded our rafts and supplies, and then waited for the other members of our group. They arrived an hour late. The other group consisted of Gary (the oldest of the crew, pushing 60), Michael who was Roger's age, mid-fifties, Jessica and her daughter (42 and 7). They all had different colorful personalities. They were here for the same reasons we all had in common. Some of it was just the pure adventure of getting in tune with oneself or just to find some answers to our complex lives. Whatever it may be, the answers were out on the River. I believe one must just have an open heart, mind and spirit to pay attention to the messages out there. For me, these trips gave me a chance to re-fuel, especially during intense working periods. I work hard; I also want to play hard. This is my balance.

We put in at the wild section of the Rogue River about five miles above the first major rapids at Graves Creek. Suzanne and her kids, it was their first trip down the rapids of a river. Mitch immediately wanted to paddle which made Megan feel more comfortable to enter the inflatable. Roger tends to throw a "curve ball" at me each time I go down the Rogue. In '86 it was my first time down the river in an inflatable. I was a novice and had no idea what to expect. In '96, I was more prepared. However, I went down the river in a hard shell without a complete roll. This year, as my skills were much better, Roger had me captain a raft for the first time along with my lovely wife Suzanne. This raft was filled with many of the camping supplies. I quickly found out that rowing a raft was a totally different animal compared to the inflatable or kayak. For me this was going to be yet another challenge, not a joy ride. And, it was a true challenge.

Our group now entered the river. Roger was in his raft with Linnaea and his oldest daughter, Nina (for the first five miles, until his girlfriend Sue would pick her up). Michael paddled his raft alone. Gary was in the other with Jessica and her daughter. In my raft was Suzanne and Megan's friend. Spencer, Mitch and Megan floated in their own inflatables. Of course, Suzanne was extremely nervous about her children in the river paddling the strong current. The river flow this year was at 3,600 cfs as compared to the normal 1,800-2,400 cfs. The current was strong.

It did not take long before Megan flipped her inflatable at the first rapid. She handled it well and Spencer helped her get into the boat and find her paddle floating down stream. We all paddled down the 1st five miles of the Rogue working out the cobwebs. We came upon huge cliffs on the right side where some teens were jumping from heights of up to 30 feet. I initiated the stop and many of us got out of the boats and climbed to the top of the rock. We lined up for the jump. Typically, Megan would have been apprehensive of jumping; however, since the other kids all showed interest, Megan followed. The kids had a ball jumping into the cool 60-degree water, time and time again. After 45 minutes of the swimming activities, we headed to Graves Creek, the River put-in, to drop off Nina and prepare for the 100 rapids ahead of us.

The first Class 3 rapid was Grave's Creek. The tongue of the rapid was to the left with rolling waves in the middle. Roger paddled down first, and the inflatables followed. Spencer and Megan flipped and swam while Mitch rode the rapid like a pro. Mitch seemed to be a natural for this sport. In my raft we went to the right and ended in the worst section of the rapid, getting caught on the rocks, inches from tipping over. This shook my confidence and made me realize that paddling the big raft was going to be more of a challenge than I had thought. We continued to paddle several smaller rapids and came upon Rainy Falls, a Class 5 rapid.

No one was going to run Rainy, at least not our group. The plan was to head to the left down the Fish Ladder, which was a steep narrow passageway. We paddled to the left side and got out of our boats to scout Rainy Falls. We took photos in front of Rainy and watched the intense water flow. Rainy will eat many skilled paddlers and not-so-skilled boaters with its natural strength. After photos, we paddled over to River Right. For safety, I would paddle the raft solo and my passengers would walk down the pathway to wait for my descent. We all ran the Fish Ladder section smoothly, except for getting turned around at the last part of the rapid.

We paddled 10 plus miles for the first day even though we had a late 2:00 pm put in. We took out at the first camping area along Whiskey Creek. During the trip from Rainy Falls to Whiskey Creek, I noticed the canyons were to the left and right of the river. The River carved its way through the valley. There was a river trail along the canyon walls that started at Graves Creek and I was told ended at Foster Bar, 45 miles way. There was a trail run that was held each year along these difficult narrow trails, one slip and runners would tumble down 100 feet to the river shoreline.

Whisky Creek Campground is also famous for a gold miner's cabin. There were remains of a cabin of a man who lived in the mountains of the Rogue for many years away from society. The cabin was 500 yards from our campground that sat on the riverbed. Whiskey Stream divided our campground from the campground above us. We all unpacked, took the heavy kitchen gear along with food, supplies and sleeping equipment up a high, secluded sandy beach to a flat area for our campground. This always was the tedious part of the trip, setting up camp. We all pitched in to get the kitchen in order and then set up our sleeping quarters.

As everyone was getting ready for a much-anticipated chicken dinner, Spencer and the girls walked up the pathway towards the Whiskey Cabin. The three girls were ahead while Spencer followed behind keeping his eyes open for any insect, bug or snake he could find. He did find one - a baby rattlesnake crawling on the trail. Naturally, Spencer did not think it was a rattlesnake, so he went after it, trying to catch it with his hands. His plan was to capture the snake and chase the girls. As he reached for the snake, it bit Spencer on his right middle finger above the knuckle. Spencer immediately yelled out "I got bit by a snake!" The snake slithered away in the grassy area as Spencer showed the girls his bite mark. The snake bite had opened a wound and immediately his finger began to swell up.

The adults were sitting at the camp as Spencer and the girls came around the cooking quarters. We all pulled chairs up around in a circle and began to eat. Spencer told his dad, that he had been bitten by a snake. Roger looked at the wound as did the other adults. Spencer became much quieter as time passed. The adults put ice on the bite and kept a close eye on him. Spencer kept saying that there was nothing to worry about since it was a garden snake and he did not think it was a rattlesnake. Spencer started complaining that his left cheek and jaw were becoming numb. Gary came over to me and said, 'I think we need to get Spencer out of here." In the meantime, Roger went over to the other campsite looking for medical help. I believe at this time, Roger knew this was serious. Roger discussed the situation with others at the camp. A gentleman from the campground thought it would be best to hike out of the campground, follow the narrow Rogue trail to Graves Creek to signal for help.

In the meantime, at our campground, Spencer's situation was becoming worse by the minute. He was now complaining of pain in his armpit. Gary said to me that I should go get Roger. I ran over to the other campground and found Roger talking with a group of adults about the plan. Roger asked me to run the trail and catch up with another man who already hiked out to get help. It was now an hour after the snake bite and darkness was settling into the valley. I immediately ran back to the campground, informed everyone that I was running out to Graves Creek (5 miles) to get help. Despite Suzanne's insistence that I not go along, I put on my headlamp and off I went. Suzanne had to stay with the other kids and Roger needed to be with Spencer. Currently, Spencer was lying down on a cot around the campfire with Roger monitoring his body signs.

It was just getting dark as I hit the trail, running at a steady pace on the narrow trail. Three miles into the run, I was becoming dehydrated due to the lack of water and the two beers I had around the campfire earlier. Outside temperature was in the 80s. As I was running down a decline, I tripped on a rock in the pathway, stumbled along the edge of the trail, falling with half of my body off a one-hundred-foot cliff. Below me was the sound of Rainy Falls. This narrow miss could have ended my life. I got up, brushed myself off, and continued to run. I made it to Graves Creek within 39 minutes, a sub-8-minute mile. I caught the older gentleman as he was walking up the road to the bridge and explained to him who I was. I asked him what the best way would be to reach someone. He said, "Galice, 5 miles south." I said that I would run ahead, and the gentleman said that he was going back to the campground. I tried the cell phone again to see if I could get 911. It was 9:10 pm and no luck. I started running down the road heading to Galice when I spotted a pickup with a kayak on top by the side of the road. I ran up to the pickup and started banging on the window. I kept yelling that an 11-year-old boy had been bitten by a rattlesnake and that I needed help. The man in the back of the truck came out and I asked him how I could get help. He said up the road was a Ranger's station and that they might have someone there. He said he would take me, so I jumped in his truck and off we went speeding down the road. We arrived at the station and he beeped his horn as we entered the driveway. There was no sign of anyone at the main area.

We then took a road down toward a house next to the ranger station. I jumped out of the truck and ran over to the door. We banged on the door aggressively. A young woman came to the door cautiously and I explained the situation. I asked her if I could use a phone. I called 911 and got through to the operator. I explained the situation and the operator said that medical attention was on its way and would meet us at the ranger station. I thanked the woman at the cabin and asked her what her name was. She said "Kelly." I said, "Kelly, can I have a glass of water." I downed the water, thanked her again, and I ran back to the truck.

As we were waiting for the ambulance, I asked the driver his name. He said, "Randy Stark and I shook his hand and told him mine. Now we were in a waiting game. It seemed like it was forever before we saw the blue lights. During the 45-minute wait, Randy and I got to know each other. Randy was on a week get away, kayaking and relaxing around the river. He is a 1st grade schoolteacher, and his wife taught kindergarten. He seemed to be an honest, caring human being who loved life and was sincere. I was lucky to run across him.

At approximately 10:00 pm, the ambulance arrived. There were three men in the front. I ran up to the truck and told them the situation. The men asked if I knew where the access road in the mountain was to the Whiskey Creek cabin. The medics asked Randy and he said that when he was 15 years old, he went down that road but did not know exactly how to get there. Time was ticking and Randy knew that since the snake that bit Spencer was a baby rattler, it released a lot more venom than an adult rattlesnake. Randy was preparing me for the worst.

Randy, through the goodness of his heart, said he would try to lead the medics to the access road. We all jumped into the vehicle and off we went. Randy flew up the pitch-black road up the mountain. Within miles, the blue lights were in the distance. The road came to a V and we needed to bear left to a dirt road on top of the mountain. We traveled 5 miles from the ranger station and then 4.2 miles to the V. We waited another 10 minutes for the ambulance to catch up. We then traveled down the mountain on a narrow dirt road. After the second bridge, we drove another mile and on the left was an even more narrow dirt road that Randy believed was the access road that would take us to the cabin. We drove another mile down this beat-up pathway. At times, I was not sure if Randy's truck or the ambulance could make it through and feared that both vehicles would get stuck.

We finally made it to the gate, only to find the gate locked. The medics decided to walk down the road to get to Spencer. By the time the three medics unpacked all their gear, it was now 11:15 pm. At this time, I feared the worst. We all walked the very steep pathway down to the campground, although no one was sure if this was going to lead us to where we needed to go.

As we got closer, we could hear the river. That was a good sign. We finally reached the campground at our very campsite and Roger came out of Spencer's tent. Spencer had been lying on a cot with Roger and Mitch at his side. The medics immediately began to work on him. I saw Suzanne with happy eyes as the last time she saw me was over three hours ago as I ran aimlessly down a wilderness trail. We were very glad to see each other.

The time now approached midnight. The medics administered morphine to Spencer and placed him on the stretcher with the plan of getting him to the hospital. I introduced Randy to my wife. As we were talking, I took off my eagle feather that I earned running the Grand Canyon, JFK 50-mile run, and the 100-mile run. I offered him the feather and told him that the feather meant a lot to me and I thought he earned it. He thanked me. I was proud that he was one that the feather now belonged to.

The medics called the operator and asked for the 4-wheel drive ambulance to assist and come through the gate to transport Spencer instead of walking up the steep 1-mile hill. The operator confirmed a positive ok and we waited another 45 minutes. Eventually, Randy and I thought we would meet them up top to make sure they knew where to go. We hiked up the 1-mile hill. When we got to the top, 30 minutes later, there was no sign of the ambulance. We waited another 30 minutes. The ambulance finally arrived. They got out of the ambulance, a man and a woman medic, and brought keys to open the gate. But, no luck, none of the keys would work. They radioed down stating that they cannot open the gate and will be bringing in a stretcher with a rolling wheel. They traveled down to meet the other group. We thought maybe it would take another hour by the time they would arrive back up to the ambulance. Randy offered to take me to the Grants Pass Hospital 45 miles away to be with Roger and Spencer. I again said, "Yes and thank you."

At 2:00 am and still no sign of the group, Randy and I decided to go down and meet them. We were getting antsy. Unfortunately, we did not see them until we got to the bottom of the hill. And once again, the journey up the one-mile hill began. The medics surrounded the one-wheel stretcher and pushed it with Spencer in it all the way up. They had to stop several times due to the physical strain. We finally arrived at the ambulance around 3:00 am. Roger struggled (but of course would never complain) walking up the mountain with a damaged left foot that was shattered 6 months prior as he broke all the bones in his foot falling down a ladder. In September, he needed another surgery that would lay him up for 6 months.

Once we got to the top, Spencer was put into the ambulance. Roger went with him as Randy and I followed the blue lights to Grant's Pass. We sped on the winding roads and at times thought we would lose control. We made it to the Emergency Room by 4:30 am; nine hours after Spencer had been bitten.

Spencer was admitted into the hospital under the care of the Oregon physicians. I could not go into the Emergency Room, only Roger could. I thanked Randy again and we exchanged addresses. I promised to mail him a carved Native American walking stick for his efforts. He said if we needed a ride back to the campground to not hesitate to call him on his cell phone. I ended up sleeping in the waiting room, 5 minutes at a time. Roger would pop in and give me updates. It was touch and go for a while since the venom was in his system for over seven hours. It took 17 vials of anti-venom medicine for Spencer to finally react positively. At 6:30 am Spencer was put into a hospital room where he was expected to stay for several days.

Spencer did stay until Thursday, three days after the bite. The worry of losing his life or his hand was over. However, his middle finger might never be the same as it could lose skin and feeling. We called Randy and he drove us back to Whiskey Creek access road at 8:00 am. We said our goodbyes, and Roger and I headed back to the campground. We arrived at 10:00 am. With no sleep for over 24 hours, it was going to be a long paddling day for us. I arrived at the campground and Suzanne was there to greet us. Some of the crew members were up around the morning fire for breakfast. I told Suzanne that I wanted to try to sleep for a few hours back at the tent, but I was too wired to sleep. My mind kept reflecting to the events leading to the rescue. It was then that I finally realized how I could have been in the hospital with Spencer if I did not catch myself from falling off the cliff.

After trying to sleep for 30 minutes, I got up and began to take down the tent and prepare for loading up the raft for our busy day paddling down the Rogue. We did not get moving until 2:00 pm that afternoon and spent four hours paddling Class 2, 3, and 4 rapids. I was numb all day from the lack of sleep. The day was a hot dry Oregon summer day in the 90's. We spent most of the day paddling through rapids and exploring historic areas. At the end of the day, we were trying to find a decent campground to set up camp for the 4th of July. However, due to the commercial rafting companies, they got ahead of us and found the best campgrounds.

We finally settled a mile or two from Mule Creek Canyon. We set up camp and many of us used the outdoor "groover" bathroom. We sat around the fire that night after dinner dressed in 4th of July apparel and celebrating with fireworks. Roger and I were pretty lit up after a couple of beers and with no sleep. We proceeded to put on a song and dance for everyone. That night I slept well. I was trying to get ready for the biggest rapids of the trip, Mule Creek Canyon and Blossom Bar.

The next day was Wednesday July 5th and we all awoke with anticipation of the rapids ahead of us. My stepson Mitch did wonderful handling the Rogue in his inflatable. He looked like a pro, although the biggest whitewater was ahead of him. My stepdaughter Megan decided to stay in the raft the rest of the trip, now that Spencer was no longer beside her.

Just before Mule Creek Canyon, we had the opportunity to go to the historic farm along with the riverbed in the valley. It was one of the only access points to a road to get out of the Rogue. Here we had lunch, walked over to the ranch and Roger called via Ranger station to see how Spencer was doing. We were all very happy to hear that Spencer was doing fine. However, he needed to stay in the hospital until Friday.

We got back into the boats and got ready for Mule Creek. The water flow was 3,600 cfs, 1,500 cfs higher than my travels down the Rogue back in '86 and '96. The water flow was going to be pumping down the Canyon channel. Mule Creek lived up to its signature challenge. It was fast moving and a challenge to stay off the canyon walls. At the end of Mule Creek as everyone accomplished their journey without trouble, we paddled to the left wall of the canyon to the waterfalls and enjoyed watching the kids paddle into the waterfalls.

After Mule Creek, the most technical rapid, Blossom Bar, was ahead of us. We scouted Blossom from the right bank and studied the course of action. Roger coached us to stay away from the left current, catch the Eddy behind the rock on the right and then follow the tongue. Roger was the first to descend and Suzanne and I followed. Roger played it perfectly, caught the Eddy and then went down the tongue. I followed; however, we went too far to the left. The current was so strong and I could not catch the Eddy. The current took us to the worst possible spot into the "Picket Fence" (a series of rocks that will flip a raft). We went right onto the picket fence and were pinned along the rocks. I thought for sure we were going over. I was preparing for the worst and luckily, we were able to push ourselves away from the rocks and down the current. We then went way to the right, bouncing off rocks and onto safety. Suzanne and I were a good team on the raft. I paddled as she was the look out and provided encouragement.

Mitch once again paddled with expertise down the rapid. We have a great photo of Mitch and his success. We all had another class 3 plus drop – the "Devils Staircase" right after Blossom Bar. This was a fun shoot with a large tongue that flowed into a pool of water below. This was the last of the major rapids for the lower Rogue. We paddled the rest of the day hitting smaller rapids, pulling off to the side to relax and swim. We found a wonderful sandy beach for camp that night.

The challenges of the rapids and the nerve-racking ordeal was over. That night around the fire after a hearty meal, I spent time looking up to the beautiful clear sky staring at shining stars that filled the horizon. It was another peaceful moment that seemed to stay still for a while, another perfect moment.

The next day, I got up as the sun was rising and peeking at its rays on the riverbed. The sound of the river was all I could hear as I was the only one up. I walked to the shoreline and found a big boulder on the river's edge. I climbed up on top, sat down, closed my eyes and meditated with the energy of the Rogue with me.

I began to hear people moving around after a half hour or so. Our group started to get breakfast prepared and pack up for a short day on the river. We had another two hours of paddling before the takeout. And then we were off to San Francisco again to stay overnight before heading back to the East Coast. The trip after getting out of the river was a blur in time. We spent a lot of time on the road, a short night in the hotel and a 6-hour flight back to Boston and finally a 3-hour drive back to Maine. The river was behind us along with the emotional adventure until….

Five years later while sitting at my desk at work, my secretary informed me that Charlotte Glover is on the line and wanted to speak with me. "Is this a sales call?" I asked. "I don't know, she said that she is interested in talking with you about your Rogue River trip."

Charlotte immediately informed me that she was a producer for the show "Got Home Alive" and they were interested in talking to me about the snake bite ordeal. After a few more phone calls, the producers of the show agreed to put together an episode to be aired on Thanksgiving Eve 2011.

During a Walsh family reunion weekend that summer at my sister's house in Westchester County in New York, a film crew flew in to film Roger, Suzanne, Spencer and me. The filming lasted the entire day. We were the talking heads for the episode while they hired actors to play our parts. I traveled back to Oregon in September to be a part of the filming along the Rogue River with Roger and a few others.

On November 24th at the Silver Street Tavern in Waterville, many of my Board members, staff, and friends gathered to watch the episode live. It was something else to see me and my family on national TV. I must say the producers did a great job covering the story without too much sensationalism.

Happily, Spencer is now living a wonderful life, pursuing his dream to be an actor and producer. All's well that ends well!

Journey 31

Sean going for a ride with Dad during a 5K race, October 12, 2008

"Anyone who tells you fatherhood is the greatest thing that can happen to you, they are understanding it."
Mike Myers

Sean Chooses Us

It was official! Suzanne and I would be bringing into the world a piece of us. Suzanne's announcement rang out at me on the 12th day of October while I was at a BGCA Workers Association meeting in Jupiter, Florida, at the Spa and Resort Hotel. When I called Suzanne at 10:30 am from my sixth-floor balcony overlooking the East Coast Florida beach, Suzanne gave me the word.

In 2004, days before Thanksgiving, I had come home after a lengthy discussion with my Martial Art Instructor, Renshi Javier Diaz. We discussed children and the importance they play in life. I had resigned myself to the fact that I was not going to have children since Suzanne already had two of her own from her previous marriage and now that I was forty-three and Suzanne thirty-nine it seemed too late to begin again. After the conversation with Renshi, he turned on the light switch that the love of your own child is something that I must experience. He said how you love your own blood is something that cannot be explained. It is truly remarkable. The conversation set me back a bit as I was flying down the pathway of life not thinking of having my own children, although the thought about being a father was always there, especially with all of the work I have done with youth. I have been like a second father to many. With Renshi's strong influence, I decided it was time to be a dad. Age to me was a non-factor. Both Suzanne and I were healthy and well established in our careers. We had lots to live for and lots of love to give. So, when I came home that November day and told her that I would like to have a child of our own, Suzanne embraced it even though she had been through the raising of two children already.

For the next year, we made our attempt to bring a new soul into our world. Unfortunately, nothing was happening and it was getting frustrating. After a year went by, I concluded that if it was going to happen it was God's will. In late spring of 2006 at the age of 45, I was invited by my friend and Passamaquoddy leader Buck Altvater to join him and other tribal members for a sweat on the reservation. I gladly accepted. Buck knew how I was trying for a child with no luck. Even with modern medicine, we had no answers other than using expensive options to conceive. Suzanne and I decided that we did not want to travel that pathway and wanted to make it happen naturally. If it was meant to be, it would be.

At the sweat lodge ceremony after the four rounds, Buck asked me to stay in the lodge with him. He told me that I did not need to worry about a child coming into my life. He said Native people believe the spirit of the child chooses their parents. At the right time that spirit will choose you and Suzanne. It will be coming. I appreciated Buck's words and it relieved stress from the process. When I got home, I told this to Suzanne and it seemed to relax her as well.

We still went through appropriate medical testing and all the tests came back negative. All systems were working well for both of us. We were a go, although nothing was happening. The doctors at this point said if we didn't get pregnant now it was slim chances that anything would happen. One doctor told us that we had a 2% chance of conceiving at this stage of the process. So, our options were to continue with medical intervention or go natural and let Mother Nature run its course.

On Labor Day weekend a few months after the sweat lodge ceremony, Suzanne and I decided to head to Moosehead Lake for the weekend, just her and I. We decided to forego the annual K100 spiritual run that year to get away on our own and continue to train for the NYC marathon. We were both excited about our first marathon together and my brother Rob who worked for the mayor's office arranged our passes in.

We packed up our SUV with camping equipment and rented a lean-to on the water's edge at Seboomook Campground on the northern part of Moosehead Lake. Our plan was to go through extensive training doing major long runs along the back log roads. We still had about two months left before the November 5th race date. We had a few long runs under our belt although this was going to help develop our base for the marathon.

After our 3-hour ride north, we set up our camp late Friday night and settled in. The next morning after breakfast, we ran 16 miles along the log roads. The road was not what we hoped. Lots of trucks and log trucks cruised by us kicking up clouds of dust. Many times, we had to cover our faces with our running shirts to prevent from inhaling the dust. The course was challenging and long. We were spent by the end of the 2 ½ hour run. I remember getting back to the camp and crawling into the tent; lying down to get my energy back. It took a few hours. Suzanne recovered quickly and looked like she could go out for another round.

Early in the afternoon, we decided to go fishing at Seboomook River. It was known for great salmon fishing. Of course, being a rookie in the fishing world, I thought I would just bring my pole and throw a line in. We drove to a spot where we could pull in our SUV and find a good area to throw in a line. I was naive enough to not realize that this area was known for mainly fly fishing and I saw a few men upriver near the falls fly fishing. We followed a path along the shoreline to an area that I thought might be a good spot to cast a line. There was an eddy that created a nice pool of water right where my line was cast. On only my second cast, a sixteen-inch salmon pounced on the line. I was shocked but extremely elated, yelling to Suzanne. We could not believe it. The men upstream were not too impressed. We were not fishing for the sport as they were. We aimed to bring the fish back for dinner and we did. That night we had a fantastic evening after dinner sitting around the campfire on this clear night. Stars were covering the sky. The salmon dinner was almost ready as we had cooked it on the fire in a pan blanketed in cut up potatoes and asparagus. Eating our catch looking out on a calm Moosehead Lake with the brilliant sky above was a moment that I certainly embraced. We settled in not long afterward, cuddling in our sleeping bag.

We left a day earlier than planned before some heavy rains approached the area. We stopped by Auntie M's restaurant in Greenville for a hearty breakfast before heading back home to Vassalboro. Little did we know that the spirit of Sean was with us.

Not knowing after our Moosehead trip that Suzanne was pregnant, we continued to train for the NYC marathon. And we continued to up our mileage. One weekend we ran a 5K road race at the Alfond Youth Center where Suzanne took 5th and I took 3rd. After the race we decided to run another 13.5 miles on a hot September day. Suzanne was struggling and not feeling well on this run.

On Tuesday September 19th I came home after work and was sitting on the couch with Suzanne having dinner while watching a Red Sox game. Suzanne and I were discussing how her schedule may change next year as she would not have to take care of two kids after school since Mitch would be driving and Megan would be going to Erskine, thereby giving us a chance to work out in the morning. I agreed and said that would be great. She continued, "I don't know what we will be doing with the other one?" I did not get her meaning right away. She repeated her comment and I looked at her stunned. She said she did a pregnancy test and it came out positive. I was happily shocked and at a loss for words.

A month later we went back to Moosehead on the weekend of Oct. 13th. We ran for an hour and went back to our cabin to discuss baby time. We were both excited to get away and be alone to discuss our future. While I was in Florida, Suzanne's doctor heard our child's heartbeat for the first time. When she got the heartbeat, she heard a steady healthy beat at 148 beats per minute. I was sad not to be there. Suzanne cried with joy; our baby Sean was on the way.

Journey 32

The Forbidden City, Beijing

"Somewhere, something incredible is waiting to be known." Carl Sagan

Trip to China

Some of my adventures lead me out of the country and this journey brought me to China in 2008. That year, I flew to China with one of my Board members of the Alfond Youth Center, owner of Champions Fitness Center, and longtime friend, Charlie Giguere. We were also workout partners and had many grueling tennis matches over the years. More importantly, we both have a great sense of adventure.

Ken Walsh

Our initial destination was Shanghai, then to Chongqing to conduct a seminar to recruit Chinese students for our AYC summer camp program. The day started early at 4:00 am, leaving from the Portland Jetport to Chicago, then on to a 14-hour flight to Shanghai. Traveling across the world brought us to Shanghai the following day since China is 13 hours ahead of us.

For me, the trip was emotional, leaving behind my 9-month-old son, Sean, and my wife. Sean was crawling now and a lot more engaging. I was a very blessed father and I would miss them both very much being so far from home and in a different time zone.

When we arrived in Shanghai, Min Poulin, who was raised in Chongqing, met us at the airport. She was our guide for the entire trip. Back in 2007, Min and her husband, Gary, met me in my office to discuss the possibility of recruiting Chinese students. I thought this was a brilliant idea to bring kids from the East and West together like the Seeds of Peace project. And so, it began.

In Shanghai, Min picked us up and we drove off to a 5-star hotel in the downtown area. The next day we had a few meetings with high profile executives to discuss hosting a recruitment office in China. For the past few months, I had studied the Chinese culture to help us to develop positive relationships with the Chinese people. My business cards were made up in Chinese. I was told that Chinese people never say "no", although a "maybe" is a no, and a "yes" truly means yes. Our objective during this trip was to obtain the "yes." I was also told that it was proper to address businesspeople by their surname first. Honor and respect are very important to the Chinese people. What I learned was that titles are extremely important and always will be in front of the surname. Business was also usually conducted over a meal. Final decisions were made with a toast of hard liquor. A toast that is typically given by a guest must be held lower than the person being toasted. When we present our business card, it must be presented with two hands holding the edge of the card. In addition, business usually was not conducted unless there was an established relationship and Min Poulin had those relationships.

It was a long travel day and when I finally arrived at the hotel, I was beat. We had been up for twenty-eight hours. All I was thinking about was sleep, but Charlie had other ideas. He was interested in attacking the nightlife and seeing where it would take him. The last view I had of Charlie that evening was of him bumming a cigarette off a Chinese man and smoking with him on the sidewalk in front of the hotel.

Since we had a long week of meetings and a lot of travel ahead, I did not want to be dragged down for the rest of the week. And I knew Min would keep us at a high pace. We only slept 3 to 5 hours per night during the whole trip. Although our energy level was high, the next day was long, carrying our luggage from place to place; taxi rides, checking into another hotel, meetings and another

Passion For Life

late night before crashing. We were planning the seminar in Chongqing for a group of over 250 people scheduled for Sunday.

The pollution in China was terrible. Min suggested that we clean out our nose each day to get rid of the toxins. I noticed that many Chinese people smoked and spit a lot. The taxicab drivers drove extremely fast without regard to pedestrians. If one did not look both ways before crossing the street, your life was in the hands of the taxicab driver. During one of our many taxi trips, one of the drivers looked back at Charlie and me to ask if we were English. We said no and asked why. He said we were too skinny to be Americans. I thought how sad that is for the perception of our culture.

Even though pollution in China seemed to be a problem, the city of Shanghai was very beautiful, clean, and quite interesting with its unique architectural designs. During our so called "leisure time" which did not amount to much, we traveled to downtown Shanghai and visited one of its highest skyscrapers – 88 floors. The view of the city was tremendous showing off the many buildings with the river winding through the city streets. The population was over 18 million people. Charlie and I took many human-interest photographs throughout our travels and Shanghai had many interesting subjects. The elders and young were most accommodating and welcomed being photographed. On one of our nights, we had dinner along the city street outside with heat fans. The outside temperature at this time of the year was still cool. The food was fantastic although many times we were interrupted by street vendors trying to sell us watches.

We got up early the following day, March 6th, and flew to Chongqing. The flight was 3 1/2 hours. When we arrived, a friend of Min's was waiting for us at the airport and drove us to the city to our 5-star hotel in the middle of downtown. The population of Chongqing at that time was around 32 million. The city is surrounded by mountains and is like Los Angeles although the dense fog stays in the valley of the city from November to April, creating an unhealthy atmosphere of pollution from the exhaust of millions of cars and factories. In World War II, the Chinese moved many of their factories to Chongqing to prevent the Japanese from the constant bombing. During that time, the Chinese were safe from the attack.

We checked in at the Empark Grand Hotel. This high-rise hotel overlooked the city and the many malls associated with its surrounding. The City square sat right below us. During the first two mornings, Charlie and I ran outside in the smog since there were no workout facilities available. This was not the healthiest workout due to the pollution although it was a great cultural experience. Each morning from 7:00 am to 8:30am, the Chinese people by the hundreds would enter the square and practice Tai Chi in different groups according to friendships, family or skill level. It was an amazing sight to see the uniform movements in waves of togetherness. It was a terrific way to start their morning before work and show their spiritual wellness expression. We stood out like a sore thumb with our running gear on and our baseball caps on backwards.

We ran around the square eight times estimating by my watch that each time was a half mile, making for a 4-mile run. Each time around, we would make eye contact with one of the older men in the group practicing Tai Chi. After the 4th loop, we started to get nods and slight smiles. The recognition from the elders was a nice feeling of acceptance.

While in Chongqing, Min had us on the move with many back-to-back appointments before the planned seminar scheduled for Sunday morning. Many of these individuals were high-powered women executives. They made a lot of money during the Chinese economic boom. I could not get over the many new buildings being built. The streets were surrounded by cranes. Every direction had cranes from one block to the next. Business opportunities during this time seemed to be endless. According to Min, the Chinese government provided many tax breaks that stimulated the economy. Most of the Chinese people took these new opportunities since it was a major change from the strict communist rule. Even though China is Communist, their business practices seemed to be like capitalistic ways. This new philosophy really helped the women's movement into business.

We met a Chinese businesswoman (English name – Joanna) who took us to visit an elementary school. We were scheduled to meet with the Superintendent of the schools of that district. Joanna owned many businesses and her headquarters was in a beautiful marble building with high-end office equipment. We rode in her Mercedes Benz to the school and met Mr. Laio. Mr. Laio was a seasoned Superintendent who was paid extremely well. He showed us around the school and we discussed the possibility of bringing some of his students to Maine. The school was modern with a U shape design and large open spaces for play in their center court. Mr. Laio expressed his philosophy of allowing his students to have as much creativity in their learning to accelerate their abilities. Many of the classrooms had art, music (rows and rows of piano rooms) and there was a grand performance entertainment auditorium.

As we were making our rounds and looking over their new turf field, I noticed the lineup of parents waiting for their children to come out from their classes for dismissal. I wondered why there was not a Boys & Girls Club need in China. The answer was simple. The kids stayed in school until dinnertime. They have many more learning hours than our American society. Before leaving, I extended an invitation to Mr. Laio to come to Maine to visit our schools and other Superintendents. He seemed pleased with the invitation.

Joanna and her assistant Jiang invited us to go to dinner with them. We gladly accepted and we went to a local restaurant near the hotel. Once again, the food was tremendous. I recognized a young Chinese camper that had been at Camp Tracy the previous year. I did a double-take and he caught my eye as well.

Passion For Life

I immediately went over to him and extended my hand out to him. His parents and our table were amazed that we would run into this camper across the world in the middle of 32 million people. The parents and their friends had me sit with them as they toasted my presence. It was a joyous moment of knowing warm friendships are among all of us no matter our race or color. If our heart is open, good energy and spirit will be allowed in.

After dinner, we were invited to go to the local Chinese Karaoke establishment. Karaoke is a big market entertainment in China. It is so much different than how it is run in the U.S. The karaoke rooms are private with their own server. Couches are placed in a circle, and everyone takes turns singing. We all belted out tunes with enthusiasm. On the way out, Chinese National soldiers and friends were next door and, of course, Charlie found his way into the room. We investigated the room to see Charlie toasting with the soldiers and quickly we were dragged in. The soldiers welcomed us with a toast that flowed throughout the night. Min finally shut the nightlife down and reminded us that tomorrow was going to be another long day. The soldiers kept telling us, "one more, one more." We finally did get out of there without too much damage.

On Saturday, we got up early for our morning run in the square, and then we were off to Min and Gary's satellite Boys & Girls Club office in downtown Chongqing. I was pleasantly surprised to see the operation. The office was on the seventh floor. The Boys & Girls Club logo was outside of the doorway and inside there was BGCA promotion including posters, articles, and certifications. There was a big round table for the weekend English tutoring. While we were there, parents brought seven students for classes.

We were then off to Min's Spa. Charlie and I volunteered to receive massages and to give an evaluation. Happily so. The massage from Min's employee was much better than the one in Shanghai. The Shanghai massage was more of a soft touch that spent lots of time on the feet. This massage was two hours from head to toe and focused on deeper muscle pressure.

After the massages, we went downtown for lunch at the circle of the square where thousands of people filled the area. It seemed like we were shoulder to shoulder with people all the time. I was surprised how many disabled Chinese people there were on every corner panhandling for money.

After lunch, we went back to the hotel to meet with the editor of the largest newspaper in Chongqing – The Chongqing Daily News. Jing Lee was asked to host the gathering on Sunday. She already helped with an editorial of our arrival and a news story. Jing Lee had also expressed her interest to be one of our volunteer counselors for the summer kids at Camp Tracy. Jing always seemed to have a smile on her face. She was very charming and lighthearted. She was also one of the few heavy-set women I saw in China. Jing and I hit it off. We seemed to communicate well even though there was a language barrier. She was very spiritual and had psychic training. She informed me that the spirits have informed her that my current marriage with Suzanne will be the last marriage in my life. I agreed and was happy to hear this!

The next morning, we hosted the seminar at the hotel. It was Sunday morning and we were not sure how many people were going to show up. Even with the advertisement in the paper and the articles, it was tough to know if people would come. We walked into the ballroom at 9:00 am to see a line of people registering to get into the banquet hall. The final count was over 350 people. They all came to listen to our presentation about the camp opportunities at Camp Tracy for their kids. I put together a power point presentation as Min was in the front of the room translating. The result was victorious with many new sign-ups and follow-up phone calls.

That night we celebrated with a traditional Chinese "Hot Pot" celebration dinner which originated in Chongqing. We traveled to the mountainside outside of the city with Min's friend Mig (I called him Lee). Mig was a very successful young businessman, 31 years of age and running his own furniture stores. He picked us up in a brand-new Audi and took us to the local restaurant. I remember the road to the mountaintop was steep and curvy. He knew every turn and corner, thankfully for us, as he sped up the mountain.

When we got out of Mig's car at the restaurant, many locals stopped what they were doing and stared at us. The restaurant owner knew Mig and brought us to our table overlooking the valley into the city. Our table was outdoors. The temperature was in the low 60's and a bit chilly. It did not take long for us to warm up as Mig ordered a round of drinks to toast the beginning of the evening. This of course led to shots and beer chasers before dinner was even served. Soon I was calling Mig his new nickname "Lee" (after the famous Martial Artist Bruce Lee) and he was wearing my Chicago Cubs baseball hat.

We were feeling no pain when the meal came out. It was a big platter with fresh meat on it. We dipped the meat in the center of the concave table where a hot liquid of spices was boiling. Within seconds, the meat was cooked and ready to be eaten. Each of the strips of the meat tasted great. I asked Lee, "What is this, it's great?" He soon informed us that the meats were cow stomach, cow throat, duck intestines, etc.

Lee continued to toast us during the dinner as it was customary to follow with a toast. The food continued to taste even better with every drink. After dinner, Mig insisted that he show us the nightlife, so we headed to a high-end night club with Karaoke singing. He called his friends on his cell phone to meet us there. When we arrived at this nightclub, I was surprised how upscale it was. It was something you would see in NYC. Mig reserved a Karaoke room with plush decorations and furniture. The room looked down onto the dance floor where hundreds of Chinese people were out on the floor dancing along with many dancing on the tables. Mig ordered drinks and once again the toasting began.

Mig's friends arrived and before long we were all the best of friends, singing and dancing together. By the end of the night, we were well toasted, literally, and figuratively. We stumbled out of there for a long taxi ride back to the hotel. We only had to stop once to let Charlie out as he got sick. The next day was a difficult one. Many aspirins were a welcome relief.

The next morning, we all paid for it, rising way too early for our train ride to the University City of Cheng-Du. The train ride was a grueling four hours. We carried our luggage to catch the train with only minutes to spare. The train ride was challenging with the constant rocking motion and no bathroom to speak of. Charlie was entertaining a little girl around the age of 3, smiling with her and laughing, the common communication of the world. The train took us outside the city crowds into the mountains. I enjoyed seeing the open country fields and the small huts where families lived. It was a very nice transition from the Chinese city life.

We arrived in Cheng-Du at lunchtime and took a cab to a hotel right near the University. Min had us on a fast pace once again, taking us to the US Embassy to talk with officials about our program in the US and to help with the VISA process. A VISA is not that easy to obtain. Unfortunately, the officials were very busy and could not let us in. Min would have to go back later. We had hoped to add to our camp the prospect for HOST family opportunities. Charlie started taking photos of the Chinese military guards in front of the Embassy Gate. They quickly grabbed Charlie by the arm and took his camera. They made him delete every photo of the guards. Min thought Charlie was lucky that he was not detained. Only Charlie....

That night Min's sister, a General in the National Chinese Army, invited us over for dinner. Her apartment complex overlooked the river. Min's father was also there. I enjoyed speaking with him through eye contact and arm motions. He indicated that he knew Tai Chi. He happily demonstrated a few of his forms. He looked very fit for a seventy-year-old. While having dinner, the "Chinese White Lighting" was served. This time Min's brother-in-law (a doctor) toasted us over and over. Once again, no one was feeling any pain during dinner and the doctor was trying to take advantage of us. Every time he toasted us, he would fill his shot glass only half-full and fill ours to the brim. Charlie called him on it and instead of a potentially dangerous situation, we all laughed until we almost cried. We ended the night as Min and I went for another two-hour massage at a local parlor while Charlie went off to a Japanese Hot Spring massage.

Min left the next morning after securing our boarding passes for the flight back to the US. Finally, Charlie and I had some leisure time. We spent the first part of the morning catching up with physical fitness, a little lifting and running on the treadmill. We were the only ones in the gym. Typically, when Charlie and I are working out we grunt and yell while pushing out our last few reps. Shortly, we had a few Chinese hotel workers gathering around outside the glass window staring at us. In their minds, I am sure they were looking at two crazy Americans in some sort of a crazy ritual. We followed this with a walking tour through the City, visiting the University Campus. The Chinese athletic facilities for a University was not as immense as the US although they had several indoor and outdoor basketball courts and soccer fields throughout. I was impressed with the Arts. They had different venues of theater opportunities. Chinese musicians were throughout the campus playing instruments. We could not get over the number of bikes throughout the campus. At one area there seemed to be hundreds of bikes all stacked up.

We left the campus and found an Irish Pub nearby. We ordered a traditional American breakfast of scrambled eggs, toast, bacon, beans and sausage along with a pint of Guinness. When the Guinness arrived, I was excited to take my first sip. Charlie reached over to get his camera for a photo and spilled the entire pint on my lap. So, I wore Guinness and then drank one.

That night we had our final massage at a Japanese massage hall. I did not find it as complete as the other ones we had that week. We ended up in Charlie's room for a final nightcap, a shot of Jameson Irish Whiskey knowing the next day we were heading our different ways. Charlie was extending his trip another week heading to the border of China and Tibet with plans to explore the countryside of China. I was envious of his plans, but I also missed home.

The next morning, I prepared for the 31-hour travel time and arrived at the airport 90 minutes before flight time. As I handed my ticket to the agent, she looked at me funny and shook her head looking at the date. The date was for the next day the 13th not the 12th. Two Chinese men realized my issue and offered to help. I had to pay pretty much all the Chinese cash I had on me in order to rectify the situation. Luckily, it all worked out and I was on my way to Shanghai for my connecting flight.

While on the flight, I reflected on the trip realizing all that I learned about the country and its people. I was surprised by how the cities are modernized and full of life. The three cities I visited, Shanghai, Chongqing, and Cheng Du, had a total of 60 million people. The traffic was always congested even though I did not see one traffic accident. I was also surprised by the lack of regard for people crossing the street and the constant violations of driving rules. Cars would stop on a dime and change direction immediately. The people in China seemed to look physically healthy but I could not imagine they were with all the smoking that took place.

In general, the Chinese were very polite and helpful. They are determined to be educated and to get ahead in the business world. Relationships seem to be high on their list and that is where one gained trust with sincere honesty. It would be very difficult to gain any real contacts without trusted connections. Min helped open many doors for us due to her relationships.

Also, education for Chinese youth is high on the priority list. Many Chinese parents go to great lengths to educate their children. They especially want their children to learn English. The timing of our trip to China was perfect. We were there at the right time especially with the economic boom and the world Olympics held in Beijing. I hoped to make my way back at the next opportunity. It is funny to think that this chance would not have happened if I had not had an open mind during my early discussions with Min and Gary Poulin when they first came into my office to discuss helping their Chinese guests in Maine. My climbing out on a limb provided an enormous opportunity.

Trip #2 to China

I found myself back in China again in early December 2017 when I was lucky to be invited to Beijing to be one of the keynote speakers at the Mind Education conference. Min Poulin helped me obtain my VISA and bought me first class tickets out of Boston to Newark and then to Beijing. The total flight time was 14 hours. Fortunately, the first-class ticket gave me the opportunity to sleep in seats that lay flat like beds. There was endless food and drinks during the entire time along with hundreds of movies to choose from. I sat next to a Chinese woman who had been in Boston on business and was now heading to Beijing. She was delightful to speak with especially since she had knowledge about baseball and was an avid Red Sox fan.

When I arrived in Beijing, a driver was waiting for me. Every Chinese person I talked with had an English name along with their Chinese name. The driver's name was Nicole and she was also one of the ambassadors of the conference. She had to drive an hour to get to the hotel. We arrived around 4:00 pm China time. My flight took off on Thursday in the US and I arrived on Friday around 3:00 pm. When I finally arrived at the hotel, I was extremely hungry and I tried to order food. It was challenging since the Chinese workers at the front desk did not speak English. Using hand gestures, I was able to get a sandwich, French fries and bottle of beer.

The conference started at the next morning at 9:00 am. I didn't know what to expect, but I was treated like a king. When I registered, I was surrounded by many different Chinese and international participants asking to take pictures with me and sharing their business cards. They had me sitting at the VIP table along with dignitaries from Russia, Finland, China and Taiwan. I was scheduled to speak to 500 participants after the Finland speaker. Min put together a slide show to go along with my speech. I had no idea what she put together although I was able to wing it and speak to each slide. The content was about the development of our exchange program with the Chinese. Participants were hooked up with translation ear pods. I thought I did a good job talking off the cuff.

After the conference and an autograph signing, speakers were invited for dinner at an authentic 160-year-old restaurant a block away from the hotel downtown. I sat with the organizers of the conference along with new friends that I met from the Japanese school. We sat at a big circular table with endless food served in the middle along with "white lighting." My Japanese friends did not take long to indulge in white lighting, toasting and celebrating our new friendship. It did not take long to feel merry. Thankfully, it was a short walk back to my hotel.

The next morning, Min's sister, Emily, picked me up along with her co-worker Lucy. We stopped at a bank to exchange money. It was Sunday and in Beijing banks were open along with most businesses. It took an hour to complete the transaction. After we received our exchange, Lucy had a driver take us to the next hotel near the Forbidden City. The hotel "Novel" was Western style with many English-speaking workers. It seemed like most of the area near the hotel was Western. Familiar shops and restaurants were in the area. Christmas trees and holiday decor covered every street. The Novel also had a twenty-foot Christmas tree in its lobby.

After we checked in, Lucy took us to the Forbidden City. We ate first at a local restaurant filling our bellies with delicious dumplings and noodles. Admissions into the Forbidden City was a lengthy process. There were many security checkpoints with Chinese police and National Army throughout the area. The Forbidden City was enormous. The photos do not do justice to being there and seeing the 800 rooms in the palace. The temperature was cold and raw. I was amazed to see the thousands of years of history of the Chinese emperors that was preserved.

Lucy arranged another driver to take us back to the hotel. This ride was quite interesting. The driver had no patience as he attempted to avoid the traffic and drove down one-way streets and onto sidewalks to get to our hotel. I was very nervous on this trip, although looking over to Lucy she seemed to be fine with the driver's actions. By the time I got back, I was ready to relax a little bit. It was not to be. They had scheduled another meeting with a Chinese Government official to discuss my advice on developing a summer camp operation. The officials were building a new camp on one of the lakes outside the city of Beijing. The dialogue went well and they appreciated my advice.

My night was still not over. Lucy, Emily and their friend Venus brought me to a massage studio for a wonderful 90-minute full body massage. It was much needed, and it was my first time ever having a pedicure. The gentleman doing the service was laughing at my disgusting toenails that had layers of nails over each other from running marathons. He laughed away as he cut through them. My toes had not looked that good in years. After the pedicure, the massage specialist came in to work on my back that was beat up from playing touch football and the long plane ride. The masseuse worked the next forty-five minutes on my feet and back. I almost felt like crying at times when she found the trigger points. Following the massage, we went to dinner to end the night. Once again, the food was tremendous. Lucy told me that evening her brother Lucas was going to take me to the Great Wall of China the next morning. I was pumped up to hear the news. Later that night as I was settling into bed, I realized that the Chinese extend the day to its full length. Early to rise, late to bed.

After I had breakfast, I met Lucas in the hotel lobby. Lucas understood very little English. Most of the time we communicated via Google translation on his cell phone. Lucas was in his twenties, married, and had two young children. He was working with his sister and Min developing the American Chinese exchange. He was anxious to spend time with me and develop a relationship. I really enjoyed his company. He had a good soul that I could tell by looking into his eyes. Our drive to get to the Great Wall of China took approximately 2 hours due to heavy traffic that serves a city of 31 million people and has 5 million cars. Once we drove through the city borders, the area mountain ranges became more prominent. The distant mountain ranges were clearer that day since the city smog was not as strong. The mountain area reminded me more of Los Angeles where the city was surrounded by mountains capturing the pollution from the industries and car exhaust.

Today in Beijing, the smog lifted due to the very cold weather and wind currents. Lucas informed me that the temperature was 3 below zero on top of the Great Wall. When we arrived at the entrance of the park, we parked the car and took a commuter bus that was packed with visitors to ride on a ski lift to the top of the Great Wall. I was lucky to have prepared with three layers of jackets with a winter hat and gloves that helped me stay warm during the visit. Otherwise, I would not have lasted 10 minutes. It was incredible learning the length of the wall, 5,500 miles. That length is like going to Florida five times by car. If one drove without stopping it would take five days to get to the end of it. I cannot comprehend the people power it took to complete this wall. When we finally got to the top, the wind was fierce, dropping the temperature well below zero. We spent the next four hours climbing and descending the pathways along the wall. I was able to capture some amazing photos, viewing the endless horizon.

After we finished hiking along the Wall, we took one person go-carts down from the top. It seemed like a ride you would find in an amusement park. Then Lucas had another treat for me. He asked me if I was hungry. He knew the answer. He said, "How would like traditional Hot Pot lunch?" I replied quickly, "You kidding me, yes!"

Driving away from the Wall, we went off the main road to a dirt road into a small village. He drove up to a family restaurant. The door entering the restaurant was high, around 9 feet high and 3 inches thick. We were the only people there. The family owners sat us on the second floor in front of the in-house waterfalls and cooked the meal in front of us. I watched in amazement as they grabbed fresh fish from the pool of water in the waterfalls and carved them with a sharp knife for our lunch. The vegetables and fish were seasoned perfectly and it was spectacular.

After the hearty lunch, we drove back to the city arriving around 5:00 pm. We found parking underneath the 20-story corporate building along the crowded streets and took the elevator to the 8th floor for our next meeting. Min and Lucy set up a meeting for us with the international global network owners. Their mission is to send kids from China to countries throughout the world. In China, this is big business. Many Chinese parents want their children to receive higher education in the United States. During the meeting, I discussed the opportunity for them to promote baseball and how they could be part of the cutting edge as the game has not grown quickly in China yet. I told them that Americans love the game and as the Chinese students get more engaged into the game, higher education coaches will want them to come to the US. I also pushed our 2020 World Series and invited them to recruit a team from China. The meeting went well, although like always the Chinese businesspeople do not commit during the first meeting. For them it is the beginning of a relationship and the start of the trust factor.

We left the meeting feeling good and Lucas drove us back to the hotel arriving around 8:00 pm. Since it was my last night in Beijing everyone wanted to go out one more time for my last dinner in China. I wanted to call it a night although they persuaded me calling out, "we want Wang Ken," "King Ken," to come out. I finally agreed. We walked across the street into a modern mall and ate at a fantastic restaurant. The food once again was out of this world delicious. We told stories over dinner and laughed a lot. It was a perfect conclusion for the trip. Min did mention that they may want me back in April to meet up with officials from Beijing University to discuss the possibility of conducting baseball clinics. I was certainly interested. I really enjoyed my new friends and asked them to be my guest and visit Maine soon.

The next morning, I was flying off to Chicago, then to Boston before my 3-hour drive back to Maine. I slept on the plane knowing my days back at work were going to be hectic with interviews for architects for our new wellness construction project and a board meeting to follow. Also, jet lag was going to be a factor this coming week. My traveling plans did not stop and the next month I was off to Seattle to celebrate my cousin Roger Funk's 70th birthday. Then in February I headed back to Florida for another trip. In my travels, I discovered that the world is flat with so many adventures to be made if you let them happen. And human souls are all the same. If we all could look past the color of the skin, gender and language, we can find the soul of the individual. And many souls are good ones.

George and his wife Mary at The Villages, Florida, February 2018

"There may be people who have more talent than you, but there's no excuse for anyone to work harder than you do." Derek Jeter

George Yankowski – 1942 MLB Catcher

I first met George Yankowski in 2009 when the Alfond Youth Center hosted its first Golf Outing and Fundraiser with the Major League Baseball Players Alumni Association (MLBPAA). Thanks to a connection with the Cal Ripken Sr. Foundation and my good friend, the CEO/President, Steve Salem, we were set up with Geoff Hixson, COO of MLBPAA, to work on a partnership once the Maine Fenway Park was built. Geoff brought in 15 alumni players from throughout the country to run a clinic at Mini Fenway. We concluded with a golf tournament at Belgrade Lakes Country Club to support youth programs. Over the years we have had over 100 MLB players attend the event including Jim Rice, Cal Ripken Jr., Luis Tiant, Fergie Jenkins, Lee Smith, Keith Foulke, Mike Torrez, Tommy John, Bobby Grich, Bill Lee, Jim Lonborg, Goose Gossage, Bucky Dent and many others including George Yankowski, our oldest alumni.

George lived in Massachusetts and came up to our event with his wife Mary. I immediately enjoyed George's company. He was a well-spoken modest individual who had plenty to share about the history of the game and life stories. He was in good shape for his age and still played a good game of golf. He stood around 5'8" and shook your hand with a strong grip. I could see why he was a catcher playing a few years in MLB. He loved wearing his wool Irish golf hat and he always hit the ball straight. He was great to be around, on and off the links.

Over the years, I stayed in touch with George and his wife. In 2013, George and his wife moved to The Villages in Florida and could not attend our events. In 2015 and 2016, I went to Florida to see them. It was helpful since Doug and Rita Sukeforth also spent their winter months at The Villages. They were great AYC supporters, and I would visit them when I was in Florida each spring. In 2016, when I visited the Sukeforths, the Yankowskis and I got together for a reunion dinner. Most of our conversation was around George's experiences with the MLB. At the young age of 94, George was as articulate as ever describing memorable moments. I videotaped him and downloaded two of his stories onto YouTube.

At the age of nineteen, George was drafted into the Major Leagues after being scouted in 1942 by the HOF famous coach and player Connie Mack to play for the Philadelphia A's. George was a sure hand catcher though not a large man and he was an intelligent player who studied the game. He was gifted enough to be recruited, although he played only a few years as backup catcher. He remembered the first game he ever played. He was called in after the A's were getting beat by the Red Sox by at least 12 runs. In the 7th inning he was called in from the bull pen to catch a rookie pitcher who had a strong arm. After the warmup, George noticed the first batter coming to the plate was the legendary Ted Williams. George called for a fastball. The first pitch was a perfect pitch on the outside corner, but the umpire called it a ball. He stared back at the umpire, which the ump did not appreciate. Ted Williams took the next pitch that, in George's view, was right down the middle of the plate - another ball.

He turned around to the umpire and said, "Hey, my pitcher can't throw any better than that! Where was that pitch?" The umpire responded, "Hey rookie, I call the game and you keep quiet." The great Ted Williams added to the conversation by saying, "Ump, give the kid a break, he's new."

Passion For Life

Another story George enjoyed sharing is about another famous Hall of Fame player, Satchel Paige. Many ball players and coaches complained that Satchel threw a spitball although no one could catch him. Then during a game one of the coaches who was watching Satchel closely from the dugout yelled out after one of Satchel's deliveries, "I got him!" The coach called time out, went to the umpire and told him what he found out.

The coach explained that after each delivery, as the ball was thrown, everyone watched the ball to plate. While everyone was watching the ball, Satchel would spit on his hand during the follow-through, giving him the ability to place it on the ball as he got it back from the catcher.

His favorite story that George liked to tell was about the Celebrity All Star game that he was invited to play in during 1943 at Fenway Park and that also included greats like Ted Williams, Dom DiMaggio and others. The coach for his team was the home run king Babe Ruth. In the sixth inning, he was called into the game to hit and catch the next inning. At his time at bat, he hit what he thought was a lazy fly ball to short left field thinking it was a sure out. The ball hit the top of the Green Monster wall for a long single. He rounded first base and turned back, where the great Babe Ruth put his arm around the 20-year-old and said, "Way to go, Kid."

The most important moment in George's career was when he enlisted into the military during WW2 even though he had a promising baseball career. He fought in the Battle of the Bulge and was assigned as a sharpshooter, placed on the enemy line as a sniper. During one of the fiercest battles, George was in front of the line firing at the enemy. His platoon was driven back leaving George in between the Germans and the US. The US retreated as the Germans moved toward his ground. George said as a kid he thought his days were numbered and he ran in the field between machine gun fire to make it back safely to his platoon. He said he was never so scared in his life. George earned many medals for his bravery in the military along with receiving one of the highest honors from the French.

George, in his mid-90's, still played golf three or four times a week. He said, "I can't hit them far, but I can keep it in the middle." He spoke at many engagements always entertaining those in the audience. George lived a fruitful life. He told me his greatest accomplishments were the time when he taught school. That is where he felt he made the biggest impact.

In the winter of 2020 right before the pandemic hit the US, on February 25th, George passed away at the age of 97 at The Villages in Florida. I was passing through around that time, having just finished playing for the Cincinnati Avalanche at the Roy Hobbs World Series. I called his home and got no answer. Unfortunately, I did not discover his death until a few months later. I was stunned even though I should not have been. George was larger than life. One never expects people like that to leave us. And, truthfully, they never do. They live on in their stories and their spirit.

Even though George had a Major League Baseball statistic of only a .161 batting average, he will always be a Hall of Fame star in my eyes. I am not alone in this sentiment.

Journey 34

Katie going for a 5K ride, born November 7, 2010

"The unexpected moment is always sweeter." Unknown

Our Pleasant Surprise – Kate Shine (My Little Angel Katie Kate)

After Sean was born in 2007, Suzanne and I were content and happy with our family of Sean as well as Mitch and Megan (Suzanne's teenage children). With a full house, we felt complete. At least that is what we thought at that moment in time.

In the early months of 2010, the Alfond Youth Center suffered the aftermath of the 2008 stock market crash. Our endowment, fundraising, grants, and programs were challenged due to the down swing of the economy. I had to make difficult decisions to change the course of action at our organization to survive the downfall without effecting services to the youth. Cost-cutting adjustments had to be made with our staffing. That year, we made $250,000 in wage cuts that affected 12 staff members, both part-time and full-time employees. In order to make these difficult cuts, I hired an outside consultant to help guide the best direction with the goal to make the least impact on our programming.

I called our Board Chair Mike Levenseller and said that I should be the first staff member to be cut. I told him the buck stops with me. The Board did not accept my offer and asked me to help put together the reconstruction strategy. Once the study was complete and approved by the Board, I had the difficult task to inform the staff who had to be let go.

Over the many years of service, this was one of the most difficult moments in my life. I had many sleepless nights and never recovered well from the emotional roller coaster during that time. I vowed to make sure that this situation would never happen again during my watch. Thus, I put forth a major effort to build our endowment to set the stage for long-term sustainability for the organization.

After a long day in March, I had staff members enter my office one by one with our HR Director, Heather Breznyak, to let them know that their position was to be eliminated. Difficult discussions, shock, and tears transpired during the eight hours of my revolving door.

I arrived home late that night, stressed and exhausted. Suzanne was in the living room sitting quietly on the couch facing the TV. I grabbed a beer out of the refrigerator, sat down next to her and turned on the Red Sox game. Suzanne just stared ahead in a fog.

"You look worse than I feel, what's going on?" I asked. She replied, "You are not going to believe this, but I'm pregnant." The sudden shock came upon me. I just looked at her with a wide-eyed expression of disbelief.

She went on and said, "I don't know how we are going to do this. Between our work schedules, Mitch, Megan and now Sean, I don't know how this is going to work?!" I kept quiet for a moment and then took a deep breath and said, "Suzanne, after this day of challenges and sorrow, this is definitely a bright spot. I can't think of a happier moment."

It did not take long for us to embrace our new surprise. We began to get engaged with the planning for our second child by converting the guest room into the new baby room. We waited to hear the results of what gender was given to us before we fully decorated the room. During the same time, Megan still lived with us and was finishing her senior year at Erskine Academy, while Mitch and his girlfriend Miranda moved in as I converted the basement playroom into a bedroom for Mitch. We had a full house.

Only 6 weeks into the pregnancy, while I was at a Boys & Girls Club conference, Suzanne had her check-up with Dr. Waldron and an ultrasound. That night she called me and said, "I have more news about the baby. The ultrasound showed two babies. We might be having twins." (This early ultrasound showed two babies, but only one heartbeat. At this point, it was too early to know for sure what would develop next.)

Once again, I was shocked and didn't know what to say. "Are you still there?" Suzanne said. I said, "Oh my, twins, holy smokes."

As the weeks went on, at each check-up, there was still only one heartbeat. Our doctor assured us that this sometimes happened, twins initially develop but only one is viable. Oftentimes parents don't even know. Another ultrasound would be scheduled with a specialist to see what was going on.

At the twenty-week mark, we had an ultrasound planned in Portland to make sure all was healthy and to determine the sex of the baby (or babies). That day, as I remember, was a beautiful sunny day. We were in the waiting room for a while before the assistant brought us back in the room for the testing. I didn't really care if the babies were male of female at this point; I just wanted our babies to be healthy and Suzanne to be safe.

The assistant had Suzanne lay down for the ultrasound test. Just like the last time with Sean, I was able to see the baby on the screen as the monitor was placed on Suzanne. As I looked at the monitor, I could only pick up one image of a baby and two amniotic sacs. I told the assistant that we were told that Suzanne might have twins. She said, "I only see one baby but perhaps the physician coming in will clarify what we are seeing."

When the doctor came in and checked over Suzanne, she did verify that it was only one baby. She confirmed what we suspected that sometimes twins develop initially but one baby does not continue to thrive and is absorbed by the body. She told us that this is what has happened and that over time, the second amniotic sac will be absorbed as well. The good news was that the baby looked healthy and was growing as expected!

She said, "Do you want to know if you are having a boy or girl?" We both said "Yes!"

"Well, I see the legs and arms. Here is the head. And.....you will be having a girl."

Suzanne and I both looked at each other with great big smiles, very pleased to know that Sean will have a little sister. Now we could start decorating the baby room for a girl!

During the last month of pregnancy, Mitch and Miranda came into our living room one evening to share with us their good news. "Mom and Ken, Miranda and I are excited to let you know that we will be having a baby," Mitch said. Suzanne and I looked at each other in shock although pleased about the news. It was odd having our little one coming soon and knowing that our child will be an aunt to Mitch and Miranda's child. With everything going on with our life at the moment, it was overwhelming.

We quickly settled on our baby's name once we knew it was a girl. She was going to be called Kate, although the middle name was more of a challenge. We first thought of the name Theresa after my mother since Sean had my father-in-law's middle name (Thomas). In the eighth month, we changed our mind and decided on "Shine" after my grandmother's maiden name. It had a nice ring to it, Kate Shine Walsh.

On November 7, in the early evening, Suzanne was taking Megan into town to get her Flu shot. She pulled into the Cumberland Farms gas station in Winslow to fill up the tank. As she proceeded to pump the gas she felt a gush of water flow down her legs. She immediately stopped pumping the gas, got in the car and said to Megan, "I think my water just broke."

Megan responded, "What does that mean?" "I am having the baby tonight." Suzanne responded. Megan said, "Well, let's get to the hospital and get Kate delivered."

"I have to call Ken and have him with me," Suzanne said. Megan replied, "No, you don't, this could be fun, just you and me."

"Megan, it doesn't work that way."

Suzanne called me from the car as I was at home with Sean. As soon as I got the news, I was in full panic mode. Suzanne calmed me down and said, "Don't worry, it may take a while. I am not even in labor yet."

Still I was anxious and ready to go on. Suzanne called Doctor Waldron and she said to go to the hospital when contractions start and most likely the baby will arrive tonight. Shortly after Suzanne and Megan arrived back home, we had everything packed and we were at the door by 7:00 pm. As we arrived at the hospital, Suzanne's contractions got heavier. By the time she settled in the room, Dr. Waldron arrived and started the delivery process.

Childbirth is an amazing thing. I feel blessed to have the opportunity to be a part of the process. The roller coast ride of watching your loved one giving birth is intense. Men could never deliver a baby! During both deliveries, watching Suzanne go through the process, gave me the ultimate respect for her. She was tough as nails.

When Katie arrived at 11:31 p.m., Dr. Waldron handed her over to Suzanne and then over to me. I had my SF Giant hat on looking down at my little baby girl – Katie Kate. Once again, I cried like a baby seeing her for the first time. She has been a joy for us every moment since then. Her beauty, intelligence, and personality brings a unique "Shine" on our family.

Bubbe holding the Native American Warrior Stick

"This is the miracle that happens every time to those who really love; the more they give, the more they possess."

Rainer Maria Rilke

Barbara Jolovitz – Bubbe's World

Lester Jolovitz was another important mentor to me and he was one of the Founders of Camp Tracy. Well into his 80s and retired, Lester still had a lot of energy and the knowledge to provide me with insights about life and work. Lester, a former lawyer and judge, was always concerned about making life better for the less fortunate. Many of our conversations were around the kitchen table where I would share my vision with the Jolovitz duo about the direction of the AYC. This is where I became closer to Lester's wife, my Bubbe. Barbara, who much of the time stayed quiet and in the background, absorbed all of our discussions. Bubbe's viewpoint certainly was expressed in the later years as she mentions often, "gifts from the grave."

As years went on, I spent more and more time with Lester and Barbara. Our conversations continued in Naples, Florida, where they spent the winter months. Lester hosted a few parties for the Alfond Youth Center at his home to help us further develop our philanthropy efforts with the Boys & Girls Club and YMCA alumni. Lester took on the role of President of our Founders Club. His connections and wealth of knowledge brought many of the grass root supporters of the Y and Club to the organization. Many of these individuals were former CEOs and business owners who were retired but wanted to stay connected with our organization. It became a win-win. This new direction helped us build a strong endowment for the AYC over time. Lester and Barbara also set up their own endowment funds, focusing on youth development and giving scholarships to our members going to college, our youth attending camp and a baseball scholarship fund for our Fenway camp.

One summer day during one of our Founders Club events at Camp Tracy, Lester supported us with another gift. I had all of our youth campers on a wooden stage below a hilly area where the Founder's Club members watched them perform a skit. The skies opened up and started to rain. Lester looked at me and said, "Ken, we need to get a cover over that stage for the kids." Of course, I agreed. Not long after that day around the kitchen table over Bubbe's blintzes, I showed them a new theater design that was put together by our Maintenance Director Steve Aucoin. Lester and Bubbe loved it and then funded it. Within two months, it was built. Now at our Camp Tracy location, hundreds of kids enjoy a state-of-the-art Jolovitz Outdoor Theater, thanks to their generosity.

During my visits in Naples, Lester and Bubbe always insisted that I stay with them. This is where I met their grandchildren, Will and Ben. After a few golf games with them, Lester and I nicknamed them Will the Thrill and Happy Gilmore. Their mom and dad, Deb and John, were also salt of the earth. They became my extended family, all led by Bubbe. Our family gatherings also centered about the kitchen table. Bubbe was famous for spoiling us with her famous blueberry blintzes among other tasty treats. Bubbe and Lester always encouraged me to bring new people over to visit. Blintzes started becoming a verb. I hear Bubbe's voice echoing in my mind, "Who are we going to blintz today?"

On February 29, 2012, at 94 years old, Lester passed away while in Naples. I got the call from Bubbe while in my office in Waterville. She said, "Our Zayde died today." The words did not register nor did I want to believe them. He was family to me and now he was gone. I remember seeing him for the last time in Waterville at Halloween. Suzanne and I had brought the kids to their house on Halloween to Trick or Treat. Lester adored them, especially little Katie who was just under two years old. Lester's face lit up when Katie sat on his lap. I will always remember that moment. I remember giving him a big hug before leaving knowing that his trip to Naples was the next week. I did not realize it was going to be the last hug. I remember staring out of my office window for a few minutes after the phone call from Bubbe, looking out over the North Street playground. I didn't want to do anything else. Lester was gone.

Bubbe continued to stay in my life and became a powerful influence for me. She blossomed and continued to do the good work that Lester started, but in her way. The kitchen table blintz meetings occurred more often with new individuals invited to the table for discussions. My mother who was fighting with melanoma cancer for a few years died on March 20, 2014, two years after Lester. Barbara, who in many ways became my second mother, asked if I and my family would call her Bubbe, a Yiddish term for Grandmother. I certainly agreed. Thereafter, our meetings around the table were called "Bubbe's World." The AYCC executive secretary, Felicia Lambert, and I designed a "Bubbe's World" tee shirt and surprised Barbara during one of our lunch gatherings. We had the shirt on under our other shirts and waited for Bubbe to get up to serve coffee. When she came back, she saw the tee shirts and laughed uncontrollably. We also established a sign at Camp Tracy leading to the Jolovitz Theater, "Bubbe's Way."

Bubbe and I published two books together, "Behold the Turtle" and "Fields of Dreams". She encouraged me to publish the Depot Hill book and she gave me confidence to follow through on my project. Bubbe is truly a member of our family. She is and always will be my Bubbe. She only shared that title with her circle of loved ones. Her kind soul has been a magnet to so many that have met her. They all have benefited from her love and wisdom. What I loved most about Bubbe is that she always had a positive perspective on life. She knew how to ignore the small stuff in life that sometimes got in the way. She always reminded me that she has been granted "gifts from the grave." For years, she acted on Lester's needs, always in the background while they were together. Bubbe took the lead during her last stages of life to be in the forefront leading the charge of a passionate life.

On March 31st, 2023, Bubbe passed away after a short illness. During her illness she never complained. Many of her friends had no idea of her illness. They were shocked about her passing. So typically, always staying positive right to the end of her life.

USTA Waterville Team 1993 – Bill Batten, Sam Shapiro, Steve Pecukonis, Chris Hatch, Ernie Clark, Jim Vigue, Ken Walsh

"If you don't challenge yourself, you will never realize what you can become."
Unknown

Left-handed Tennis

For many years, I have played tennis at Champions Fitness Center & Tennis Club in Waterville, Maine. I usually played in the Men's League. Although I have never had any formal tennis instruction, I was still competitive. I mostly learned to play the game in Amenia, New York, at the local tennis court on Main Street, playing with my family. I had good hand-eye coordination, so it did not take long for me to keep the ball in the court and serve well enough to compete in a novice game. However, anytime I played against skilled players, I could clearly see the difference in the level of play.

It was not until after college that I started playing the game more seriously against many of my buddies who competed with me in other sports. In New Rochelle, New York, we developed our own Fall and Spring leagues by playing on any courts that were available. I developed a good forehand and a strong first serve. My speed and good hand-eye coordination helped me land on top of the league playing against my buddies.

When I arrived in Maine to work at the Boys & Girls Club as Executive Director, I met Charlie Giguere, the past President of the Board of Directors and former alumni of the Boys and Girls Club. Charlie owned Champions Fitness Center and played competitive tennis. The Center had four full tennis courts and Charlie had played for many years. He and his staff ran the local United States Tennis Association for Central Maine. Charlie invited me to play a few games with him and to join the league, which I did. I had trouble excelling in the Men's Open, so I played in the A division. The Open Division had many of the serious players who played in the ongoing USTA leagues rated at the 4.5 level and higher. When I started playing, I was rated between a 3.0 and 3.5 player. I had a weak backhand, so I ran around it using my speed to get to the ball. The other disadvantage was that I had severed the ACL in my left knee from a touch football game in 1990 and it was still not repaired at that time. Often, my knee would give out on me while going after a ball in the corner.

I enjoyed the game of tennis and now that semi-pro baseball was over for me, tennis became my new athletic interest. In the off-season, I played in the Park & Recreation Softball League in which our team went undefeated for three seasons. This was highlighted by beating the Governor's Greatest Hits Team led by State of Maine's Governor John McKernan. We ended up beating his team by 20 plus runs.

I started playing in the Waterville Men's League and ended up winning the league championship for the A Division. Then in the spring of 1995, I was asked to captain the Men's A Team. I recruited a good team of 10 solid players, including a very good competitive doubles team of Jim Vigue and Chris Hatch (two local financial investors). I played number one singles. Our team excelled, not losing a match in Maine and went into the New England's tournament, undefeated until the semifinals.

I continued to play and challenged myself to move up to the Open Division. Even though I was competitive without the proper fundamentals and the strength of a backhand, the top seeded players beat me handily. I bounced back and forth in divisions and then in 1996 had knee surgery to repair my ACL, knocking me out of league play for several years. As I took on a new challenge of running marathons, ultra-marathons and triathlons, tennis took a back seat. In 2004, I married Suzanne, my son Sean, came along in 2007, and then Kate in 2010. Not until 2012 did I go back to the tennis court to compete in league play. I started out in the Men's A and won the league with an undefeated record during the winter/spring league. I then played in the Fall 2012 Open League going into the semifinals before losing a tough match. That is when I decided to challenge myself to do the unthinkable: learn how to play left-handed.

I skipped the Winter/Spring 2013 league and called up the Tennis Pro Jason Tarif to tell him of my plan. Jason was game to assist. Following our conversation, every week for seven months in 2013, I took 30-minute lessons to learn how to hit left-handed. From learning the grip to proper fundamentals, it took some time for my mind to connect with my body. It was very difficult to learn how to swing my forehand with power and serving was even more challenging. I easily picked up the two-handed backhand with control and strength. Going into the summer, my serve was the skill I needed to work on the most. At best, I was able to get the ball into the court, but without much power.

I signed up for the Men's A League play and word was traveling fast that I was coming back into the league playing left-handed. The first question from the other players was the big "Why?" followed up with, "Did he hurt his right arm?" When Jason or I explained that it was just a challenge for me to tackle, the other players looked at me confused.

My first match in September was against a player I had played against the previous season and beat him in two sets. He quickly won the first six games, beating me in the first set 6 to Love (zero). I had a hard time getting my forehand to be consistent and I had a lot of unforced errors hitting the ball into the net and not following through appropriately. My opponent, said, "Hey, Ken why don't you just switch back to your normal hand so we can have a match." Those words got me fired up and helped me refocus.

On the next set of the match, I concentrated on my follow-through and keeping the ball in the court. I knew my legs would also keep me in the game chasing down the ball and sending it back to the other side of the court. I was a retriever right-handed and I certainly could play with the same philosophy left-handed. The goal was to make the other player make the mistake. It worked. I won the second set, surprising my opponent. However, I knew the third set was going to be a little more difficult now that my opponent understood my strategy. The third set was even better as I won 6 games to Love. He walked away shaking his head.

The rest of the season continued that way. The matches were closer and some continued to go into three sets. I ended up winning all of my matches, giving me the berth as number one seed in the playoffs. During my first match, I won in two sets, setting up for the championship match. But that match never happened. My opponent did not want to play and told Jason that I was just trying to show everyone up. That was far from the truth. I set a goal and challenge; and I accomplished it. This was a great satisfaction.

After the Fall season, I entered the Men's Open League playing right-handed. It was amazing how learning to play left-handed helped me improve my right-hand game. It was interesting how training one side of the brain helps define the other side of the brain. I played the best tennis I ever had at the age of 52, losing only in the finals against a better-skilled player.

    I gave up tennis in the Spring of 2015 when one of the Alfond Youth Center Board Members and Colby College Professor Dan Shea asked if I was interested in playing squash. Good-bye tennis after forty years, Hello squash - my new adventure. Squash was short-lived after two years as baseball training became my focus for seasons to come.

"My idea of Christmas, whether old fashioned or modern, is very simple: love others." Bob Hope

Christmas Spirit – 2015

Suzanne, Kate and Sean and I had just arrived back at home after watching The Nutcracker Ballet at the Waterville Opera House for the second straight season thanks to the tickets given to us by our Bubbe (Barbara Jolovitz). Bubbe thought that it would help enhance our holiday spirit by bringing the family to this event. Even though Sean at eight years old was not as thrilled as his little five-year-old sister, Kate, we all had a great time getting into the spirit of the moment.

Christmas has always been my favorite holiday especially since my mother and father made the spirit of Christmas special. Being the youngest boy in my family, my oldest siblings played up on the Santa Claus thing. I can remember from a very young age hearing the bell ring around 2:00 a.m. when my parents arrived home from midnight Mass in Brooklyn. The bell meant Santa had arrived and it was time to run down the stairs of our four-bedroom home to open our presents. I tried to go to bed, yet fighting to stay awake, and then finally falling asleep until Santa's bell rang downstairs.

The Walshes' younger children, Dennis, Rob, Nancy, and I rushed down the stairs into the hallway that led into the living room where my older brother, Jim, and my two other sisters, Janice and Ellen, would be there with my mom, dad, and grandma Tumminelli. Sometimes guests of the family would witness the mayhem of wrapped boxes and bags being handed out from the tree loaded with gifts. We stayed up into the early hours of the morning playing with our presents until we could not keep our eyes open any longer. I do not know how my parents made it happen to provide an unbelievable Christmas for all of us. I imagine they sacrificed many things for us to have these special times.

One Christmas, Jim made deer tracks on the roof to make sure I really believed in Santa. While we were sleeping, he went up on the roof with a cane and made tracks. Then at the magical 2:00 am hour, he made the sound of Santa before crawling back into the window. We ran to the window to see the sleigh marks and reindeer tracks. Santa was certainly real at that moment. I remember with excitement explaining to Mom how I saw Santa and the evidence of his tracks.

Our Christmas family gatherings seemed to multiply as time went on. When we moved to Amenia, New York, our country Christmas expanded to our extended family. It wasn't uncommon to have 30 to 40 people at our house before and after midnight Mass. It was typical to stay up most of the night. My mom tried to get to bed by 4:00 am so she had a few hours of sleep before getting up to start the turkey for Christmas dinner. We would all gather around the kitchen table in the morning after a few hours of sleep for coffee and a small bite to eat before Christmas dinner. Many different conversations went on all at the same time.

For several years, I was charged with retrieving the Christmas tree. I started the tradition in junior high school and it carried on until I graduated from college. Most of the trees came from Murphy's Farm located at the base of Rattlesnake Mountain. I hiked up above Depot Hill following a trail to the end of the field.

There was a cluster of trees that I found and selected one to cut. It truly got me into the spirit of things. I had enough rope to drag the tree for the mile plus journey back to the house. Many of the trees were around 10 feet tall and very full. Mom was always impressed and I took pride in my selection. Sometimes I scouted out the tree during the summer, marking the one I would take. Even though the trees were on a private farm, it never seemed to be an issue.

As I got older and moved away from home, the Christmas celebrations continued. After I moved to Maine in 1992, my Christmases back home were less frequent. My parents eventually traded in the real tree for an artificial tree as my other siblings would also miss the Amenia Christmas due to being with their significant others for the holiday.

In 2013, while my mom was battling with cancer, I was going to make it back to be with her as well as my brothers and sisters. Even though it meant leaving Suzanne and the kids in Maine, I planned to spend that Christmas Eve in Amenia and then return to Maine early Christmas morning. However, that would never be. I did make it to Amenia, but on Christmas Eve a bad ice storm hit Maine. Many homes lost electricity and Suzanne called to tell me that our house was without power, too. I told my mom and, with disappointment in her eyes, she knew I had only one choice and that was to go back to Maine. I wished everyone a Merry Christmas and drove the 6 hours back home. My mom passed away three months later.

Although there was no electricity in Maine, that Christmas was still one of my best. We gathered around the fireplace for heat, which kept the house warm for quite a while. Suzanne and I played games with the kids, talked about Santa under the candlelight and went to bed early. The morning came with still no electricity so we bundled up and celebrated Christmas anyway. That afternoon the power came back on just in time for our family dinner. What I remember most was that we had no distractions: no video games, no TV or iPads, just us. Perhaps that was Mom's present to us. In her weakened state with no gifts to wrap, no energy to cook, and far away in New York, she gave us the spirit of Christmas.

My family's spirit of Christmas taught me how to share it with the less fortunate. At work, assisting many children of need at the Boys & Girls Clubs and YMCA, I came across many youth who deserved a better holiday season. For years, our donors gave us the support to buy gifts for these kids. And because of these contributions, less fortunate children and youth did have a better Christmas. At times, I dressed up as Santa Claus and handed out the gifts. One time I did it from the rooftop of the Alfond Youth Center and threw down gifts to kids in front of the building.

Christmas in 2001 was also very special. There were six-year-old twin boys, Josh and Jacob who came to the Boys and Girls Club every day. Their hard-working mom did all she could to support the kids on her single income. They had a small two-bedroom apartment in the South End of Waterville and the boys attended the Club every day while their mom worked and went to school. I heard that the twins were going to have a limited Christmas. That is when I started rallying the troops at the AYC to help support their Christmas. And they did! Before I knew it, the kids had gifts such as skateboards, baseball mitts, footballs, ski jackets, games, toys, more than anyone could imagine. I talked to the kids' mom ahead of time to let her know that I would be coming over early Christmas morning to deliver gifts. She was thankful and excited for the boys. She assured me the door was going to be unlocked for my visit.

    I rented out a Santa suit and on Christmas morning got up with Suzanne at 4:30 am to travel from Vassalboro to Waterville with two large duffle bags of gifts from Santa to deliver. We arrived at their apartment around 5:00 am. The city streets were still and quiet with snow on the ground and Christmas lights still on at some homes. The apartment door was unlocked and there was a night light on as we crept in. The twins' room was directly across from the doorway and their door was open about six inches. Josh and Jacob were sleeping in their bunk beds. I turned on the hallway light and opened the door fully and shouted, "Ho, Ho, Ho, Merry Christmas." The boys jumped up with their eyes wide open. It had to be unnerving having a big fat man in their doorway in a red suit. Their Mom came to the bedroom door and the boys finally got what was going on. We all went into the living room around their small Christmas tree and I started handing out one gift after another. They were in disbelief. I handed the last one out and said, "Now I have to go to deliver more gifts!" The kids started following me out the door. Their Mom said, "Let Santa go, he still has lots of work to do." I said, "Be good to your mom and Merry Christmas." And off I went.

    Josh and Jacob continued to come to the Club until their teen years. They both excelled in academics and sports. They became all-star athletes, earning scholarships to college. At our awards dinner in 2015, at the age of twenty, they spoke to our crowd thanking their mom for her unconditional love and for giving them an opportunity even though the challenges were difficult at times. They did mention that special morning and said they learned the spirit of Christmas and the meaning of hope that morning. They said that they recently found out who was behind that red outfit and they thanked me publicly for that day.

    These fond Christmas memories inspire me to make the holiday spirit as real as possible for my own kids, Sean and Kate. At our new house on Crowell Hill Road when Sean was 2 1/2, I dressed in a Santa outfit early in the morning when it was still dark and waited for Sean and Suzanne to come down the stairs. The only light was the glow of the Christmas tree. I was sipping hot cocoa and having a cookie when Sean spotted Santa for the first time in his house. I remember him being very cautious as he came down the stairs holding Mom's hand. Mom, of course, kept saying, "It's Santa, Sean." Sean had recently watched the Polar Express for the first time and understood the bell, his first Christmas gift. I handed him his very first bell. I said my Ho Ho Ho's and I went into the garage. When I left, Sean cried out "That was Santa!"

I went outside, entered the house from the basement bulkhead and dressed in the cellar. I came up the stairs while little Sean was busy opening his first Santa gifts. I said, "Sean, I heard something outside, what was that?" He said in his sweet little voice, "That was Santa!" In that moment, the spirit of Christmas was pure and completely magical for all three of us.

During many summers, we would spend a week camping in New Hampshire, near Santa's Village. Even during the hot summer, the magic of Christmas is at this park. We all love going there. On another year at the Alfond Youth Center, I dressed up as Santa and walked the hallways as kids arrived for our After School Program. I went into the preschool childcare program where little Kate was attending. I did the entire Santa act with the Ho, Ho, Ho's and what do you want for Christmas. Luckily, Kate at the age of five did not pick up that it was me. That night I asked her if she saw Santa. She said, "Yes, Santa sounded just like you, Daddy!" I knew then that my days playing Santa for my kids were coming to an end.

2017 Team photo

"Thanksgiving.... A day to stuff my face and play and watch football." KAW

Annual Thanksgiving Touch Football Game

    On the eve of our annual Thanksgiving touch football game, I always reflect back to the many games played in my life during this wonderful holiday. Ever since I was a little boy, my brothers and I, along with the neighborhood gang, would play this classic game from the city streets in Brooklyn to the country fields in Amenia to the football fields in New Rochelle, Briar Cliff Manor and now in the great State of Maine at Maine's Fenway Park.
    The tradition started when I was nine with my brothers, Rob and Dennis, throwing passes in front of our house in Brooklyn. From there the games would be carried out onto the city street playing 3 on 3, no first downs and the street sewer caps marking the TD. Many of our skills developed on these streets as cars lined up along the narrowed street where we had 12 feet to work with for passes. However, the real strategy of the game developed when there was a gap between

cars or a junk car that sat on the street for weeks. I remember it like it was yesterday playing a game and the neighborhood quarterback would say, "Johnny, you do a stop and go, Tony, a button hook and Kenny a down and out in between the junk car and the blue car."

With running plays, it was next to impossible to get anywhere unless the player had good blocking and the spin move was key to get around your defender. As a little kid, I had good wheels and used the juke and often fake to one side, the other side and then off to the end zone. I was also able to cut on the dime, which helped years later in other sports.

When we moved to Amenia, the football games changed to playing Kill the Carrier, which turned out to always be a short game due to bloody noses or worse — broken fingers or jaw. The game was simple. Whoever had the ball was open target to get tackled by all the others playing the game. This game worked well for someone fast or a strong fullback type. My strategy was to outlast everyone using my speed and my "jukes." Since I was a little guy as soon as someone got a hold of me, I released the ball for someone else to pick up. I also remember the many games in junior high and high school. We played full tackle games with no pads, just a straight-out brawl.

I vividly recall one game during my junior year on Thanksgiving weekend. At Webutuck High School, I played Varsity basketball, soccer and baseball. I was also the Class President and rallied the troops to play a full tackle football game at Amenia Elementary on the same field that the semi-pro Amenia Monarchs baseball team played. Many had played in our school intramural team, the Mario Nostrum Fugaroller (MNF) Gang. The turnout was tremendous that Saturday morning after Thanksgiving. We had 20 players show up. It was an intense game and many of our players were good athletes. If our basketball coach Earl Sussman ever knew we were playing this game, especially in the beginning of basketball season, he would have flipped. The game went back and forth with scores and good hits. I clearly remember during the kickoff; I received the ball and was heading up the left sideline and out of nowhere my good friend Tom Flood came flying at me. Tommy loved football and since we only had a soccer team, he unleashed his energy on the field that day to show his passion for the game. Tommy was short but built like a linebacker. He was pumped to hit and hit hard. I came running up the sideline with the end zone in sight and then came the Mack truck. Tommy cleaned my clock sending me into the sidelines and knocking me out of my cleats. I am sure everyone else on the field thought I was dead. Tommy was lying on top of me, crushed into my body. He pulled me up by my NY Jet number 14 jersey and said, "You OK little buddy. I finally caught up to you. Isn't this game great!?" All I could say in a daze was, "You betcha," thinking I need him on my side next time.

During college days, our family would have the traditional big Thanksgiving dinner at our house. My mom would stay up half the night getting ready for the feast, knowing all the family would be home with their significant others or friends. Not one Thanksgiving could I remember that less than twenty of us were at the table. Before the feast, many of us ran the Murphy Hill five-mile loop. It was a one mile straight up hill that led into a 5-mile run. Of course, Dennis, Rob and I would start off talking about this being a fun run and would lead to a competitive road race. Dennis typically had the advantage and would pass us at the end, even though Rob would push the pace to get into Dennis's head. After the run, our cool-down was 3 on 3 football on the street in front of our house. We recruited our oldest brother, Jim, our brother-in-law, and boyfriends of our sisters and would play for an hour or so before dinner.

One game that stays in my mind was a three-on-three match in the mid '80s. The teams were me, my brother Rob and my buddy, Andrew Erskine, against my brother Jim, his brother-in-law, Norm Fontaine, and Dennis. Our game plan was simply to run them to death. Rob called for one fly pattern after the next (the bomb). For the first few series, they tried to stay with us, but eventually they were spent, and it resulted in a blowout game. Rob could not help but gloat at the "Top of the Stretch" bar that night as we enjoyed our holiday drinks.

Thanksgiving football continued and I got more serious in the game playing for the New Rochelle N.Y. Giants touch football team in the Westchester league. We played football every Sunday from September to the end of December. We had one of the craftiest quarterbacks in the league, Rich Marano. He planned many plays ahead of time to get any advantage against the opponent. We won many more times than we lost. Unfortunately, my playing days ended abruptly early in the 1989 season when I tore up my left knee with an ACL injury at 29 years old. Although the recovery was quick, the knee was never to be the same. My quick cuts and explosive push-off were limited.

When I moved to Maine in 1992, I continued to bring my enthusiasm for the game to Waterville. The first year I was there, I recruited friends and Board members of the Boys & Girls Club, most all in their forties, to play a touch football game at Drummond football field. It was an icy cold Thanksgiving weekend. Seven on seven filled the field. The game was played on the full field, which made it very challenging to keep up with the fast pace and wind sprints. The game did not last long. Half the players were on the sideline with pulled muscles, hurt shoulders and bruised bodies. This was their first and last time playing with me.

Soon after that game, I started thinking about how to bring a touch football league back for the fall of '93. Recruitment started immediately. The first was finding a good quarterback and I did: Joel Lavenson. Joel was a strong, intelligent athlete who had played college football as QB. Then, I went after big receivers: Doug Frame and Joe Jabar Jr. both were six feet four with good hands. I rounded the team off with a gutsy athletic rugby player, Jay Saulter. We filled in the other two spots with other players. The next three seasons we played other teams in the area without losing a game. Our game was at a fast pace with great plays drawn up by Joel.

But once again, after a few injuries, our team faded. However, we all remember those magical games. There was one play that we were famous for that usually resulted in a touchdown. It was the fake drop downplay. Doug Frame would take three steps and fake falling on the ground. Joel would pump a fake pass to Jay and then Doug would get up for again an easy wide-open pass for a TD.

Now years later, after building the field at Camp Tracy in Oakland, Maine, Maine's Fenway Park is where we play each Thanksgiving weekend. Some die-hard Board members show up every year along with many of my younger staff members at the Alfond Youth Center. My good buddy and longtime friend and former University of Hartford QB, Joel Lavenson, in his '70's with a hip replacement still plays with us. The games have been played in all kinds of weather and no cancellations. One year, we had 6 inches of snow on the ground. It was a slow-moving game, but a good competitive one. Playing to seven points, it came down to a tie at six when the team I was playing against won on its last drive.

The body does not do what it used to do now that I am in my early sixties, but I use my other abilities to play the game and have fun. Where my speed was a factor in the past, my knowledge and sense of space is more important now. For me, Thanksgiving will always relate to touch football. There is nothing like being on the Grid Iron.

Its meaning became even more important to me in 2017 when my ten-year-old son, Sean, played with us for the first time. He played on my team along with Patrick Guerette and Mike Levenseller. Most of us were 50 years and older and he was the new young rookie. His fresh young legs made some key defense plays. Sean caught his first catch on the Grid Iron. For Sean, it is the beginning of many more years of playing Thanksgiving football.

It is a great Walsh family tradition!

Todd and Steve Waite with Baseball HOF Peter Gammons at Fenway Park. Reunion 2014.

"Don't limit your challenges. Challenge your limits." Unknown

Steve Waite, The Quality of Courage

I met Stevie Waite in 1980 while I was working as the Director of the Millerton Day Camp in New York. I was 19 years old. It was my first job overseeing staff and running a summer recreation program while on college break.

Stevie and his gang came from the hill off Main Street. Every day they came down to play ball; either stickball, softball or basketball. During the mornings, I developed a curriculum similar to what I remembered as a kid attending Amenia Recreation. Sports, arts & crafts, swim lessons and games in the morning, then open swimming in the afternoon. Millerton had the only in-ground pool in the area and it was a big attraction for many kids.

That summer my brother, Rob, took a job as the Amenia Recreation Director. Our dinner discussions around the Walsh family table were always comparing and challenging each other to the point of creating the first Amenia versus Millerton Olympics. My brother, a junior at Fordham University, studied politics and quickly shared how he was going to make the challenge into a circus in the local paper. I had a different approach. I was a coach at heart and thought about how I was going to prepare my kids to get ready for the event and give it their all while also having fun.

A month away from the Olympics, Stevie, a mild-mannered and polite 12-year-old, helped round up the Millerton athletes and brought them down each morning to prepare for the Olympics, scheduled for August. With Stevie came the Lalonde brothers (Judd, Jake, Ben and Joel), Greg Babet, Trevor Stickles, Brian Watkins (Webutuck HS gym teacher's son) Gary Burke, David Carson, Steve's younger brothers Rob and Todd along with Yvonne, Malcom and Violette Davis. This was the core crew. All of these kids had heart, but it was not until years later that I realized none of them had the tremendous drive and heart of Stevie Waite.

That summer we trained religiously each day with a set schedule to prepare for the Olympics. My brother and I discussed the schedule of where and when each event would take place. We had the strength in the pool while Amenia had the strength on the tennis court since the pool was in Millerton and the tennis court in Amenia. The other events were up in the air. Thirteen-year-old, Yvonne Davis, committed to playing tennis and practiced with her dad on her own time. She ended up winning the gold. She also won the gold in life years later in supporting international training and supporting others.

Leading up to the competition, Rob reached out to the Amenia and Millerton newspapers to get coverage and, boy, did he! The front page in the sports section had photos of Rob and me, with me pointing at Rob saying, "I want you." The Rocky movie motivated me to make that gesture, while Rob was photographed licking his fingers acting like he was throwing a spitball. The paper played up more on the rivalry of the Walsh brothers rather than the kids. That set the stage for a competitive event that lasted a week.

Stevie was our captain and set the attitude for the rest of the team. Even during the hottest days, he rallied the group to come to practice. He competed in almost all events and won gold medals in his events. In contrast to Rob's leadership, our team had matching navy blue shirts with the Olympic Rings and our logo on them. We made our own Millerton Olympic flag and we practiced how to march onto the field. When we got off the bus, our team of six 13-year olds looked like the West Point Cadets getting ready for battle. On the other hand, Rob's kids came off the bus looking like the little Rascals, hats on backwards, tee shirts hanging out of their shorts, and kids scattering in all directions.

The weeklong competition went to the wire with our team behind in points and only the Cross Country event left. I had my top runners, including Stevie, out against Amenia's top five. The run was one mile, four times around the baseball field. Stevie started off in the middle of the pack and paced himself until the final lap before he kicked it in to take the gold medal and helped us win the Track event. This created a tie in the Olympics.

Pride developed from that summer and for the Millerton kids. It was a foundation that was built for years to come. The following summer, we shut out Amenia by 100 points to their zero. We also competed in the Dutchess County Olympics in which many of our kids took home the Gold including Stevie's 8-year-old brother Todd who earned four gold medals.

After the summer of 1981, I went on to be Director of Kent, Connecticut's Park and Recreation Department during my summer college recess. I slowly lost contact with Stevie and the gang. I did follow them through high school sports where Stevie excelled being a natural athlete in soccer, basketball, baseball and track. He was All-County in each of them and could have gone on to play college sports, but the Air Force was his calling.

In 1985, I received my bachelor's degree from SUNY Cortland in Physical Education and was soon offered a job at the Boys & Girls Clubs of New Rochelle as Unit Director of one of their three branches. It was two years later that I got the dreadful letter from Stevie.

I was in my office preparing for the Spring softball leagues when a letter was dropped off on my desk by my secretary. On the white envelope was choppy handwriting addressed to me and the return address was from the veteran hospital located in Westchester County. I opened the letter, which I still have today. The letter was a typed message from Stevie (someone must have helped him) informing me of his accident.

He told me in his letter that he first wanted to thank me for giving him the drive to take on challenges and to never quit even though he now has his most difficult battle in front of him. In 1987 while on military leave, he was asked to join his friends for a party. Stevie wasn't drinking although his friends were. While horsing around, one of his buddies picked him upside down and slipped. Stevie came crashing to the ground headfirst, breaking his neck. It severed his C6 vertebra. He went on to say that no matter what his physical life may be, he will continue to work on fulfilling his dreams even though that was now altered.

He said he wanted to see me, so I made the trip. I braced myself, preparing for the worst. As I entered his hospital room, I found Stevie in bed propped up with his neck in a brace. When he saw me, he immediately had the Stevie Waite bright smile. "Ken, about time you got here".

"How are doing buddy. It's been a while."

"I could be better." He explained what happened and had no ill feeling towards his friend.

I was blown away not knowing what to say or do. Here was a vibrant young man now physically immobilized. I tried to put my game face on and launched into how it is early and with good hard work, I thought things could change. Stevie stopped me after a few minutes of my lame attempt to motivate him and said, "Ken, you have nothing to worry about. I will be fine with or without my body. You taught me the don't quit attitude and I intend to move on in a positive matter."

His reply stopped me in my tracks and the conversation slowed down. I wished him well and told him that if he needed anything, I was 30 minutes away in New Rochelle. We stayed in touch for a while although what I understand now Stevie was focused hard on his recovery. As a former athlete, he hit rehab with the hopes to gain strength in the areas of his body that could respond. He never would walk again but through hard work he gained limited activity back into his arms.

We lost touch after a few years and I moved to Maine to take my new position at the Boys & Girls Club in Waterville. Not until 2014, nearly twenty-seven years later, did we reunite when I was asked to participate in a book signing event for the Depot Hill Gang book at the Millerton Library. I was excited to go back to the town where my Recreation career was developed. Former teachers, friends and family came for the signing and speech.

Then, the door opened in the back of the library and a middle-age man in a wheelchair came through. It was Stevie Waite. Steve had his typical wide bright smile. "Kenny, I couldn't miss this." "Hey Stevie, how are you doing buddy, what have you been up to?" "You know, hanging in there and causing trouble."

Steve got me caught up on his life. He worked hard in the gym to strengthen his body, soon setting goals to compete in the Special Olympics in which he excelled. He went back to school showing interest in writing and motivating others. He visited many high schools, including our former high school speaking to students about challenging oneself against all odds. His former soccer coach, Ron O'Keefe, asked him to help coach the Varsity Soccer team. The two developed great squads during their time together.

At one point, Steve moved to Florida for a while and then came back home to Millerton, buying a home, a van, and a small house with a backyard for his dad. His family has rallied around him, supporting his condition and bonding as a family. Then tragedy struck again. In the early '90s Steve's youngest brother and our Millerton Olympic star, Todd Waite, committed suicide at the young age of 20. This hit Stevie hard and to this day, he is still working through it.

I caught Steve up with my adventures and family. I told him that I was proud of him and that I would not let go of this reunion. We both promised to keep the connection going. This is when the bucket list conversation started. I told Steve I wanted 100 items to be sent to me within a week. Steve, said, "Do you think you are still my coach?" I did not answer the question, just gave him my coach's stare, and told him with my eyes to just do it. He said, "I get it. I'll work on the list."

I watched him wheel over to the van. He pressed the button and a door opened with the platform for his wheelchair that came down even with the parking lot. I saw Steve rise into the van, position himself into the driver's seat and

Passion For Life

close the door. We waved to each other as he drove away. A week later, I received an e-mail with his 100 bucket list items. One stood out to me immediately - see a baseball game at Fenway Park.

During the summer of 2014, I was working on getting Larry Gowell, former Yankee pitcher and Maine resident, the opportunity to sing the National Anthem at Fenway. This was one of his bucket list items and since he helped me each year with our annual golf outing and baseball camps, I pushed to make that happen. Gena Borson, the Red Sox Foundation Executive Director, had me working with Dan Cassidy who lines up entertainment. Larry was able to perform the National Anthem on a July day to a full house. While there, I talked with Dan about Stevie and his bucket list to watch a game at Fenway. Dan told me he would get tickets and give Steve the VIP treatment. Within weeks I received three tickets.

I called Stevie and said "Hey, are you available on September 9th?" He asked, "Why?" "We have a date at Fenway." I said. "You are kidding me, No way!"

Stevie had no idea that it wasn't just tickets to the game, but also a tour and field access. On that Sunday afternoon, Stevie drove to Boston with his nephew, Todd, who plays for the men's baseball team, the Monarchs. I met him at the front of the stadium at Gate D. Of course, the energy was high as the Red Sox were playing the Blue Jays and it was another sold-out stadium. As Stevie was pushed in his wheelchair by Todd down Yawkey Way, he had this great big smile on his face.

We entered the stadium with Dan's assistance early enough for a grand tour. We went through the stadium level and right onto the field. Stevie's eyes bugged out and glassed over with joy. We were right on the field. We went over to the Red Sox dugout and the famous Hall of Fame reporter Peter Gammons was there. I asked Peter if he would be willing to take a photo with Stevie and Todd. He was glad to. We went to the outfield and met some of the Red Sox and Blue Jay players warming up. They came over for photos as well. Stevie just kept shaking his head in disbelief. For me it was a dream come true to be able to provide this opportunity for my good friend. We ended up in the stands at our seats and watched the Red Sox win a great game. Our photos during that day told the story. One Bucket List item checked off for Stevie and many more to take on. And Stevie is doing it one by one. He has had a lot more adventures for a man in a wheelchair than many people do with all physical abilities. He is an inspiration to mankind.

In the summer of 2015, Stevie befriended my dad who was 91 that year. Stevie often took him out to lunch and they had great discussions. I always appreciated the friendship that dad had with Stevie, which lasted until my father's death. It was that summer when he called one day with news. "Kenny, how about we go back to Fenway for another game." "Sure thing you name it", I said. I could feel over the phone a big Stevie smile as he said, "Well, keep the date open for September 27th. The Red Sox are playing the Blue Jays and we have box seat tickets on the first base side. It's me, you, Todd and Gary Burke, a reunion."

Gary Burke was his best buddy who was in more emotional pain than Stevie over these years since the accident in 1987. Stevie was in the process to help mend that pain. You see, Gary was the one who dropped Stevie that unfortunate evening that broke Steve's neck.

We arrived at Fenway that beautiful Sunday afternoon for a 1:05 p.m. game. I hadn't seen Gary since 1981. He turned out to be a great family man, now retired from the Air Force and living in Connecticut. I watched the magic happen as Stevie and Gary reflected back to their childhood. Their bodies were older although their hearts and minds were back to being kids connecting once again at the most beloved ballpark in the country. Even though this was not on my bucket list, it should have been. It would have read, *reuniting old buddies once again*.

In 2016, my dad passed away. Before his death, I brought Steve to see my dad at his Depot Hill home. I knew this visit would spark my dad's spirits so I let them have alone time as I listened and watched from the other room. Dad loved Stevie and the feeling was mutual.

Shortly after dad's passing Stevie had tickets to a Notre Dame versus Syracuse football game at Met Life stadium in New Jersey. My brother, Jim, joined us along with my Board member, Brian Kelly, who shares the same name as the coach of ND. We watched Notre Dame win a thriller. Weeks later, Steve finally made it to Maine. I set him up to stay at the Pine Tree Camp that had all the equipment for his needs. Pine Tree Camp sits on North Pond and from his cabin was a picture perfect Maine view of the pond on a chilly late October weekend.

Stevie Waite is truly my hero. He has more zest for life than many people, even with his challenging disability. His taxing routine, each and every day, makes him mentally strong and gives him the discipline to take on life. Stevie is my mentor, my coach, and a brother forever.

Journey 40

Just before the sweat: Judd, Dale Newell, Yvonne Davis, Me, Johnathan, Brain Altavator, January 8, 2014

"Great things never came from comfort zones." Anonymous

Sweat Lodge Ceremony – 15 Below Zero

During the summer of 1980 while managing the Millerton summer recreation program, I met Yvonne Davis. I was going into my sophomore year at SUNY Cortland. My brother, Rob, and I have been competitive all of our lives so we came up with a plan to develop a summer Olympic competition between our rival recreation programs. The timing was perfect since the USA had just come off the dramatic win over Russia in ice hockey to win the Gold. This began a challenge between brothers and neighboring towns for the first Recreation Olympics between Amenia and Millerton. We set a date near the end of summer, deciding on the events and rules.

As I formed my players for the events, I came across a dynamic young teen, Yvonne Davis one of the few African Americans in Millerton. As kids growing up, we were all color blind and I do not remember any prejudice feelings, ever. If there were, the energy, intelligence, and desire of Yvonne would have won out anyway. During the summer of 1980, I relied on Yvonne along with Stevie Waite to help organize the older kids and keep unity. She was perfect for the task and she helped us tie Amenia in our first Olympics. The following year we shut out Amenia in every contest. Over the years, I lost touch with Yvonne until I heard from the grapevine that she excelled in school and went off to college.

Fast forward to 2014, after I completed my first book "The Depot Hill Gang," I had a book signing at the Millerton Library. Stevie came by and we caught up on old times. During the discussion, he said I should reach out to Yvonne. Shortly after the conversation, I did just that and realized that we had the same passion to help others. However, Yvonne took it to the world level working for the Bush and Obama administrations helping countries around the world develop their economy and unity. During our many early conversations, she talked about how she wanted to help the Alfond Youth Center. I was game for any of her expertise and support.

Over the years, I assisted the five Native American tribes in Maine to develop Boys and Girls Clubs on their reservations. Since Yvonne helped over 70 different countries, the Native Americans intrigued her and she wanted to know more about what we had done and what more could be done. Since I made my best connections and relationships with Maine Native Americans through a sweat lodge ceremony, I asked her to join me during a visit to Maine.

That week in January produced an extreme cold front that swept the Northeast. Temperatures dipped well below zero with no relief in sight. Even with talk of the extreme cold weather, Yvonne was still game and more excited. The journey to the Passamaquoddy tribe on Spiyak Reservation was nearly four hours away on a remote road heading "downeast." Spiyak was on the bay across from New Brunswick, Canada.

While in Maine, Yvonne stayed at our home with our family. Yvonne and my kids got along famously. After the kids went to bed, we all stayed up for a while discussing Yvonne's unique adventures serving under Presidents Bush and Obama.

Five a.m. arrived quickly. I had anticipated the trip through a sleepless night. I have done sweats before during extreme weather, but mostly hot with 90 plus degree temps. Freezing temperatures were another thing. When we awoke and checked the temperature, it was 9 below zero. My thoughts immediately went to "how is this going to happen?"

As I packed our gear Suzanne helped with Yvonne's clothes, adding leg warmers and extra jackets. Suzanne thought we were nuts and worried about our safety. The cold temperature did not phase Yvonne. She was determined to make this happen. We set out entering my frigid car in the garage at 6:30 a.m. and drove to the Alfond Youth Center to meet Bill Atchinson, a volunteer of the

AYC, who was joining us for the journey. Bill was our number one volunteer at the Club and served as our spiritual leader, mentoring many individuals. He was the right person to join us.

At 7:00 a.m. the three of us headed northeast and the temperature dropped to 11 below. While we were driving, Yvonne and Bill had many discussions on the ceremony logistics. The temperature was so cold that undressing was a concern. I explained that the lodge was heavily insulated and once the hot rocks are placed into the center circle things heat up quickly.

Yvonne was interrupted by a phone call from a Caribbean radio station for an interview. While I was driving, Yvonne was on their station giving her professional perspective on terrorist groups. The interview went on for 30 minutes while the temperature continued to drop to 15 below as we got onto Route 9 traveling toward Down East Maine.

I pulled off to a landmark spot on Route 9 that was a picture-perfect photo opportunity. I asked Bill and Yvonne to get out for the photo shoot with the endless horizon of Maine frozen tundra behind them. We quickly took the photos as every breath from our mouths froze while we posed. At the last stretch of Route 9, I pulled into a country market for a pit stop to pick up snacks and take a bathroom break. The sweat lodge ceremony was in an open field with no facilities.

The last part of the ride was on the back roads to the towns of Meddybemps and Charlotte. Buck, the Passamaquoddy spiritual leader, called me to get an indication on how far out we were. I told him 30 minutes. It was around 10:30 am before we arrived. My Toyota Camry struggled a bit getting up the farm roadway into the snow-covered field. However, the other cars' pathway helped propel the Camry forward.

We pulled up to the field and I saw the familiar smoke from the heated fire baking the rocks. Buck and his crew got there early to set up the lodge, covering it with layers of tarp, setting the fire and preparing the ground. Buck has always been gracious and hardworking even though he was leader of the ceremony. He worked harder than most to prepare for the sweat lodge. Buck, a traditional spiritual man, passes on the traditional Passamaquoddy beliefs not only to his tribal members but to others. He is as humble as they come; a strong, wise, and soft-hearted individual that I respect more and more over the years. I am lucky to call him my friend.

With Buck, around the fire circle and preparing for the sweat, was Dale (Penobscot), Judd (Penobscot) and Jonathan (a good friend of Buck's). These warriors were all in their 50's and 60's. They were in great shape as they had run many marathons over the years, all finishing in less than 3 hours. The chemistry among them was beautiful. Like Brian, they are very humble and spiritual. They are not judgmental and are open minded. I had a feeling Yvonne and Bill would be a perfect fit for the ceremony and they were.

Since the temperature stayed around 15 below, we all stayed close to the fire. The fire was extremely hot and gave us immediate warmth as we stood close. Between the fire and the sweat lodge door was the altar. On the altar was sweet grass, an eagle feather, a turtle rattle and a bear pipe.

When it was time, the men undressed around their cars and got in their shorts. Before we climbed into the lodge with Buck, we were all smudged with sweet grass. This was important in removing any evil spirits. Buck sat facing the opening toward the East side. Yvonne and Bill followed, and I was asked to bring in the first four rocks. Stripping down in the cold weather was painful, especially staying outside using a pitchfork to bring in one hot rock at a time. By the time I got into the lodge, my toes were frozen, and I was chilled all over. I crawled in sitting near the door beside Jonathan, trying to get warm by the rocks. Since I was closest to the doorway, the chill continued and would remain until the flap came down, shutting out the cold air. The rest of the participants seemed to be OK as they huddled into the lodge around the circle of rocks.

I got in and Buck said whoever has any jewelry on including rings may want to take them off and place them outside. I took my wedding ring off and Jonathan handed me his. I crawled back out in the cold blowing air and placed them on top of the lodge.

The ceremony began as Buck explained the process of the four rounds. He put together his carved bear pipe, added tobacco and lit it up. The pipe passed clockwise around the circle. Buck said if anyone had used drugs or alcohol in the past 48 hours, they could not smoke the pipe. Also, if anyone wished not to smoke, they did not have to. The pipe made the rounds four times representing the four directions, North, South, East and West. The flap stayed open during the pipe sharing.

By the fourth round of smoking the pipe, I was certainly ready for the flap to come down to gain warmth. Buck said, "Close it up." Jonathan struggled to shut the opening, pulling the army tarp down. Finally with a pull and tug, the flap was secured. We were in total darkness. Buck began speaking in his Native tongue and started splashing water from the bucket onto the rocks immediately creating the welcome hot steam into the closed air. Soon the temperature in the lodge felt as if it was well over one hundred degrees. We now officially experienced extreme temperatures from freezing to hot.

The sweat began to form on our bodies as if the water faucet within was turned on. I love that feeling, the cleansing of the body. Dale began singing a traditional song. The repeated beat and words were easy to pick up so we all joined in. While in the sweat lodge in the middle of Native country during one of the coldest days of the year, half naked, we were protected by the hot sacred rocks while many others in Maine would not dare to even go outside. Within the lodge, we sang with a unified voice, celebrating, praying and dreaming of a better tomorrow.

Passion For Life

The first round was the East round representing the Eagle and the color red. A few of us prayed openly. The second round was the South representing the Turtle and the color blue. This was the female round and the most powerful round. The female energy in the lodge comes with strong spirit as they give birth to all of us. "They are the power of the life," Buck explained, "That's the reason why this round is the most difficult." It did seem to be the hottest. The third round was the West, the animal the Bear and the color yellow. My native name West Wind comes from this round. Finally, the last round was from the North, the White Buffalo and the color white. We all prayed at different times during each of the rounds. I was impressed that open prayers were for others and not ourselves. The prayers wished positive energy and asked the spirits to help those in need. Each time the round ended, Buck would pound the Turtle rattle at the top of the inside lodge four times and the bottom four times. That was the indication to open the flap. Many of us who knew the medicine man, Dave Gehue, gave thanks and shared stories of his impact on us.

The flap opened and the rush of cold air came in. The initial effect wasn't too bad since the temperature inside was still extremely hot, but it did not take long for the frozen air to chill our uncovered skin. We all rushed to get out of our wet clothes while we had residual heat on our bodies. We then got around what was left of the fire to gain some more warmth before taking down the Sweat lodge. Yvonne looked up in the sky and shouted, "Look at that big bird." Dale added, "Not just a bird –an eagle!" What a perfect conclusion to the Sweat ceremony.

On a typical day we all would have crawled out of the Sweat, rolled over on the ground, and sucked in the cool air thankfully. Not today. I was amazed how quickly our team worked to dismantle the lodge, folding up all of the tarps, removing the rocks from the middle and placing the gear into Buck's truck, within 15 minutes.

Buck invited us all over to his house on the reservation for dinner. I gave Yvonne and Bill a quick tour of Sipayik showing them the tribal office, school, and the Boys and Girls Club before going to Buck's home. Buck prepared a terrific stew with deer and bear meat. Jonathan came up to me and asked if I had his wedding ring. His question hit me like a ton of bricks. I forgot all about the rings that I left on top of the lodge. We excused ourselves and drove back to the field. Unfortunately, the rings could not be found.

Back at the house, Dee, Buck's wife, gave me a hug and said I remember the day Buck lost his ring as well. It was a difficult day. Buck said that he will go back up there especially after the first rain and will look for them. He said the Sweat lodge spirits would watch over them.

I debated whether to tell Suzanne about the ring, or just get another one. It's funny because for the last couple of years I had wanted to switch my wedding band to a ring that has Suzanne's birth stone in it. This certainly now was the motivator.

We drove back to Waterville in the darkness, having great conversation about the transformation of ourselves to become better people than what we are now. Yvonne was flying high with emotional strength. What she hoped to get out of the sweat lodge turned out to be much more. It was a day to remember. A day when many Mainers were huddled to stay warm at their workplace or home, we created a memorable adventure that will last a lifetime.

Unfortunately, my wedding ring was never recovered, however, Buck did find Jonathan's ring. And I got a new wedding ring while the spirits held onto mine. The new ring on my finger is an Irish Claddagh ring with three birthstones representing Suzanne, Sean, and Kate.

This wasn't my last below zero sweat lodge. In December of 2016, we planned another sweat. The weather was even colder on that day.

Journey 41

With former Depot Hiller, Irwin Nachinsom, in Los Angeles

"Some friendships are timeless."

Southern California Trip

Over the years, I've had many opportunities to meet up with my baseball heroes from the past. I grew up watching these players and followed them during my young playing years. This year, thanks to the Depot Hill Gang book that I published, I reconnected with an Amenia friend who lived on the Hill years ago. He left before we built our own baseball field in Lango's cornfield. Irwin Nachinsom lived in a house down the block from me and was 3 years younger.

Irwin moved to Los Angeles with his family, received his Bachelor's degree at UCLA and his Master's degree from USC, and now is a partner at a major accounting firm. He contacted me through Facebook and thanked me for writing the Depot Hill Gang book. He said it brought back great memories of growing up on the Hill. He too has a love for the game of baseball and coaches his son's team. He follows the LA Dodgers throughout the year. Irwin's firm is also involved with the Professional Baseball Scouts Foundation. They sponsor a table each year at the annual event honoring baseball icons and raising funds at one of the major hotels in LA. And, he is good friends with the Chairman of the Board of the Baseball Scouts Foundation. This year they were honoring the outgoing Chairman Bud Segel and past San Francisco, Cincinnati Reds Manager, and former Dodger star Dusty Backer. Former Red Sox player Kevin Millar was the Master of Ceremonies and Hall of Fame players and Managers such as Dave Winfield, Paul Monitor, Goose Gossage, Jim Palmer, George Brett, Tommy LaSorta, Bobby Cox, Bobby Valentine, Bobby Grich, Phil Neikro, Larry King, and HOF announcer Vince Scully were all going to be there.

Irwin invited me to attend and it did not take long for me to book a flight to LA in January 2015 to make it a week of adventures, meeting new people and finding new opportunities.

Our family had just recently picked up a Black Lab puppy and my trip was the week after bringing home our new family member, Koko. Suzanne was a real trooper and supportive of me going even though it was during the coldest of winter with Megan home from college, two little ones, plus a new hyper and untrained puppy.

I arrived in LA late Friday night with jet lag and slept into the next day without being disturbed by the kids, the puppy or Suzanne, who gets up at 4:15 a.m. every day for her workout. It was weird to be able to sleep in and have only the event to be concerned about. It was a rare occurrence, and I appreciated this opportunity. I only wished that Suzanne was with me to share in it.

I had an early afternoon workout at an upscale LA spa and a short run around the Avenues of the Stars neighborhood. I then dressed in my monkey suit for the event. I arrived at happy hour and walked into the silent auction area. I could not believe the items up for bid. The memorabilia covered two large banquet areas. There must have been thousands of autographed, framed photos of many athletic and celebrity stars. It was very impressive.

I watched the celebrities come and go as they were interviewed, and I talked to a woman who was doing a documentary on scouting. I mentioned what I did for work and she asked if it was OK to interview me. I said certainly and was recorded talking about the importance of scouting in baseball.

I saw Irwin with one of his partners coming into the ballroom as I finished the interview. Irwin was glad to see me and brought me over to the table that was reserved for us. There had to be at least a thousand people in the banquet hall. With just the people attending the dinner they must have raised a cool million dollars plus millions more in sponsorships and auction items. It was a good day for the scouts.

At the end of the evening, I had a chance to speak with Commissioner Bobby Grich and George Brett. Bobby attended one of our Alfond Youth Center Golf Outings a few years back. He and his wife recognized me and talked about how they loved Maine. Irwin and I talked a little more and vowed to keep in touch. I left and got ready for bed knowing the next day was going to be a three-hour ride to Palm Desert.

The next morning, I rose out of bed around 8:00 a.m. and opened the curtains on the 11th (Room 1139) floor of the Hyatt Century Hotel to see the brilliant blue sky and temperatures in the mid-seventies. What a perfect day for a road trip I thought. I set my GPS for Palm Desert to meet up with Geraldine Snyder, a former Waterville resident and a friend of AYC board member Phil Roy and his family. Geraldine was a pilot during her younger years. At 83, she spends much of her time traveling and dancing with her boyfriend.

Driving down Route 10, I could not help but notice the awesome mountain range to my left. I was hoping the trip to Palm Desert was going to take me over those mountains. One mountain stood out above all, the major ski area for the California, Arizona and Nevada residents; Bear Mountain. The mountain top had a white peak. I had an urge to redirect my plans and cruise to the mountain, but my work discipline kept me on course.

I-60 took me toward Palm Desert, up and over the mountain range. It was such a beautiful drive weaving in and out of the mountain valleys. Once over the mountain into the desert I could not get over the fields and fields of windmills as far as one could see. My secretary, Felicia Lambert, did a fine job setting me up with my accommodations, the Marriott resort overlooking this great mountain range and sitting on a golf course. My nephew, Tim Walsh, now serving his twelfth year in the Marines stationed at the Oceanside base near San Diego, was meeting up with me. We had plans to go to the pool bar to get something to eat, have a few beverages and watch the AFC/NFC football championship games: the Packers vs. the Seahawks and the Patriots vs. the Colts.

We saw one of the most exciting finishes in playoff history as the Seahawks battled back, within 4 minutes, down by two touchdowns, to win the game. It was an incredible finish. It was great catching up with Tim, especially since I hadn't seen him since he returned from his latest tour. We planned to meet again in San Diego with his girlfriend (now wife) Michelle. The next day Tim was heading to compete in the Spartan 5K challenge competition. Tim has come a long way in his life. He came to Maine in the late nineties after graduating from high school. He didn't have much direction in life at that time, although he always wanted to be a Marine.

I took him on as an employee at the AYC as a lifeguard and teen coordinator. Although he always wanted to serve our country, he had a knee injury that made his acceptance questionable. He worked hard to rehab his knee. After a few years living with me in Maine, his dream was accomplished. He enlisted and now has served three tours, two in Iraq and one in Afghanistan. He is an outstanding individual reaching Gunny Sargent and leading his company every day.

The next morning, I met Geraldine Snyder at her home just a few miles away. She was waiting for me outside her house. Here was a spry 83-year-old lady full of energy and loving life. She immediately invited me in and we talked about her days living in Waterville. She loved to dance and when she was 50 years old, she decided to learn how to fly a plane. Only just a few years ago she gave up her pilot's license after moving from the high desert. She crashed her plane once while flying with her son. She said she got caught in the warm wind currents and flew her plane into electric wire and her plane did a nosedive into the ground. Thankfully they both survived the crash. Her son lost his front teeth but had no major broken bones or cuts. The crash was reported in the LA times.

Now living in Palm Desert, she goes dancing every Friday night at Elks Lodge #1905 with her boyfriend, drinking wine and enjoying her friends. She travels, visits her grandchildren, and has passion for life. I took her out to lunch, and we didn't have any loss for words at any moment of time. She talked about the old days of Waterville and her years at high school dancing at the sock hops and working at the gas station. In later years, she partied at the Melody Ranch in Fairfield, Maine. Not too long ago, she made a trip to the East Coast flying her own plane to spend time with her friends and dance once again at Melody Ranch.

After lunch, she insisted that she take me for a tour of the Palm Desert. She wanted to show me Bob Hope's estate and her son's house sitting on top of a ridge overlooking the city. She drives her car like a fighter pilot with a lead foot and sharp brakes. I only hope that I have her energy and spirit when I am her age. I departed around midafternoon. She suggested that I head over the mountain on Route 74. After saying my goodbye and promising to visit a few of her friends in Waterville, I was on my way.

The trip over the mountain was ideal for what I was looking for. The road went straight up and over the mountain and the views were spectacular. I took my time and stopped at as many turnouts as possible. The road went through some towns and state parks. It took me approximately 3 hours to get to San Diego where I had plans to meet my former college roommate and rugby team member, Eric Leitstein. Last time I saw Eric was a few years ago when he and family came across country as his son was signed up for our New England Baseball Camp at Camp Tracy. Since college, Eric had developed a successful business owning several pubs and restaurants.

I got onto I-5 heading south to Balboa Avenue. I took Balboa to its end at Mission Beach. One of Eric's restaurants, Pacific Beach Ale House, was right in front of me. I parked and walked a block to a new restaurant that Eric had recently bought and was renovating. We were excited to see each other. Eric told me to follow him in his car to the place I was going to stay for the next three days, his new condominium on the beach that he bought as an investment and for guests. The two-bedroom condo's front door was just steps away from the beach.

Passion For Life

I dropped off my stuff and we headed to Union Street, one of his other establishments in downtown San Diego. Eric's new establishment is 7,500 sq. ft. and just blocks away from the Padres Stadium and the Conference Center.

The next day while Eric had business activities, I slept a little later. I once again took advantage of this opportunity since there were no kids and no puppy around to get me up early. I got out of bed and had a quick cup of coffee sitting out on the deck and taking in the Pacific Ocean before a morning run. The running trail and beach was full of energy from individuals from all walks of life running, walking, surfing, playing volleyball, etc. I wore my Asics running shoes along with shorts and a tank top for a long overdue run. My plan was to run for about an hour. I was feeling refreshed and well rested with no responsibilities. I was to meet up with Eric later during the day. I ran with an extra hop in my step. For the first time in a long while I felt that I could run forever. I looked at my running watch and I had run over an hour. I kept running for two hours straight, the first time since the Sugarloaf Marathon. It felt great, though I knew that I was going to pay for it the next few days.

I got together later with Eric to visit some of his other restaurants and then have dinner with my nephew Tim and his girlfriend Michelle. That night I drove back to the condo and parked the car in the basement garage. As I was getting out of the car, the automatic garage door shut on me. I was locked in the garage under the condo! I looked for switches, door buttons, a lever, but there was nothing in sight. After a while I went to the back of the garage to another automatic door, and I was able to open it up. At this point, after a few phone calls and texts to Eric with no response that I was not getting out, I was about to give up and camp in the car for the night when I spotted a door at the back of the storage area. I lifted the latch and I was free.

Once again, I had a great sleep. After a quick run, I drove 30 minutes to Del Mar to meet up with Nelson Vails, the 1984 silver medalist in cycling. He was the first African American to ever earn this honor. Nelson was born in the Bronx and was inspired by a mentor and coach to take up cycling. Nelson had the drive and the ability to excel in his field and to earn the right to be in the Olympics to compete against the world's best. Nelson shocked the world in 1984 to take the Silver Medal.

I met Nelson at the local Starbucks. Now in his fifties, he still trains and rides his bike 45 miles a day around the San Diego area. He speaks to different groups and encourages them to engage into healthy alternatives. His program is called "Riding with Nelly." We had a great discussion about how his message would be a terrific one for the BGCA movement. I thought Yvonne Davis and I could get him in with the right marketing people. For many underprivileged youth, cycling could be a way to inspire them. Nelson said he would also help with a Celebrity Dinner in San Diego.

The next day I flew out of San Diego to head home after a long week. Suzanne was a real trooper taking care of our two little ones with a new puppy on top of it all. Of course, her busy job as Chief Operating Officer at a non-profit community action agency added to the challenge. I knew I had lots of work to do to give Suzanne overwhelming support since I was gone to sunny California and left her in the Maine winter. My relationship bank account was depleting and I needed to deposit more funds quickly for my wonderful teammate in life.

Journey 42

Legging out a hit and turning two; playing for the Central Maine Wave at Colby College Field at the age of 55.

"I am convinced that God wanted me to be a baseball player." Roberto Clemente

It is Never Too Late

In the Spring of 2016 I decided that it was time to consider playing baseball again, not softball but fast pitch hard ball. As we were planning the spring Cal Ripken baseball program, I talked with Nate Stubbert who had played in a wooden bat league in the area for years. Since Colby College in Waterville renovated their baseball and softball diamonds, with a seven-million-dollar turf project, I thought that perhaps it was a good time to organize a Waterville team and play at the new field. Unfortunately, I had a few business trips out of state that prevented me from following through on recruiting a team and securing sponsorships.

Shortly after I returned, the President of the area wooden bat league, Kris Targett, called me and said if I was interested in playing ball, I could join his Winslow team called the Green Wave. To say I was delighted would be an understatement. I was pumped up with the thought of playing for the first time since 1989, twenty-seven years ago. I thought I should break the news to Kris that I was older than the rest of the teammates, as I would soon be turning 55.

Ken Walsh

I said to Kris, "By the way, my glove is most likely older than you." I used the same glove when I played with the Amenia Monarchs back in 1980 until 1989 with Bronx Braves. I believe Kris was thrown back by my age, although he still encouraged me to play.

A week later, unexpectedly, Bill Alfond, one of the Boston Red Sox partners stopped by my office and left gifts on my desk. I was surprised to see two wooden baseball bats. One was an official MLB 34" bat signed by Mike Bordick, and the other was a non-signed 34" 1986 World Series Red Sox second baseman, Marty Barrett's, bat. This came right from the dugout with ball marks on the barrel of the bat. I said to myself, "I'll keep the Mike Bordick bat as a memorabilia item, and I'll use the Marty Barrett bat in game play.

This past year, during the fall and winter months, I played a lot of squash and injured my right elbow. I thought it was tendonitis but worried that it could be something worse, like a torn tendon. I carried that injury into the beginning of the season. Each practice and during the game, I taped my right elbow and wore an elbow sleeve to keep the pain at bay. Every throw to first was difficult. My first practice was on the Winslow High School field in April. I met a few of the Wave players; many of them had played with Kris for several years. Batting practice went well using my "Marty Barrett" bat, which I showed to the other players. They looked at me as if I was crazy. Some of them said, "Why use that bat? If it breaks, what would you do?" I replied that I would then tape it and retire it for good.

I seemed to hit the ball well, making good contact, lining the ball throughout the field. During batting practice, a new teammate and the second oldest guy, Kevin Guertin, observed that I liked the pitch low and inside so I could turn on the ball. He also noted that I had trouble with the outside pitch. The next few Sunday practices went well with meeting more of the players, but more importantly, no new injuries. It was great to play second base again, but I noticed that my glove certainly did not have much padding left as each ball smacked into my palm with a sting. I decided it was best to wear a batting glove under my mitt for better cushion.

Our first game was on May 1 against the Pittsfield Pirates at 10:00 a.m. at the Winslow field. Before the game, I suggested that two ball players join our team, former Waterville HS stand-out and hit record holder from the University of Southern New Hampshire, Chris Hart, along with one of our interns from the Alfond Youth Center who had just graduated from a college in Massachusetts and had played for the Monarchs, Patrick Argentina. His dad played triple A for the Yankees and his skills were close to his dad's. Those new additions helped our team through the season.

I also called my friend and former Board member of the Alfond Youth Center, Chris Gaunce, whose family owns Central Maine Motors, to see if he would consider being a $500 sponsor of the team. He gladly accepted. We ordered our uniforms from David Winkin at Joseph's Sporting Goods store with Central Maine Motors printed on the back. Thankfully, the uniforms arrived in mid-May as our team wore different variations of uniforms for the first few games.

The night before my first game on May 1st brought butterflies to my stomach waiting with anticipation for the game. I stopped playing squash to make sure that there were no injuries. I stretched a lot and I used the foam roller, taking my wife Suzanne's advice.

That Sunday morning, I got up at the crack of dawn and prepared a meal. I left the house early to arrive before game time to stretch and loosen up. Cruising along in my black Camry, I listened to my inspiration music from Rudy, Rocky, and Braveheart soundtracks to get mentally up for the game. Twenty-seven years later I would once again be on the baseball diamond, this time the oldest guy on the field.

Our team's pregame practice was a lot different from what I was used to when playing college and/or with the Monarchs years ago. We usually had batting practice and took infield/outfield. With the Wave it was everyone for themselves. I jumped in the batting cage with Kevin Guertin, Jeff Burnham, and Andy Kilber to get a few swings in before the game.

As Kris read out the starting lineup, I was happy to hear that I was starting at second base. The first pitch of the game came to me to my left toward the middle. The ball got by me and I knew that I should have had it. That would be the last error I made during the season. I made a couple of good defensive plays during the game as we pounded out hit after hit and beat the Pittsfield Pirates badly 19-4. My first at bat was a line drive up the middle against Gary Moen. Gary was a warrior on the mound, pitching with a replaced knee. The rest of the season, I struggled at bat and hitting on top of the ball. With the game under my belt, I grew more confident that I could get back to the game I used to play. I always played with hustle and tried to get on base any way possible - walk, bunt, beating out grounds, whatever it took. Now, at 55, I was not as quick as I used to be although I did have good speed.

The following game was against Farmington. I got another hit and I played a solid second base. In the 6th inning, I hit a ball between third and shortstop knowing in my younger years this would be an easy play to beat out for a hit. I took off out of the batter's box kicking my legs into gear, pumping my arms, and accelerating to full speed only to strain my right quadricep. I knew immediately that I was toast as I limped to the bag, injured. I did beat the play but was out for the rest of the game.

During the next game, I played but did not run at full speed in order to heal the injury. We played so-so ball. Sometimes, we played error free, other times our bats were quiet, and we made senseless errors. In any baseball game, I believe pitching can dominate a game. I suggested to Kris to invite former Major League Baseball player Matt Kinney to pitch for us. Matt was drafted by the Red Sox and then traded to the Twins before pitching for the Brewers and SF Giants. He also played a year in Japan. At 39, I assumed he could still throw. We found out that he certainly still had life in his arm.

Matt got on the mound for us during our weekend series playing on Colby College's new field under the lights. We played against first place West Paris Westies. The game was excellent as both of our teams had a no-hitter going into the 6th. The Westies finally did get a hit; however, Matt shut them down with his high 80 mph fastball and spot on breaking pitches. We struck back in the 7th leading off with batters on base with a walk and hit by pitch. Then our veteran first baseman and St. Joseph's graduate, Ben Muniz, blasted a triple over the center fielder's head. He was driven home with Kris Targett's hit and we pulled ahead 3-0 leading us to victory. At that point I thought to myself we would be the team to beat if all our players show up for the playoffs.

We played the next night against the Rumford Cardinals who were tied for first place with the Westies. Rumford had a good quality team coached by their local high school coach, Ryan Palmer. He recruited good skilled players along with young stars from the area. Rumford jumped on our pitchers early, leading the game by four runs. We battled back scoring two runs. The game stayed that way until the 8th inning. Rumford scored two more runs. In the 9th inning we were down 6 to 2. Our leadoff hitter, Jody Jose led off with a double, hitting the ball in the gap. Lefty Tim Kinneson lined a base hit to the right field scoring Jody with no outs. Tim's son Peyton popped up for the first out. Then Rumford's pitcher walked two of our batters loading up the bases with one out. Chris Hart, another lefty hit a base hit out to right field driving in one run with bases loaded again. Our next batter popped up with me on deck.

Here was my chance with the bases loaded and two outs. A base hit would tie the game. An extra base hit could win the game. This 55-year-old had the opportunity to be the hero. I grabbed my Marty Barrett bat to warm up with extra warmup swings on the on-deck circle. I walked over to batter's box at 9:30 PM at night under the lights returning to the game for the first time in years. My heart was racing knowing the circumstance. I stepped up in the batter's box, placed the bat on the plate and took a few warmup swings. I assumed that the Rumford pitcher would attempt to get ahead of me with a fast ball early in the count. I dug in preparing to swing at the first pitch in an attempt to drive the ball. The right-handed pitcher wound up and threw the expected fastball right down the middle. This was the perfect pitch; I swung and made contact, topping the ball for a grounder toward the middle. All runners were on the move as the ball progressed quickly up the middle toward the left side of the short stop. He caught the ball stretching out as I ran down toward first base. The short stop flipped the ball over to the second baseman for the final out. One inch away from me being a hero and tying the game. I felt disappointed for letting the team down. We got in our line at the end of the game to shake each other's hands and got our stuff in the dugout before heading to our cars.

As I was walking to my car, I did not have negative thoughts of what could have been, but thought about how amazing what had happened. After 27 years of not playing baseball, I was playing with players half my age and was able to compete with them. I was still able to perform at a level to have fun even though it was not at the skill level of what I remember being as a younger athlete. I thought to myself, "Wow! This is cool."

The season went on and our team got progressively better. We ended the season in the middle of the pack and won the first two playoff games. The quarterfinal game was against Rumford, the team that beat us in the regular season. The game was held in Rumford on August 14th, the day after my dad passed away. I was not going to play until Suzanne told me that the best thing I could do was to play in honor of him. I took her good advice and drove two hours to Rumford. I was able to reflect on my dad's life and put life in perspective for that moment. Even though I was subdued, I was focused on playing. Not many times did my dad see me play ball, but I was certain that he was watching now.

The ballfield in Rumford was near the paper mill in town. As I took grounders at second base, I could see the tall smokestack in the background. I assumed that some of the Rumford players and family members were employees of the mill.

Matt Kinney could not make the game, so Kris started first baseman Ben Muniz on the mound. I was unsure how that was going to work since he never pitched during our regular season. He was brilliant. Our team also hit well jumping ahead of Rumford for six runs as Ben shut out the team. Ben left after seven full innings giving way to Kris to finish the game.

Unfortunately, Kris's arm was tired from throwing a lot during the season. The Rumford batters hit Kris hard and scored three runs in the bottom of the 8th. In the ninth we went down in order, we were still leading 7-3. In the bottom of the ninth, Kris walked the first batter. He then hit the second batter.

Now runners were on first and second with no outs. Their strongest hitter, their third baseman, was up. Kris's first two pitches were balls and with a 2 – 0 count the third baseman took Kris deep, hitting the ball over the left center fence. The score was now 7-6 with no outs. The momentum changed quickly. Kris walked the next batter, a base hit followed along with another walk to load up the bases with no outs. The next batter hit a line shot to shallow left center and the runner on third thought the ball was going to drop in, so he started to celebrate by jogging home only for our speedy centerfielder Brain Bellows catching the ball at knee level and almost making a double play throwing back to third base. The runner got back in time. With one out, the bases were still filled.

The following batter hit another hard shot right at our center fielder who was playing in. The runner on third still could not advance. With two outs and the bases loaded we were one out from going into the semifinals. The next batter, who was a lefty, had two hits coming to the batter's box. With a 2-2 count, the lefty hit a looping fly ball toward Ben who was playing first. He was able to leap perfectly to catch the ball at the tip of his mitt, snow coning it for the final out. I would like to believe that my dad shared some of his magic from heaven to make all these circumstances work for us to win the game. I was satisfied with that thought.

Our season ended abruptly the following weekend playing in South Paris against the Westies, a team we beat before. Only nine of our players showed up and we had no pitching. Ben's arm was toast along with Kris's. We had six different men on the mound trying to stop the Westies with no luck as they pummeled us. It was a horrible way to end the season.

I decided that if the Central Maine Green Wave wanted me to play, I would continue only if I didn't hurt the team. I was committed to come back next season batting left-handed. I figured since most of the pitchers are right-handed, batting lefty would give me an advantage especially with my dominant eye being on that side. I thought I would be able to pick up the ball from the pitch much better. During the off-season I worked extremely hard on my flexibility and bat speed. During the winter I converted my basement into a makeshift batting cage by cleaning out my wood shop and placing nets and turf inside. I hung a ball from the ceiling dangling from a string to hit into the net repeatedly. For Christmas, Suzanne gave me an automatic pitching machine. While she worked out in the next room balls would fly into her space. I did hit a few balls up the middle through the netted hole, breaking a few picture frames and a window. I did not mind at all picking up the glass and fixing the window since each hit was a good one. I took over 7,000 swings to get ready for the season. My good friend, Joel Lockwood, a 35-year-old insurance agent and manager, who had played ball in the past, aspired to play this coming year, his comeback. We had been practicing together since the season ended and I was confident that 2017 would be my baseball breakout year, batting left-handed.

However, 2017 wasn't a breakout year. I did start out batting left-handed against right-handed pitchers but after a few games went back to my comfortable right side. Our 2017 season went well enough especially during the beginning and middle of the season, however, we lost three straight at the end of league play along with our first round in the playoffs to the Bethel Braves. A veteran right-handed pitcher Levy Brown kept us in check to beat us 5-2. It was disappointing knowing that the season was over until I received a call from the Winthrop Red Sox baseball coach Dave Ricker. His team won 4 straight Pine Tree Wooden bat championships. He asked me if I was interested in playing in the Roy Hobbs Baseball World Series 53 and over Division in Fort Myers in

November of 2017. I would be playing for the Northeast team, the Kennebec Cubs coached by Bill Arsenault and his brother-in-law from Philadelphia, Grady Ragsdale. The team was made up of 8 guys from Maine, 4 from Kentucky and 6 from Philly. Bill Arsenault called me soon after I agreed to play and asked if I would join some of the Maine guys and play in the Fall baseball league every Sunday until the end of October at Old Orchard Beach baseball park to get prepared for the tournament. I gladly accepted. I had a decent Fall, hitting over four hundred and playing mostly short stop. The guys who played on Sunday were from Maine although they came from out of state as well. The ages of the players ranged from 45 to 75. Along the mid-coast there are two leagues, the 45's and 65's. Many of these players also have played in the Roy Hobbs World Series over the year. Dick Hill started the league along the coast having passion for the game and still playing in his 70's and a pretty good pitcher at his age. He played in the minors in his younger years and like many of us who are still playing, not willing to give the game up.

    I met some of my teammates during the Sunday games and really enjoyed meeting up with a 62-year-old right-handed pitcher Larry Murphy from Portland. He has played the game for many years and he is a Roy Hobbs veteran playing for over 10 years in the World Series, mostly on the mound. He had great control of the ball and was able to move the ball in and out of the strike zone, a crafty pitcher who always had a game plan. The first time I met him, he was in full Detroit Tiger uniform wearing his number 17. He immediately introduced himself and gave me the background on some of the players on the field including the founder, Dick Hill. Also on my team for the Fall was our manager Bill, along with short stop and pitcher, a hard-throwing right-handed, Walt Foster, catcher Mike Wentworth who was the best built athlete standing 6'2" and physically strong, a former math teacher Denis Mencine our dependable second baseman, and another short stop/pitcher Steve Curtin.

    The Fall season brought outstanding weather. We only had to postpone one game due to rain. During the second game of the season, I pulled my left hamstring running out a base hit. That set me back for a few weeks although I kept playing through the injury. I met Don Holmstrom, a 74-year-old who is still playing ball and lives in Winslow. He and I carpooled down to Old Orchard taking turns driving. Don is a retired schoolteacher and has never given up the game. He also makes the trip to Fort Myers every year and now is playing in the oldest division. Don still puts the barrel of the bat on the ball and plays a good infield. I asked him how he prepares for the season. He said during the winter in Florida he runs along the beach throwing a heavy ball to keep his legs and arm in shape.

    I started planning for the trip to Fort Myers as soon as I got the invitation. Suzanne helped with all the travel details and was undecided if she and the kids were going to come. The kids would have to take time off from school. They certainly didn't mind the possibility, but it was going to fall during Katie's birthday. We had to take that into consideration for a 6-year-old. We also had another issue. The Alfond Youth Center Annual Charity Ball fundraiser fell on that Saturday night of November 4th. Therefore, we had to fly out on Sunday rather than Saturday. I was not too happy about that since I was going to miss the first two games. After much discussion, we decided to make it happen. Thanks to Suzanne's diligent work looking online for flights, we got great deals. She also booked an Airbnb online and found a house in Lehigh Acres only 15 minutes from Jet Blue Park where most of the games are played. The house was a three-bedroom home in a quiet neighborhood with a pool. It was perfect for our family.

The week before our journey South, we had a major windstorm blow through Maine with winds up to 75 miles an hour. Half of Maine's population lost power including us. We had the generator running from Monday morning all the way until Saturday before the power finally came back on. We were not sure if we could leave the house without power. Lucky for us it all worked out.

After a late night at the Alfond Youth Center Charity Ball event, we drove down to Boston leaving at 6:00 a.m. and arriving at 9:00 a.m., ready for our 11:00 a.m. direct flight out. Our flight down was uneventful and I was antsy wondering if I could at least catch the end of that day's doubleheader. After we picked up our upgraded car rental - a black Cadillac - we headed to the Players Development Complex for registration. The atmosphere was tremendous with an unbelievable baseball buzz going on. Players throughout the country were around the 6-field complex. Our division, the 53 and over, had the largest draw of teams with over fifty teams. They broke the divisions to single A, AA, AAA, and AAAA. After the Wednesday game, the tournament directors placed teams according to win-loss record, runs scored and runs against. Last year the Cubs played in the double AA, which was expected again this year.

We checked in at the Airbnb house after grocery shopping and the kids immediately got in the pool. I was disappointed to not arrive in time to play the second game, which I eventually found out that we lost 11-2 against the Minnesota Bees. However, we did win the first game playing against the Silverhawks 12-7. That evening into the night, I could not settle down, anticipating our next game scheduled for 1:45 p.m. at the Player Development Complex against a team from Cincinnati, the Crosstown Traffic.

After a good yoga stretch in the morning with my beautiful workout partner, Suzanne, I was ready to go. I had a 30-minute drive to the field. I got to the field area early and saw some guys sitting around the picnic tables wearing our team colors and KC hats. I introduced myself and found out they were all from Kentucky: Dean Doak first baseman, Denny Wheeler Centerfield and Schievy our right fielder. I had a great time talking with these guys, all core baseball men who love the game and the strategy of the game. They all had been playing in the tournament for years as well.

We walked over to field number 5 for our game as the other players began to arrive. Our other co-coach, Grady Ragsdale, introduced himself along with some of the other players – Gary Loewenstern, Drew Kellock, Jim Kevin, John Pecora and Doug Chumbler. Everyone but Doug was from Philly area.

I found out that I was going to bat leadoff and start at third even though I was told by Bill that I was most likely going to play outfield to use my leg speed. We were the away team, so I was first up hoping to immediately help the team.

Bill came up to me and said, "Ken, we need you on base." I came to the plate using my LaCasse Ash 33" bat made in Maine. On the mound was a seasoned left hander that was throwing strikes in warm up and seemed to be all around the plate. I thought I would take a pitch and then get ready to find my pitch to hit.

The first pitch was a strike down the middle. I was hoping to see it again. It was not to happen. He hit the corners and had me down one ball, two strikes and threw a fast ball on the outside corner for a swinging strike out. I was thinking to myself, "Hell, that was a great first impression for my team." It would be my first and last strike out for the rest of the week.

The next time I was up was in the third inning with a runner at third and two outs, I didn't waste a good pitch. The lefty threw a fastball middle and away so I drove it to right field for a hit and an RBI. Then I stole second and third.

Next time up, I crushed a fastball down the middle over the left fielder's head for a double. My last time up, the left fielder stepped back 10 yards, otherwise this hit would have gone way over his head as this ball was hit harder than the double. The outfielder reached up, going back and caught the ball over his head. We won this game 6-1. Walt Foster pitched a gem of a game, throwing hard all game and going the distance.

The next game on Tuesday was a closer battle beating the Midwest Pirates 6-3. The spirited John Pecora from the Philly team pitched an excellent game keeping the Pirates off the bases. John is a rugged linebacker-built man who does not seem to take any bull. He is a straight up guy who calls it the way it is.

Our third game was at Century Park, the home of the Minnesota Twins spring training field. The field was absolutely beautiful. The field was groomed in every which way, and I found the infield very hard, making the ball travel with speed. Sliding was fun especially since I slide headfirst. I came home that evening with skin burns on both my elbows and knees.

Our next game was against the Atlanta Astros, a 3-1 team who won the AA World Series in 2016. I batted last in the order and played third. This game helped determine our seed ranking in the playoffs. Our old reliable Larry Murphy started on the mound for us. He pitched his heart out. We pulled ahead quickly the first four innings for a 5-1 lead. Slowly the Astros bounced back with a few runs off Larry, and he was eventually taken out for another reliable pitcher Steve Curtin. Our fielding during the three games was fantastic, playing errorless ball. With one out and a runner on first in the seventh, a ball was hit to our short stop Walt who picked it up and threw it over to our second baseman Denis. As he turned to pivot for the double play, an Astro player came in hard with elbows up hitting Denis in the jaw as he released the ball. I don't know how Denis completed the double play, but he made a perfect throw to first. John Pecora who was now playing left field almost came out of his skin protecting Denis running in from the outfield ready to rumble. The umpires got in-between the player and John backed off. The player apologized and the game went on. Denis was a little shook up.

In the bottom of the ninth, the Astros rallied again, scoring two runs to make it 5 to 4. Runners were on second and third with one out. I was playing third with the sun glaring in my eyes. On a one-two count, the left-handed batter hit a lazy fly ball over to the third base sideline. I had a beat on it until I lost it in the sun just as I was getting close to it. I dove near the sideline fence to just catch it in the end of my glove to make the second out. We ended up getting the third out and winning the ball game. Suzanne and the kids arrived back from the beach in time to watch the last few innings and saw my catch.

With the victory, we ended up 4-1 and waiting for the decision for what seed and what division we were going to play in. We had Thursday off to rest a bit. Suzanne and I took the kids to the zoo and played around the pool for a relaxing day and evening. That night at 8:00 p.m. we finally got word that we were ranked 5th and would play in the AAA division. Great news! Unfortunately, Suzanne and the kids were heading out the next morning to fly back to Maine.

After I drove the family to the airport, I headed to Jet Blue Park for the playoff series. Our game was against the Cuyahoga Indians, the World Series champs from single A. After the pep talk from our Manager Bill, we were ready to play. I started at third and batted first splitting innings with Doug. On the mound for the Indians was a solid left pitcher that did not throw with much speed but kept the ball down and in the strike zone. I led off with a base hit to left field, although our next hitter grounded to the short stop causing a force out at second.

We were up by one run, but it was short lived. With our ace on the mound, Walt Foster, we knew we would be in the game if our defense played the way it should. It was not to be. Errors killed us keeping the Indians in the game with unearned runs. We hit the ball hard but into the ground. They had a strong infield, especially on the left side. Their short stop and third baseman were flawless making play after play.

I continued to hit the ball well. I was 2-3 going into the eighth inning and down seven to one. But our bats came alive! I hit a broken bat base hit, stole second and then scored on a run. We put two more runs on the board with the bases loaded with two outs. The Astros got out of the jam as one of our Cubs grounded out to first. We shut the Astros down in the bottom of the eighth with one inning to score three runs. I was able to get up again and beat out an infield grounder for a hit finishing 4-5. We scored two more runs making it a one run game with runners on second and third with two outs. Denny was up and he hit a solid ground ball right to second baseman. Game over, we lost 7-6.

This was a bittersweet ending. Even though we lost, our team played well together especially since this was the first time that we had all played together. The chemistry of the team was excellent. Many of us made the right plays at the right moments to keep us in the games all week long. The last game did not show the strength of the team. If it was double elimination, I am certain that we could have gone farther.

For my first Roy Hobbs World Series, I was pleased with my performance going errorless at 3rd and 2nd base, batting mainly as a leadoff hitter, going 7 for 13, batting a .538 with one walk, 4 RBI's, 4 Runs, 4 stolen bases and a double. I was and am still excited about the future and playing for years to come, God willing. It felt great after a twenty-five-year layoff from the game and playing at this level.

Journey 43

"You can be a kid for as long as you want when you play baseball." Cal Ripken, Jr.

An Epic Baseball Day – BP at Fenway Park in Boston

For all the years of loving baseball, I never imagined being in a Major League Baseball stadium playing the game. For me, becoming a professional ball player never came to be, although the love of the game was always there, even knowing that the dream was not to happen.

As destiny would have it, at the age of 55, I found out that dreams do come true.

In the Fall of 2015 during a discussion with the AYC's Development Director, Kim Fleming, I came up with the idea of creating a new auction item that would bring in a good sum of money – a baseball fantasy batting practice event at the Boston Red Sox Fenway Park. Kim thought it was a great idea and asked me to pursue the opportunity. I e-mailed a Boston Red Sox partner and friend

Bill Alfond about this being a possibility. He said he would investigate it. A few months went by when I received an e-mail from Fenway's Facility Operations Director, Peter Nesbit, asking me for more details of what I was looking to do. After I explained, he said he would line it up. Game on!

At the AYC Charity Ball event that year, we had a wonderful new auction item that we thought could garner high bids and raise good money. The auction item description stated *"Batting Practice at Fenway Park for Two, Pitched by Ken Walsh."* It was music to my ears. The event was well attended, and the BP at Fenway auction item went for $3,100 and was won by Chris and Linanne Gaunce, the owners of Central Maine Motors in Waterville. Their plan was to give this as a Christmas gift to their teenage sons, CJ and Daniel who were both passionate baseball fans. When the kids opened the gift, they were blown away and very excited about the adventure.

The next part was the choice of a date. Peter Nesbit and I went back and forth all winter long attempting to set a date that would work for everyone. In late spring, Peter finally gave me a few dates that worked for the Red Sox. One of the dates was July 20th, the same date the San Francisco Giants were in from the West Coast. I did not hesitate and locked it in after confirming with the Gaunces. The last time the Giants were at Fenway was in 2007. That year, Home Run King Barry Bonds was still playing for the Giants. It was his last year. It was also the year my son, Sean, was born. That year, in the stadium was a bat-making company and I had them make a bat for Sean engraved "San Francisco vs Boston, Sean Thomas Walsh, June 16, 2007".

Around the same time that I locked in the date; I received a phone call from my cousin Roger Funk. He said he was coming in from the West Coast for a week and asked which week might be best. I explained the situation and he thought it would be wonderful if he could come to the game since he was a big SF Giants fan. I told him that I would take care of tickets. He quickly replied that he would buy tickets for the 19th. So, we had tickets for the two-game series. Things were really shaping up, two Giants vs Red Sox games, both teams in first place and the chance to hit and pitch on the historic Fenway field. The Fantasy trip was becoming a reality trip.

Roger flew into Boston on a Thursday. Suzanne, the kids, and I went to Boston to meet Roger. We spent time the next day going to George's Island to tour the old Civil War fort, eating good Italian food, and then heading back to Maine. That weekend my Wave Baseball Team had a game at Colby's new seven-million-dollar turf field. I was excited to have Roger see the game since I spent many of my summers in the late sixties watching Roger play for the Monarchs as their catcher. Now it was his turn to watch a 55-year-old second baseman on the field.

That Saturday, on the eve of the game, I asked Roger if he had any interest in going to the batting cage to take batting practice. He jumped on the suggestion

Passion For Life

and asked my 9-year-old son Sean to join us. I was delighted because just this past spring Sean decided that he was not interested in playing baseball anymore and after 4 years of playing tee ball and rookie ball, he was done. I remember very clearly when he told me. I had just returned from my spring training trip in Florida. I was working out in the basement while Sean was playing in the family room. I went to the room and said, "Son, it's baseball season. Let's go out and have a catch." Sean replied, "Dad, we need to talk. I know baseball is your thing but I'm not a sporty guy. I don't want to play this year."

I replied, "Sean, it's OK as long as you are doing what you love to do, and you are doing something that interests you." I looked over to Suzanne and said, "Please take over while I get sick."

Now Sean wanted to go to the cage and hit balls. We went to Colby's batting cage at their new turf field. Sean batted first. Batting lefty, he hit his first pitch line drive right back at Roger, almost taking him off his feet. Sean had a great big smile on his face. It was a wonderful way to start the evening full of good hitting.

The next day was my ball game at Colby College against the Rockland Tigers. We ended up beating them 12-4. I went 0-4, although scored a run hitting the ball each time without striking out. Roger kept score and seemed to have a good time.

The next day I had to go to work while Roger stayed around the house. He spent most of the day stacking our three cords of wood into the garage. Roger and our black lab Koko got along great as he stopped work every once in a while to play fetch with him.

On Tuesday, Roger and I headed to Boston and checked into a Marriott Hotel in Waltham around 30 minutes from Fenway. We got rid of our luggage and went to the stadium to be there a few hours before the game. We parked near the stadium and began exploring the Fenway area. We soon found a pub and restaurant across from Yawkey Way. We had a few beers and dinner before heading back into the mainstream. I walked into one of the souvenir stores off Yawkey Way and found the perfect hat to add to my collection. It was a black golf hat with Fenway Park in white print along with the Red Sox and Giants logos. Roger, a lifelong Giant fan, had his SF hat on. At around 5:30 pm the crowds began to thicken. I was amazed by the wave of Giants fans coming from the West Coast wearing their orange and black shirts and hats. I had never seen a guest team take over the stadium like what I saw on the 19th and 20th of July.

Roger and I got into the stadium early enough to watch the Giants on the field for batting practice. We watched as the Giants took the field and went through the pre-game routine with the Giants' starting lineup and past World Series winners taking Batting Practice that included Pence, Posey, Belt, Crawford, and Panic. Coach Bruce Bochey watched from behind the batting cage as each player rotated in and out for swings.

Our tickets were just to the right of home plate under the overhang. We were pumped! I was with Roger, my childhood mentor, and watching two teams that we both loved. The game was a perfect matchup between the former Giant and World Series winner Jake Peavey returning to Fenway against the Red Sox hot pitcher Rick Porcello having a great career season. He ended up winning over twenty games and the Cy Young Award that year. That day, Red Sox player, Brock Holt, hit a solo homer and David Ortiz smacked a three-run home run leading the Red Sox to a 4-0 win. The stadium was electric.

We drove back to our hotel around midnight knowing the next day was going to be an historic one for us. We were to report on the field at 10:00 a.m. and I was going to throw batting practice to 15- and 19-year-old Daniel and CJ Gaunce. Roger was excited about just the thought of being on the field at Fenway to take pictures.

We arrived at Fenway Park and parked a few blocks away from the stadium. We waited at the gate until security checked us in. The Gaunce's were held up with traffic but got there in time. Peter Nesbit came down from his office and escorted us into the ballpark. He first took us on a tour around the stadium ending up at the Green Monster wall. There was another group taking batting practice as we watched from the top. All the batters sprayed balls throughout the field although no one hit the wall or jacked one out for a home run.

I was anxious to get on the field to pitch and maybe, just maybe, hit one depending on the time. Peter brought us down to the third base side and on to the field. This was really going to happen. It was hard to believe. We entered at the away team dugout and walked onto the field.

For Chris, Linanne, CJ, Daniel, and Roger it was the first time on these sacred grounds. These were the same grounds that legends Yaz, Fish, Rice and Williams all played on. Peter asked if we would like to go into the dugout. It didn't take long for all of us to say "Yes" and we all hung out in the dugout acting like players and coaches for the moment.

Now, it was time for me to take the mound and throw batting practice to the kids. Daniel got up first as his parents and Roger were set to take photos. His brother CJ ran on to the field to shag flies. I had a bucket of MLB baseballs and started to fire away. Daniel immediately made great contact driving the ball throughout the field. The echo of the wooden bat throughout the stadium will be a lasting memory forever. There I was on the mound where great players of the past took this spot throughout the long history of Fenway.

After Daniel finished with hitting his bucket of balls, CJ got up and he pounded out hits. We had more time, so I pitched to Chris. For a guy who had never played organized ball, he hit the ball well. We still had time and I pointed over to Roger and said, "You want to hit?" He looked at me as if I just told him that he was called to play for the Majors. He said, "You kidding me. Of course, I want to hit."

Passion For Life

Roger, at the spirited age of 68, had the stance from the early days of playing for the Amenia Monarchs. His bat was back, elbow high, stance parallel waiting for the speed of the bat to meet the ball. I threw the first pitch and brushed him back with an inside chest level throw. He looked at me with a smile and a nod to throw him another one. CRACK, he slammed a line shot down the line. Another CRACK, he hit a line drive up the middle. CRACK a line drive driven 3 bounces and hitting the green monster wall. He was in a groove and loving every bit of it.

After Roger's epic batting moment, I had the chance to bat. Daniel offered to throw, so I got into the batter's box, gripped my 34" Marty Barrett wooden bat and took a deep breath. Daniel threw steady lob pitches that I sprayed throughout the field. I was trying to tee it up with the hope to hit the Green Monster Wall. Even when I thought I caught the ball square; I was just shy of the warning track. It gave me new respect on how good these MLB players are as they crush ball after ball over the wall.

When batting practice was over, we still had not fully realized the opportunity that we just had. How many times did we all think how it was so far from reality to just be on the field at Fenway. But to take batting practice at Fenway – now that was far from reality.

The day was not over. We all departed the stadium and went our separate ways. Roger and I went back to the hotel as the Gaunce's toured the city. When we got back, we headed to the jacuzzi to relax and replay every minute on the field taking BP. Around 4:30 p.m. we headed back to Fenway to witness the circus of the crowds before the next game. I went to the WILL CALL area to pick up the tickets and to wait for Mike O'Connell and his two buddies to arrive.

We were going to be sitting in the Budweiser section together. Roger went to take photos and walk around the stadium as I sat on the curb across from Yawkey Way to wait for them. Once again, I couldn't get over the number of Giants fans that were here for this two-game series. I sat next to a couple from San Francisco who flew in just for the game. We talked for 20 minutes about the West Coast, the Giants, and Boston. They were impressed with Fenway and enjoyed being in Boston.

When Mike O'Connell and his buddies arrived, we went straight to the right field roof top Budweiser section and began toasting and drinking. Roger was one of the few wearing a Giant's hat in this section. He was proud of it and let everyone know who he was rooting for. The Red Sox fans were polite as they gave it back to Roger, especially when the Sox started to pound the Giants. The game was a seesaw with the lead going back and forth between the Sox and Giants until later in the game when Hanley Ramirez put on a show hitting his third home run and driving in his 6th RBI of the night. Both teams pounded out 31 hits tying an American League record for most hits in a game. The Red Sox won 11-7.

Ken Walsh

That special Wednesday on July 20, 2016, will always be a moment in time as one of my top baseball moments in my life. Like in the movie Field of Dreams, where Shoeless Joe Jackson asks Ray, "Is this heaven?" I felt as if I was asking the same question over and over that day. Yes, heaven sometimes is on earth and I had a piece of it on this day.

Journey 44

The undefeated Champions: Coach Wayne Gendreau, Garrett Gendreau, Corbin Anderson, Dustan Hunter, Cam Brown, Coach Brian Bellows, Coach Ken Walsh, Joel Retamozzo, Eli Kerr, Gabe Pouland, Cooper Tardiff and Sean Walsh.

"Perfection is not attainable, but if we chase perfection, we can catch excellence."
Vince Lombardi

The Perfect Season

In the early spring of 2016, my son Sean told me that he was not going to play baseball in the minor league division that year. To be honest, I was disappointed. My only son not having interest in the game that I loved so much was hard to take. At the same time, I wanted to support all of his interests. That is what dads must do.

Sean is a talented boy and I knew he would be successful due to his interests and skill set. So, after this news, I continued with my business of building Purnell Wrigley Field, playing in the men's wooden bat league, and taking swings in my home indoor batting cage. Then it happened.

A year later in Spring 2017, Sean came to me after one of my sessions in the batting cage and said, "Dad I would like to play baseball this year." I am not sure what inspired him to change his mind and I attempted to hold back my enthusiasm to not show too much emotion and scare him away. I took a deep breath to try to hold back my joy and said, "Sean, if that is what you would like to do, I'll sign you up for the Alfond Youth Center Cal Ripken League."

Of course, I could not hold back my excitement with Suzanne. I ran up to see her in the living room and quietly whispered to her, "Hey, Sean wants to play baseball this year!" We were both happily surprised and pleased with his change of heart. We both love the game of baseball and know that it can be the launching pad for so many other great things in life.

I did not want to interfere with Sean's interest to get into the game, so I told the Alfond Youth Center's Athletic Director that I was willing to help teach fundamentals but did not want to coach. Sean had a series of clinics and practices in the gym that March before teams were selected. Sean and I practiced in the cellar throwing back and forth and taking batting practice. He was starting from scratch, but he had interest to learn. And best of all, he was having fun.

In early April, we had a family trip planned to go to Florida and the Bahamas in which Sean would miss two weeks of practice. During this time, the coaches were going to pick the team. Before I left, I found out that one of my Wave teammates and Sean's AYC counselor, Brian Bellows, was going to coach. I asked him to consider choosing Sean. He said he would. For our trip we packed a baseball glove and during down time we had a catch on the beach and around the pool. When we got back from our trip, we happily discovered that Sean was going to play for Coach Bellows. His team was the Waterville Alfond Team.

The weather conditions in Maine that spring were horrible for baseball. The snow took a long time to melt and the weather was very wet and cold in April. Luckily for Waterville, we had the new turf field at Purnell Wrigley Field. For many towns, their baseball programs were postponed. At Purnell Wrigley due to the turf, we were able to get in a majority of our practices.

I really tried to stay out of practices and watch from the sideline, but my Physical Education background and experience in teaching fundamentals would not allow me to step aside. At the first practice on the field, I quickly jumped in after watching for 15 minutes and troubled by seeing the old method of kids standing around doing nothing and waiting for the next batter to hit. I asked Coach Bellows if I could step in to support him and take some of the kids for ball rolling line drills and then work on outfield play while more kids did soft toss. In a short time, all the kids were engaged in moving from station to station, each having more touches with the ball rather than standing around. I was hooked and a welcome addition to the coaching staff.

Uniforms were handed out before the first game. Sean received the number 4, the same number I wore on my uniform many times over the years. The opening season was during the same time of the Purnell Wrigley Dedication with All Star pitcher Lee Smith as our guest. After the ceremony, I took Lee Smith and his wife back to Portland for their flight out. That same day, Fran Purnell and I went to Fenway Park to watch the Chicago Cubs and Boston Red Sox play in a

Passion For Life

game at 4 PM. Unfortunately, I was going to miss Sean's first official baseball game at Purnell Wrigley Field. His game time was at 4 PM as well.

While watching the Red Sox and Cubs game, I could not help but wonder what was going on in Waterville. Suzanne texted me to provide updates on the score. The Alfond Team was behind. Every inning the other team, Central Maine Motors, scored more runs. Going into the last inning – the sixth inning - I saw the final text; it read Central Maine Motors 7 Alfonds 0. I did not see another text for a long while and figured that Sean's team lost their opening game. I assumed that our pitching was not up to par and the lack of hits had led to defeat.

In minor league youth baseball, pitchers at the ages of 8 to 10 have a hard time reaching home plate. Most of the game consists of walks and passed balls that become the majority of the scoring. That is how it is most of the season until the kids begin to understand fundamentals and improve their skills. The pitcher and catcher are key ingredients for success. The pitching position is even more challenging due to a limit on pitches for most age groups and many teams do not have much depth in pitching. Therefore, when your number one pitcher is out due to pitch count, the game can get out of hand with walks. I believe the minor league structure should be changed to give kids chances to field balls and bat rather than the passed balls and walks.

On my way home around 7:00 pm, I got a text and update from Suzanne. The game ended with a tie 7 to 7. Alfonds came back in the bottom of the 6th to score 7 runs using all of their 10 batters (a team can only bat 10 batters per inning). Sean got up 3 times, struck out twice and walked once. He told me when I got home that his "On Base Percentage (OBP)" is .333. I said to myself, "Where did he get that from?"

The season went on with practices twice per week and games two to three times per week. May was all about baseball. Late nights meant many dinners out since our home was 20 minutes from the field. By the time we got home, it was homework and baths.

The Alfonds were on a roll, playing four games in two weeks, winning each of them and outscoring the opponents 57 runs to their 5. Sean's OBP was well over six hundred, batting both left and right-handed. The team's starting lineup was becoming more set with our star pitcher Dustan Hunter on the mound while our solid steady catcher Garrett Gendreau was behind the plate. Garrett and Dustan would switch spots later in the innings for Garrett to finish up pitching duties. We had Logan "Kong" Dodge playing short stop. I gave Logan the name "Kong" after seeing him launch some long shots in batting practice. He was also a foot taller than the rest of his teammates. To round out the defense was Corbin Anderson at first base, Cam Brown at second, Joel Retamozzo at third and in the outfield Gabriel Pouland, Austin Lee, Cooper Tardiff, Eli Kerr and Sean. Our secondary pitchers were Logan, Joel and Corbin.

Ken Walsh

On May 16th, my 56th birthday, we had a game in Sidney who had a solid team. Sidney scored quickly to take the lead, two to zero. The score stayed 2-0 into the 4th inning when our team erupted with 7 runs and then 9 runs in the fifth. Corbin Anderson had his debut as pitcher, becoming the surprise of the day by throwing strikes and getting the last batters out. My personal highlight was when Coach Bellows moved Sean to second base in the last inning. A ball was hit in his direction, and he moved in front of the ball, gobbled it up and threw to first base to make his first official out. After the out, he put his arms up in victory as the parents cheered him on yelling "Hey, Coach Walsh, that's your present today!" I had the biggest smile on my face. The gift of seeing Sean succeed was the best birthday present I could get. I was thinking to myself that evening and laughing inside, "How about that! What a great day, especially for a boy who didn't want to play baseball."

The next two games were against a Winslow team and a Waterville team. The Alfonds won easily playing good defense, smart base running and excellent pitching from Dustan and Garrett. That led us to the last game of the season. We stood in first place with 8 wins, no losses and one tie. The game was against an Oakland team. Their record did not indicate the level of talent on the team. One player played for the State AAU team and was one of Sean's Club Naha karate mates, Sean Achorn. This little blond-headed dynamo had a competitive spirit and the skills to go along with his drive. He pitched a sound 3 innings keeping them in the game. He also had key hits to make the game close.

That evening at Purnell Wrigley the game was a battle right from the start. Both teams scored runs quickly. In the top of the 6th we were up seven to five with two outs and runners on first and second. The next batter hit a ball to Logan at short stop. He picked it up cleanly and threw it over to Corbin at first for what should have been the out to end the game, a play that typically we counted on all season. Unfortunately, the ball bounced out of Corbin's mitt permitting the game to go on.

Corbin, cool as a cucumber, took it in stride and did not let the emotions get to him and played on. With the bases loaded, two outs, and Alfonds leading 7 to 5, the Oakland team's power hitter was up. He took a 1 ball and 1 strike count before he swung on the next pitch driving the ball deep left center field hitting the turf and rolling all the way to the fence clearing the bases for a grand slam. The score was now 9 to 7. We ended up getting the last batter out although now we were down by two runs going into the bottom half of the last inning.

The Alfond team got a few batters on base, but Oakland quickly struck out two of our other batters leaving runners on second and third with two outs. That is when little Cooper Tardiff came up to bat. This boy has a heart of a giant. His life has been full of struggles with illnesses. According to his mom and dad, Cooper had 15 different surgeries, but his will and love of life is unmatched. Here he is now at the plate, game on the line for the undefeated season with

Passion For Life

runners on second and third with two outs. This would make any ball player shake in their pants. The first pitch was thrown for a strike. On the next pitch, Cooper swung with all his might and missed the ball. Now it was two strikes and two outs as Cooper waited for the next pitch. The pitcher went into his wind up to throw a pitch down the middle. Cooper's little arms swung the bat with all he had. The bat hit the top part of the ball bouncing in between first base and the pitcher. The two runners rounded the bases as they moved on the hit to run home. Cooper sprinted out of the batter's box as the ball was bobbled by the pitcher and dropped. Cooper was safe as he raced by first base. The two Alfond runners scored to tie the game! The Waterville parents went crazy, shouting at the top of their lungs and engaging the players. Our next batter struck out and we were now in extra innings. During the next inning, Oakland left two on the bases, scoring no runs. The bottom of the seventh started with our top of the order and Dustan leading off with a hit, stole second and went to third on a passed ball. Garrett followed at the plate with a hit to second base to win the game and keeping our regular season play undefeated.

We were the number one seed going into the playoffs. The first round we had a bye and then in the quarter match-up we played the Oakland team again. Their star player Sean Achorn did not play due to a conflict with his other travel baseball team. This time we beat Oakland with a lot less dramatics for a score of 10 to 5. Sean got on base twice and scored once.

The next game was scheduled at Fenway against the Winslow team that had a star athlete playing for them. He had the most home runs in the league, was a great defensive catcher and could run as fast as lightning. We had to play it smart on who to pitch. In the league if a pitcher went over 40 on the pitch count, he could not pitch for two days. This game was scheduled for Sunday and the championship game for Monday evening. Coach Bellows, Coach Gendreau and I agreed that we were going to save Dustan for the Championship game and start Garrett. Garrett was our number two pitcher all season long. Although, he did not throw with velocity, Garrett threw strikes. After Garrett we planned to put in Logan "Kong" to hopefully finish the game.

The game was scheduled for 10 AM. This meant that Brian and I were going to miss our Sunday Wooden Bat League Men's baseball game in order to coach this game. That was an easy choice. For a minor league game, the parking lot and the Fenway stadium were filled with spectators. It was a beautiful sunny day for early June.

Since we were the home team, Winslow batted first and loaded the bases. Their star player, Joey Richardson, was up. Garrett's pitch was perfect for Joey right down the middle. He crushed it with a sweet swing driving the ball over Gabe Pouland's head in centerfield for a grand slam. Garrett ended up getting the final outs of the inning although we were down 4-0. The Winslow team started their all-star player Joey Richardson on the mound. He pitched well although we scored enough runs to gain a good lead in the first two innings. We scored 7 runs to pull ahead. Garrett's pitch count ended his performance on the mound after three good innings.

We brought in Logan for the 4th inning. Even though he got the first batter out, he struggled and walked a few batters. With one out and the bases loaded again. Joey (Number 14) was up. It did not take him long as he hit another tremendous shot way up high and deep to left center field that hit the wall after four bounces. With his speed it was a certain homerun. Joey almost caught the runner ahead of him as he rounded third.

We were losing 8-7 going into the bottom of the fourth inning. Joey was now catching, and a new Winslow pitcher was on the mound. During the next two innings, we scored 11 runs and they picked up two more leading into the final inning. The score was 18-10 and looking like a sure victory, but Winslow battled back to score 5 runs. Logan's pitch count had exceeded 75 so he had to leave the game. We brought in our third baseman Joel Retamozzo who made excellent plays at third base and pitched one time for us. Joel was a quiet steady ball player that did his job without looking for fanfare. With a runner on first, Joel walked the next batter. On a passed ball, the runners moved up to second and third with one out. Joel faced a good hitter who batted third in the lineup and struck him out. The next batter was number 14, Joey, who hit two grand slams and had 8 RBIs already.

Brian looked over to me and said, "What do you think about moving Logan out to leftfield and putting Dustan at short?" I said, "Let's do it."

With runners on second and third and two outs, if Joey hit another homerun the score would be tied. With the count at one ball and no strikes, Joey swung at the next pitch driving the ball deep to left field. For me it seemed like everything was slow motion. Logan drifted back toward the warning track, let his feet jump up and the ball found its way into his mitt. Game over! The Alfond team all ran out to meet Logan jumping on him and celebrating a tremendous victory. The parents were all standing and clapping to salute the effort of these young boys.

As things settled down, we huddled the boys together after the traditional handshakes. One game left for an undefeated season – a perfect season. Coach Bellows said, "Boys we have one game to play, be ready for tomorrow."

The next day was a cloudy overcast and rainy day. The forecast for Monday June 5th was rain on and off with temperatures in the low fifties. It was not your perfect day to play baseball although playing on Maine's Fenway Park's turf prevented a cancellation.

We also got word that Cross River Film Company from New York City wanted to be there to tape the game. They were covering mainly Brian Bellows for the film they were producing called "Safe at Home," a story about our baseball program and our replica ball fields.

Passion For Life

Sean and I arrived at 4:15 pm, 45 minutes before game time. Already the field was full of the baseball players and the crowds of people were gathering outside the fence to watch the game. The inclement weather did not hold back the many spectators on both sides between the Winslow and Waterville teams. The parents who were the faithful followers of our team were there in force along with their extended families. They gathered in the bleacher area right behind home plate with their rain jackets on and umbrellas above their heads.

Even for 9- and 10-year-olds the excitement of the championship atmosphere was building. Our star pitcher Dustan Hunter even told me that he had butterflies. I said to Dustan, "Just focus and throw strikes and you will be alright." Having the film crew on the field with their commercial cameras one would see at MLB games seemed to be surreal. For many of the spectators they did not know what was going on and some assumed that the game was live on TV. The camera followed the kids and coaches around before, during and after the game to get the live action. That piece of the activity added even more excitement for the kids.

The opening ceremony included all the kids being called out on the first and third baselines as they introduced their name and number. After the National Anthem the game was on. We were the home team, and you could feel the energy and excitement in the air.

Dustan pitched the first inning perfectly, shutting down Winslow with a one, two, three inning. At the bottom half of the first inning, Dustan led off with a hit and was followed by Garrett hitting a double. With runners on second and third, Corbin Anderson got a hit driving in two runs. The inning ended with the Alfonds leading two to zero.

For the next two innings, Dustan shut down the Winslow team and the Alfonds erupted with more hits, walks, and passed balls to add another 4 runs. After 3 innings we were up 6-0. In the top half of the 4th inning, Dustan got into trouble walking the first two batters. The middle of Winslow's line-up added a few hits driving in two runs before Dustan got out of the jam. In the bottom of the 4th, we added another run going into the fifth inning leading 7-2. Unfortunately, Dustan had thrown his 75th pitch and had to leave the game. We brought in Corbin who had pitched only a few innings during season. He was successful getting the ball over the plate despite not much velocity. With the score 7-2 and six outs to go, we felt confident that Corbin could finish off the game. And he did.

After a rocky start in the 5th inning, walking the first two batters and giving up a few hits resulting in two more runs, Corbin struck out the side. With the bottom of the order for our team, we did not score heading to the final inning, leading 7-4.

Corbin got the first batter to ground out to Camden at second, walked the next batter with the top of the order. The leadoff batter hit a single up the middle.

Our centerfielder, Gage Poulin, kept the ball in front of him and held the runners at first and second. The next batter struck out although a passed ball sent the runners over to second and third with two outs. For the Winslow team their reliable hitter who batted third in the lineup was up. This was a real threat to drive the runners home. Corbin with his calm composure got set on the mound. He threw the first two pitches for balls low and in the dirt. Garret did a fine job keeping the ball in front of him to prevent the runners from scoring. Corbin then threw a ball down the middle and the batter took a hard swing fouling the ball back. Corbin went back to the mound, stepped on the pitcher's plate and threw his fourth pitch high and away. The count was now 3-1. It certainly was a hitter's count. Corbin threw his 5th pitch right down the middle and the batter took another hard swing and missed. Now the count was full, with two outs, runners on second and third in the last inning.

Corbin Anderson, a 10-year-old boy who only pitched a few innings all season, was on the mound with the game on the line. Parents were standing and shouting encouragement for both teams. In both dugouts the kids were standing and shouting support. The camera crew was capturing each second on film. Corbin with his incredible focus took the ball in his hand, went into a full wind up and threw the pitch. The ball was a perfect throw right down the middle. The batter watched it into the catcher's glove. The umpire shouted – "Strike three."

The Waterville Alfond supporters erupted with joy. The players and coaches leaped to their feet in excitement, rushing to the pitching mound to surround Corbin. The celebration continued on the field as an extraordinary moment transpired. The kids walked behind the plate and put their hands through the fence as parents pressed up against the fence area celebrating with their children. The players showed respect to their parents for their support all season. It was an amazing moment that I will remember forever. My eye caught Corbin's parents. There they were with proud smiles. I knew this moment would always be special for them.

The kids then lined up for the traditional handshake. The sportsmanship shown by the Winslow team was incredible. They congratulated our team and kept their heads up high. This was an indication of excellent coaching from Head Coach Beckwith.

Athletic Director, Isaac LeBlanc, requested that all the players and coaches line up on the field for the ceremonial recognition. Isaac named all the players on the Winslow side handing them trophies. And then to the Champs, first recognizing the coaches followed by the kids one by one alphabetically. As the kids were named, high fives and hugs were given to each player.

Sean getting a hug from Dad

When Sean was called, we gave each other a great big bear hug. This hug will last for eternity. The perfect season came to an end. A moment in time that I can reflect on that will never be taken away from me and my son and all our family.

Fran Purnell at the Red Sox vs Cubs game in 2017, after the Wrigley Field dedication.

The one constant through all of the years, Ray, has been baseball." Field of Dreams Movie

Mr. Baseball – Mr. Fran Purnell

I call him "Dad." Fran Purnell has insisted that I call him Dad since my own Dad passed away in 2016. I have known Fran since I moved to Waterville in 1992 although I started to really get to know him in 2014. That was the year he decided to retire after 45 years from volunteering for his services running youth baseball. He came to my office at the Alfond Youth Center and told me that after thinking long and hard that he wanted the AYC to run the program. He said some of the current coaches did not want us to oversee the program fearing that we would ruin what Fran had created. Fran said that his conclusion came after talking to his close circle of friends and family. He saw what we did with the building of Maine's Fenway Park in Oakland and knew of my passion for the game of baseball.

I said, "Mr. Purnell, I am honored that you thought of us and me. I will not take this lightly and will make sure we continue to build the successful baseball program that you are giving us."

From that point on, it did not take me long to push the concept to build another field in honor of another great person, Fran. After Fenway was completed, I always had a replica Wrigley Field on my mind. It was off to the races as I set my sights on accomplishing this goal.

I did mention to Fran that I had an idea to enhance the field that he built from scratch, although I don't believe he knew what I was really up to. My first call was to my good friend and Boys & Girls Club National Government Relations employee, Jack Glazebrook, to discuss how I could get a licensed agreement from MLB and the Chicago Cubs. I know the secret to raising funds was having the licensed agreement as this made the fundraising much easier. Jack directed me to the MLB Marketing Director Tom Brasuell. At a Boys and Girls Club of America (BGCA) conference in Chicago, I had the opportunity to meet up with him to discuss this possibility.

After our meeting, he said he would make a few calls. Months went by before action developed. In the meantime, I flew out to Chicago once again to meet with the head of the LISC Foundation, Kerri Blackwell, to ask for a lead gift since they have given dollars to build ball fields and for her endorsement for the naming rights. After our lunch at Harry Carry's restaurant, Kerri agreed to make a few calls to help. Finally, Tom called me and said that he had a conference call with the Chicago Cubs and Red Sox officials and they agreed to issue the license to us. The Cubs had to receive permission from the Red Sox since the Boston Club market base is in Maine. Thanks to Bill Alfond, a minority owner of the Red Sox, it helped move this agreement along.

Now that I had the licensed agreement, the only one in the nation to build a replica Wrigley Field, I was off making fundraising pitches to leadership supporters in the community. The Gaunce family was the first to join in with a leadership pledge followed by Bill Mitchell, the Borman Foundation, Doug and Rita Sukeforth, and the Harold Alfond Foundation. Our initial application to the MLB Tomorrow fund was denied. Although like I always say, a no is a maybe and a maybe will become a yes, and that is what happened.

After our application was denied, we started digging in to find out why. Our AYC grant manager who is a fellow Brooklyn boy also believes in never accepting a no for an answer, started a dialogue with the Tomorrow Fund staff administrators. They said even though this was a worthy project, since they had given

Passion For Life

a leadership gift to our Fenway Project they would not give more funds to the same community.

I called my good friend, Jim Hughes, who serves on our Board of Directors, to see if he could give a helping hand. He had a friend who knew the MLB Commissioner, Rob Mansfield, well enough to call him and make a pitch. Within weeks Jim called me back and said, I got good news. Cathy Bradley, the Executive Director of the Tomorrow Fund, will be calling you and asking you to put in another application for funding.

Cathy flew up to Maine to meet with our AYC team to discuss the project, visit the current Purnell Field and collect her notes for our application to be presented to their Major League Baseball Tomorrow Fund Board. Within months we got even better news, the MLB Tomorrow Fund granted us 100 thousand for the project.

The fundraising had a good start although the total cost for the project was estimated to be around $1.4 million. We raised over $800,000 in cash and earned the other $600,000 through in-kind services. The City of Waterville through the efforts of the Park & Recreation Director Matt Skehan and his Public Works sidekick Mike Folsom, helped with the demolition of the field and site work saving over 200 thousand, while Central Maine Power supplied the poles and local electricians supported putting in the new lights from Musco. Philip Lamantia, a Chicago native with his volunteer workers, built the dugouts and the framework for the concession stand.

The project continued to push on and Fran caught wind about what we were doing. Being a baseball man, he was thrilled and could not believe that this was happening at his field. Fran's home is just on the other side of home plate on the next street. And now, the field that he developed for over 40 years was going to be a turf Wrigley field with new lights, dugouts, concession stand and the landmark centerfield score board. Fran at many times offered to help with the project, which he did by assisting with fundraising, pounding nails, sheetrocking, and being the person around the field to give the workers direction and answer questions. Fran couldn't help but get involved since for years he built this field using lots of in-kind support attempting to open every door imaginable to make his dugouts, press box, concession stand, and batting cage. His labor of love brought many people in the community together to set concrete for the fence, work the concession stand, to umpire, coach, announce the game, keep score or just watch the boys and girls play. And all of this came from enormous volunteer hours lead by Fran. In the early '90s, Fran did get recognition from the Waterville Mayor at the time, Tom Nale, officially giving the ball field a name – Purnell Baseball Field.

Fran's drive to support this project stems back from the '70's when he got involved in the baseball program after one afternoon he was asked to help assist and coach his son's team. From then on, Fran could not get away from supporting the program and became a head coach, a commissioner and a key person in the development of the field. For Fran, his wife Joyce, and his family, the ball field became their second home. In the late '80's Fran saw a young man in a wheelchair watching a game from the other side of the fence and after that moment he knew he had to do more.

The next season he committed to never ever letting kids with disabilities be prevented from playing baseball. He teamed up with the Challenger program and for 25 years on Friday evenings, kids and adults with disabilities have been on the field playing ball because of Fran. Fran tells the story of how one young boy got involved in the Challenger program and never missed a game. Unfortunately, due to his illness several years later, he passed away. His mom told Fran that he wanted to be buried in his Challenger uniform.

The objective was to have most of the field done by the fall of 2016. The timing was perfect since the Chicago Cubs were playing one of their best seasons in 108 years, when they won the last World Series. The Cubs were in first place heading for 100 wins and surely heading into the playoffs. At the same time, we were building the replica score board. The vision was to have this scoreboard celebrating the first World Series for the Cubs in 108 years and we, in Waterville, would have the only replica licensed field. The Cubs kept us all on the edge of our seats through the playoffs beating the Giants to get into the World Series to play against the Cleveland Indians managed by former Red Sox Manager Terry Francona. The series was a battle right from Game One. The Cubs found themselves down three games to two. After winning Game Six to tie the series, the team had to play in Cleveland for the final game. Battling back in the late innings the Cubs won at 12:47 am, to be the World Champions. I was watching this great historic baseball moment at home in Vassalboro and wanted to text my new "Dad" to congratulate him. He beat me to it. The text read; "We did it son, the Chicago Cubs, our World Champions. Now let's finish the score board."

The next day I contacted Peter Schutte who was the President of Graphic Color who did all of our graphics and said, "Peter, we need to freeze the clock on the score in time at 12:47 a.m. The time the Cubs became World Champions once again.

With all the excitement of the new Purnell Wrigley Field also came the challenges of life. Fran's wife Joyce had developed lung cancer. Every winter Fran and Joyce headed to Florida, this time they had to stay back to take on their most challenging opponent. Through the winter season into the New Year of 2017, Joyce had her taxing appointments with chemo and visits to the ER. It was wearing on Fran as well. I needed to lift their spirits.

In early May, the first weekend of our baseball season, was the date for the dedication of the Purnell Wrigley Field. Hall of Fame Pitcher Fergie Jenkins, who was our honorary Chair, called me that he could not make the dedication due to illness in his family. I immediately called Lee Smith, All Star and former pitcher of the Cubs, Cards and Red Sox. He gladly accepted the invitation. Lee received his long-waited call in 2019 to enter the Hall of Fame.

On a Saturday in May, over 200 local kids playing baseball arrived at the field on a beautiful but cool Maine morning. The field was completed with the beautiful turf fixed on the ground with the fresh white line on the foul lines and batter's box. Our announcer was on the second floor of the concession stand prepared to make the formal introductions of the teams with city officials, sponsors, players, and Lee Smith. After the players marched in, including our son, Sean, wearing his white baseball pants and navy-blue Waterville Alfond jersey, they lined up along first and third base line leading into the outfield.

I came out to thank the sponsors and the City of Waterville for the collaborative effort. Lee Smith was introduced with a loud round of applause. After he was done, I asked Fran and Joyce to come out. The thousand plus people there gave them a thunderous applause with everyone standing on their feet saluting them for a lifetime of support to the game of baseball.

I then told Fran and the crowd that I had a surprise. "Everyone, please meet me in the parking lot in front of the first base dugout."

There was a four-foot by eight-foot stone covered with a tarp. I asked Fran and Joyce to come in front of the tarp for an unveiling. While everyone was around the tarp, I read a proclamation recognizing that day as Fran Purnell Day. I proceeded to take off the gray tarp exposing the new monument with Fran Purnell's face on it wearing a Chicago Cubs hat with the description of the history of the field and Fran's leadership. Fran was taken aback, speechless.

"Son, you got me. I would have never expected this."

"Dad, you deserve all of this and more, and I got more, today we are heading to Boston to see the Red Sox play the Cubs."

That day we drove down together to meet up with Philip Lamantia who rented out a limousine as well as bringing his daughter Samantha. We had a terrific day as the Red Sox beat the Cubs in a classic baseball game. My favorite part of the day was having the 6 hours in the car with Fran talking about baseball, family and life. I absorbed his years of wisdom and advice as it flowed out of his mind through his lips. That evening as I drove into Waterville with Fran, he said, "Son, let's go to the field."

I drove into the parking lot pulled up close to his new monument. He shook his head again and said, "You certainly got me."

On the other side of the fence was a father and son having a catch on the turf field. The games were over, the sun was setting and the sound of a ball hitting into the glove of the father and son's mitt echoed. We both looked over enjoying the sight.

"Kenny, this is what it is all about. I love this game. You get home and see your family. You've had enough of me for one day."

I said, "I'll take you home."

"No. I'd rather walk home."

"Hey Dad, thank you."

He knew what I meant; he nodded and turned and walked away. I watched him walk as he admired his new field, walking past the third base dugout into the outfield spectator area disappearing beyond the wooden fence leading to his street. The same walk he has taken for forty plus years.

Fran passed away on the morning of May 2, 2023, at the age of 82. I lost a second father. Prior to his passing I tried to get him to the traditional grand opening ceremony of the baseball/softball season in which all players, parents, coaches, and family members show up to mark the beginning of the season. I had Waterville Police Chief Bill Bonney there to throw the first pitch. Colby coaches along with the players showed up to show support to the kids as well. I talked with Fran's son Kevin to see if we could at least have Fran show up even if he was in a wheelchair. In the nursing home he made the attempt to get in the wheelchair, unfortunately the pain to sit upright was to be challenging. 2023 would mark the first opening that Fran would miss.

I had the first pitch signed by the police chief along with the Colby coaches.

Vic and me at the on-deck circle

"You beat cancer by how you live, and in the manner in which you live."
Stuart Scott

Spin the Bottle

We never know what may happen in the course of our life. Some things we control and other things in life we do not. It is like playing Spin the Bottle. Sometimes the spin might not be a good one. That is what happened to my friend, fellow teammate and coworker, Victor Garay.

Vic, to say the least, did not have the rosiest upbringing. He grew up in the projects of the Bronx without a father and raised by his grandmother along with his other siblings. Fortunately, he found basketball as an outlet at an early age. His skill in the game kept him focused and away from trouble. Thanks to his high school coach and guidance counselor, he considered options to go onto college and away from city life. That brought him to Bangor, Maine, to play at Husson College. That is where he became a star point guard, finishing and graduating with a four-year accounting degree. After graduation, he worked as an assistant coach at Husson and a basketball referee.

Ken Walsh

In 2016, Vic joined the AYCC staff as Account Assistant. During conversations together, I discovered his love for sports and his family. The Bronx kid had settled down with his wife and three young children in the town of Winslow in a very nice neighborhood far from his start. The Bronx city boy was now a family man. He continued to play recreation basketball and softball as a point guard and shortstop. He loved the Yankees, especially Hall of Fame short stop, Derek Jeter.

In 2018, I convinced Vic to play for our Brooklyn Dodger men's baseball team in Bath. At the age of 48, he still had the skill set to play hardball even though he had never played organized baseball before. He agreed and started practicing with our team and played the entire season starting at second base then moving over to shortstop. He was our leadoff hitter and the spark plug for the team. During his rookie season, he made some spectacular plays at short leading us to a 10-6 season and playing for the championship at Hadlock Field. The following year, we had another excellent season, finishing with a 12-3 record and first in league play.

In the fall of 2019, I invited him to play for our Cincinnati Avalanche team in February in the 2020 Sunshine Classic series in Fort Myers. He was extremely excited and started practicing with our other teammate Don Sawyer. We spent a few months at the Colby batting cages and field to prepare for the competition. Even on New Year's Eve with the temperatures sitting around 10 degrees, we took batting practice in the cages. We booked an Airbnb in Cape Coral and planned to fly out on February 13th. Then it happened.

Vic went in for his 50-year-old routine colonoscopy procedure on February 6th. It was then that they discovered he had stage four cancer in his large intestine and a few spots on his liver. Vic, as well as all of us around him, was devastated with the news. He had to cancel his trip to Florida to begin treatment. He was told in baseball terms that he was down to his last strike and he needed to hit a home run with the cancer treatments. He cried on my shoulder in fear several times not knowing what lay ahead. He tried to keep positive with his chin up, although he knew as we all did, he was fighting for his life.

Before I left for my trip down south, I went to Joseph's Sporting Goods Store in Waterville and ordered new Dodger uniforms. These uniforms had Vic's number, the number 2, sewn on the sleeve of each one in honor of him.

In Florida before our first game, Larry Murphy and I gathered the team together. Even though the Cincinnati boys did not know Vic everyone was down about the situation. Larry asked me to say a few words to the team. We gathered around the dugout on a hot Florida afternoon. Our manager, Jeff Butcher, asked everyone to circle up. He said, "Kenny has something to say."

I hesitated to clear my mind before I said, "You all know that Vic can't be with us today. Last week, he was diagnosed with stage four cancer, and he is now fighting for his life. We are here because we love the game of baseball and play with our hearts every day. I am asking you to pray with all your hearts for Vic. He has a wife and three young children that need him. Today let's play for Vic." At that moment, everyone put their hands in the circle and shouted, "Vic."

What followed was a classic finish. We played against a team from Pittsburgh. Through the entire game they stayed in front of us. Their pitcher, a tall righty, kept us off balance while our pitcher, Clyde, kept us close going into the last inning and down 6 to 4. I batted second, already 3 for 3, scoring 2 runs, stealing 2 bases, and driving in an RBI. At the bottom of the inning, we filled the bases with one out. The Pittsburgh team brought in a relief pitcher, their third baseman. He was warming up throwing fastballs low and away. Our leadoff hitter, Bill Pike, stepped up to bat. After falling behind on a 1-2 count, he popped up for the second out.

It was my turn to bat with two outs, bases loaded and the game on the line. I dug in with my spikes, tapped my red model 271 on the plate and said in my mind, "Vic this is for you." I assumed the pitcher was going to live on the outside of the plate as he warmed up throwing fast balls in that area. I was looking fastball all the way, intending to drive the ball to the right side. I stepped 6 inches away from the inside of the box waiting for a knee-high pitch. That pitch came.

I put the barrel of my bat on the ball sending it over the first baseman. Immediately, the runners at second and third scored to tie the game. I rounded second, saw Don Sawyer rounding third and stopping halfway to the plate. The first baseman reached the cut-off and fired to the catcher. It sailed over his head and Don scored the winning run. Our benched cleared, celebrating and mobbing me at third base. My walk off hit gave me my 5th RBI and fourth hit for the day.

I could say it was my day, but it was really Vic's. For Vic, it was the first win in a long battle ahead as he battles not for just one game, but for his life.

Journey 47

2020 Colby College win against Bowdoin.

"When life gives you lemons, make lemonade." Elbert Hubbard

Colby Baseball Championship Season

After getting back from my Florida trip with the Cincinnati Avalanche baseball team, I started coaching as an assistant coach for the Colby College Mules Baseball team. Head Coach Jesse Woods, in his second year with Colby coming from Norte Dame along with his Assistant Coach Tad Skelley asked me to help. After talking with Suzanne and getting the nod, I gladly accepted even though I knew that my time was going to be limited due to the demanding work at the AYCC as CEO. But my love for baseball was overpowering and I managed to help coach according to what my schedule would allow.

The hardest part of coaching a college team is getting to know the players quickly during a short season. From February until the end of April is pretty much the whole season. Ahead of time, I asked for the roster and the bios of all the team members in order to get a feel for the team chemistry. What I found out quickly is that Coach Woods recruited a strong sophomore and freshmen class and weeded out the junior and senior class that he inherited. All the players were kids from around the country. There was only one Maine player. The high expectations were set as soon as Coach Woods got to Colby. With his expectations, Colby would no longer be the door mat, they were going to be contenders each and every season. The freshman class, a mix of infielders, pitchers and a catcher, was the foundation for the future. He also told me that he worried about the current pitching staff although the recruiting class coming in had four strong pitching prospects.

I was excited to start even as Maine's winter was upon us. We got outside several times, had practice in the cages and on the turf field. Two of the Colby seniors Taimu Ito (DH and Catcher) and William Wessman (IB and Pitcher) stood out as leaders of the team. Taimu was more vocal and a spokesman while William was the quiet leader, leading by actions. I enjoyed talking baseball and life with these two men.

Practices were going well. With thirty-six players, we were able to scrimmage often against each other. One evening right before preparing for a scrimmage during a weeknight under the lights, Coach Woods looked over to me and said, "Hey Coach Walsh, we need a second baseman tonight for one of the teams, you want to play?"

It took a matter of a nano second for my response, "Hell ya," as I immediately ran out and took my spot at second.

As it always happens, the most unexpected does happen. The first five batters in the first two innings were lefties. Each ball hit went right to me for plays at first. One, I had to dive to my left coming very close to a diving catch. The Colby players cheered in unison, appreciating the hustle from a 58-year-old. I was pumped up to be able to get on the field with Colby ball players and hold my own. I did get up once to bat, grounding out to the third baseman.

Practices continued despite the unrest in the world because of the COVID-19 pandemic that was first identified in the Chinese city of Wuhan in 2019. It spread rapidly across the world eventually hitting the US. The first case in the US hit Washington State on January 21, 2020. The lack of containment led to it spreading through the country. Eventually gathering places shut down. NHL, NBA and MLB began to cancel games and then pulled the plug on the season including NCAA March Madness. Coronavirus was becoming dangerous for seniors and those with compromised immune systems. At the AYCC, we postponed all tournaments and gatherings in and out of our facility. We had to be prepared to shut down the facility. The stock market plunged in record drops. The economic US engine was stopped in its track for the time being.

Colby's baseball team was scheduled on March 21st to head to Florida for spring baseball. On the weekend of March 14th two doubleheaders were scheduled. But on March 9th the NESCAC (Colby's athletic conference) canceled all league play and the season was suspended. That afternoon, Coach Woods addressed the players in the dugout telling them how he was disappointed and had hoped that perhaps that they can play teams within the State that have not canceled their season. The next day, President David Greene ordered all students to leave the campus by the weekend. Colleges and universities across America were shutting down. It was a dark time in our history.

Coach Woods was able to schedule one last and only game on Thursday afternoon against Bowdoin College, one of their biggest rivals. Game time was at 4:00 pm and I had a few things going on that day for work. That evening, I was scheduled to be at a fundraiser for the Augusta Boys & Girls Club. I planned to attend the first half of the game and then leave. But, by mid-morning I wasn't feeling the greatest and decided that it was best to go home, get away from staff and kids to make sure that I didn't place anyone in jeopardy. Therefore, I would miss the fundraiser and the one and only game Colby was playing.

That evening around 8:30 pm, I texted Assistant Coach Skelley asking for the results. He texted back that Colby had won in the bottom of the ninth on a walk off single to right field by the senior catcher, George Schmidt, with the bases loaded, winning 5-4. He had to fight off a full count, fouling the ball off three times before hitting the winning two run RBI. I watched the replay on Facebook as the players ran out of the dugout mobbing George at first base. Colby's 2020 undefeated record would be in the history books, 1-0, a bittersweet ending for the seniors. Another Senior and the only Maine player, Emery Dinsmore got the start and pitched four innings giving up only one run.

That Friday night all the players and coaches got together at Amici's restaurant in Waterville for their final dinner together. At the end of the dinner, Taimu addressed the players and coaches with emotion, thanking them for the opportunity to play with a great group of men. The room stood still for those moments as the thought of the season being cut short took hold with the question of what might have been. Although what did happen was a strong memory of one game, one walk off, that led to an undefeated championship season.

Journey 48

Championship victory over the Pirates at Old Orchard Beach stadium

"The strength of the team is each individual member. The strength of each member is the team." Phil Jackson

Dodgertown

Life changed for all of us around the world when the COVID-19 Pandemic invaded our civilization. Our way of life was altered. Schools were shut down, businesses stopped operating, travel from State to State was discouraged, and in some cases banned, and all sports leagues were canceled. By June 2020, there were already two million people infected by the virus just in the United States. Millions more were infected worldwide and the numbers continued to rise.

Despite the negative effects of the Coronavirus, many good things happened including great human compassion and spirit that rose to the call of duty. This was clearly demonstrated at the Alfond Youth and Community Center each and every day.

I was on the ball field practicing with the World Series 2020 Cal Ripken U12 Team on Sunday March 15th when I received the call that all of the schools in

Central Maine were shutting down due to the virus. At that time, they made the statement it was going to be two weeks and then they would reassess the circumstances to figure out if the kids would be going back to school. Children of all ages would now learn remotely.

From that point on, there was a chain reaction that hit like a wave with businesses, colleges and many institutions closing their doors. The AYCC continued to provide the needed services to the community by providing over 35,000 hot free meals throughout the spring, along with offering essential childcare services for the area school and medical staff. It was truly a great call for service. I was so proud of the AYCC staff and volunteers as they stepped up to the challenge and delivered the necessary care. We never closed our doors although many modifications had to be made to comply with CDC protocols.

During this time, all recreation and sports activities were in question. Just like Colby Baseball, spring sports across the country came to a halt along with the pro sports billion-dollar industry.

I, along with my Maine Brooklyn Dodger teammates, was looking forward to getting back on the baseball field and seeking payback from getting knocked out of the playoff round against the Giants the year prior, especially after finishing in first place with a 12-3 record. During the managers meeting with the commissioner of Maine Woods Baseball League, the season was in question due to the pandemic. After much discussion and back and forth negotiations with the Bath Park and Recreation Department, we thankfully could begin play and use Kelly Field for the season. The season was delayed until the first of July, eliminating the first five games of the season and limiting us to a 10-game schedule.

Manager of our Dodger team, Dan Simpson, a seasoned baseball player and veteran of the league and in my opinion the best hitter in the conference discussed with me the holes that we had with our roster especially losing our starting pitcher Larry Murphy to shoulder surgery. Also, we knew Vic Garay was in question because of his battle with cancer and three other players who decided not to come back. That left our Dodger roster down to eight players, however, the eight remaining players were all solid.

Dan made the case to the other managers during the drafting of the free agents that the Dodgers needed help and negotiated the first pick and a waiver for an immediate add-on. Dan pleaded his case and finally got his way. We locked in a new left fielder and big lefty stick, Tim Kennison who I had played with in the Pine Tree league. Our second pick was Braxton Bell, a southern player from North Carolina that had just moved to the area. Bell was a switch hitter and a solid infielder that was billed to be a solid replacement for Larry Murphy. Surprisingly, our third pick was Mike Foshay a solid leadoff hitter and a dynamic center fielder coming from the Portland league. He had just turned 45 and Murphy thought he would be one of the best players in our league. Finally, for our last pick, we chose "Coach" Don Sawyer, the former Waterville High School

Passion For Life

Varsity Coach who won two State titles and knew the game of baseball inside and out. He was a crafty pitcher, solid infielder and he could consistently put wood on the ball.

With these picks, we had no holes in our lineup. Everyone could play the field, hit in the lineup and knew the game of baseball. Our pitching staff was solid with our starting pitcher Tommy Walker taking the responsibility followed by Don Sawyer, Bobby Bowen, Braxton Bell, and Dan "Meesh" Michaud. The season looked promising.

After my trip down to Florida in February to play in the Roy Hobbs World Series with the Cincinnati Avalanche, I was anxious to get back on the field even when it was the dead of winter. Don Sawyer came down to play as well and was hooked after the four-day weekend was completed. Don pitched well and had a few key hits that gave him the confidence to play ball again at 60 years old. Don and I reached out to a few other players from the Dodger team to start spring batting practice in the cages at Colby College. Their batting cages had a hitting system inside and the facility was covered in tarp to keep in the heat. Each weekend until the end of March we took our swings. Occasionally, we would hit on the turf field especially in between snowstorms. The temperatures at times were in the high 20's into the 30's creating a nice sting on the hands for several swings. It was a good incentive to hit the ball on the sweet spot of the bat.

As temperatures broke and spring started to settle in, more players showed up to our weekend batting and fielding practices. At times we would have seven to nine players chasing balls in the field. We conducted practices at Maine's Fenway and Wrigley replica fields, Colby College and Lawrence High School. By the time the season started, we were way ahead of schedule with comfort at the plate. And it showed during our first game.

We came out of the box quickly in the first game to beat the team that won the league championship the prior year. On the day after the 4th of July, we pounded out 20 plus hits, played flawless defense and our new starter, Tommy Walker, shut down the Pirates bats winning 17-1. I started off the season going 2-4, including 2 runs, 2 RBI's and 2 stolen bases. The combination of our new leadoff hitter, Mike Foshay, along with me batting second, Dan Simpson (the best hitter in the league) batting third and Rick Comeau, our RBI machine, batting fourth was a strong force for any team to face. Everyone in the line-up could hit and drive in runs.

Our new draft choice, Braxton Bell, had a tremendous day at the plate pounding out four hits and six RBI's to lead the offense. For the rest of the season, however, he was quiet at bat until the playoffs. Vic Garay, battling stage four cancer, started at shortstop and switched on and off with Braxton at that position. But this was the first and last game that Vic took a break during the season. For the rest of the season, he started at short and stayed there every inning, every game.

Beating the 2019 championship Pirates at a lopsided score raised eyebrows throughout the league. Our team continued to roll through the summer in which each game had a new hero for the day. Tommy Walker, our starting pitcher, continued to shut down teams followed by our relief pitching of Don Sawyer and Bobby Bowen. Braxton Bell who we hoped would see some innings hurt his arm the first game and was limited to pitching time. Meesh filled in for a few games as our closer along with Bobby. The Dodger machine kept rolling along, beating the Cards 18-10 and then the Braves 7-2. In three games, I already had seven hits adding to Dan Simpson and Mike Foshay's strong bats. By August 8th completing a double header sweep of the Giants 15-1 and 8-5, and taking down the Pirates and Cubs, 9-2 and 9-4 respectively, we were undefeated at 7-0 going into mid-August. Sweeping the Giants was a nice payback after last year. In the semifinals with a 12-3 record and sitting in first place as number one seed in the playoffs, the Giants beat us 10-5.

With three games left in the season, the rest of the teams were gunning for us, doing whatever they could to prevent us from having an undefeated season. Our three remaining games were against the Cards, Braves and Cubs. Any one of them had the ability to win and prevent the undefeated season. On August 15th, playing with our manager and best hitter, Dan Simpson, we faced the Cards. The Cards had not had many strong victories this season, losing several games by only a few runs and losing leads in the last inning of play. Nonetheless, they were a good hitting team that we could not take lightly and let down our guard.

In our game against the Cards, they scored quickly in the first inning to lead by one. Going into the 4th inning, we were ahead by only 2-1. Then our bats erupted mostly from the bottom of the order. Bobby Bowen, Greg Frizzle, Tim Kennison and Tommy Walker all had key hits for a seven run fourth inning.

The next few innings continued in the same way, pounding the ball and beating up the Cards 15 to 3. The final score concluded with a 15 to 5 score, bringing the Dodgers to an 8-0 record. Dan, who was not at this game due to family obligations, received texts from Larry Murphy, our scorekeeper, to keep him up to speed.

Over the next few days as Dan and I reviewed the line-up and discussed strategy, he told me how he was going out of his mind not being there at the game and more so knowing the game was tight. Every week during preseason and during the season, Dan and I discussed strategy for each game. We discussed our lineup, our strengths and pitching possibilities for the upcoming game. It was one of the best parts of the season, talking baseball with Dan "Skip" Simpson.

Our next game was against last year's 0-15 team, the Braves. Their team during the off season changed dramatically with adding a core of solid players coming from the Portland league and players who played in the Roy Hobbs World Series including hard-hitting solid defensive players and pitchers, Ed

Simmons, Chris Rolfe, Jeff Howland, Dan "Doc" Proctor, Ed Mayer, and Clair Crandall. These players made the Braves very competitive, and I thought they were the only team that could stop us from our championship run.

The game against the Braves was a great fight right to the end. Not until the last innings did we pull ahead with timely hitting, solid pitching and critical defense to beat them 8-3 heading into the final game of the season. The next weekend was the final game of the regular season against the Cubs. We lost to the Cubs in the 2018 season in the championship game 7-3. The majority of their team members were still participating although they lost a pitcher and a strong utility player due to the pandemic. The first game we beat them handily. That Saturday of game time, it was one of the few weekends in Maine this summer that the weather did not cooperate. It rained throughout the day into Sunday morning. The Cubs Manager, Bill Arsenault, wanted to preserve his pitching staff for the playoffs and preferred to play on Sunday evening for the makeup game rather than during the week. We could not get enough guys to play on Sunday and wanted to play during the week. Since we could not come to an agreement, the Commissioner, Mike Doucette, decided it would come down to a coin toss. Since the victory had implications for the Cubs more than Dodgers, they needed the win. Unfortunately, it did not land their way and we got the win of the toss and remained undefeated. The Cubs dropped to 6 and 4 and into third place.

The playoff picture was now set with the Dodgers and Pirates receiving the first-round bye and the Cubs and Cards playing along with the Braves and Giants playing against each other.

Week one of the playoffs turned out interesting. The Cubs had to fight back in the bottom of the 9th to squeeze out a victory. The Braves also came back in the late innings to overcome the Giants. The following week set the stage for the semifinal games. We were matched up again against the solid Braves team that had fire power to upset any team especially with Dan "Doc" Proctor, one of the best pitchers in the league on the mound. He threw as hard as anyone and had a rubber arm that never got tired. Lucky for us with the league rules, Doc can only pitch 5 innings.

The Pirates over the years had the Cubs' number beating them in key match-ups. This match-up followed history. The Cubs were ahead going into the bottom of the 9th by one run. With two outs and the Pirates up with runners on second and third, a play to third base turned disastrous. The third baseman picked up the ball and threw a wild throw over the first baseman's head with the winning run rounding third and heading home. The right fielder picked up the ball, made a good throw to home but was too late as the runner slid safely into home base. Game over. The Pirates were headed to the championship game.

The semifinal game was played at the Old Orchard Beach stadium, a beautiful little stadium in Maine that has around 3,000 seat capacity. Our team was edgy going into the game knowing the capabilities of the Braves and the middle of their lineup that had long ball strength. We also knew that Doc Proctor and Clair Crandall were strong pitchers that could make the difference. Dan and I discussed the strategy of our lineup throughout the week. I was going to move over to 3rd base to give strength in the double play combination switching on and off with Braxton. When Meesh was not catching, he would move over to 3rd and having a catcher's arm was going to help there. Danny, who had played most of the season with a broken finger, was going to switch on and off with Bobby Bowen at right field while Greg Frizzle and Rick Comeau would switch off at first base. All the other fielders stayed in their place with Tim Kennison in left, Mike Foshay in center, Vic Garay at short, Lucky Buzzell as catcher and our starting ace on the mound, Tommy Walker.

The game on a beautiful Maine fall day was a tight one going into the 4th. That is when our bats came out swinging to score 4 runs and bring our lead to 3 runs. From there we continued to chip away more runs and with our pitching shutting down the Braves big hitters; with runners on when it mattered most. Our defense was solid throughout the day. I had a good day at the plate going 3 for 4 with 3 RBI's, 2 runs and 2 stolen bases. My only out was a 3-2 count and the umpire called me out looking on a low and outside pitch. I had started to head to first base knowing it was a ball and the umpire rung me up for showing him up. That was a lesson learned.

I also strained my right hamstring running down a ball heading into centerfield. It was not fully pulled, and I had hope that it would recover by the following week. Dodger first baseman, Greg Frizzle, had the highlight of the game. In the eighth inning, we were leading 8 to 1 and a looping foul ball headed toward the first base side dugout. Greg, a big guy, rushed toward the foul ball tracking it down only to take a wrong step on the top of the concrete dugout steps and crashed onto the hard floor, bouncing on the steps. The thud was an awful sound and we all thought he was seriously injured if not dead. After everyone rushed over to see him and surround him to help, he got up after a few minutes and insisted that he continue to play. He stayed in the game and the following inning, behind the relief pitching of Bobby Bowen, we shut down the Braves to win and head to the championship game. Once again, the Dodgers stayed undefeated.

The match up was now set, the 2019 championship Pirates versus the undefeated Dodgers. Game time on Sunday Sept 20, 2020, was at 1:00 pm at Old Orchard Beach Stadium. During the week, our centerfielder relayed a message to all of us that the Pirates' Manager and catcher Mike Wentworth told him that we were the "worst undefeated team he ever saw." Our players did not take his assessment kindly and it only added fire and focus to our players.

Once again, we had beautiful Maine fall weather with temperatures in the high 60s. The field was in great shape and the grass recently cut, the infield dirt was smooth as silk along with the white marking lines perfectly set. Surprisingly, for an old men's game, we had around 100 spectators watching the game

Passion For Life

including some of the former Dodger championship members from the 2006, 2008, 2010 and 2015 teams.

Tommy Walker and the Pirates' ace, Gary Moen, hooked up in a great pitching duel into the 5th. I already had two hits, scored a run and stole two bases. With two outs in the fifth, Greg Frizzle came up with the base loaded. Greg had not had much luck this season at the plate. He was hitting under .300 and many of his solid hits were right at players. He was due. With a 2-2 count, Greg put his bat on the ball on a low pitch, looping a fly ball over the head of John Corey, the Pirates' first baseman. Their second baseman came running full speed behind John and dived for the ball. It hit the tip of his glove bouncing away into foul territory, allowing us to score 2 runs and giving us a 4-1 lead. The score remained that way until the 8th when the Pirates scored one and we did as well. Braxton Bell filled in at second base in the 8th and made a nice diving catch going to his right with the base loaded with one out and perhaps preventing the Pirates a rally late in the game. Although the highlight of the game came when the bases were still loaded with Manager Mike Wentworth stepping to the plate with Bobby Bowen on the mound in relief for Tommy Walker. Mike worked the count to 3 balls and 2 strikes. He went down swinging hard on a 3-2 curve ball. That moment let the air out of the tires for the Pirates.

In the top of the ninth, we shut them down and it was fitting that our short stop, Vic Garay, who was battling with cancer the entire season, caught the final out on a pop up. The Dodgers all ran to the infield to celebrate in joy, hugging each other, slapping high fives and enjoying the undefeated season finale. Mike Wentworth brought over the championship trophy to our team while Danny and I held it up high and all of the players circled around it. After we had our team photos taken by different friends and family members, we all went to our dugout to gather our stuff. Off to the right of the dugout was Vic all by himself. He was holding his head in his hands in full tears. I walked over to him, placing my hand on his back and telling him, "It is amazing, God wanted you here and to be here at this moment. You were meant to be here."

That day, I had another good game at the plate going 3-3, 3 stolen bases, 1 run and 1 RBI. With my playoff run and 6 hits, I ended the season with a .476 batting average and .522 on base percentage.

During the entire season Suzanne and the kids came to every game. The players called Suzanne, the Dodgers' lucky charm. We ended up a few weeks later hosting a celebration party at our home in Waterville. Besides good food and drinks, we handed out championship Maine Brooklyn Dodger baseball tops.

For a season that almost did not happen due to the Pandemic of 2020, it ended in a celebration. Our Dodger team will never ever have to ask ourselves, "What if we did play, how good would we have been?" No need to wonder. We did play, and we won, and we were undefeated!

Journey 49

Team photo after winning the extra inning game to get into the playoff round.

"If there's a Goliath in front of you, that means there's a David inside of you." Carlos Rodriguez

Maine Black Bears – Roy Hobbs World Series

After the successful run of the undefeated Maine Brooklyn Dodgers, the thought of anything matching that championship season was far from my expectations. With the pandemic invading our lives worldwide and the contentious election between Donald Trump and Joe Biden on the minds of many of our millions of citizens, heading to Florida to play in the Roy Hobbs World Series seemed to be a great way to make lemons into lemonade.

Unfortunately, due to COVID-19 many of my teammates that I have played with over the years for the Kennebec Cubs elected not to play, including our manager Chris Rolfe, and our administrator Mike Wentworth - both good hitters and our catchers. Shortly after their decision not to play, our short stop/pitcher

Walter Foster, our centerfielder Bill Pike, and Pitcher/infielder Steve Curtin decided to opt out as well. Mike Wentworth asked me to take over as the administrator for the team. I agreed although I had no idea what I was getting myself into. Now I was up against organizing the team as well as recruitment of new players in order to be competitive for the RHWS. My first call was to Ed Simmons a veteran player in Maine's league and in tournament play around the country. He advised me to also contact Rick Caruso from Albany, NY, who he has played with for years and helped manage many teams during tournaments. After a few text messages and phone calls it did not take long to find replacement players to represent the Kennebec Cubs AKA Maine Black Bears.

Our recruitment all started with a pitching stud from Puerto Rico, Wilson Reyes. Wilson played in the minors in Puerto Rico and played for many years in tournaments. He had played in seventeen championships in all divisions including in AAAA divisions. When Wilson agreed to join us so did his circle of friends including his Puerto Rico teammates. Wilson brought with him two former AA ballplayers, his catcher Harry Martinez along with shortstop and pitcher Israel Gonzales. Along with these outstanding pickups, outfielders and solid veteran hitters Steve Hutchinson and Tim Lysik joined the Maine based team of Simmons, Caruso, Jeff Howland, Dan "Doc" Proctor and Ed Mayer. We then added three other players, Mike Hall from Michigan, John Pecora and Steve Doran from New Jersey. Finally, we recruited a pitcher, JT Tomlinson from Orlando, Florida, that we hoped would pitch two key games for us, one in the beginning and then in the playoff games.

I flew down three days before the tournament in order to participate in the coach's meetings and to get the lay of the land. I was also able to see the Maine Black Bear 45's team managed by Simmons and Caruso in action. I watched a good game in the playoffs, but unfortunately the Bears lost an elimination game after a gallant rally late in the game. I was able to catch up with some of my buddies watching the game, including Dino Doak who played with me a few years. He was now playing for the Tennessee Dirt Bags. He would be playing in the 53's the upcoming week in our division. I also ran into some of the guys from Philadelphia that I played with as well as they are now on all different teams. What I did find out was that many teams were in the same position that we were in. Players opting out from playing and many teams were scrambling around picking up new recruits.

On the eve of our first game, we got together for batting practice at the cages of the Roy Hobbs World Series Players Development Center. We were able to assess our new teammates and immediately knew that they could hit. A day on the field truly determines the level of play. In the morning, we knew that for the first game we would be playing without a shortstop. Gonzales was not going to be able to make it until Game 2 of the double header. This was going to be interesting since our first two games were against two AAAA teams. While we

Passion For Life

were around the cages, Wilson Reyes got on the phone and made some calls to Puerto Rico. He had good news as he lined up another short stop to play; former minor league player, Jose Visquez. They were going to fly him in to Tampa and arrange a driver to get him to Fort Meyers for Game 2.

The next day, on a typical sunny day in Florida at historic Terry Park field at 10 am we started the tournament. It did not take long right from the start to see that we were going to be competitive. I had an idea how the week was going to unveil with the depth of our core fielding, hitting and pitching. We were all surprised that the tournament directors placed us in the AAAA division right from the beginning. The three years I have been playing in the RHWS we have played mostly in AA. Our first game was against a team out of Seattle - the Rangers. They had a hard throwing righty on the mound that mixed up pitches very well to keep us off balance. Even without Gonzales and Vasquez, we played the first AAAA team well. With no short stop, Ed Simmons placed me there. It was my first start at short stop for any league in the past three years. I played well enough making 4 of 4 chances. The game was tight until the 8th inning with the Rangers ahead 3-2. In the bottom of the 8th with two outs and the bases loaded a routine ground ball went through our second baseman's legs, allowing three runs to score and taking us out of the game. We ended up losing 6-2.

In the second game of the doubleheader starting at 2 PM, we played against the Omaha Indians, a seasoned team that had won championships in the past. Our high recruit from Orlando, a hard throwing righty, JT Tomlinson, was on the mound for us. He started the game challenged with throwing strikes and walking in runs which allowed early scoring for the Omaha Indians. He did settle down and started to cut away on our 9-run deficit. In the 7th inning, we took the lead with big hits and driving the starting pitcher out of the game. We held on to win 12-9. In the middle of the game due to dehydration from the hot weather and hampered by my left knee, I got injured diving after a ball over the first baseman's head while playing second. The injury to my right leg strained the hamstring and IT band. This caused challenges for me the rest of the week and took away any foot speed that I had for base running. And for the first time in tournament play, I would end up finishing without a stolen base.

After the game, I headed to Hilton Hotel to check out and drove to Cape Coral to meet up with Suzanne and the kids as they had arrived in Florida while Game 2 was going on. We rented out a three-bedroom house on the canal with a screened-in pool. I got to the house around 9 PM hardly able to get out of the car due to my strained right leg. It was a good reunion with the family. It took a while to settle down. Kate was in bed already and dinner was late. Thankfully, the next game was not until 1:45 PM against the Massachusetts Chiefs, another AAAA team.

The next day came too soon. Getting out of bed was quite difficult although I managed, thanks to my friends Advil and Aleve. I was ready to play ball.

Our next game against the Chiefs was at Jet Blue Park. The wind was blowing hard coming in from the outfield. Despite the strong winds, our team played solid defense, Reyes was excellent at the mound with controlled pitching, and our bats came out swinging to score eighteen runs beating them 18-6. Reyes only had one tough inning. Gonzales, Vasquez, Hutch and Proctor combined for 11 hits to lead the team. I went 1 for 3 driving in two runs for the day.

Going into the last day of pool play to determine divisional play, we faced our fourth AAAA team - the New Jersey Twins. The game was played at the Players Development Complex. This time heavy winds were playing out to right center field. Our Center Fielder Tim Lysik was telling me how sweet it would be to beat this team. Their manager told Tim that he was not good enough to play on his team as they were stacked with so many good players.

With the score tied two to two in the third, Tim got up with the bases loaded. Pitching against him was the Twin's manager. On a 2-2 count, Tim connected with a fast ball to drive it deep to left center field and rounded the bases for a grand slam. It was his only hit of the game. After that inning we never looked back, winning 15-5. I started at second although only played half the game out in the field in order to rest my injured legs. I went 2-2 with an RBI by hitting two line shots to right center. This game completed pool play, ending up 3-1 against four AAAA teams. Now we had wait and see where we would be seeded in the playoffs, AAA or AAAA.

Suzanne and the kids came to both games on Monday and Tuesday. They have been my good luck charms not losing one game while they have been present extending all the way back to our undefeated Dodger team. After our victory, all the team members followed John Pecora to his black SUV to celebrate over coolers full of beer. Suzanne and the kids dropped me off so I could enjoy the tailgate party and came back to pick me up an hour or so later.

On Wednesday, our team had the day off while the officials figured out the playoff system. All the teams would be divided into either A, AA, AAA, or AAAA. AAAA was the highest ranked and only eight teams would be included in this division.

While we waited, Suzanne, the kids and I had the day to ourselves hanging around the house and the pool. We got up late, ate brunch, fished on the canal, Sean skateboarded, and we just chilled out for the rest of the day. Later that day, we got the word that were rated number 4 in the nation and placed in the AAAA division with our first game against the Borderline Brewers, a powerhouse team that had a lineup of Hall of Famers. It was a double elimination format. Therefore, losing one game would not eliminate the team from the playoffs, rather it would place the team in the losers' bracket. Being in the loser's bracket is challenging although not impossible to come back to win the tournament.

Our first game started at 9 am at the Player Development Complex against the Brewers on another windy clear blue-sky day. I started at second and batted eighth. Borderline City jumped on us quickly hitting off Israel with connective base hits, finding balls and finding holes in our defense. After 4 innings they were up 7-1. We battled back to score 3 runs in the 6th and 7th but it was not enough, and we lost 9-3. At bat, I went 2-4 with an RBI. I learned a valuable lesson on one at bat to not to show up the umpire. I worked the count to three balls and two strikes. After fouling off a few pitches the next pitch came in high and outside. I headed down first base line before the call was made and the umpire rung me up. I could not believe it. The umpire was a big man standing 6'6" and intimidating behind the plate. When I got into the dugout Rick Caruso said, "He rung you up because you didn't wait for the call and the umpire took it as you showed him up." Of course, that was not my intention. The Maine Black Bears were now in the loser's bracket with the long journey ahead in jeopardy of going home early with another loss. Our next game was at 1:30 PM against the number one seed, a team from Seattle.

It seemed like we were done and the odds were against us. This team had seasoned teammates that had played together for years in AAAA. The beginning of the game seemed like it over before we got one at bat. By the second inning, they were up 9-1, crushing the ball in the gaps hitting double after double. In the 5th our offense came alive exploding with runs to tie the game. Our catcher Harry Martinez and Jeff Howland started the assault hitting back-to-back triples from Martinez and Howland. Ed Simmons lined a hit scoring Howland from 3rd, after Ed taking second base from a wild pitch, I hit a liner up the middle scoring Simmons. In the 6th and 7th, we scored more runs tying the game 10-10. The score stayed that way going into extra innings leading into the 12th. At the Players Complex the fields have no lights therefore games can be called for darkness. We were the last game being played as the other ones were over. In November, the Florida sky around 6 pm was getting dark. RHWS officials who were watching the game discussed postponing the game if it continued into the 13th.

In the top of the 12th, Israel Gonzales doubled, and Jeff Howland knocked him in with a double as well. We were now up 11-10 going into the bottom of the 12th against a very good hitting team. Dan "Doc" Proctor came into relieve to attempt to shut the door down. Quickly the Seattle team rallied with back-to-back singles. Jose playing short stop and Mike Hall stepping in for me at second base made some good defense plays for force outs leaving the runners at second and third with two outs. The next batter who had two hits already and had good power could win the game with a walk off hit. On a count of two balls and two strikes, the hitter made solid contact out to left center field. Israel Gonzalez playing center field glided under the drive and the ball found the web of his glove for the final out. Game over! The Black Bears knocked out the number one seed in AAAA moving on to play another day.

Now there were four games to go in order to win the AAAA championship. For this to happen we must win in back-to-back doubleheaders. Our challenge was the depth in pitching. We had to lay it all on the line with the pitchers we had left on the squad. The only live arms we had available was John Pecora, Doc and Wilson Reyes. Doc started the first game against the Rangers losing 6-2. Now we have him facing the Seattle Rangers again.

The Rangers jumped on Doc immediately in this playoff game scoring a run on three consecutive hits before he settled in and shut them down by striking out the 6th batter. In the third, we bounced back after a hit by Lysik, Martinez and Gonzales loading the bases for Vasquez who hit a two-run single followed by Howland's scoring another two runs. The Rangers came back the following inning to score two runs creating a tight game until the 7th inning where the Bears came out swinging scoring six runs cruising to victory 13-3 for a final score. Doc picked up another win pitching a solid nine innings.

We were now in the quarterfinals playing in the afternoon at Terry Park stadium against the AAAA champions from last year, the Tennessee Dirt Bags. They just played their first game in the morning, beating the Staten Island Yankees. My good friend and former teammate from the Kennebec Cubs, Deano Doak, now played on the Dirt Bags. We caught up before the tournament started and had dinner together at my favorite Italian restaurant "Two Meatballs in the Kitchen". Before our game, we congratulated each other and wished each other luck.

John Pecora, our fiery lefty from New Jersey, got the start. He had trouble finding the strike zone in his warmups leading up to the game. We were the home team and when the Dirt Bags got up, they scored early from a few walks and a hit. John got out of the first inning without major damage thanks to an inning ending double play. In the bottom of the inning, we bounced back with three key hits scoring three runs to pull ahead. Now up three to one, John went back to mound only to still have issues finding the strike zone. He walked two consecutive batters. Our manager Ed Simmons had seen enough and pulled John from the game. He motioned over to Doc to indicate that he was in. Doc had just finished pitching nine innings that morning and was now back on the mound to give all that he had left to keep us in the game. He pitched brilliantly inning after inning, keeping the Dirt Bags off stride, throwing strikes, and letting our solid defense and hitting propel us to an 11 to 5 victory. Winning two games on Friday brought us into the final day of the tournament. Saturday morning's game for the Semi Finals had us matched up with South Dakota Rushmore's. The winner would play in the afternoon against the Borderline Brewers for the AAAA championship at City of Palms Stadium.

As for me, I was all banged up with a pulled IT Band, pulled hamstring and a swollen right knee. But, at this point, nothing was going to keep me off the field. I pounded down a few Advil and an Aleve to help relieve some of the pain. Both legs were taped up, keeping them tight, so I could move without pain.

Passion For Life

We were back at Terry Park Stadium for the early 9 am start. On the mound for us was our stud from Puerto Rico, Wilson Reyes, who had 17 championships under his belt. He could stay on the mound all day. Wilson had strong presence on the bump and showed confidence with each start. If we won, with Reyes on the mound, we really didn't have a plan for the next game. Our Florida recruit JT Tomlinson could not make the weekend as planned due to his football coaching responsibilities. Our pitching tank was empty.

For the semi-final game, we were going to leave it all on the line with Wilson on the mound. The match-up against South Dakota was a good one. We battled back and forth, each team scoring a run in each of the first four innings. I started at second and hitting 7th behind Steve Hutchinson. In the second inning with the runners at first and second, I got the bunt sign from Eddie Mayer. I went after a high and outside pitch to bunt and I missed. I looked down to Eddie and he gave me the sign again to bunt. This time I got a perfect pitch and laid down the bunt only for it to trickle foul for strike two. With two strikes on me, I thought I would get the sign to hit away, but no, Eddie gave me the bunt sign again. I stepped out of the box and gave him a questionable look. He repeated the sign and the bunt was on.

This time, with two strikes on me, I placed a perfect bunt down the third base line for a hit. The ball was picked up by the pitcher. He attempted unsuccessfully to throw out Ed Simmons at third and threw it by his third baseman to allow us to score two runs. The game stayed tight at 4 to 3 into the top of the 7th with South Dakota up. After a walk and two hits, the bases were loaded. Wilson stuck out the next batter. With one out, the next batter popped up to our shortstop for an infield fly rule. Now with two outs it looked like we might get out of the inning. The next batter hit a rocket to the left of third baseman, Steve Hutchinson. He was on it to make the final out until the ball took a bad hop, bouncing high over his glove and shooting down the line past our left fielder to score three runs. After that inning, the Rushmore's cruised on to an 8 to 3 victory. They went on to play the Brewers but lost to them in a tough game.

It was a bittersweet ending of our magical tournament. We were all pleased about how we played and fought hard throughout the World Series, playing the best teams in the Nation and competing in AAAA. Lined up along the first base side of the stadium, we all were awarded the Bronze medal by the Roy Hobbs World Series officials. Team photos, congratulation, hugs, and goodbyes were exchanged.

The tournament was special for me. I learned a lot about myself. I had to fight hard to stay mentally in the game with the injuries I had and knowing the best part of my game (my speed from my legs) was gone. I was happy with my performance as I played a solid second base and still chipped in with 10 hits ending up with a .385 batting average. It was fun coming together as a team and playing with guys I never played with before. The positive attitudes and desire to win were among us all. I also learned that there is another level of play. Playing with the Puerto Rican players gave me a better understanding of the baseball excellence. They made the game look so simple with the smooth fielding, solid hitting and playing the game with enjoyment.

The best part was having my family with me. They were at all of the games cheering us on. Even little Katie was a trooper. Our last game was on her 10th birthday. She sat there in the stands watching her old man play the game he loved even on her special day. I also had the thrill of having my son, Sean, at age 13 in the press booth announcing my name and number when I got up for the last time. "Now batting number 14, Ken Walsh." A surprise magical ending!

Passion for Life starts with a story about baseball and ends that way. For me, so many lessons of life are discovered on the field. The field of life is the same as being on a team that is striving for the same goal. If the chemistry is right, you respect one another, play hard and have the right people playing the right positions anything can happen. In life, whether it is your family or work, the same applies.

We are in this world for such a short period of time. Every minute is precious. Every day is a gift. Make sure you chose your right vocation. Remember half of your day and more than half of your life you will get up in the morning and head to work. Make sure that work is not about a job, but a passion of life so it is not a job but a way of life.

The same goes with your family. Make magical moments happen. Listen, share and speak from your heart and do not take these fleeting moments for granted. How many times have we all heard of elderly people saying, "I wish I made more time for my family." Do not be one of them, make the time. Play every day like it is your last game and play every moment in your life like it's your last at bat. We all will have challenges that we face in life, during these times step up to the plate and swing with authority. Go down swinging if necessary and keep swinging until you make contact. Don't stay in the dugout, pick up your bat and get into the box for another swing. Don't ever give up. With drive and perseverance, you will make each and every year a championship season.

Have no regrets. Live life with Passion.

Journey 50

"Rest if you must but don't you quit." John Greenleaf Whittier

The Journey Forward

It happened again. While in Florida playing in the Roy Hobbs World Series Sunshine Classic my good knee, the right one, was injured, taking me off the field.

After a successful November World Series bid and coming in third place, Eddie Simmons and I assembled a team to represent the Maine Black Bears in the 50's division. This time we were missing from our roster the Puerto Rico players and had to fill in with others we knew from previous play. Our team was made up of half Maine guys and the rest from Florida, Michigan, Missouri, New Jersey, New York, Massachusetts, and New Hampshire.

Since I was coaching at Colby College, I spent a lot of time throwing batting practice; sometimes throwing over 1,000 pitches during an afternoon practice session. My arm was stronger than ever. I also was hitting often with some of the Black Bears in my basement. Eddie Mayer, Ed Simmons, Larry Murphy and Chris Rolfe participated in these cellar-hitting sessions. The used "Jug" machine from Colby challenged us all as it was placed 40 feet away and could easily fire a ball at 100 miles an hour. On top of that, I was training hard at the Alfond Youth & Community Center with the physical trainer to prepare for a week filled with base running. My left knee swelled up often with no cartilage on the inside of the left knee. Although, my training helped rehab the knee to its best potential to perform.

I rented an Airbnb outside of Fort Myers with Bobby Bowen and Chris Rolfe. It was Bobby's first experience in the World Series play and he was pumped. Our first game was on a Thursday, followed by doubleheaders on Friday and Saturday, and one game on Sunday. We were all excited to get on the field and play, especially the guys in the northern region where the snow was still on the ground.

Game time was 2:00 pm and half of our team had never played with one another. It was a beautiful warm sunny day at the Lee County Players' Development Park. The wind gusts were strong at times. The first inning was not what we hoped for and we were the home team. On the mound was our righty from Missouri, Chris Fuemmeler. He pitched well although we didn't help him much, making costly errors. Casey Stingley said what captured the moment, "You don't win games you lose them."

On the first play of the game, the opposing lead-off hitter smacked a mile high fly ball in the bright sun with the wind blowing out and causing the ball to drift from the pitcher's mound to first base. Our first baseman called it and then called for me to get it. I was shading deep in the hole at second for the right-handed hitter and had to hustle hard to get to the area. I tracked the ball just two feet behind first base, losing sight of it for a second. The ball came off the tip of my glove hitting me in the forehead. That was the beginning of a four-run deficit with other players muffing ground balls and pop ups. Four unearned runs.

At the bottom half of the inning, I was up. On a 1-0 count, I hit a line drive over the shortstop's head for a base hit. On the second pitch and leading off at first, I took off for second, safely sliding in for a stolen base. The ball got by the second baseman into the outfield as I headed to third. There were no outs and I was standing on third. On the next pitch to our batter, the ball got by the catcher. The backstop was a short distance from home plate, so I had no intention to go home especially behind by 4 runs and nobody out, but our third base coach Clair Crandall had a different idea and yelled for me to go. I hesitated before taking off and ran down the line. I could see that I was a dead duck as the catcher got to the ball with the pitcher waiting for me at home plate. I typically slide headfirst although knowing that I had no chance to score I slid in feet first. As the pitcher tagged me out at home, my right knee buckled. I felt the twinge on the medial side of my knee. At that moment, I did not think much of it, except perhaps I strained a muscle. I continued to play at second the next inning with the knee compromised.

Passion For Life

It was now the top of the seventh with a runner on first. Our pitcher caught the base runner sleeping and fired over to Ed Simmons who was playing tight to the bag. The runner, knowing he was in trouble, took off toward second. I moved into the pathway to receive the ball from Ed to tag the runner. The ball was a little behind me. My compromised right leg stayed grounded and pivoted. When I caught the ball, my right knee popped. Everyone on the field heard it go. I felt like I was shot in the leg and immediately landed on the ground in terrible pain. I went out for a moment, coming to with players around me. The tournament Athletic Trainer was called to the field as I lay in the dirt infield. Some of the players carried me off the field and the Roy Hobbs World Series Athletic Trainer brought the golf cart over to bring me to the trainer's area to examine the knee.

During the initial examination, the trainer thought the pain was just an MCL strain and not the ACL. It was hard to figure out the diagnosis with my right leg muscles restricting motion and preventing them to give them any other indication. I asked the trainer if I would be able to play the remainder of the series. He said he didn't recommend it. Ice and painkillers were given to me. The next two days were double headers and I kept score watching from the sidelines until the final game of the World Series.

I convinced our manager, Ed Simmons, to put me in the lineup for the last game. That morning, I got to the batting cage early to try to swing a bat. I took about 20 swings from John Pecora in the cage. I felt good enough to play. Ed said he would place me back at second base although questioned me about batting. Perhaps I should have listened although I was anxious to at least hit once more before the end of the tournament. He reluctantly put me in at the end of the batting order.

Suzanne and the kids did not travel to Florida with me this time. She was in the parking lot at the AYCC and waiting for Kate's swim meet to begin. At that time, Meg Giffin, the daughter of Tom Giffin who is the organizer for the tournament, was sent out to video tape live some of the games. Meg and Suzanne got to know each other over the years from the different tournaments. Meg was pleasantly surprised to see me back on the field playing even though she thought I was done for the tournament due to the injury.

I played the first few innings at second, stumbling around the field with one good knee while the other was wrapped up tight. It was good enough to get by for the first few innings. At the top of third, it was my turn to bat. Meg took notice and messaged Suzanne that I was about to hit. I was watching the opposing pitcher set up batters and noticed he started off with a curve for a strike. My plan was to time it and bang the ball back up the middle. As I walked to the plate, I could hear Meg with her portable video announcing, "for the Maine Black Bears, # 3 Ken Walsh is approaching the plate to hit. Suzanne, your husband is getting up."

I planted my bad right leg in the dirt at home plate, kicking in a groove to get settled. I took a few practice swings while waiting on the pitch. On third with two outs was one of our runners. Just as I thought, after the pitcher wound up, he released a curve ball breaking knee high in the strike zone. I was ready for it and made good contact, driving the ball up the middle only for my right knee to twist. Like being shot once again, the knee could not manage the tort of the turn and immediately, I found myself face first in the dirt in front of home plate, writhing in pain. This time my knee almost dislocated and that could have damaged the main artery to the knee area. Later I found out that in some cases like this when the artery is damaged and restricting blood flow, it can lead to amputation. Meg abruptly said, "Sorry Suzanne, I'm going to sign off!" Suzanne's last vision was of me in the dirt holding my knee in pain. She did not know anything more until 30 minutes later when I called from the bench.

The catcher of the opposing team didn't know what was going on. He thought I tripped and stood over me chuckling until he saw the agony of pain. My teammates and other players gathered around and then carried me off the field. Once again, I felt like "Rudy" being lifted off the field, although these past few times not for the right reasons. Ed Simmons just shook his head letting me know, I told you so. At this point, I knew I had to get home and have the knee examined and find what the damage may be.

When I arrived home, I set up an appointment with the Maine General Hospital Sports Medicine Athletic Trainer Coordinator, Rich Garini, to examine my knee and give me next steps for rehab. I was fortunate that the Sports Medicine office was located across the hall from my second-floor office at the AYCC. This had been a real advantage for me during the past few years. I was one of Rich's regular visitors especially for rehab of my left knee that has taken years of abuse. The left knee swelled up mainly on the medial side. It was all bone on bone. Rich's initial assessment determined that the MCL was compromised but he also thought that the ACL (anterior cruciate ligament) might be also affected. He did not think cartilage was a problem. He set me up with an appointment on March 8th with Dr. Chris Lutrzykowsko of the Maine General Orthopedics for further examination and an MRI. I dealt with Dr. Lutrzykowski in the past, evaluating my left knee. His philosophy matched up with mine. He always discussed how to get athletes back on the field rather than not allowing them to play again. His visit and MRI confirmed that my MCL was compromised, and ACL was ruptured. He told me I had the choice of repairing the knee or rehabbing it so the structure was strong enough to continue to play yet knowing that at any time the knee could give out since the ACL was not in place. He also mentioned it might not be a bad idea to talk with a surgeon to discuss options as well. He set me up with an appointment with Dr. Ben Huffard from Portland Orthopedics to discuss possibilities. I thanked him and said in the meantime, I would work with Rich Garini to get the knee in shape.

Passion For Life

A few weeks later, I met with Dr. Huffard at his Brunswick office. He also is a sports physician and worked for the Portland Pirates minor league hockey team with the objective to get the athletes back on the ice. Again, this is attitude I wanted in a doctor. My visit with Dr. Huffard went well. He understood that I wanted to play ball this summer with the Dodgers and would consider the repair surgery for September. He also mentioned in some cases when the knee structure is strong enough, surgery might not be necessary. I did play tennis for 5 years without an ACL with my left knee. Eventually I had that repaired in 1995 by an Olympic doctor suggested by Harold Alfond and Waterville native Dr. Doug Brown. My left ACL has held up for 30 years despite being pounded on with numerous ultra-marathons, triathlons, tennis, and football. We decided that if I changed my mind and wanted the surgery done earlier, I would give him a call. Otherwise, he would just wait to hear from me.

For me, I felt as if I got the green light to continue to play this summer for the Maine Brooklyn Dodgers. For the next six weeks, I set up weekly rehab training sessions with Rich Garini. Rich had me working my leg on strengthening exercises using the cables and fitness machines. We eventually worked on agility and balance exercises and graduated to running on the indoor track. Within four weeks, I felt as if my right knee was back to normal. The MCL was still tender, although it seemed as if I could play ball without any concerns. However, the sleeping enemy impacting a full return was the ACL. Like back in 1990 when I lost the ACL in my left knee while playing in a touch football game in New York, the same situation was a concern. The stability of the knee would never be the same until surgery. Since I played competitive tennis for 5 years without the ACL, I thought I could easy do the same with baseball. I found out quickly that assumption was wrong.

I was psyched to get back on the field. On Sunday May 2nd the Dodgers opened the season against the Giants. For Dan Simpson, it would be his last game of the season due to prostate cancer and impending surgery in Boston. Dan is the best hitter in the league. This season we would lose our number one hitter who batted third for us and led the team in hits, averages and RBI's last year. I was in the 2nd spot right before Dan and playing second base. Between both of us, in 12 games, we had nearly 50 hits.

Against the Giants, the Dodger team pounded out 16 hits and scored 15 runs to win the opener 15-6. Our defense was solid, committing only 2 errors. I had a good day at the plate going two for four with 3 runs, 3 stolen bases and a diving catch at second base. All indications looked as if I was back and ready to go for the entire season. The second game would prove me wrong.

Our second match up was against the Pirates who we played for the championship last year. This match up brought a lot of chatter during the week between our ball players. The Pirates wanted this game bad, especially since Mike

Wentworth coached the Pirates and had relationships with some of our players. There was a lot of pregame conversations prior to the game.

And the game lived up to expectations. Tommy Walker did a fantastic job keeping the Pirates in check for the first 5 innings. Since losing two of our relief pitchers, Don Sawyer and Bobby Bowen, we were trying to figure out who could replace them. The replacements did not do as well as Tommy. They gave up a few runs later in the game mainly with walks, bringing the Pirates within one run. We missed Dan Simpson at the plate and some key Dodger errors kept the game close. In the 4th inning, I led off with a base hit, then stole second. I reached third on a passed ball. Our next batter, Dan "Meesh" Michaud, our catcher, grounded a ball towards the middle of the diamond. I took off to home, turning on the gas. Just three steps from home plate, my right knee buckled causing extreme pain around the knee. As soon as I hit the plate (scoring a run), I went down hard onto the dirt, holding my knee and moaning in agony. Unfortunately, Suzanne, Sean and Kate had to see me rolling around in the dirt in pain before being lifted off the field. This came from nowhere. I could not understand why in the last game, I did not have the same issue. I was surprised but also knew at that moment that I was gone for the season and needed to think about surgery sooner than later. We ended up winning this second game 6-5. I ended the 2021 season 3 for 6, 3 stolen bases and 3 runs. Now it was my time to watch from the bench.

From that point on, our Dodger team faltered, losing the next four games and ending the season with a losing record of 8-9 and being eliminated from the play offs in the second round. Dan Simpson had his surgery and recovered well, coming back to play in limited action for the last game of the season and two playoff games. The best part of his return was that he received a positive report and was cancer free. I had my reconstruction knee surgery on June 14th with a 9-month rehab plan. Dr. Huffard used the patella tendon as the new ligament replacement. For the first time in five years, I would not be playing summer ball or the Roy Hobbs World Series tournament games in November.

The road to recovery was hard. Not the rehab since I took it as a challenge. The first two weeks, I stayed home from work icing the knee with the ice machine every 30 minutes. Advil was my best friend. After one week, I got rid of the crutches and hobbled around slowly. I went to Brunswick Orthopedics twice per week and stayed religious to their protocols. It was the most challenging watching my teammates on the field without me.

My dedication to the routine helped me rebound back stronger than ever. The physical trainers called me the poster boy of rehab. I hit all the benchmarks ahead of schedule although I had to be patient for the patella tendon to fully heal even though I felt strong enough to get back on the field. Even though I could have played in the 2022 February Roy Hobbs Tournament, I stayed on the side of

Passion For Life

caution and elected not to. I continued to work hard to build muscle strength, flexibility, and agility to come back strong for the 2022 Dodger season.

And I did! I made it back on the field playing for the Dodgers in 2022. As a team we had an OK season, finishing league play at 8-7 after a rough start. We were hampered by key injuries to our starters including the pitching staff. I found myself back on the pitching mound for the first time since varsity high school baseball as a Webutuck Warrior. I also played third and second. I led the team in at-bats, hits, RBI's, and stolen bases. We had a nice second half, winning our first playoff game then losing in the semi-finals in the bottom of the ninth. Our starting pitcher Steve Lockard pitched one hell of a game, but our relief pitching couldn't find the strike zone, walking in the winning run against the Pirates. It was a tough way to end the season.

2022 ended up being a special year for me. Not only was I back playing baseball, but I was honored in Belfast, Ireland, with the Bronze Medallion Award for Community Service. My great great great grandfather and grandmother, Raymond and Kate Walsh, were born in Belfast and their Irish heritage qualified me for this honor for the "Coming Home" recognition. Suzanne, Sean, Kate, and my brother Rob attended the ceremony at the Titanic Hotel in Belfast. Belfast was a fascinating city that is now celebrating 25 years of peace due to the good efforts of Senator George Mitchell who is from Waterville, Maine, and was the Majority Senate Leader that developed the peace treaty between the Catholics and Protestants. Their former Lord Mayor of Belfast, Mairtin O Muilleoir, showed us around the City including City Hall. He also had a connection to Eadaoin Hamill who has been instrumental in organizing the youth Belfast (Ulster League) baseball program. Mairtin brought us to Hyde Bank Park where the only baseball fields are located. When we arrived late in the day, before our dinner party, there were two dozen players on the field practicing. My brother Rob and I threw batting practice in our dress shoes to the Irish players. My Dad had to be smiling down at us in that moment. And, this moment helped jump start my next level of interest in helping out kids internationally. The next day, I met with the Belfast Baseball officials to begin working on plans for an exchange program. During the summer of 2023, we will bring 12 Irish youth to our Camp Tracy location to attend baseball camp. Our Maine Black Bear Senior team will be traveling to Ireland in the fall to play an exhibition games in Dublin and Belfast. I also joined the Baseball United Foundation led by John Fitzgerald and supported by MLB great Steve Garvey, to assist in fundraising efforts to support these opportunities for international and US kids.

On top of all of this, I was honored in the fall of 2022 with induction into the Maine Baseball Hall of Fame. This award is a reflection on my wife, Suzanne, who has been my biggest champion in my life. She is the true Hall of Famer.

Life is weird with its twist and turns. When one door closes, another one opens. We must look for it. I believe we must stay to the fight that life challenges us with and we always must pursue opportunities that result in positive outcomes. It's attitude, its perseverance, it's believing in yourself and in others that good can come out of anything. Having the "Passion for Life" will always lead us to the top of the mountain.

Name Index in Participating Chapters

A
Acorn, Sean (44)
Alfond, Bill (11,42,45)
Alfond, Dorothy (11)
Alfond, Harold (11,24)
Alfond, John (11)
Alfond, Peter (11,12,24)
Alfond, Ted (11)
Alkeman, Robbie (4)
Altvater, Brain (20,22,31,40)
Altvater, Denise (20,40)
Anderson, Brain (44)
Anderson, Corbin (44)
Anderson, Judith (12)
Anderson, Rebecca (44)
Argentina, Patrick (42)
Arsenault, Bill (42, 48)
Athinson, Bill (40)
Aucoin, Steve (11,35,38)

B
Babet, Greg (39)
Baker, Dusty (41)
Baldacci, Gov. John (11)
Barbezat, Debra (45)
Barlock, Deb (35)
Barlock, Will (35)
Barrett, Marty (42)
Bartlett, Doc (5)
Batten, Bill (36)
Beckwith, Jesse (44)
Bell, Braxton (48)
Bellows, Brian (37,42,44)

Belt, Brandon (43)
Benn, David (19,29)
Benner, Bob (14)
Blackwell, Kerri (45)
Bledsoe, Drew (11)
Bochy, Bruce (43)
Borson, Gena (39)
Boucher, Fred (24)
Bowen, Bobby (48,50)
Bradford, Julie (29)
Bradley, Cathy (45)
Bradley, Keith (4)
Brancia, Sam (6)
Brasuell, Tom (45)
Brett, George (41)
Brewer, Charlie (6)
Brodick, Mike (11,42)
Brody, John (11)
Brosius, Scott (11)
Brown, Cam (44)
Brown, Doc (14)
Brown, Dr. Doug (50)
Brown, Levy (42)
Brown, Mardie (14,16)
Budd, Jim (5)
Buffet, Warren (11)
Buker, Jennifer (24)
Burke, Gary (39)
Burnham, Jeff (42)
Bush, Pres. George W. (28,40)
Butcher, Jeff (46)
Buzzell, Lucky (48)
C
Callaway, Robbie (11)
Campion, TJ (5)
Caroll, Bill (5)

Caroll, Joe (5)
Caroll, Phil (5)
Carson, David (39)
Carter, Derek (27)
Caruso, Rick (49)
Cassidy, Dan (39)
Christianson, Mark (1)
Chumber, Doug (42)
Clark, Ernie (36)
Clemens, Roger (11)
Collier, Frank (2)
Comeau, Rick (48)
Corey, John (48)
Cormier, Gerry (16)
Couch, Eric (11)
Cousy, Bob (11)
Cox, Bobby (41)
Crandall, Clair (48)
Crawford, Brandon (43)
Cummings, Rich (2,4)
Curtin, Steve (42,49)

D

Daiz, Renshi Javier (7,8,12,31)
Dana, Barry (14,18,21,24,27)
Dana, Lori (24)
Datillo, Gate (6)
Daughty, Pat (4)
Davie, Bob (11)
Davis, Ann (11)
Davis, Jim (11)
Davis, Malcom (39)
Davis, Violette (38)
Davis, Yvonne (39-41)
Declemente, Hank (6)
Dent, Bucky (33)
Denver, John (24)

DiMaggio, Dom (33)
Dinsmore, Emery (47)
Doak, Dean (42, 49)
Dodge, Logan (44)
Doolan Jacob (37)
Doolan, Josh (37)
Doran, Steve (49)
Doucette, Mike (48)
Downey, Tom (1,5)
Dunlop, Jeff (1)
Dunn, Joop (28)
Duquette, Dan (11)
E
Edwards, LaVell (11
Erskine, Andrew (2,4,38)
Eskelund, Kenneth (24)
Eskelund, Shirley (24)
Estes, Karen (24)
F
Farra, Tracye (4)
Figlutsie, Jerry (6)
Fisk, Carlton (11,43)
Fitzgerald, John (50)
Fleming, Kim (43)
Flood, Tom (4,38)
Folsom, Mike (46)
Fontaine, Norm (37)
Ford, Mark (12)
Foshay, Mike (48)
Foster, Walt (42,49)
Foulke, Keith (33)
Frame, Doug (37)
Francis, Chief (20)
Francona, Terry (46)
Frizzle, Greg (48)
Fuemmeler, Chris (50)

Fuerst, Morton (6)
Funk, Linnaea (30)
Funk, Nina (30)
Funk, Roger (1,7,12,26,30,43)
Funk, Spencer (30)
G
Gammons, Peter (39)
Garay, Vic (46,48)
Garciaparra, Nomar (11)
Garini, Rich (50)
Garvey, Steve (50)
Gaunce, Chris (42,43,45)
Gaunce, CJ (43)
Gaunce, Daniel (43)
Gaunce, Linanne (43,45)
Gehue, Dave (22,40)
Gendreau, Garrett (44)
Gendreau, Wayne (44)
Giguere, Charlie (24,29,32,26)
Giffen, Meg (50)
Giffen, Tom (50)
Giroux, Paul (5)
Glazebrook, Jack (45)
Glover, Charlotte (30)
Gonzales, Israel (49)
Gossage, Goose (33)
Gowell, Larry (39)
Grant, (4)
Greene, David (47)
Grich, Bobby (33,41)
Grosso, Dan (6)
Grosso, Grace (6)
Grover, Eva (14)
Grubert, Bob (8)
Grubert, Dan (8)
Grubert, Sean (8)

Guerette, Patrick (37)
Guertin, Kevin (42)
Guimond, Barbara (21)
Guimond, John (14,20-22,27)
Guimond, Nicole (21)
Guscoria, John (9)
H
Hall, Mike (49)
Hamill, Eadaoin (50)
Harrington, John (11)
Hart, Avis (24)
Hart, Chris (42)
Hartley, Bob (22)
Haskell, Ray (37)
Hatch, Chris (36)
Herring, Don (6)
Hesseltine, Steve (12,21,24,27)
Hill, Dick (42)
Hillman, Chris (25)
Hodsdon, Al (11)
Holmstrom, Don (42)
Holt, Brock (43)
Hope, Bob (41)
Hosier, Greg (5)
Howland, Jeff (48,49)
Huffard, Dr. Ben (50)
Hughes, Jim (45)
Hunter, Dustan (44)
I
Illiano, Joe (2)
Irizarry, Jose (12)
Irons, Grant (11)
Ito, Taimu (47)
J
Jabar, George (24)
Jabar, Joe Sr. (11)

Jabar, Joe Jr. (38)
Jackson, Larry (5)
Jenkins, John 14,33,45)
Jeter, Derek (11)
John, Elton (3)
John, Tommy (33)
Jolovitz, Barabra (24,35,37)
Jolovitz, Lester (35)
Jones, Julius (11)
Jose, Jody (42)
K
Kaat, Jim (11)
Kellock, Drew (42)
Kelly, Brian (39)
Kelly, Gordon (8)
Kennedy, Pres. John F (11,28)
Kennedy, Robert F. (28)
Kennison, Peyton (42)
Kennison, Tim (42,48)
Kerr, Eli (44)
Kevin, Jim (42)
Kibler, Andy (42)
King, Larry (41)
King, Steve (11)
Kinney, Matt (42)
Knoblauch, Drew (42)
Kourht, Mike (5)
Krieling, Jim (2)
L
Lababarra, Sam (6)
Laio, Mr. (32)
LaLonde, Ben (39)
LaLonde, Jake (39)
LaLonde, Joel (39)
LaLonde, Judd (39)
Lamantia, Philip (45)

Lambert, Felicia (35,41)
LaPierre, Jim (5)
LaSorda, Tommy (41)
Lavenson, Joel (38)
LeBlanc, Isaac (38,44)
Lee, Bill (33)
Lee, Jing (32)
Lee, Ming (32)
Lefferts, Doug (26)
Lefferts, Karly (26)
Leitstein, Eric (41)
Levenseller, Mike (38)
Lewey, Noel (20,22)
Loewenstern, Gary (42)
Lockard, Steve (50)
Lombardi, Vince (2)
Lonborg, Jim (33)
Lord, Bill (12)
Lord, Joyce (12)
Lord, Tyson (12)
Lord, Zack (12)
Lovejoy, Dave (9)
Lunder, Peter (11)
Lutrzykowski, Dr. Chris (50)
Lysik, Tim (49)
M
Mach, Connie (33)
Mann, Howie (5)
Mansfield, Rob (45)
Mascaro, August E. (6)
Marano, Rich (6,8,38)
Martinez, Harry (49)
Martinez, Pedro (11)
Martinez, Tino (11)
Mathies, Kurt (38)
Matolla, Charlie (4)

Mayer, Ed (49)
Mays, Willie (1)
McClay, Paul (11)
McCarver, Tim (11)
McEniff, Helen (1)
McEnroe, Karin (18)
McGraw, Tug (1)
McKernan, Gov. John (36)
McLaughlin, Joe (3)
McQuarrie, Megan (24,26,29-31,34,41)
McQuarrie, Mitch (24,26,29-30)
Menicine, Dennis (42)
Merrithew, Logan (27)
Merrithew, Tim (22,27)
Merwin, Dan (4)
Michaud, Dan (48)
Milar, Kevin (41)
Mitchell, Bill (45)
Mitchell, Butch (21)
Mitchell, Sen. George (50)
Mitchell, John (11)
Moen, Gary (48)
Molitor, Paul (11)
Moon, Rev. Sun Myung (8)
Mould, Dr. Mike (5)
Muniz, Ben (42)
Munson, Thurman (11)
Murcer, Bobby (11)
Murphy, Gary (1,4)
Murphy, Larry "Cowboy" (42, 46, 48,50)
Murphy, Larry (5)
N
Nachimson, Irwin (41)
Nale, Tom (45)
Neikro, Phil (41)
Neptune, John (21,27)

Nesbit, Peter (43)
Nixon, Trott (11)
Norton, Shawn (14)
O
Obama, Pres. Barack (40)
O'Connell, Bill (22)
O'Connell, Mike (22,43 - 44)
O'Connell, Steven (6)
Offerman, Jose (11)
O'Keefe, Ron (39)
O'Leary, Troy (11)
O'Muilleoir, Mairtin (50)
O'Neil, Paul (11)
Ortiz, David (43)
P
Page, Satchel (33)
Palmer, Ryan (42)
Panarelli, Dave (22,25)
Panarelli, Jodi (44)
Panarelli, Megan (25)
Panik, Joe (43)
Parker, Bill (4)
Peavey, Jake (43)
Pecora, John (43)
Pecukonis, Steve (36)
Pence, Hunter (43)
Penigar, Dyanna (44)
Pike, Bill (46,49)
Porcello, Rick (43)
Poretta, Mike (6)
Posey, Buster (43)
Pouland, Gabe (44)
Poulin, Gary (32)
Poulin, Min (32)
Powell, Greg (11)
Proctor, Dan (48,49)

Purnell, Fran (45)
Purnell, Joyce (45)

R
Racanello, Dennis (8)
Ragsdale, Grady (42)
Reid, Ian (8)
Remy, Jerry (11)
Retamosso, Joel (44)
Reyes, Wilson (49)
Reynolds, Brie (31)
Rice, Jim (11,33,42)
Ricker, Dave (42)
Riley, Deb (22)
Ripken, Cal Jr. (11,33)
Riveria, Mario (11)
Rolfe, Chris (48, 49)
Romano, Tom (2)
Rooney, Dennis (1)
Rooney, Mike (1,22)
Roy, Phil (9,41)
Runser, Mike (11)
Ruth, Babe (33)
S
Saberhagen, Brett (11)
Salem, Steve (11,33)
Saulter, Dr. Jay (38)
Savage, Andy (1)
Sawyer, Don (46, 48)
Schievy (42)
Schiffer, Bob (1)
Schimidt, George (47)
Schutte, Peter (45)
Scully, Vinc (41)
Seager, Bob (14)
Seaver, Tom (1)

Selig, Bud (41)
Shapiro, Sam (36)
Shaw, Ed (22)
Shaw, Janice (22,37)
Shea, Dan (36)
Shufelt, Dave (4)
Silvernale, Mike (2)
Simmons, Ed (48,49,50)
Simpson, Dan (48,50)
Sims, Billy (11)
Skehan, Matt (45)
Skelley, Tad (47)
Smith, Lee (33,44,45)
Smith, Nancy (37)
Snyder, Geraldine (41)
Sockalexis, Louis (21)
Stanley, Mike (11)
Stark, Randy (30)
Steinbrenner, George (11)
Stickles, Trevor (39)
Stengel, Casey (50)
Strawberry, Darly (11)
Stubbert, Fred (11)
Stubbert, Nat (42)
Sukeforth, Doug (33,45)
Sukeforth, Rita (33,45)
Sussman, Earl (38)
Swanson, Erica (8)
Seuk, Dr. Joon Hoo 8
Singleton, Ken (11)
Swanson, Terri (6)
Swift, Billy (11)
T
Takahichi, Kensaku (8)
Tardif, Cooper (44)
Tardif, Jason (36)

Targett, Kris (42)
Thorton, Charlie (5)
Tiant, Louis (33)
Tomer, George (27)
Tomilinson, JT (49)
Torrez, Mike (33)
Trottier, Joe (6)
Tumminellie, Josephine (22,37)
V
Vails, Nelson (41)
Valenti, Jerry (6)
Valentin, John (11)
Valentine, Bobby (41)
Varitek, Jason (11)
Vaughon, Mo (11)
Vigue, Jim (36)
Visquez, Jose (49)
W
Waite, Rob (40)
Waite, Steve (29,40,41)
Waldron, Dr. Rosalind (35)
Waite, Todd (40)
Walker, Tommy (48)
Wallace, Sparky (5,22)
Winkin, Dr. John (11)
Walsh, Arthur (7,22,24,28,37,39,45)
Walsh, Dennis (7,12,24,37-38)
Walsh, Ellen (22,37)
Walsh, Jim (22,24,38,39)
Walsh, Kate (35,38,41,43,49,50)
Walsh, Katherine (50)
Walsh, Liam (22)
Walsh, Lilly (22)
Walsh, Michelle (42)
Walsh, Raymond (50)
Walsh, Rob (1,2,22,31,37,38,40)

Walsh, Sean (32,37-9,41,44,45,46, 49,50)
Walsh, Shawn (11)
Walsh, Suzanne (14-19,21-24,26-31,34,36-37,40-43,48-50)
Walsh, Theresa (4,7,22,24,37)
Walsh, Tim (42)
Wayne, John (29)
Wentworth, Mike (43, 48, 49)
Wessman, William (47)
Wheeler, Denny (43)
White, Kevin (11)
Williams, Bernie (11)
Williams, Ted (34,44)
Woods, Jesse (47)
Wright, Bill (4)
Y
Yastrzemski, Carl (43)
Yawkowski, George (34)
Yawkowski, Mary (34)
Yeoman, Sue (26)

Milton Keynes UK
Ingram Content Group UK Ltd.
UKHW021014241024
450188UK00013B/772